Dac
me...
...Love,
Ken and
Kelley

DRAGGERMAN'S HAUL

Ellery Franklin Thompson (1899-1986)

ELLERY THOMPSON

DRAGGERMAN'S HAUL

THE PERSONAL HISTORY OF A CONNECTICUT FISHING CAPTAIN

FOREWORD BY
BERNARD L. GORDON

PUBLISHER'S AFTERWORD BY
STEPHEN JONES

FLAT HAMMOCK PRESS
MYSTIC, CONNECTICUT

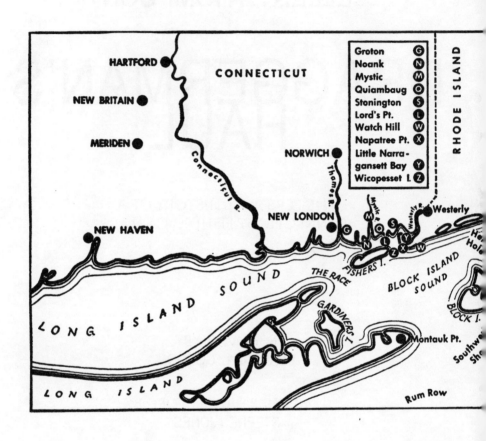

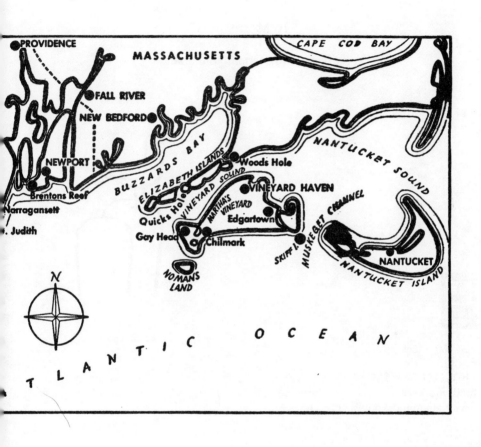

To Morris

A darned good fisherman and brother

Flat Hammock Press
5 Church Street
Mystic, CT 06355
(860) 572-2722
www.flathammockpress.com

Draggerman's Haul originally published 1950, Viking Press
Come Aboard the Draggers originally published 1958, Stonington Publishing Co.

Printed in the United States of America

10 9 8 7 6 5 4 3 2 1

ISBN: 978-0-9795949-3-9

Contents

Contents

Foreword

ELLERY FRANKLIN THOMPSON
FISHERMAN, AUTHOR, AND MARINE PAINTER

By Bernard Ludwig Gordon

Stonington, Connecticut, has been home port to many notable mariners. Among the most famous in the eighteenth and nineteenth centuries were Captain Edmund Fanning, who with his brig *Betsey*, hunted seals, circumnavigated the globe, and discovered a South Pacific island that now bears his name. Another Stonington son, Captain Nathaniel Brown Palmer, at twenty-one skippered the fifty-foot sloop *Hero*, hunted fur seals south of Cape Horn, and is credited by some geographers with the discovery of the Antarctic continent.

The most colorful Stonington mariner-fisherman of the twentieth century was Captain Ellery Franklin Thompson, who commanded a fifty-foot fishing vessel about the size of "Nat" Palmer's *Hero*. Ellery Thompson was born on Easter Sunday, 1899, on Pequot Hill in Mystic, Connecticut. His mother's family included Chapmans, Rathbuns, and Packers, while his sea captain, fisherman father was descended from Denisons and Wilcoxes, making Ellery a descendent of many generations of nautical families.

Captain Frank E. Thompson (1873-1936), Ellery's father, commanded passenger steamers between Norwich, New London, Mystic, Stonington, and Watch Hill. For ten years he was captain of the *Governor Winthrop*, the ferryboat that crossed the Thames River from Groton to New London before the highway bridge was built. He also skippered the local passenger steamers *Gipsy*, *Summer Girl*, and *Watch Hill*. Frank Thompson also owned a small fishing boat, and he is believed to have been the first Connecticut fishermen to use the newly introduced otter trawl, which is dragged along the sea bottom to scoop up fish. While fishing with him on the *Florence*, Ellery gained the rudiments of dragging for fish from his dad. Ellery went to sea at age fourteen and for almost five years worked on the coastal steamer *City of Lowell*. He also served as crew on his father's fishing boat during his spare time.

When he was twenty-one years old, in 1920, Ellery borrowed four thousand dollars and bought his first dragger, the *Grace & Lucy*, named after his backer's daughters. While Ellery was extremely proud to be captain of his own fishing dragger at twenty-one, he soon found that his new boat was not entirely satisfactory. Constructed too flat forward, she did not respond well in heavy seas, rolling and pounding heavily. Ellery advanced to a second dragger, *Louise*, named after his older sister. This vessel also had its faults, rolling and pounding in heavy seas.

In order to have a more sea-kindly fishing dragger, Ellery decided he would design one. Purchasing drafting equipment from the local art supply store, he drew plans for his next fishing vessel. Rather than have the boat built locally, as his first two had been, he ordered his new boat from the Rancocas Construction Company in Delanco, New Jersey.

The new dragger was named after his younger sister, Eleanor. In may 1927, with some trepidation, Ellery took the *Eleanor* on her maiden voyage from the Rancocas shipyard to New London. The new vessel handled beautifully; its design proved effective. Stonington, Connecticut became the *Eleanor's* home port for the next twenty-five years. Ruggedly constructed the *Eleanor* was one of the few Stonington fishing draggers to survive the famous 1938 hurricane, and resumed fishing shortly after the storm. Ellery gained a reputation as a practical fishing dragger designer and drew up plans, at the behest of his friends, for a number of Stonington fishing vessels.

Ellery was a highly respected Stonington fisherman from the time he tied up his dragger *Eleanor* at Bindloss Dock in 1930. He became an East Coast celebrity in 1947, when *The New Yorker Magazine* ran a feature article about him in its 4 and 11 January issues. The article, written with warmth and affection, depicted Ellery as a "sad-eyed, easygoing Connecticut Yankee and the most respected fishing captain in Stonington, Connecticut." Joseph Mitchell, author of *The New Yorker* article, also devoted fifty pages of his 1959 book, *At the Bottom of the Harbor*, to Captain Thompson. Ellery himself wrote two books, *Draggerman's Haul*, first published in 1950, and *Come Aboard the Draggers* in 1959.

In June 1943, Captain Thompson developed a friendship with Daniel Merriman, Director of the Bingham Oceanographic Laboratory at Yale University. Merriman and his co-workers, Herbert E. Warfel and Jim Morrow, went out collecting fish specimens with Ellery on Long Island Sound at least one day a month during the 1940s. Thus, the *Eleanor* became a part-time research vessel. At least six significant marine survey reports on the fishery resources of Long Island Sound were based on data collected during these trips.

During the late 1940s and early '50s, I occasionally served as a crew member on board the *Eleanor*. Captain Ellery would usually head out of Stonington Harbor about 5 A.M. in quest of flounders, or "flat fish" as he would call them. He would drag his eighty-foot-long otter trawl net in Block Island Sound. Sometimes Ellery would head "down the beach" to drag off the Rhode Island shoreline at Misquamicut or Quonochontaug. Occasionally, we would go out to the "Hell Hole" or the "Mussel Bed" east of Block Island. Ellery sought out black-back flounder, yellow-tail flounder, and fluke, or summer flounder. When he unloaded his catch back at Binloss Dock in Stonington at 4 P.M., it was packed in wooden boxes and shipped to the Fulton Fish Market in New York City.

In 1951, Ellery astonished his fellow fishermen at the Stonington dock by shipping a woman as crewmember. Nineteen-year-old Edna Butlin was one of the first female crew persons, not related to members of the crew, to be seen working on a Stonington dragger. She got the knack of sorting fish and mending nets with skillful proficiency.

In the late 1940s, Ellery decided to record on paper his forty years of adventures off the coast and along the shores of Southern New England. The result was a full-length, illustrated, autobiographical book, *Draggerman's Haul*, published by Viking Press in 1950. Full of marine adventures, humorous anecdotes, and Ellery's philosophy, it proved to be a popular book for its original publisher. (Prior to this edition it was reissued by the Book & Tackle Shop of Watch Hill, Rhode Island.) Warner Brothers Studios in Hollywood took an option on the story but never produced a movie of it.

Ellery's first book proved so popular that he wrote a second volume called *Come Aboard the Draggers*, which was printed in 1958 by the Stonington Publishing Company. Shortly after his second book was published, Ellery began writing a regular column in Mystic's newspaper, *The Compass*, which continued for many years.

Ellery was also a prolific marine painter. His mother painted landscapes and still lifes, so painting was not a totally foreign endeavor for Ellery. His paintings are unsophisticated in composition and detail, yet some capture the feeling of a boat at sea quite accurately. It is estimated that E.F. Thompson painted over one-thousand seascapes, including whaleships, clipper ships, lighthouses, and almost every commercial fishing boat in Southern New England. The walls of hundreds of Connecticut and Rhode Island business establishments display his oil paintings. Ellery would frequently present a painting to a friend in return for a favor, yet he sold many of his paintings in his later years at prices ranging form $50 to $400.

Ellery was a member of the Mystic Seaport staff in the late 1950s and early '60s. He served as guide and occupant of the fisherman's shack near the rope-walk. There he would relate to visitors endless anecdotes on fishing off Southern New England. During this time he lived in a small apartment on Main Street in Mystic and would frequently be seen with his paint-covered cap at a jaunty angle, bringing a newly completed painting over to Archie's Soda Shop or Maxwelton's paint store. During the winter months, Ellery would paint up a large quantity of seascapes, and at the annual Mystic Art Festival he would display his latest productions for the crowd that gathered in front of Archie's Restaurant.

During the early 1970s, Ellery moved away from Main Street to an old house at 44 Water Street on the Mystic River facing sunken barges, the railway trestle bridge, and the boatyard. Here, in an appropriate setting, he spent his final years painting, corresponding with friends, and writing and rewriting his memoirs. He gradually filled many boxes with manuscripts about his halcyon days offshore and along the coasts of Connecticut and Rhode Island. Ellery was always friendly, astute, and a keen observer of the changing maritime history of Southern New England. In the mid-1980s, Ellery developed medical problems that prevented him from living alone. He died in a nursing home in April 1986 at the age of eighty-seven, well remembered by his many friends for the nautical legacy he left behind.

Ellery Thompson

I. Birth of a Draggerman

To one who has launched upon the fearsome business of writing his autobiography, the story does not seem to begin on the day of his birth, but in some respects long before that, and, in others, much later. In my case I think it begins really on the day I decided to catch fish for a living-though there was a lot before that to explain the decision.

That was when I was in my teens, but when I was a boy, living in a New England seaport, one never heard the appellation "teen-agers." When a fellow wore diapers he was a baby; when he shed them he was a kid; when he dropped his first teeth he was a boy; and when he got a couple of his supposedly permanent teeth kicked out in an argument, he was a man. Whether he shaved or not had nothing to do with it.

For better or worse I got pushed out of the boy stage in 1914 when I was fifteen. Already I loved everything connected with the sea and ships, and despised anything that was connected with hard work on land. And as for high school—well, my interest fell to a new low as I felt the pressures of approaching manhood pushing at me. And so, in the spring of 1914, Mom and Pop decided that it was time to put the inevitable New England seaport question to me: "Do you want to go to sea? Or would you rather continue the unequal struggle with school? Or do you want to work for a living?"

The last two choices scared me, and anyway, as I look back at it now, I think I must have realized that it would be useless to struggle against fate. The sea had been the natural habitat, and fishing the accustomed occupation, of my people for generations. Sea-going ancestors on both sides of my family came from England in the seventeenth century and settled on the New England coast. Mother's family tree bore Chapmans and Rathbuns and Packers, and Father's Thompsons and Dennisons and Wilcoxes, and practically every twig on both became a fisherman or a fisherman's wife.

Of course their fishing methods were different from those I have followed for over thirty years. "Dragging" or "drag-fishing" came to Connecticut at the end of the first decade of the twentieth century, and Pop was the first Connecticut man to use the new method. Today New England draggermen catch a large proportion of the Eastern Seaboard's edible fish, `dragging huge cone-shaped nets along the ocean floor behind small (usually Diesel-powered) boats, generally thirty to sixty feet long (though some are larger) and scooping up whatever may lie in their paths. Something like fifty such boats, including my *Eleanor*, work out of Stonington, Connecticut, alone.

When a Draggerman, using a power winch, pulls up his net, the mouth of which may be as much as eighty feet wide, and dumps its contents, the haul may include the darnedest and most unexpected assortment of objects which ever cluttered the deck of a ship—a lot of fish, of course, if he has been lucky, ranging in size and character from flounders, whiting, goosefish, sea-robins, trash sculpin, and skates, to a five-hundred-pound shark or an equally vicious-looking mollykite; a few lobsters maybe; some dead-man's finger sponge; and perhaps the bone from an actual dead man's finger, or a skull or tibia or pelvic bone; an unexploded bomb, reminder of the futility and inevitability of war; parts of machinery; a bird cage; a half-ton of coal from the wreck of a coal barge (very useful in the ship's stove); a faded, water-logged Yale pennant; a pair of corsets; a bit of metal work from a sailing vessel of generations dead and gone—almost anything which can sink. I have dragged up all of these things and many more, and still look at a haul when it comes out of the depths of the sea with the same eager curiosity which drove me as a barefoot, nightshirted boy into our sitting room on Christmas morning long before sunup.

But none of my ancestors before Pop ever had this particular kind of fun. Their commercial fishing was done by a variety of methods. For example, a large part of our fresh edible fish was once caught in stationary nets that were set along our coastline from the sandy shores of Cape Cod to the western limits of Long Island Sound near New York City. They were held in place at strategic fishing locations by long stakes, poles, or anchored floats. Each net generally had leaders (long fence-like sections of netting) beginning near shore and running off to the main body of the trap, in deeper water. When the moving fish struck these leaders, they turned off shore as a rule and were led into the mazelike center section where they remained until removed. On the larger traps, set at some distance from the shore, a passageway was left open to allow small boats to pass through the leader, saving them the worry, time, and trouble of running out around the whole net.

The Cape shore, Nantucket and Vineyard Sounds, Buzzards Bay, the area off Sakonnet and Newport, Narragansett Bay, Block Island, the beach between Point Judith and watch Hill, Fishers Island Sound, the shores of Connecticut, and the shores of Long Island were all dotted with these nets.

There were handliners, too, boats that set trawls with hundreds of hooks, purse seiners and gill netters, and in their season they brought in swordfish, tuna, cod, haddock, sea bass, pollock, mackerel, flounders, and other fish. But because of the irregularity of trips, especially in the fall and winter months, the average catch fell far below the quantity caught nowadays, when large and powerful engines drive vessels through calms and storms.

From the beginning of my family the majority of its men have been fishermen, mariners, sealers, or shipwrights. And the majority of women have probably said, "No son of mine shall go to sea!" And how many won?

If mom had any such thoughts in her head about me she never expressed them. And Pop apparently had the right idea from the start. They both told me to take the summer to think it over, but Pop added, "Going to school is a great thing for anyone, they say, but attending a big school of mackerel out in Block Island Sound isn't the worst thing in the world, either."

"Sure, I'll think it over," I said, but both he and I knew pretty well right then what the answer would be.

Ten minutes later I was helping him steer the ferry boat *Governor Winthrop* across the Thames from Groton to New London. Pop, who had been captain of the boat for ten years, was at this time acting as spare captain. He was a master mariner, had served his time on large steamers, and had spent most of his life on the water—at least most of what I can remember. Like many another New Englander of his day he was a part-time fisherman and mixed fishing with other jobs—a little farming at times, but mostly steamboating and piloting. He had patrolled the minefields across the New London Harbor on the *Gypsy* during the Spanish-American War; acted as a mate on the ocean-going tug *Minnie*, hauling coal barges from Norfolk, Virginia, to New England ports; filled the post of quartermaster on a Fall river steamboat, *The City of Worcester*; and piloted the steamer *Chelsea*, the "slow boat" to New York from eastern Connecticut.

Transportation along the coast was chiefly by boat during the days of my father's greatest activity and during much of my early life, and sometimes Pop's jobs consisted of running small steamers from Norwich to New London, and over to Mystic, Stonington, and Watch Hill. Since a steamboatman's home was usually established where his longest stopover occurred, and since this changed with changes in my father's jobs, we seemed to live all over the Connecticut coast. As I look now at a list, arranged in chronological order, of the places in which Mom and Pop and we kids, as we came along, lived, I get a little dizzy: Quiambaug, Mystic, Norwich, New London, Mystic again, Groton, back to Quiambaug, back to Groton, Willow Point, and again to New London, where Mom and I still hold forth. In addition to moving here and there, I went on as many trips with my father as was possible, so that very early in life the coast itself, and the waters which stretched in fascinating mystery away from the coast, and the islands which they surrounded, seemed almost as much my home as any single spot on it.

During a period when he was working out of Norwich, Pop met Avery Smith who owned the *Gypsy*, and his friend Walter Dennison who operated the *Summer Girl* that ran between Norwich and Mystic, and in one summer Pop was offered three jobs at once—the *Summer Girl*, the *Gypsy*, and the *Watch Hill*. Pop was a fellow who hated to pass up any experience and was always willing to try anything once, so he settled down to three-year plan, running each of the three ships for a year. But he always remembered best, and talked most about, the *Summer Girl*.

In fine weather the run was one of the pleasantest and easiest on the coast—from Norwich, fifteen miles down the winding Thames River valley past the colorful water fronts of New London and Groton, out into Fishers Island Sound, then eastward several miles before turning northward past Noank and continuing two miles up the lovely Mystic River to Mystic. But in foul weather, especially in fog, it was one of the most treacherous and hazardous performances ever to torture the nightmares of a sea dog. There were obstructions which had to be cleared by inches, and sharp turns which must be made in split-second timing. Pop knew his fogs and his coastline and riverbanks, and while he was on this run he joined that category of admired river pilots known as "fog-eaters." Nautical regulations demanded that in fog the whistle be blown every sixty seconds, and Pop told me that one of the secrets of shore-line fog navigation was to listen like the devil for the echo of every blast., If a man knew the coast and had a good ear, he could learn to tell from the echo's strength and direction just what was opposite him and approximately how far away it was. (Actually, radar is a modification of that principle.)

But there was a lot more than that to good navigation. Pop used to say to me that, in addition to listening to echoes, barking dogs, bells, and horns, and watching what lights you could see at night, and knowing where they were, good navigation consisted of knowing yourself—that is, the accuracy of your own senses—the tides and winds and the speed of your boat under various conditions, and then in developing skill in split-second timing while running between channel buoys.

Another thing he used when he was running between Connecticut hills in a fog was his valve trombone, an instrument which he played for his own, rather than other people's, entertainment. Some hills seemed to respond better to "America," Pop's favorite piece, and some to "Nearer, My God, to Thee," and he knew which piece to use on which hill. Later I asked him why he talked so much more about the *Summer Girl* than he did about the *Gypsy* or the *Watch Hill*, and he said he liked the *Summer Girl* the best of the three because the acoustics on her were much better for his trombone.

If you look at the map you will see what that stretch of New England coast and the waters off it, between Niantic, Connecticut, and Watch Hill, Rhode

Island, are like: the Thames, the Mystic, the Niantic, and the Westerly Rivers flow serenely through wide mouths into Long Island Sound, and the Connecti-cut hills proceed inland from the coast in stately ranges. The many inlets along the coast make it look like a jagged-toothed saw that hasn't been sharpened properly. Islands, reefs, beaches, mud flats, and sand bars make the region as mysterious as any land of dreams conjured up by the imagination of a nine-teenth-century writer of boys' books. And the water itself! There are hidden coves; there are shoals where a rowboat would strike bottom, yet a few miles out there are rock-covered pits three hundred feet deep in the ocean's floor. And the restless fury of the tides sways back and forth, foaming and fretting, inviting and threatening. Any boy who didn't like this section of America, or who shut his ears to the call of the sea, would be crazy. And I wasn't crazy—at least not when I was a kid.

I was born on Easter Sunday, 1899, on Pequot Hill at Mystic, not far from where ninety-eight Englishmen from Hartford wiped out a thousand Pequot Indians in one night in the seventeenth century. The massacre was a dirty, even though courageous business, and I have always been annoyed at the ugly mon-ument on the hill near my birthplace, which memorialized the white men from Hartford rather than the Indians who gave the place its name. I was the second in the family, my sister Louise having been born three years before in Quiambaug.

I can't remember much about my first residence in Mystic, because almost before I could bat a baby-blue eye we had moved to Norwich, from there to New London, then back to Mystic, and, before I was six years old, to Groton. I do know that throughout my memories of childhood there is a constantly recurring picture of a horse-drawn moving van owned by the B.B. Gardner Moving Com-pany, standing in front of our house, as through Mr. Gardner had left one con-stantly parked there.

We hadn't been in Groton very long during our first go at the place when one of the best days in my life came along—August 6, 1905.

My father left the house bright and early to steer the ferryboat *Governor Winthrop* on her maiden voyage across the Thames between Groton and New London. He seemed awfully excited and a little worried as he looked at Mom before he left. I thought he was excited about the ferryboat, of course, which was enough to get anyone stirred up, and I was mad because he wouldn't take me with him. And when he said to Mom, "You're sure it'll be all right, now?" I wondered whether he was worrying about the boat. But Mom just pushed him to the door, smiling, and said, "Of course it will. I'm not sure yet. Anyway, I've done it before and I hope to do it again after this one. Hurry, now, or you'll be late." Then I *was* puzzled.

Just then Harold McLaughlin, my cousin, who later became a well-known Stonington Draggerman, came along, and we sprawled on the lawn and began to talk about the things that matter. I told him about my mother's mysterious remarks and he said, looking speculatively at the roof, "I'll bet she's going to shingle the roof or something. It needs it. Your pop's probably afraid she'll fall off." But that didn't satisfy me. Mom had said she'd "done it before," and I couldn't remember her having shingled any roofs, though she'd done practically everything else in the way of hard work.

Half an hour later my sister Louise, nine years old and practically grown up, came hustling out of the house looking very important, and rushed away, shouting at us as she ran, "I'm going to get Grandma Thompson, over at Aunt Annie's, and you boys are to stay out of the house *all day*. Don't you dare go in!"

Now the whole business was over my depth and I lapsed into wondering silence while Harold burbled on and on without my even hearing what he said. I knew that Grandma had been staying at Aunt Annie's for over a week, but didn't know why. Later I learned that Ma and Aunt Annie had been running sort of a race, with odds on Aunt Annie, but Ma won.

In a few minutes Grandma Thompson arrived, literally on the run, and rushed into the house without even a glance in our direction. Close on her heels came the doctor, carrying his black bag and looking eager and serious. He didn't look at us either. Like Grandma, he was, as they say on the New England coast, "bound."

A little later I heard a sound in the house that was something like the mixture of a seagull calling and a calf blatting. It went on and on, and after a while Louise said that I could come in, and there was my kid brother Morris, and I was delighted. He looked pretty red and wrinkled and wormy, but I had a hunch right then that he was going to be a swell guy, and I was as proud of him as Mom was herself. And when I saw Pop's face after he got home, I knew I had shown good taste, because Pop liked him too.

Then Pop put it up to me. "When I'm away from home, on the steamer or fishing, you've got to be the man of the family and take care of your mother and your sister and your brother. You're going to spend a lot of time around the water with the kid, and you'll have to look out for him especially there. Someday I want you to teach him how to swim. That's something I can't do."

Pop belonged to the Knights of Pythias and took it quite seriously. After he'd talked to me a little about the specific duties of an older brother to a younger, he told me, in order to give me a good example, the story of Damon and Pythias, and how one friend had sacrificed for the other.

When Morris was about a year old Pop got restless again. So we loaded our gear in the B.B. Gardner van and moved us to Quiambaug. The family was larger by two members than it had been when he and Mom and Louise had lived there before, and one bigger than when we had lived in nearby Mystic. We were like a snowball.

Quiambaug (which had another name—Mistuxet-by-the-Sea—but no one ever called it that) is a little sea-coast village between Mystic and Stonington. Of course it's much larger now. I counted the other day and found that there were eighteen houses there. But when we came to it there were only twelve. There was no store, but Oliver Dennison drove a meat wagon. The old residents used to say you could always tell when Oliver was coming by looking for a small dark cloud moving along the road. The cloud would be gulls or flies or both, and Oliver and his wagon would be just ahead of it. Mom seldom bought meat from him, though, because of his high prices. "I simply won't pay fifteen cents a pound for sirloin steak," she said.

To the south were clam flats and pebbly beaches littered with fishing shacks, tar barrels, and drying reels for seines and traps. To the east was the cove, into which Quiambaug Creek emptied; and up from the cove was Lord's Hill, littered with more rocks and boulders per acre than any other land for miles around. As a Quiambauger would tell it, it took a lot of rocks to make New England, and the good Lord got together all he could, so he'd be sure he'd have enough. When he got through he had a lot left and dumped them on Lord's Hill. That's how it got its name.

Three miles east of Quiambaug is Stonington, a real fisherman's town, where a man can go swinging down the narrow streets, wearing hip boots and a plaid shirt, with maybe a couple of shots of rye inside for ballast, and be pointed out as one of the town's leading citizens. Its harbor, protected by ` breakwaters, is easy to enter even on the darkest and stormiest nights, and on shore four long docks jut out into the channel. There is a boatbuilding yard, two fish-packing plants, and two marine railways. Stonington was then, and is now, a great place for any boy—or any man, for that matter.

We settled on a small farm, where a quarter of an acre of land was waiting to be cultivated. If it had been left to me it would have kept on waiting until the Lord blew the trumpet of doom, but Pop had different ideas, so we compromised. When he was out on the steamer or fishing, I just pretended it wasn't there. But when he came home he put a hoe or a spade in my hand without giving me a chance to express my opinion, and we both cultivated the land while I secretly cultivated a strong dislike for everything connected with farming—especially a hoe.

There were beasts, too—a horse and a cow and chickens, which had to be fed and watered and kept clean. It was in those days that I began to see what a fine job a fisherman had. You didn't have to feed or water the fish, or clean out their stables, or hoe the seaweed out of their feeding rounds. You just caught them. I kept envying Morris, who was of course too little to do these things, and Louise, whose work in the house exempted her.

Louise had a little lamb; its fleece was very dirty and I despised it. It baaed and butted, ran into burdocks and got its wool all matted with burrs, and looked silly all the time. It served one useful purpose, though. At two years of age Morris was still taking his nourishment out of a bottle, which made me very impatient. I wanted him to grow up and go to sea with me, and I couldn't imagine a fisherman or a sailor going for that kind of bottle. But nothing Mom could do seemed capable of breaking him of the habit. He would just look disdainfully at food in any other form, and if Mom forced it into his mouth he would spit it out.

One day she had an inspiration. Before giving Morris his bottle she gave it to the lamb, who sucked at it avidly, butting its silly head and twitching its dirty burr-matted tail in ecstasy. Morris set up a howl, and when Mom offered him the bottle he struck it away angrily. After that he began to eat like a person.

As I envied Louise and Morris, I envied my father too. He could spend so much time out on the water, at the fascinating business of fishing or captaining a boat, while I was playing nursemaid to a lot of silly finless creatures ashore.

Yet some of my happiest memories are connected with Quiambaug. The little village overlooks Fishers Island Sound, and on a clear day the view extends all the way to Long Island. It was the hub of the Connecticut fishing industry, profession, and art—for fishing is all three.

It was Mr. Fishingtown himself. Quiambaug was dominated by fishing and by Wilcoxes, that famous New England coast family which has more members connected with fishing than any other, and of which Pop's mother was a member. There were two families of Wilcoxes, besides the Dennisons, the Clarks, the Miners, the Noyeses, the Davises, and other fishing families; and the air at all times was quite literally redolent of fish in various forms and stages. Much of the stimulating aroma drifted over the village and surrounding territory from Latimer Point across the cove (later a favorite hide-out for rum-runners). Here stood the Wilcox factory, where the small, bony, and inedible menhaden was turned into various useful oils, fertilizers, etc. It was this strong odor which the old-timers said gave the villagers so much strength and good health, and I believe there was something to it, thought it would be hard to make a stranger, smelling it for the first time, understand. Certainly people believed it then, and many were the friends and relatives who came to sit on the Wilcoxes' porch for the sake of the health-giving odors that drifted up from the fertilizer factory. On Sundays and holidays it was sometimes difficult to get through the crowd to the Wilcox front door.

Menhaden, or "bonyfish," were among the chief prizes of the commercial fisherman. When I was a boy these fish were plentiful and schooled up and down the Atlantic Coast from Nova Scotia to Florida. They were caught in huge purse seines manipulated by men in two double-ended "seine boats," and a third rowboat called a "striker boat," working from a mother-steamer; and were brought back from the sea literally by the millions on the decks of Quiambaug fishing boats, chief among which were the white and buff Wilcox steamers, and delivered to the Wilcox processing plant. The result was the building up by one family of Quiambaug Wilcoxes of the largest fortune taken from the sea by Connecticut men of their generation, and a reputation for a fertilizer so laden with magical properties that a little of it sprinkled around a dead stump would make the stump either send forth living branches again, or get up and walk away to escape the odor.

From our doorway in Quiambaug we could see where the original Wilcox homestead had once stood—the great double house with the widow's walk at the top, from which Wilcox women had watched the sea on stormy evenings with anxious eyes, awaiting the return of delayed Wilcox vessels. Here both the Elias Wilcox family (active chiefly in fishing for menhaden and in operating the Wilcox factory) and the Nathan Wilcox family (trap fisherman and later draggermen) had lived, one in each side.

In the Elias side of the house my father and his sister Lena had lived as children. Pop's mother was a Wilcox, and since her husband, my grandfather Thompson, died three months before my father was born, Great-uncle Elias had taken the two children into the already large Wilcox family, and had set out to raise the boy as a fisherman. He put my father on Wilcox boats under his son, also named Elias, who taught him at an early age to steer, to navigate, to mend nets, and much else from the rich store of Wilcox sea and fishing lore, and worked him as if the life of the body and the salvation of his soul depended on work alone. Great-uncle Elias took quite literally the maxim "The Devil still finds work for idle hands to do." Hard it was, but as a result Father had no difficulty getting his master's license at twenty-one.

Until he had married my mother, Florence Chapman, Pop worked with his uncle; and then one day, fretting at the constant domination to which he had been subject for years, he said he was going to quit. Uncle Elias said that if he quit he would not get his Christmas bonus. Father told him what he could do with the bonus, and quit. I'm sure that Father never regretted it, but I don't believe Uncle Elias ever quite forgave him for his act, or for his words.

The old double Wilcox house was gone before we moved to Quiambaug. It had burned to the ground one Sunday afternoon while all the family, except my father's sister Lena, were at church. Aunt Lena remembered that a cache of money accumulated for the purpose of buying a boat was hidden in an upstairs room. She went up and rescued it, though she failed to get out twenty patchwork quilts packed away in chests, the evening work of many Wilcox women.

After the old Wilcox homestead burned, the two families scattered somewhat. Most of Captain Nathan's growing family settled in the immediate vicinity and engaged in farming and fishing. The elder Captain Elias retired to become a gentleman farmer, while his son Elias headed the rapidly growing bonyfish enterprises. Another son, Rowland, became chief skipper of the Wilcox fishing fleet; Steve became part-time manager of the fertilizer factory; and another son, Orrin, whom Pop called Uncle Al—he is still living, over ninety—moved to Mystic to take charge of the Wilcox office there. After the fertilizer factory was sold his young second wife, Clara, opened the Wilcox store at Mystic.

I can still remember Great-grandmother Wilcox, who lived in a small house near the ruins of the old homestead. Pop was her favorite grandson, and even after he was grown up she would keep tidbits to give him, as though he were still a little boy. I can remember more than once going to her house with him and watching while she bent over to haul a pan of apples from under the couch, and, handing one to Pop, said, "Here's a nice red apple for you, Frankie." And Pop would grin like a kid as he thanked her, and stick the apple in his pocket.

As the younger Elias prospered, he built his white house—with a widow's walk—on a grassy knoll south of the highway, overlooking the coastal waters, And here, on high ground, he built a tower, something like twenty feet tall; and on top of it he set an old pilothouse from a steamer, with a powerful telescope inside it, so that he could keep watch on the Wilcox fishing fleet at sea. To get the telescope into focus he often trained it on the near-by landscape, sometimes to the embarrassment of those who inhabited it. After a session up there on a clear day Elias would come down and report whether the horses of the farmer plowing on Fishers Island, four miles out, wore blinders or not, or whether the man he had sighted on Watch Hill, seven miles away, wore suspenders or a belt, with side comments on the fitness of these things.

He also had frequent, and often acid, remarks to make on the general conduct of men working on the Wilcox steamers. He picked out unerringly those who hadn't pulled their weight, sometimes referred scathingly to the impropriety of performing certain functions on the landward side of the vessel, and at times made his men almost believe that he was a lip reader. Every man on a Wilcox steamer sighed in relief when a fog settled between ship and shore.

The pilothouse was blown off the tower and carried away in the 1938 hurricane, but the tower itself still stands, reminder of the days when Captain Elias was a mighty power in Quiambaug.

Concern for Wilcox fishing luck permeated every nook and cranny of Quiambaug life, for half the population was made up of Wilcoxes and men and women connected with Wilcox enterprises, and half the rest owned Wilcox stock; even Pop had a little of it. One Wednesday evening, so a story goes, the voice of a Wilcox steamer came right into prayer meeting and, for a few minutes, stopped the proceedings cold.

For several weeks fishing had been very poor. The fertilizer plant had been running at less than half capacity. There was illness in the village, too, and one of the most active fishermen lay in bed with a leg broken by a nasty fall on shipboard. It was a sad and discouraged-looking folk who gathered that Wednesday evening in the little white church near Quiambaug to lift their hearts in prayer to an almighty and merciful God, who traditionally had a special sort of interest in fishermen. A Wilcox steamer had gone out that morning, provisioned for a three-day trip. Perhaps if they got their prayers in early enough, God would be kind.

The meeting settled down as usual, and the minister began his prayer. "O Lord," he said, "we are gathered in Thy house, a humble people. Like Lazarus, we are bowed down and afflicted. Our burdens—"

Just then there drifted in from the Sound an unmistakable toot from the whistle on the Wilcox steamer which had left port that morning, and one of the deacons, who owned some little Wilcox stock, held up his hand, stopping the minister in his tracks. There was nothing unusual in a Wilcox steamer blowing its whistle as it approached the shore. It was a custom which had been established to let the factory and the village in general know what the catch was like. Each toot stood for twenty-five thousand fish. What *was* unusual was for one of the large steamers to come in the day she went out. Usually two or three days passed before her hold was filled with fish or she ran out of provisions. So surprised glances ran around the meeting, and everyone listened, minds at least momentarily diverted from the minister's melancholy prayer.

At the second toot, the minister, who also owned some stock in the Wilcox factory, looked at the deacon, his face showing appreciation. Fifty thousand fish! Not too bad! The minister sighed happily and bowed his head, about to begin again, when a third toot came joyfully over the water and into the house of prayer. A slow smile lightened the stern features of the deacon. The lines about the minister's mouth softened also, and looks of satisfaction spread throughout the congregation. You could almost tell who owned stock in the Wilcox factory and who didn't by the looks of relish and of envy on different faces. Everyone waited, almost holding his breath. And then a fourth toot came, and a fifth, and sixth! By then everyone in the place would have believed anything, and so there was no real surprise as the tooting went on—ten toots in all! And even after that the minister waited a long time in silence. So did everyone else. But there were no more toots, and finally the minister bowed his head again, scarcely able to abandon his broad smile and force his face into serious mien proper for prayer. Two hundred and fifty thousand fish! A quarter of a million! Truly, the bounty of the Lord was great!

The minister began his prayer again. "O Lord, we thank Thee! We are gathered here in joyous and humble gratitude and praise. As Simon Peter saw the work of Thy bounteous hand at Gennesaret, so are we constantly aware of Thy goodness to us in every way. Give us wisdom and make us, too, fishers of men. Amen."

There was a chorus of hearty amens from the congregation, and there were no more melancholy prayers begun that evening.

The Nathan Wilcox family were—and are—no less remarkable than that of Elias. There were two girls—Lucy and Jennie—and four boys—Jesse, Moses, Elmer, and George. Every one of them except Jesse is alive as I write, Lucy at ninety-five, Moses at ninety-one, Elmer at eighty-eight, George at eighty-five, and Jennie at eight-two, and all are active. Jesse died in 1944 at ninety-three, having fallen out of a strange bed after working fourteen hours of the preceding twenty-four. I met Elmer the other day going to mow a neighbor's lawn. The street was so rough that he got mad trying to push the mower over it, so he hoisted the thing to his shoulder and carried it along with the ease of youth.

Elmer and his wife, Phoebe, and their two daughters, Lillian and Anna, were our nearest neighbors when we lived at Quiambaug. Everything was arranged mighty handy at Elmer's. Not more than ten feet form the back door was their three-holer (the Wilcoxes always did things on a grand scale—most people were satisfied with two) and banked against the north side of it was their ten-foot-high woodpile, handy to the kitchen door, and a fine windbreaker for the privy in cold weather. Elmer was a good neighbor. Every May Day and Halloween he and his wife "hung" our family a holiday basket from their garden or cellar. It always came in handy. But Pop had a cow and Elmer didn't, so Pop always "hung" Elmer, and some of the other cowless Wilcoxes, a gallon of milk each.

The present-day fame of this family of Wilcoxes rests chiefly on the shoulders of Elmer's brother George, who is actively engaged in operating the largest fishermen's supply house between New York and New Bedford. In his small net factory at the rear of his home at Quiambaug, George, with the help of his daughter Gladys, his nephew, and his grandson, makes every type of net, from a small hand scoop net to an otter trawl. A short-wave radio receiver keeps them informed on developments at the fishing grounds. Not long ago they heard a Draggerman talking by short wave to another captain and bemoaning the loss of a trawl net. A replacement would have to be specially made, and he envisaged a long wait in idleness. When he rushed over to George's that night to put in his order, the net was ready for him. George generally has orders for nets months in advance, but when a fisherman is up against it, that man comes first—if his credit is good.

George has accumulated enough money in his fourscore years of honest toil and shrewd business so that he has nothing to worry about, but he still works hard and is still cautious. A while ago he called on a slightly younger friend who had just bought a television set. George was charmed with it and asked questions. When he was told that it cost nearly five hundred dollars, he shook his head. "I'll wait five or ten years until they come down a bit and I can afford it," he said.

The other fellow looked at him sternly. "George," he said, "as a friend, I'm telling you that what you can't afford is to wait five or ten years."

That brought a thoughtful look to George's face. I think perhaps it was occurring to him for the first time that he was not really young any more.

A few weeks later I called on him after an absence of months. As soon as I drove into the yard, I noticed that there was a television aerial on the roof of his house., I found him in his workshop, his hands busily and skillfully fashioning scoop nets for crab fishing, with the radio on full blast beside him. He was listening to a game between the Dodgers and the Cardinals, and rooting for the Dodgers. He talked for a little about his television set, but his mind was really on baseball, and he talked mostly about that. He knew as much about the standing of the clubs and the performances of individual players as any seventeen-year-old American boy.

When they were younger George and Elmer fished together and stuck together in most things. It seemed natural enough that they should fall in love with two neighborhood girls who were also always together. When both of the girls said yes, they arranged a double wedding, thinking they might just as well lose only one fishing day. Finally, after fifty years of fishing, Elmer got water on the knee and his doctor ordered him ashore. George said, "Okay, El, I'll go too. We started together and we'll quit together." Elmer became a gentlemen farmer, and George built up his fishing supply business.

In the course of time both of their wives died, as did also the wife of Moses, their older brother. In 1946 Moses announced that he was going to be married again. George was well past eighty now, but he, too, had thoughts in that direction, and had a girl of sixty-odd in mind. He broached the matter to her and she was quite willing, but when he began to talk about children she shook her head. Marriage, yes—but no children! So George called the whole thing off.

There are countless stories about the Wilcoxes. George himself especially enjoys telling (when his daughter Gladys is not around) about the last sperm whale ever caught along the New England coast—the one he and his brother caught.

It was while they were still trap fishing. On taking up a trap off Quiambaug one morning they discovered that a whale had gone straight through it, wrecked it, and now was lying in shallow water on the beach, weak and exhausted. He was only a little fellow—about thirty-two feet long, just cutting his eye teeth—probably a nursing whale who had lost his mother and was slowly starving to death. They were sorry for him, but more than that they were angry at him for having ruined their net, and decided to make him pay for it. They towed him into Stonington, built a fence around him, and exhibited him at a dime a look for a few days.

Meanwhile the little fellow died, so they gutted him, filled the void inside him with six oil barrels, sewed him up with netcord, and, hoisting him on to a barge, took him to Norwich, fence and all, and exhibited him there. While in the process of gutting him, they discovered that some of the anatomy of a young male whale was pretty amazing, and they exhibited part of it in a separate enclosure, as a side show for men only, and collected an extra dime from each visitor.

They were doing pretty well with their whale, taking in a lot of dimes day after day, and still public interest didn't seem to be diminishing. But finally the health authorities came down to the barge and told them they they'd have to get out. To the Wilcoxes, accustomed as they were to the odor of the fertilizer factory, the whale had a good wholesome smell, but certain inhabitants of Norwich had complained.

They'd taken in quite a few dimes by then, but this profit was only in the nature of a by-product. George and Elmer cut up the carcass and rendered ten barrels of whale oil from the body, and dipped a barrel of sperm oil from the head. By then the little fellow who had wandered away from his mother to become a juvenile delinquent had certainly paid his debt to society.

II. A Bushel of Flounders and an Old Yale Pennant

We lived in Quiambaug a year, keeping the B.B. Gardner van handy and in mind all the time, then loaded our plunder onto it once more and went back to Groton, eastward across the Thames River from New London. Here we could watch the new lighthouse in the process of construction at Southwest Ledge, the ferryboat plying back and forth between Groton and New London (this was years before the highway bridge was built), the endless parade of tugs and coal barges moving into the harbor when an approaching storm drove them to shelter. We watched naval vessels, excursion steamers, and Sound steamers, and during the hours of darkness we often watched the searching beam of a steamer's light proving a channel for a marker, or sweeping the shore for the house of a ship's officer or one of his friends. We explored the idle hulls of formerly well-known coasting schooners or fishing smacks, rotting at their docks, their owners either dead or too old to care. Many of the docks themselves, relics of the great whaling industry of the past, were falling into the river, but some of them, especially the Ferguson dock and the Hallum Street dock across the river at New London, still gave shelter to the harbor's small boats.

In many ways this period was the low point in the marine history of eastern Connecticut. At Mystic nearly all shipbuilding, which had been the life of the community, had come to a halt. Stonington seemed to be sleeping in silence after the discontinuance of steamboat lines which had used it as a terminal port in transporting freight and passengers between New York and New England cities. Noank, which at one time is said to have been the home port of fifty fishing vessels and which boasted of its Palmer Shipyard in continuous operation for nearly a century, was falling apart at the seams; it was soon to enjoy a brief boom, only to subside again, sleepily and lazily, while artists painted the picturesque ruins of its former glory.

Soon, under the impetus of World War I, all of New England was to take on new life, but we were spared advance knowledge of that. To my eyes all seemed serene, and the world a place in which one could have plenty of fun with nothing to worry about—except for school and a dozen after-school chores.

Pop, when he was out on the boat with me, or around the house, or mending his gear at night by lantern light, certainly did nothing to discourage my feeling that boating and fishing furnished the only way of life for a man of sense. After all, that was the way he felt about it, and he was an honest man. Often we would prowl the shore together, looking over every three-hundred-dollar lobster boat for miles around, and talking to the men who operated them. Everywhere it was the same story: sail was on the way out fast, and even steam was encountering a rival in gasoline. Engine manufacturers seemed to be sprouting all along the coast.

Uncle Frank McLaughlin, a marine engineer, said most of the new companies wouldn't last long. Their engines started harder than his old bird dog on scent, drank more gasoline in ten minutes than a New York fire engine, and didn't have enough power to pull a setting hen off her nest. He always ended his tirade against the cheap early gas engines by saying that one old steam engine could outpull every gasoline engine within the sound of a steam whistle. But then he would laugh and say that many gas-engine factories were making remarkable progress, so much so that he feared for the future of the small steam engine. To prove his point he teamed up with Pop on several steamboat jobs and waited for the opportunity to get into fishing alongside Pop. And I also waited for the not-too-far-off day when the family plunder would include a couple of motor boats that could take a guy fishing for something worth while.

Of course Uncle Frank was right in his worried prophecy. With gasoline motors being rapidly developed it would be only a few years before individually owned boats costing a thousand dollars or less would be replaced by company-owned vessels costing over thirty-five thousand dollars. Tremendous cargoes of fresh fish would be supplied to our great urban centers to meet the increased demand for and appreciation of food from the sea. But when we moved to Groton there were only a few bonyfish boats working, a few small trap fishermen, and a lot of small boats which were engaged in lobster fishing, their single-cylinder, unmuffled engines sounding loud and harsh in the early morning.

Well, they were "the good old days"—yet the truth is that today fishermen have better and safer boats under their feet, and tried and proved equipment designed for safety, as well as for efficiency in operation whereas when some of our fathers and uncles and friends went to sea it was sometimes only by good luck, Yankee ingenuity, and the kindly help of divine Providence that they ever set foot on dry land again. And as to their catch, fish is a much more delicious and wholesome food in the bit cities today than it was then, because of the greater sanitation which surrounds its handling and the much shorter time which elapses between its capture and its consumption.

Before leaving Quiambaug, Pop had ordered a twenty-six-foot Cape Cod dory, advertised at the time as the largest dory ever built by its makers, to use in lobster fishing. Finally, after we had reached Groton, the dory came. My father built it over to suit himself and installed a Little Giant gasoline engine, made in the Midwest. The motor ran well enough, but he wanted more power, so he replaced it with a five-horsepower Lathrop, and engine made in Mystic by the firm that was making the name Lathrop synonymous with dependability.

One day, thumbing through a 1907 magazine on the ferryboat, Pop came across a photograph of a Boston fishing vessel from whose crosstrees hung a beam trawl, a large bag-shaped net designed to be drawn along the bottom of the sea, to scoop up any sort of fish that were lying there at the time. He came home with his face alight and said, "I've never seen the net, but from what I saw in the picture I can make one."

The gear required two curved iron frames about two feet high and four feet long, separated by a twelve-foot beam or pole. A local blacksmith made the frames, and Dad made the net. When the framework was ready the beam lashed in place, the rig resembled the frame of a wide sleigh. The top or the funnel-shaped net was lashed to the beam, the lower edge laced to a chain stretched loosely between the two sides of the frame's lower part. With two lines of equal length fastened at each side, the boxlike entrance and cone of netting were ready to be dragged.

Pop, with me trailing right along, placed the gear aboard his dory and, feeling much as Ben Franklin must have when he invited the lightning with his kite, we started on our strange expedition, the laughter of pessimistic doubters ringing in our ears as we headed up the Thames.

Arriving at the cove above the railroad bridge at New London, we set the awkward outfit overboard. When it rested on bottom with the towlines fastened at the stern, we towed it over the river bottom for a quarter of a mile. Neither Dad nor I could bear to wait longer than that to see whether it worked or not, so we took it up. When we dumped its contents on the deck we found that the catch contained a bushel of nice flounders, two lobsters, three blue-shell crabs, four skates, a dozen sculpins, an old pail, a pair of shoes, a nursing bottle, and a faded Yale pennant—which beat hand-lining all hollow, the Old Man said. And he grinned like a kid when he said it. We made several more drags that day and went back to the dock with a barrel of good fish, making fishing history along Long Island Sound.

Walking home later, Pop said to me, "Ellery, this method of fishing is going to be the coming thing." How right he was! And to back up his prediction he had Jerry Davis of Noank build him his first "round-bottom lobster boat, the *Florence I* (named after Mom). It cost nine hundred dollars ready to go.

For a year or two he continued to fish that gear every chance he got between times on his ferry job, lobstering, and taking out boat parties. Then he heard about a new type of net that Captain Elisha Clark of Quiambaug had brought back from Long Island after a sea-bassing trip. Dad made a special trip on the trolley cars to Stonington, where he viewed this wonder net called the otter trawl, which differed from the beam trawl chiefly in the addition of two boards, one on each side of the net, which kept the net open. He noticed that the net was small and compact, and looked like an improvement over the awkward beam trawl.

In the spring of 1910 Dad made on of these nets, adding modifications of his own to the original design. He then made a pair of cutting boards (now called doors) and, after trying the gear in a series of experimental drags, pronounced it good.

This didn't surprise me in the least. As far as I was concerned anything that Pop made was bound to work, and anything he did was right. I was his man Friday, his dog Fido, his tag-along whenever possible. Red-letter days were those on which he took me to New York on one of the Sound steamers, sometimes the *City of Lowell* under Captain James Pettigrew, sometimes the *Chelsea* under Captain Colberg. Once in the city we headed directly for Fulton Fish Market. Then, the pleasant duty of passing the time of day with the boys in the market accomplished, Pop and I prospected farther afield—the Aquarium, Eden's Musee, Proctor's, and the street of streets, Fourteenth Street, the poor man's Times Square. I could readily see that a life of fishing—big time fishing—would give a man plenty of opportunity for visiting the big city and learning the facts of life. That was the golden period that saw the earliest *Follies*, and in my adolescent mind things were beginning to shape up.

About this time I had my first glimpse of the *Tartar*, unquestionably the fastest sailing and handsomest fishing schooner ever to call a Connecticut port her home. She was similar to later vessels that raced against Canada's *Blue Nose* for the fishing-schooner championship of the North Atlantic. When, long before her time, she was lost on a Jersey beach, she confirmed the old adage that the good die young.

The *Tartar* was partly owned and was skippered by Captain Henry Langworthy of Noank, the tile-fish king, a cultured sea dog who, when not jogging just inside the Gulf Stream while his trawl dories were out getting a trip of tile fish, was generally to be found browsing in some Fifth Avenue art gallery. I'll never forget the day when I first saw the *Tartar* sailing rail down up the Thames river, everything on her, including the cook's apron, and drawing beautifully. What chance did school have in the mind of a boy while he was looking at a sight like that and dreaming of getting at the helm of such a craft?

Meanwhile Morris was eating his victuals with a knife and fork, and in other ways acting like a human being. As soon as he could walk he began to tag along after me everywhere I went, and in my heart a great hollow of loneliness for a close companion began to be filled. I taught him about everything I knew, which didn't take long. As soon as possible, and long before it was sensible, I taught him how to to paddle a leaky old rowboat so that he could go along with me in the Thames River while I learned to swim. One day we were almost swamped and engulfed by the four-hundred-foot excursion steamer *Providence*. We both crawled home pretty wet, and Ma spanked us. Later Morris said to me, "You're twice as old now, and I'm littler than you are. But wait till you're a hundred and I'm only fifty. Then I'll be stronger than you are, and I'll fix you!"

When he started school I used to help him with his homework in the evenings. Not that most kids in first grade had any homework, but I saw to it that Morris did. We were especially active on spelling. I would spell out for him "h-o-e" and "r-a-k-e" and "s-p-a-d-e" and "w-e-e-d" and tell him that these were things to be avoided all his life. Then, to make sure he understood, I would draw pictures of them. Then I would spell "boat" and "fish" and "oar" and "sail" and draw pictures of them, telling the kid that these were the good things of life, the things for him to look forward to. And Mom and Louise would look askance, hardly knowing whether to approve or disapprove but Pop would laugh heartily, and sometimes come over to us and draw swell pictures of a tug pulling five or six barges.

Of course in school vacations I often went fishing and taking parties with Dad. But one day, when I was about twelve years old, I stayed at home. Dad came back early and seemed glum and depressed. Upon being questioned by my mother, he told his story.

It happened at a spot called South Race, south of Fishers Island, at the entrance to Long Island Sound, where the water is nearly three hundred feet deep and where the ebb and flood have cut deep channels and holes in the bottom, leaving jagged rocks to pierce and tear whatever touches them. It is the deepest and roughest hole along the coast, and on the bottom crawl the best lobsters that have never been caught. Pop had set oak-framed lobster pots in this spot, hoping to take some of them.

On the day of his adventure he arrived at his buoyed lobster pots and began to pull in the first one. It was unusually heavy, the brand-new twelve-thread line taut as a fiddle string. He put another turn around the power winch and kept pulling. Soon the extra-heavy load was near the surface, and my father peered over the rail to get a look. What he saw made his heart being to pound. Wedged against the head of his lobster gear was an old-fashioned brass-bound chest. It was almost completely covered by marine growth; kelp streamed out from it for several yards, but it could not hide the fact that the chest looked exactly like several pirates' chests Pop had seen pictured in national magazines.

The line to the chest and lobster gear was now hot and smoking, so my father carefully placed several turns around a cleat and then shut off the winch. There was a slight take-up, and with a loud snap the line parted. The chest and gear were gone for good. Pop took bearings on the land in order to record the spot, and came home immediately.

I didn't doubt his story for a moment and I don't now. I knew when Pop looked at a picture—or the real thing—he knew what it meant. The next day I went out with him. We went right back to South Race, of course, and caught on the first trawl we hauled in was an ancient brass rim from a spirit compass made in the time of Captain Kidd. I hadn't doubted from the first that Pop had almost snagged a Kidd treasure chest, but here was evidence to convince anyone! I think Pop was as excited as I was as we looked it over, snatching it from one another to examine every detail.

But the treasure! We never found it. If you want to look for it, I'll tell you approximately where to go. The spot is somewhere between Montauk Point and Fishers Island, at a part of the Race where the waters of Long Island Sound rush out on the ebb, and where the waters of Block Island Sound, backed up by the ocean, rush in on the flood. Many secrets are hidden there, and there they will always remain, for in waters three hundred feet deep, with hilly ledges and rushing tides, no man or equipment could ever hope to explore the sea bottom. My father pointed out to me that day the exact land bearing he had taken. They are no more. The 1938 hurricane did away with them.

That's not the only treasure-chest story that's still alive along the Connecticut coast. My great-grandfather knew about some men of Mystic who came into possession of a map showing where treasure was buried on Fishers Island in a pool now called Money Pond. The instructions on the map told of a curse put on the treasure. Anyone who attempted to recover the loot was advised to wait for an overcast night—no moon or stars showing—and to arrive at the pond, probing with poles. When found, the chest was not to be left until removed. That was all.

The men made their preparations and waited. They had everything they needed: sharp-pointed poles, picks and shovels, a good boat, and several hurricane lanterns. Soon a dark cloudy night arrived, and the excited treasure hunters set out for Fishers Island. It was midnight when two of the men walked out into the pond, jabbing their poles deep. They worked furiously and tensely and were so busy they failed to notice that a storm was brewing. Suddenly one of the men drove his pole into something solid, and, forgetting the admonition to keep silence, he cried out, "My God, I've found it!"

He had no sooner spoken than the storm, with tornado-like winds and driving rain, broke over the island. Forgetting the instructions not to leave the treasure, the men dropped everything and ran for shelter. Huddled beneath an overhanging ledge, they eagerly waited for the storm to pass.

Suddenly there was a terrible flash of lightning, followed immediately by a deafening clap of thunder. The ground shook and the pond steamed, for the bolt had struck directly in its center.

The squally tempest soon passed. The men hurried out into the pond, trading and poling wildly, but try as they did for the rest of the night—and other days and nights too—the thing was gone for good. Captain Kidd had done his work well.

Did I believe this story when I first heard it as a kid? Of course I did. What kid wouldn't? Do I believe it now? Sure. Why bother your head to disbelieve a thing like that?

These memories are all things any man might treasure, and I do treasure them, along with many other memories of our life in Groton, where terraced homes rose in a splendid amphitheater overlooking a great river show. Near our Granite Street house was the old shipyard cove where the huge *Minnesota* and *North Dakota* had been built by the Eastern Shipbuilding Company, and where Pop kept his boats and lobster gear. It was a natural playground for boys, and here the Lawry boys, the Coffin boys, the Ford boys, the Sprague boys, the Comi boys, the Gray boys, the Tomlinson boys, the Penleton boys, the Crandall boys, a couple of tomboys, and the rest of the shore gang, and I played at all hours of the day and night that we could get away with it. Here I took Morris as soon as he was big enough to toddle, and, with a look of awe on his face, he watched me as I showed him that I could swim in four feet of water "with no feet on bottom."

And there was the powerhouse farther up river on the Groton shore, which continually pumped a stream of hot water into the river. So we kids, when the water was too cold farther out, went swimming close by the outlet of the powerhouse pumps, where the temperature ranged from ninety to one hundred degrees. Better than Hot Springs, and a lot cheaper.

There was old Fort Griswold, too, with its colorful caretaker, Major Wessel, who told us all about the Indian fighting in the days of his youth. The Gray boys, Lloyd, Philip, and Robert, who had American Indian blood in their veins—and were proud of it—never would listen to these hair-raising tales. Nor would they play the wrong kind of Indian games with us palefaces. It was in the old Fort that I got tied, as a paleface, to a stake, and Pete Comi shot me with a blank cartridge. It took Doc Hewes a week to pick the paper wadding and bit of powder out of my jaw, but I didn't mind because I thought that it might make me a hero in the blue eyes of Pete's pretty ten-year-old sister Laura.

Out Groton home was a first-floor apartment. We had a parlor, a sitting room, a kitchen, a large bathroom (what a luxury!), and two bedrooms. Ma and Pa slept in one, and there were three beds in the other, one for Louise, one for Morris, and one for me.

Ours was one of the few houses in the neighborhood that had a piano. Ma played it, Louise took music lessons, and Pop tooted his trombone, so it was a good thing, on the whole, that the Getchells, who lived in the other apartment, were somewhat hard of hearing. When Louise's music teacher ("Mame" Morgan, descendant of Groton's most famous whaler) came to town to give Louise her lesson she would usually make a day of it and have other pupils at our house so that she could use our piano in teaching them. Sometimes one of the girls who came would get caught by a storm and spend the night with us, sleeping with Louise. The guest usually hadn't brought a nightgown and sometimes would refuse the one Louise proffered, saying that it was a shame to muss it up for just one night; and I, through half-closed eyes, learned that the nighttime is not so dark as it is cracked up to be. But I'm sure it didn't do either the girls or me any harm. It was all in the course of education, and I think Mom and Pop had figured it that way in arranging the beds as they did.

After we got into bed I listened while the girls talked about everything from Beethoven's sonatas to who put the wasp in Millie Marquardt's bloomers, and how the individual town boys stood in the local wolves' league. It was all in the course of education. I never heard anything complimentary to myself, but I learned something from that too.

My favorite among Louise's overnight guests was Nancy Colberg, daughter of Captain Martin Colberg who for years skippered the Sound steamer *Chelsea*, on which Pop and I sometimes went to New York together, and which Pop had piloted for a time. Nancy was there often, and sometimes Louise would go to sleep before she did. Nancy and I would take up the conversation, talking across the room to each other quietly, happily, never romantically—and yet there was romance in it too, in the best sense of the word. Often she would tell me stories of the sea told her by her father; I have never forgotten them. Morris, who was then at an age at which all girls seemed useless impediments, was usually sound asleep long before.

Of course the fact that these friends who now and then shared a bedroom with Louise and Morris and me were girls, and that they were lying naked or nearly so just a few feet from my bed, made such nights more exciting to me than any in which boys stayed over and slept with me, yet there were no sly intimations of sex in these encounters, no evasions or nasty giggling in our speech or in our thoughts. It was all good useful friendliness, and if (as in the case of the blond and freckled sea-captain's daughter) there was unspoken romance in my heart, it was a clean and good and wholesome thing, which raised, if anything, the standards by which I would always want to measure relations between the sexes. I have often since thought of those nights since I have grown up, and have thought back to an earlier day when "bundling" was a controversial custom in New England, and have wondered whether those who believed in it and saw that it was practiced in their households, hadn't seized upon a pretty good idea after all.

III. Easy Choice

I think that Pop had more guts than anyone else I've ever known (unless it's Ma) and that's a good memory for any man to have of his father. If he was ever afraid of anything in his life—whether it was danger, or something too big for him to handle—I never knew it. In 1912 he was master of the steam lighter *Panuco* which was used to haul rock and fill when the Duck Island breakwater was being built. He was a terrible worker, never content to stay in the pilot house as most captains did while a load was being discharged; he was always down on deck helping and hurrying things along. One day in April, as a load was being taken off the *Panuco*, a huge rock slipped out of the sling and pinned him against the rail, breaking one leg in three places, breaking his pelvis, chipping his spine, and crushing him internally. No one had any idea that he would live. He was taken up, rushed to shore, and put on a train for New London. By a strange chance, his own mother, bound for her home in Mystic, was on that train and heard that there was a badly injured man in the baggage car, but didn't learn who it was until later.

After the doctors had examined him at the hospital they gave him a fifty-fifty chance to live overnight—and they were trying to put it kindly. They really had little hope for him, and, deciding that the ordeal of operation would kill even that little, they didn't operate on him that day. Pop knew what that meant, but he couldn't be bothered with what they thought about it. He had beaten worse than fifty-fifty odds before. The next morning he was still alive, so they went to work on him, patching him up here, straightening him out there, doing the best they could. Then they told him pityingly that if he would lie in bed very quietly for a few months he might be able to walk again with crutches or a bad limp, but of course he would never be able to work hard again.

Pop grinned grimly at them. "You want to bet on it?" he asked.

Of course no one took the bet. It wouldn't have been a polite thing to do. And it's a pity no one did. Pop would have made the one bit of money in his life which had not cost him hard labor.

As soon as I learned about what had happened to Pop I remembered what he had told me on the day Morris was born about being the man of the house while he was away. My first concern was for his new power boat, the *Florence*. Getting Morris to go along, I rook the rowboat and rowed out to it, and together we pumped out the bilge, sloshed water over the decks to keep the planking from drying out, and in general tried to see that everything was shipshape. And seven-year-old Morris worked along with me, taking orders like a well-trained mate at sea. Every day while Pop was laid up we did that, unless the weather made it impossible.

Slowly but surely he began to mend. Two and a half months after entering the Old Home Memorial Hospital he was free enough from pain to be able to get along without doping. Then one day when one of the nurses mentioned that, in case of fire, they would have to carry his bed out with him in it, and that that would be a pretty awkward performance, he went into action. He called for the head nurse, the chief surgeon, and his regular doctor, and demanded that he be sent home. "If you can take me out of here in bed when there's a fire, you can do it easier when there ain't." he said. Then he told them how it could be managed.

And so we at home had the surprise of our lives when we got a telegram telling us to expect Captain Frank Thompson, who would arrive in bed. Of course it set us all to wondering just how a guy would arrive home in bed, but I had a hunch and, taking Morris by the hand and collecting two of my buddies, Chick Coffin and Harold ("Brownie") Lawry (who, years later, married my sister Louise), hurried down to the ferry dock just in time to see Pop's ferryboat, the *Governor Winthrop*, heading across the river from New London to Groton. Right away I knew Pop was on it, though, not being dead sure, I was still keeping my idea of how he got there to myself. Aloft the boat was decked with a string of brightly colored code flags, and at regular intervals the skipper tooted his whistle. I counted twenty-one toots between New London and Groton, and at each one my pride mounted. Each toot meant something a lot better than the twenty-five thousand fish that a Wilcox steamer's toot told about. Finally I could contain my feelings no longer and, turning to Chick Coffin and Brownie Lawry, said, "See what they think of my Pop? He wasn't captain of that ferry for eight years for nothing!"

"My Pop, too!" Morris protested.

"How much did he make as cap'n?" Chick Coffin asked with a competitive gleam in his eye.

"Ninety dollars a month," I said proudly.

"My old man makes twenty-five a week as a carpenter," Chick said smugly.

"Wait till we get a bigger boat for dragging and taking out parties," I boasted. "He'll make a lot more than that." Of course I had heard what the doctors had said about Pop never being able to work hard again, but I paid no attention to talk like that. I knew the old man, and they didn't.

"I'll bet he'll make a million dollars," Morris said and stuck his lower lip out stubbornly in a way he had all his life.

Brownie Lawry, whose hobby was wireless and code messages, hadn't been paying attention to our argument but had sat there, his eyes fixed on the ferry with a thoughtful look, his lips moving silently. Finally he had it figured out. "Know what those flags say?" he yelled. "They read: GET WELL, CAPTAIN FRANK!"

Just then the boat made a rather bumpy landing, which must have shook Pop up something terrible, and the first thing off it was—what else but a B.B. Gardner horse-drawn moving van, just as I had suspected. There seemed always to be one around wherever Pop was. Inside it was Pop in his hospital bed, padded on every side with great wads of thick moving-van quilts. On the back of the van someone had chalked AMBULANCE. The horses were all dolled up with ribbons and rosettes as though they were hauling a wedding carriage. In the driver's seat, holding the reins very tightly and a little too high, as if he were a bit afraid of them, sat a well-dressed gentleman with a goatee and a stiff hat. Beside him rested a black medicine case. It was Pop's surgeon, who had insisted on driving the van himself in order to make sure that there were no unnecessary jolts.

Slowly the noble vehicle started down Thames Street, the doctor avoiding all the bumps. And in shouting excitement we boys followed, picking up recruits as we went, until there were over a dozen boys and at least that many dogs in a wild and joyous procession. Folks along the way thought a circus had come to town.

Up Allen Street and into Granite Street, and finally the van-ambulance-caravan-of-joy backed up to our piazza, where there were plenty of willing neighbors' hands ready to help. The sky was darkening. Plainly a storm was brewing, and they wanted to get Pop under cover at once. They unloaded the bed quickly and gently and carried it, with Pop on it, up the steps. Then they encountered difficulty. The darned thing wouldn't go through the door. As they were hesitating and wondering what to do, the rain hit us like a wave off Napatree. The moving men were for putting the bed back on the van, but Pop said, "Not by a damn sight. Set me down and rig up an awning over me. There's some old sailcloth in the basement that'll do fine. I've been wet before and I'm going to be wet again, for I'm home now, and I'm going to stay here."

Then one of the men, who was used to moving pianos, had a bright idea. He asked for a hammer and took a window casing out of the side of the house, and they shoved Pop and his bed through the hold. And there he was, as snug as a skipper in the cabin of his boat.

He was installed in the parlor near a window facing the river, where, with his bed tilted a little, he could watch the river traffic; and he was happy. His government paycheck came in every month, and so there was no acute financial distress. But now and then I saw him looking with worried eyes at Ma, who was getting bigger and bigger. It wasn't until November, when she went to the hospital and came back thin again with my little sister Eleanor in her arms, that I knew why. For Morris and me that year was sure one of varied excitements. While Ma was in the hospital Grandma Thompson took over, and we kids had to mind our steps under the watchful eyes of the strictest disciplinarian I have ever known.

When Ma came back from the hospital with Eleanor, Grandma Thompson went home to Mystic, and Pa, with the aid of crutches, got up. We celebrated at the kitchen table that night until nine o'clock, with oyster stew and steak and milk. I remember Pa ate two dishes of oyster stew and was about to ask for a third when he sniffed the steak and sighed and went to work on that instead.

In a week Ma was apparently as strong as ever. But it wasn't until the following spring that Pa got out of the house, hobbling around on crutches. About that time government papers came to the house; they had something to do with a pension. But Pa wouldn't sign them, and sent them back. He growled to my mother, "No siree, I'm not going to life off of the government." Ma said, "Frank, you're making a mistake. You'll regret it." And the subject was dropped.

Then, as, to all outward appearances, complete recovery loomed ahead for Pa, he got ambitious and wanted to expand his boating activities. To do this in proper style—he had his eye on the *Isabelle*, a thirty-eight-foot sloop yacht, suitable for taking charter parties—he needed five hundred dollars. I heard him talking it over with my mother. "Flossie," he said, "we can sell those two shares of Wilcox Fertilizer stock to Uncle Al Wilcox, and I think he will let me have enough extra so I can get the *Isabelle*."

"I hope you know what you're doing, Frank," was all my mother said.

Uncle Al came through as expected, and the *Isabelle* joined our fleet. Happy days were just over the rim of the yachting horizon; City Island to Newport, Norwich to Block Island, one to forty fathom, and Pop and I were in our element. By the time fall came around again, he looked and acted like his old self and could really give the laugh to the doctors. Pictures which I have of him, taken twenty years after the accident, show a man as straight as a ship's mast, hale and hearty, and looking much younger than his years.

Sometimes I wonder what was the most amusing experience Pop and I had while running the *Isabelle* as a party boat. Perhaps it was that awful Fourth of July party. Pop had contracted to take out fifty representatives of a large insurance organization on an all-day boating picnic; and he was to furnish four hundred mixed sandwiches—eight for each passenger. For all this he was to get one hundred dollars. Pop set the price; he should have made it a hundred and fifty dollars. Try to get a sandwich like one of those for a quarter today, even without a yacht trip thrown in!

The day preceding the party Pop skinned out his lobster pots for all the lobsters he could get his hands on—"respectable" illegal ones included. He went to town and bought several large hams, a dozen chickens, and enough cheese to fill a wheelbarrow. After this stuff was freighted home, it was up to Ma. She went to work; she called in a neighbor, and they boiled the lobsters about twenty-five minutes—the right time for a plump, one-pound lobster; then they boiled the hams and roasted the chickens and cut up the cheese. Louise and I helped, and Morris stood around waiting for the tidbits I handed him on the sly. It was fascinating work. One chicken practically disappeared without touching a sandwich.

At midnight everyone knocked off. We all got up at daylight and finished the job of making sandwiches. Ma made most of them. The kitchen and living room were full of sandwiches. I even had my pockets full of them, and a whole lobster in my hip pocket. I wasn't hungry, but I couldn't let the opportunity go to waste.

Pa and I took the grub to the shore in a wheelbarrow—three loads. Then it rained. Only half the party showed up. Half of them got seasick. After the party was over we had two hundred and ninety-four and a half sandwiches to cart home—two loads. The Thompsons and half the neighbors went on a sandwich diet. We cleaned them up, but it was work. We even called in our neighbor's cat and dog to help out. They looked the situation over and made an agreement between themselves—the dog working on the meat, and the cat on the lobster sandwiches. As we washed the final ones down with tea, company walked in on us. And there wasn't a thing to eat in the house. Mother wept, and Father said a polite damn.

Finally came the day when the New London Ship and Engine Company began filling in the old shipyard cover near our house in Groton. Our mooring spots were doomed, our swimming hole was gone, and our spirits hit bottom for a while. Then Pop decided to take his boats to New London and tie them up there at some old dock where they wouldn't bother anyone.

This venture was to turn out better than I anticipated.

There were free rides on the ferry, since Pop was captain and during the winter I would climb down into the ferryboat fire room and bask in 110-degree heat before an open fire door as Stew Holliway, stripped to the waist, heaved in large shovelfuls of soft coal, and the blazing fire seemed to wave red hands at me through the open door. There was the fruit and candy stand in the ferryhouse. The fruit stand was outside and the candy stand inside; it was awfully convenient for a team of boys. While one bought fruit on the outside the other helped himself to candy on the inside, or vice versa. But retribution came on the wings of officially acquired virtue. Later, when this same team of boys joined Mr.

White's Knights of King Arthur in Groton, conscience made them pay back to the ferryhouse fruit dealer enough money to buy a crate of oranges from Florida.

The only trouble with living in Groton and fishing out of New London was that you were licked on getting out fishing early in the morning. The first ferry (and the only way across the river for most commuters) was about five-thirty A.M., and during summer the sun was riding high by that time. Pop said, "Ellery, some day I'm going to live in New London and not depend on a ferryboat to get me to my boats."

And in time we did, but even before that, while we were still living in Groton I spent as much of my time as possible at New London's old Ferguson Dock where Pop berthed his boats. These were some of the happiest and most instructive days of my life.

The dock was a T-shaped affair, a relic of prosperous whaling days, which lay sprawled on the waterfront near the Custom House, Bailey's Sail Loft, and Darrow and Comstock's ship chandlery. Now most of it was eaten away with rot and marine growth. It was on the south side of the New Haven railroad track—the "wrong" side—and into the area ventured every kind of humanity God ever fashioned. Some of the smaller fishing boats tied up there, and of course some people came to see them. Others came to watch the Block Island steamer land at a neighboring dock; some came to watch the government buoy-setter take on gaily colored channel buoys at the station just to the west. Some men and some women came, bent, I was told, on wickedness. But I didn't understand anything at all about that. The habitués of the place who enchanted me were the old-timers who came at all hours just to hang around and shoot the breeze and tobacco juice.

There was an old shack on the dock and a pot-bellied stove in the middle of it, on which there was usually a pot of coffee brewing, and just outside was a pile of coal picked up along the New Haven tracks. (Later, after dragging began, much of the coal was covered with seaweed, for it was brought up in nets from wrecks of coal barges lying on the bottom of Long Island Sound.) I learned there to make good coffee—a whisky glass full of coffee for every pint of furiously boiling water, and, it it's a big coffee pot, an extra glassful for the pot. I learned that a whisky glass has many uses even if there is no whisky around. It's an excellent cutter for shipboard biscuits, made from a recipe I acquired in the Ferguson dock shack. It makes biscuits about as big and about as hard as a silver dollar; some people call them "dog-watch biscuits."

One old-timer who admitted—as though it were a crime to read—that he had read a book Called *Moby Dick* said that he himself had once seen the great white whale off Nantucket. A remark like that was always a signal for something else from another—sometimes serious fact, sometimes a story in the realm of good fantastic fiction. On the day when I first heard about Moby Dick another fellow said he had seen him once too.

"It was when I was a young fellow," he went on. "And it was just before I went overboard and he swallowed me. So I know just how Jonah felt. Only I was smart. I didn't wait for him to throw me up. When I realized I was too far down to get out the front way I began to work my way toward the rear exit, and I was glad I had a lot of clothes on, because I could feel the whale's digestive juices going to work. I tried to find his ribs to use sort of like steps on the way, but he had too much belly fat. I tickled him good, though, and that made him contract and help me along, and I needed it, because bit by bit I felt things going. First my hat and pea jacket were digested, and then my boots and pants and other things. Finally, just as I was stark naked and beginning to feel my skin going, I reached the exit and swam to the surface, raw, almost gone, but still alive, and here I am."

From day to day I looked forward to tales like this, and to the lessons I learned at the Ferguson Dock Informal Academy of Fishing, Sailing, Yarn-Spinning, and Acceptance of Life, and a lot of the lessons were practical—how to harpoon a swordfish without getting tangled in the line (I think it was Captain Ed Slade who taught me this, using a keg thrown into the water as the fish, and a barbless harpoon); how to plug the hinges of lobsters' claws with little tapered plugs to keep them from destroying one another while being shipped (Captain Green, an old lobsterman, taught me this); how to scale and rip open and gut fish; how to open sea-scallops without destroying the meat; how to read charts, and where the channels were and the rocks weren't; how to tie four or five essential knots, make a couple of good splices and several hitches; how to mend a net; and how to tell what kind of weather to expect. I learned, for instance, than when a ground swell was coming in from offshore, gulls were flying high and circling, a ring had been around the moon the night before, a sundog appeared in the western sky, the barometer was falling, and Old Nate Lester's rheumatism was acting up, it was time to batten down hatches if at sea, or stay ashore if you were fortunate enough to be there.

I learned that alcohol floats, and that as often as not a drunken person does not drown; for the day a white-haired woman, boiled as a hoot owl, fell overboard from the Block Island steamer while a near-by band was playing "Rock of Ages, Cleft for Me" I saw her float ashore in better shape than she went in, before the band finished playing the second verse. A watcher said, "What a pity! She may be somebody's mother." Nate Lester snorted and said, "Somebody's damned fool the devil doesn't want."

Most people would call much of the talk I heard on the Ferguson Dock rough talk, but in using that adjective they would have missed the point. These were men who had seen life and death at close range, to whom all fundamental facts were equally noteworthy and story-worthy. Stories which, in the way of their telling, in the choice of words, and in the facial expressions which accompanied them, might have reflected a dirty mind in some more polite circles were clean, wholesome, kindly, and informative stories as my friends told them.

I remember one about a fisherman who had worked hard all his life and had little to show for it when he had passed sixty. One day at sea, after some particularly troublesome moments, he suddenly seemed to blow his top and, crying, "Work like a horse, look like a horse," he took off all his clothes, threw them over the side, and stood stark naked on the deck.

"And did he look like a horse?" the man who told the story was asked.

"He looked like an old stallion," the man said sadly, "like a very old one."

It was not meant to be funny. It was merely graphic, and the listeners nodded sympathetically and went on puffing their pipes and spitting tobacco juice into the water silently. No one laughed.

They were that way in their nomenclature, too—casually physiological and graphic, without being dirty about it. Every one of them was acquainted with the tide rips and often treacherous rock bottoms of those narrow channels between small islands, which are called "holes"—Woods Hole, Quicks Hole, Robinson's Hole, Holmes' Hole. And for one particularly nasty one they had a name of their own which wouldn't look well in print, but sounded all right when they said it and was eloquent of what they thought of it. Their directory of "heads," those promontories on land which were often welcome sights to men at sea, was similar. Martha's Vineyard had its Gay Head, Fishers Island its Fish Head, Block Island its Clay Head, Nantucket its Sankaty Head, and it is not surprising that they gave the promontory on the tiny island Noman's Land (which they always call "No Man's Land," and so do many maps erroneously label it) the name "Maidenhead."

As I grew up with these men I became used to their talk and their ways, and came to understand the hearty goodness of which they were made and to find in them a wholesomeness which some with other backgrounds might not have recognized. Here is another story which illustrates what I mean. In later years, when I was a young man and fishing, I had a fisherman friend about my age who had been courting the same girl for over a year, saving every penny he could.

One day when I met him I could see at once that he was terribly excited and happy about something. Grinning like a kid, he stuck his hand out in front of me. "Ellery," he said, "shake hands with a married man!"

Surprised, I shook his hand and said, "Did you really do it?"

"Nope," he said, "but I've got to!" And there was pride and happiness in his voice. Now he didn't have to answer any questions his conscience kept asking him about whether he could support the girl properly. Now he was going to have to do right away what he had wanted terribly for over a year to do, and everything was fine. Today he, his wife, and his several children are among the happiest people I know.

All of my experiences, which still loom large in my memory, influenced my decision to fish for a living, but I'm sure that the final shove came one day when Pop seemed hell-bent to show me as much of water-front life as possible between sunrise and sunset. Whether he intended that the day should furnish a clinching argument or not, I don't know. But that's what it amounted to.

Pop had some business with white-haired Jerry Davis, dean of Noank's small-boat builders, so we took an early trolley for Noank. Jerry was busy repairing a small boat when we got there, and Pop didn't try to stop him. And so, as I watched with fascination, I saw the old builder do one of the things for which he was famous. He was proud of the accuracy of his eye, and hated to use a rule when anyone was watching. I saw him squint at a place in the side of the boat which needed a bit of planking, saw him squint again at a board that was in his hand, then back at the boat again; and then he sawed the board off without measuring. When he placed it against the space in the side of the boat it fitted perfectly. He glared at us defiantly. Then he grinned, and we grinned back, and the talk started between Pop and Jerry, while in fantasy I wielded the old man's tools, making the best darned boats ever seen off the Connecticut coast. I was glad I hadn't been there the time one of Jerry's boards didn't fit, which was still talked about whenever Jerry's name was mentioned among those who knew him. I'd learn the trick myself, and my boards would *always* fit.

Before leaving for Mystic we went to look over Jack Daboll's twenty-eight-foot Lathrop-powered boat, a duplicate of Pop's, in which Jack had brought back a thousand pounds of lobsters and a ton of six-pound bluefish one day not long before. And I saw myself standing knee-deep in fish in the stern of his boat, with Morris standing beside me, the two of us gloating over our catch.

At Mystic we visited the factory where the famous Lathrop marine engines were made. Pop knew James W. Lathrop, pioneer in marine gasoline engine construction, and he and his son Walter showed us around. As we were leaving, Mr. Lathrop put one hand on my shoulder and said, "When's this boy of yours going to be ready for a Lathrop engine, Captain Frank?"

I answered for Pop. "As soon as Morris is old enough," I said. "He's only nine now." And both men laughed. But it was kindly, friendly laughter.

We got to Stonington in the early afternoon and went to the steamboat dock, where the retired Sound steamers, the *Puritan* and the *Pilgrim*, lay in depressing idleness. The father of Bert Ford—who was later to fish with me—was caretaker of the boats and invited us aboard. From an upper deck of the *Puritan*, now ghostly in its vast lifeless emptiness, we watched a lazy scene in Stonington Harbor. Two small trapping outfits, the Burdicks and Ostmans, were tending their traps near the outer breakwaters. A coal-laden schooner was anchored near the west breakwater, and not far from the *Puritan* were two Portuguese women trying to swim in what appeared to be at least four dresses and six petticoats. Directly beneath us, lying under the shelter of the *Puritan's* huge bow, were several small draggers, hand-liners, and lobster boats.

It was a fascinating spot. As we left the *Puritan* and the *Pilgrim* and headed up the dock, my pulse was quick with excitement engendered by the sights and sounds and smells of the harbor, and pride in my father, who knew all about these things. The pretty Portuguese women were heading up also. One of them waved, and Pop waved back. "Don't tell your Ma," he said to me. "Around the water front, strangers wave at one another, but never try it in the city park." I promised and felt proud of his confidence.

As we were about to head for the trolley line to go home we noticed a large white and buff Wilcox fishing steamer coming up the harbor, and preceding it on the wings of an afternoon sou'wester was the delightful aroma of cooked food—food which, one could tell by the smell, was fit for a king or a fisherman.

"It's the *Rowland Wilcox*," said Dad. "She's going to dock at Bindloss's coal dock. We'll go down; I want to see Uncle Rowland." And waterward we went again to turn off at the coal dock.

Apparently the steamer's crew had eaten an early supper, for, after tying up, they lined the rail—a few chewing on toothpicks, the rest chewing tobacco. A crowd had gathered; among it was Mr. William Bindloss—my father had pointed him out as the dock's owner—and with him was a small boy about four years younger than myself. My father and Mr. Bindloss were old friends and soon they were in earnest conversation, while little Johnnie and I glared at each other. (We don't any more. It is at John Bindloss's dock in Stonington that my boat, the *Eleanor*, is berthed.)

Suddenly Captain Rowland Wilcox appeared at the rail and called out to Mr. Bindloss and my father to come aboard and bring the young dabs along. After we had climbed aboard he asked us to have supper with him. An invitation to supper on a Wilcox steamer! Wow! That was equivalent to eating at Rector's or Delmonico's.

We found the Wilcoxes' reputation for good eating well deserved. The table in the gallery was loaded; none of us stopped eating until after we had stowed away quantities of bluefish and steak and cake and pie cooked by the ship's cook. Finally most of the gang in the galley got up slowly with satisfied looks on their faces and drifted out onto the deck, but Captain Rowland, Mr. Bindloss, Father, Johnnie, and I stayed at the table. Johnnie and I began ribbing each other about girls, while Mr. Bindloss told a couple of yarns about his father, who had outfitted several whalers for trips to the Antarctic region; and Captain Rowland Wilcox told about his last trip, and how, finding no menhaden, he had set around mackerel, made a good catch, and sold them over the docklog at Newport. "In fact," he said, "we just came from there."

My father had said little up to this point, but now, mellowed by two cups of

good coffee, he told about making and fishing the first beam trawl in Connecticut. Captain Rowland Wilcox said, "Come up to my stateroom a minute,
Frankie, and I'll show you on the chart where there is a smooth bit of good
flounder ground off Charlestown, Rhode Island. I think it would be a perfect
spot for your new king of drag fishing."

We all climbed up to the skipper's room aft of the pilothouse. The captain
pulled out a chart and showed Dad a spot marked by a cross—a spot which,
since then, has been named "the Hell Hole" by draggermen who have torn their
nets to tatters on the sharp rocks of the bottom. But Captain Rowland Wilcox
was right about the abundance of fish there.

As we were about to leave, Dad noticed a big hump in the Captain's bunk
and spoke about it.

"Oh that," said Captain Wilcox, peeling back his mattress. "It's only five
thousand dollars in bills from the trip of mackerel we sold yesterday. Haven't
had time yet to get it over to Mystic and bank it."

Going home on the trolley, I kept thinking of that lump in Captain Wilcox's
bunk. I also remembered the day before Thanksgiving 1908, when Pop and I
had set and towed the first trawl net in Connecticut, and my feeling that I had
helped to make fishing history. I recalled a certain Sunday in 1912 when we
had dragged up two thousand pounds of flounder, six pairs of corsets, a man's
foot, and a Model T Ford. (As a matter of fact, Pop got a Packard once.) And I
would never forget the day I caught a thirteen-pound bluefish on Bartlett's Reef
south of the Harkness estate. And I remembered that treasure chest that Pop
nearly recovered from the three-hundred-foot-deep hole in the Race, which was
doubtless still there waiting to be taken.

I was through with the fishing question: to be or not to be. Hell, I wasn't
going to be a fisherman; I was one, and had been one for a long time, only I had-
n't fully acknowledged it yet. I was just going to quit the senseless business of
going to school up the street, so that I'd have more time to spend on the important things in life.

That night at home in Groton my father saw the time was ripe. The family,
all six of us, were assembled in the living room overlooking the harbor. I could
see the beam from a Sound steamer's searchlight playing about on low-hanging
clouds. A tugboat was blowing a series of short snappy toots, signaling barges
to stand by with hawsers. A Sound fog had cleared, and another shipment of
coal was to continue along the coast. Morgan's yacht *Corsair* could be seen silhouetted against the well-lit New London water front. A similar scene could
have been duplicated in a dozen New England harbors.

But the scene in our living room was somewhat different. The last bottle of
the evening for Eleanor rolled empty to the floor. Louise was reading Camp
Fire Girl literature. Morris, by the Victrola, was picking out an Uncle Josh

record; looking up, he gave me a big grin, and I grinned back at him.

I now divided my attention between my mother's worried expression and my father's clean rubber collar, well-trimmed mustache, and blue uniform coat left over from his steamboat career.

The wall telephone jangled. My mother, looking annoyed, moved over to answer it, her dress swishing and swashing across the floor. "No, I'm not going to take the children to see Mary Pickford or Marguerite Clark....Yes, I'll ask Frank about a pinochle game tomorrow night....I'll call you later. Good-by." The shortness of her answers showed that her mind was not on the conversation. She came back and sat down again.

I looked out the window and saw the shadows of a widely strung-out water parade. The *Keeler* was moving down the harbor with her string of barges.

And then it came. "Ellery, are you going back to school, or are you going to work ashore, or do you—"

I saw Morris looking at me expectantly, counting on me, and I didn't wait for my father to finish. Hell, we had had it all settled between us long before this. I said, "I do."

And then he gave me a lot of good advice about fishing, but what I remembered best—for he had said it to me before, and he said it to me many times after that evening—was: "Keep your feet firmly on deck, never step into a coiled line, and keep away from the edge of the boat as much as possible." His use of the word "edge" was intentional. He could have used any number of nautical terms, such as "bulwarks," "rail," or "scuppers," but he said "edge," as though it were a cliff or a precipice—something over which one could fall to his death. It doesn't take a very vivid or poetic imagination to consider that speech as something composed of metaphors, and to make of it one of the soundest bits of advice any boy could have in facing any circumstance of life.

From that day on it seemed as if I was married to a life on salt water. At least, I've put more into it than most people put into their marriages.

IV. Seventeen-year-old Skipper

I started fishing steady with my father in June 1914, when the new method of dragging with an otter trawl seemed to have rosy prospects. Sometimes Morris went along with us—just for the ride, we thought. But even then, at nine, the kid was showing that he meant business. He would get into the thick of activity whenever he could, help with the net—doing the right things, too—wade into the fish when we were sorting them, often pricking and cutting his hands on their spiny fins and never squealing about it. He had a way of half opening his mouth, which denoted stubbornness, and when he did this and pulled his cap down over his eyes, his big ears sticking out from under it, and hooked one thumb in the top buttonhole of his jacket, he looked tough. He was tough, but in the way you want a man to be; and I always envied him his ability not to consider the risks before undertaking a thing, and not to be scared, even when there was something to be scared about. Then and later I felt that at every step he was about two years ahead of me, doing at nine what I did at eleven, at eleven what I did at thirteen, and so on.

At that time most of the boats around eastern Connecticut fished close inshore for reasons of safety and because there were enough fish—flounders, mostly—for the boats then in use; the fish hadn't learned to move father offshore to avoid the fishermen.

Sometimes we dragged our net in the channel of the Thames river above the drawbridge at New London. One favorite spot was just below the submarine base, where, in late June—and generally with ninety-degree heat—the crews of Yale and Harvard struggled in narrow racing shells down or up a fourteen mile course. Yachts came from everywhere for Regatta Day, their decks jammed with celebrants, to anchor just about where our best river fishing grounds were located. Many yachts had women guests, and during the weeks following Race Day we usually dragged up more odd, and frequently intimate, mementoes of the regatta than we did fish. Women on boats often do strange things, and, in moments of emotional stress, are likely to throw almost anything through a porthole.

One day my father's boat pulled up a beautiful pair of blue corsets. One of the crew remarked that they were better than those worn by his wife. He washed them carefully, hung them on a line on deck until they were dry, and took them home. The next day he appeared on the boat with a black eye. He said his wife had said to him, just before she hit him, "You've accused me of busting out all over the place. Okay. Then get me a new pair of corsets. Even a good second-hand pair bought in a store will do. But I'll be damned if I'll wear anything thrown into the mudbank of a river by a educated tart!"

The majority of commercial fishermen today do not fish quite so much in cluttered waters, so naturally the contents of a fishnet do not run to old shoes, lamps, bedsprings, corsets, clocks, automobiles, brassieres, high-heeled shoes, etc.

After a year of fishing my father decided I should follow in his footsteps and be a steamboat man. Since I had many glamorous tales of steamboat life and had watched the large white vessels go by, I didn't mind a bit. Two friends of Pop's, Valentine Chappell and Captain Howell, gave a hand, and, at the age of sixteen, I found myself bow-watchman on the famous twin-screw Sound steamer, the *City of Lowell*, under the command of Captain James Pettigrew.

The *Lowell* ran between New London and New York; she once established a new record for a passenger steamer running through Long Island Sound, making the one-hundred-and-thirty-odd-mile trip between New York City and Stonington in five hours and twenty minutes. That would be speed even today.

Those nights when the *City of Lowell* raced the water thoroughfare of Long Island Sound with a westerly gale on her tail were memorable nights for me. The nights when I prowled around New York City were too, though I never did anything very startling. I remember a night when I reached a high point in daring and bought some French postcards outside a theater. I was warned not to open them until I was in the next block, so I waited, and then, my heart beating wildly, I tore the envelopes open, only to find that I had bought a few souvenir postcards bearing photographs of the Arc de Triomphe, Notre Dame Cathedral, the Eiffel Tower, and the Louvre! And did I feel foolish and city-slickered!

Sooner than I would have liked, the Congress of the United States ended my steamboating days by passing a law barring all boys under eighteen from petty officerships on passenger-carrying coastal vessels. That let me out, so back I went from the New York water front to the water front at New London and my father's fishing boat.

Morris and I used to look at the waterfront habitués speculatively—especially the so-called "sporting girls." We wondered just what sporting events they were connected with, and it is to their credit that they never enlightened us.

My father had taught us both to treat all people alike, a sort of friendly neighbor policy and application of the golden rule rolled into one. That was why, one day, I took Morris and two of these sporting-girl characters to lunch at a popular New London restaurant. As we sat down, two well-known businessmen at the next table got up hurriedly with red faces, leaving unfinished meals, nodded coolly to us, and left the restaurant. Our guests smiled and waved at them gaily. We then continued our conversation about boats, fishing, automobiles, and Morris's school work, with which he was becoming as impatient as I had with mine a few years before.

I really didn't know why the two men had looked the way they had; I thought that it was just some strange kind of snobbery, and, remembering my father's teaching, felt superior about it. Now I'm pretty sure that they knew intimately a side of my companions' lives of which I knew nothing. But I'm equally sure that I knew a side of those girls which the men never remotely guessed, and I still think that I had the best of it. The girls I knew were nice sisterly friends.

I learned alter that that day marked the beginning of a certain amount of unjustified talk around town about "those wild Thompson boys," who were "beginning so young!"

There were a lot of questions about the facts of life in my mind in those days. Women like those I took to lunch, for instance—they were often called "bad women," though I never saw anything remotely bad about them, or anything except things that I liked. And one day I had a small adventure with one of them, which made me try in vain to make an adequate definition of what constituted good, and what bad, so far as women were concerned.

Her name was Belle. I had seen her around the dock often when the fishing boat came in—a natural enough thing, it seemed to me, for it was a fine spot to catch the breeze on a hot day, while at the same time watching the boats—one of the best of all occupations.

The scene was quite ordinary as Pop and I brought the boat in and tied her up. (Morris wasn't along that day.) Pop went ashore at once to adjust the compass on a near-by ship, leaving me alone with the *Florence*. Belle was there on the dock, in her somewhat fancy dress, strolling about, enjoying the breeze; a taxi driver I knew was looking over a pile of scrap iron, the relic of a steamer's boiler, while waiting for a fare, and a couple of small boys were playing out near the end of the dock.

Then a shopping housewife came out onto the dock and asked me how much I would charge for a mess of flounders. I said, "Five cents a pound, or six pounds for a quarter." She said, "All right, I think I'll have three pounds. Will that be twelve cents or thirteen?" But before I could get the fish weighed and wrapped up, she screamed, "Oh, my goodness! Someone's fallen overboard!" Then she turned, and, holding up her long skirts, ran as though the Pequot Indians were after her.

I jumped ashore and ran up the dock and found Belle lying on her belly at the edge of the dock, hanging onto one of the boys who had fallen into the water. The taxi driver was hanging onto her ankles to keep her from tumbling off.

Meanwhile the railroad crossing attendant had rushed up, and we all soon got the kid back on the dock. He wasn't hurt, only scared, and he began to cry. Belle got to her knees and began to wipe his tears away with an old soiled handkerchief edged with cheap lace. The taxi driver began to laugh and said, "I'll bet that's the first time anyone has seen Belle on her knees since she was a little girl."

Belle said, "Oh, shut up! Look at my clothes, I'm a mess." Someone handed her her pocketbook; she had dropped it when she started to help the boy. She opened it, took out a half-dollar, and gave it to the boy saying, "Here, kid; here's four bits my mother gave me once. Take it and beat it, and don't you come down here again until you learn to swim!"

The taxi driver said, "Come on, Belle, I'll take you home. You've spoiled that dress."

The boy on his way up the dock turned and gave Belle one last look of gratitude.

Now, could you have told that boy that Belle was a bad woman? I wouldn't have wanted to be the one to do so, and if I had, I don't think he would have believed me.

Ever since that day I have tried to be pretty careful about saying who is bad and who is good or where one classification ends and the other begins. Just where some of us belong is questionable.

That afternoon was for me the beginning of a long acquaintance with Belle.

My associations along the water front never seemed to worry Pop. I think that if his principles about such things could have been put into a couple of sentences they would have gone something like this: "Help a kid to develop as much sense as you can and then give him his head and let him decide what's right and wrong for himself. Let him stick his neck into danger even if he gets knocked down now and then. Just try to stick around and give him a hand if he needs it. As to people, it takes all kinds to make a world, and he might as well get acquainted with as many kinds as possible right near home."

In later years I have heard the headmaster of a famous boys' school say with similar wisdom: "There are times when you have to knock a boy down, and it's right that you should do so—so long as you stay there and help him pick himself up again. The unforgivable thing is to walk away and leave him lying there. And never let a boy get your goat. They'll try to, you know."

I remember the dive I took that might have been my last if Pop had let me get his goat. We were anchored off the ferry slip, and I told Pop I could "pick up bottom" at fifteen feet. "Okay, prove it," Pop said. "Only I'm going to make sure I get you back."

He tied a six-thread line around my waist and I dove off the cabin, swimming out and down until I got to the anchor. Then, thinking I'd play a good joke on the old man, I held my breath and clung to the anchor. Finally I felt a light tug on the rope. Pop wasn't going to lose his elder boy. But still I hung on, and when Pop pulled harder I brought the anchor along with me.

"What the devil's got ahold of you?" he yelled when my head broke the surface. "A devilfish?"

"The anchor," I laughed, taking in a deep lungful of air. Then I let go of the thing and it started down again, but I started with it. It had caught in the rope at my waist. If Pop had got mad and let go the rope too, my joke might not have been very funny. But he didn't let go. He never did, once he had taken hold of a thing—not until it was finished right.

He had been brought up in a hard school and he saw to it that life was none too easy for me on shipboard. I could make a minor mistake once, but never twice. A major mistake was unthinkable; it could lose a ship and lives. Pop and I often got into hot arguments when we were at sea. If they got too hot I would climb the mast and dare Pop to come and get me, knowing that since his accident he wouldn't dare. Eventually, after watching the gulls gulping down fish, I would get hungry and come down; Pop and I would shake hands and start over again. But one time he tried to turn a handshake and a pat on the back into a half-Nelson and flatten me on deck. To save myself from a bad tumble I flattened him instead, and he got a bloody nose in the process. On the way home that night he said, "Don't tell Ma what happened. We'll say a swinging block struck my nose." (Austin Rice and K.O. Palitz, famous Connecticut boxers of that day, were friends of his, and he thought a lot of his boxing ability." "Okay, Pop," I said. After that our shipboard relations improved greatly.

Of course what he had in mind was teaching me to take care of myself and trying to make me tough enough so that I could do it. Sometimes when we "took up" we would find a thighbone or a human skull in the net to remind us how extremely dangerous fishing could be.

One day when my father and I were on the fishing ground midway between New London and Fishers Island we saw a neighboring trawler run by Tony Brown fishing near by. I was watching him, and turned away for only a moment. When I looked back he and his boat had simply disappeared. I called my father's attention to this strange fact, and as I did so we both saw wreckage floating on the water. We hastily buoyed our net and ran down toward the spot where I had seen the trawler. Finally we saw Tony swimming and floundering in the middle of the wreckage.

A Navy hundred-and-ten-footer which had also seen the accident came driving wide open for the scene of disaster, with men stripped naked to go overboard, but we waved them away, for we were close enough to get a line to Tony. We succeeded in pulling him on board.

A submarine running submerged had struck the towlines from his net on bottom and had overturned his boat. The trawler was now barely floating; just the tip of the stern showed at the water's surface.

My father quickly ran a strong line through two ring bolts on the stern of the sinking craft. We fastened the line to our stern, to keep Tony's boat from sinking, and slowly towed the swamped boat into New London harbor. The next day we picked Tony's gear up from bottom and found a three-hundred-pound shark in it. We kidded Tony for a long time about the shark that had capsized him.

One never knows with certainty what is under the keel of a boat. Another underwater danger brought tragedy to our fellow fisherman Manny Nunes and his brother. While they were fishing off Hatchett's Reef, near Saybrook, where the tide and freshets from the Connecticut River make dragging dangerous, their net caught on a submerged wreck, and before they could turn their boat head-on into the tide they were rolled over and Manny's brother was drowned.

One summer day Jim Neilan, ace reporter on the *New London Day* and correspondent for the *New York World* and *Boston Post*, chartered Pop's boat and took the *New London Day* Publishing Company employees on a picnic and fishing trip. Our luck with the fish lines was poor, so finally someone asked us to "drag the net." We headed for the dragging ground between Ocean Beach and Fishers Island.

We set the net, and while we were dragging the men talked about a shark scare along the Jersey coast where a large man-eating shark had come in close to the beach and attacked and killed several bathers. After an hour of such talk we "pulled up," and there, nestling in the midst of a nice catch of flounders, was a vicious looking five-hundred-pound shark! I never heard such a varied assortment of shrieks in my life as came from the women in the party, or saw more wide-eyed awe than even the men displayed. I don't know whether he was a man-eater or not, but he was an ugly looking fellow. I wouldn't have wanted to be overboard with him.

It was a chance in a hundred—and with newsmen and photographers aboard at that. Neilan had his pictures out that night, and the next day the large city papers carried the story and displayed the monster all over their front pages. And that was how the shark scare spread to New England.

Thanksgiving Day 1916, Pop came down with pneumonia. Against my mother's wishes but with Pop's permission, I tried to fish his boat that winter around the Thames River. At times I went alone or with Morris, but more often with an additional man to help.

One man I hired was a well-known water-front character, short but strong, called "One-eyed Mike." He was very shrewd, and people said he could see more with that one eye of his than most people could with two. It was a strange and disturbing experience for a seventeen-year-old kid to have a middle-aged, experienced fisherman working under him and calling him "Captain," and I used to work my boyish imagination into quite a frenzy by wondering what I would do if he ever mutinied. One day I found out.

It was after an extremely laborious drag, during which Tony was silent and seemed disgruntled. With the fish finally on deck, he sat down beside them and said, "I'm through."

My heart started beating hard, as it did at the height of my fantasies of mutiny, but I tried to look tough. "What for?" I said gruffly.

He held out his right hand, palm up, rubbing fingers and thumb together, which in any language means "more money."

"How much more?" I asked.

"Dollar seventy-five a day; dollar 'n half not enough."

"All right, Mike," I answered, trying to hide my relief at finding it so easy. "You'll get it. Come on, let's get back to work!"

He got up and started working again; and the short mutiny, which in reality was just a little sit-down strike, was over.

At night Mike always had a market basket filled with scrap fish to take home—skates, sculpins, toadfish, etc.—to which he was very welcome. One night the bottom came out of his basket as he was getting on the dock. Back on the deck fell the skates, sculpins, toadfish, and about ten large flounders that were hidden underneath. "How long has this been going on?" I asked.

"Not long," he replied. "Only since I work here." He winked at me, and what could I do but wink back?

It was rugged work fishing in the winter in those days. We wore woolen mittens, but after they got wet our hands seemed almost colder than they would have been with none on. Indeed, I have seen old-timers throw their mittens angrily on deck and work with bare, lobster-red hands, rather than have them encased in wool and ice. Today most fishermen use rubber-coated gloves and mittens. Running hot water on the deck also makes a lot of difference in fishing comfort.

We didn't do too badly that winter when I tried to be a skipper at seventeen, and we didn't do too well. With the first sign of spring Pop again took charge of the remains of his boat, engine, and gear, and it was just as well for both his boat and my education.

He had now decided to build a larger boat, so the thirty-six-by-eleven-foot *Eleanor Louise* was contracted for; the hull to cost seven hundred dollars. With a twenty-one-horsepower Lathrop and suitable equipment, the whole outfit cost about two thousand dollars. Today the same boat would cost six thousand dollars and would be considered a sliver. But in 1917 it was the largest and best dragging boat in local waters.

The summer his new boat, built by Jerry Davis of Noank, made her maiden trip, the *Florence* was turned over to me to run. Morris was now on his summer vacation, and I needed a crew, so the satisfaction of his need and mine was the same. He "signed on" with me, or, as we say in New England, "got a site" on my boat at a dollar a day. The fish were large and plump, numerous, and cooperative that summer, and we did all right.

At twelve, Morris was still only a kid, handy around boats and willing, but with his head still filled with some of the more fantastic bits of seacoast lore, which he took as gospel truth. That first week in July when we fished the *Florence* together he thought, for a few minutes, that he was seeing confirmation of one of the old legends. We were on the Sound off New London, the water smooth as glass, and the sun shining brightly, when he suddenly shouted at me "There's a mermaid swimming!" His eyes were popping with wonder and his pointing finger called my attention to something in the water at some distance from us. I steered the boat close, and soon saw that it was a young women, in a natural swimming position, her right arm outstretched as if about to take a crawl stroke, her face submerged in the water. But there was no movement anywhere about her.

I got the *Florence* alongside her, and we put a rope around her lifeless body and hauled it aboard—with scant ceremony, I'm afraid, since neither of us wanted to let the other see how scared and inadequate he felt. I remember being a little ashamed as we looked at her lying on the deck, as if my eyes were taking advantage of here when there was nothing she could do about it. I was sure that I had seen her face before, but couldn't think where. Then we put about and hurried back to shore.

Just inside the harbor we met a fishing boat captained by a friend of my father. I told him what we had aboard, and he at once told me that we were breaking a law. Rescuing a live person who is overboard is fine, but it is illegal to take a dead boy on board. So, scared again, we turned out to sea, put the rope around the body once more, and, feeling almost as though we were deserting one who by now had become a friend, put it overboard and towed it in.

When we got to the dock and the body was taken from the water by the proper authorities, I learned that it was that of the pleasant young usher at the Crown Theater in New London, who had often shown me to a seat and smiled at me. Searching parties had been out looking for her for some time, for she had started out the night before to swim around the lighthouse two miles from shore.

We fished around New London and close to Watch Hill most of the summer, although once we made a sort of pilgrimage to Block Island, ten miles off the coast of Rhode Island. This island is the subject of much fact and fancy, a sort of Never-Never Land of legend along the New England coast, the haven of many a storm-caught fishing boat, and one of the places where New Yorkers lose their inhibitions from June first to Labor Day. We had heard the fabulous stories, of course, of how many of the islanders made their living by salvage from wrecks; of how they even enticed ships to their death by setting up false lights in line with rocky reefs where any ship would meet its doom in a storm; of how they would tie a lantern to a cow and lead it back and forth behind a haystack, to give the appearance of a mariner flashing a light; of how they could club to death, for the purpose of robbery, any survivors swimming in from a wreck. We had also heard of the minister whose only compensation for years of preaching on the island was the privilege of using a longer wrecking pole with a larger hook on it than the others, and of the fact that the waters off Block Island were a favorite haunt of mermaids.

Years later I was having lunch with some visitors in a New London restaurant when an old Block Island friend of mine came and sat down with us. After we had swapped lies for awhile, the one New York City man in the group, who had drunk quite a lot, stuck his lower lip out in a stubborn expression and began quizzing the Block Islander. "Is it true," the New Yorker asked, "that the Island has family feuds like those in the Kentucky mountains, and that just a little while ago one Block Islander, in such a feud, shot another out of an apple tree?" The Block Island man had a poker face. "No," he answered. "We got no trees." The city man scowled, but he was not to be stopped. "Is it true," he asked again, "that your people used to lead a cow with a lantern tied to it around a haystack to lure ships onto the reef?" This time the Block Island man got mad. "That's a lie," he cried. "My grandfather told me it was a horse."

We didn't see any mermaids, and we didn't find anything which could remotely have confirmed any of the Block Island legends, but, even without mermaids, wrecks, or cows with lanterns tied to them, we had fun, and Morris and I decided that we were going to make Block Island a regular port of call. But Pop laid down the law when we got back the next day to a worried family. "Next time you feel like going as far away as that, you take me along," he said, and it was some years before I became really acquainted with the poor man's New-England-coast Miami.

During the winter of 1917-1918 my father and I decided to fish his new boat, the *Eleanor Louise*, together, so he sold the *Florence* to Captain Doolittle, who was one of the first fishermen to drag from New Haven. Then we moved again from Groton to Willow Point, and then from Willow Point to New London. Most of the B.B. Gardner moving vans were now horseless, and it was one of the new gasoline-driven trucks which, doing the last job we ever called on the Gardners to do for us, finally took all of our stuff from Willow Point and dumped it at 265 Crystal Avenue, New London, where Ma and I live to this day.

From the point of view of a boy, there were a number of fine things about living in New London. There were the T.A. Scott Corporation's tugs and lighters and other equipment for salvaging wrecks anywhere from points on the bottom of the sea to mountain-top sites; there were the three Sound steamers that ran to New York, the clipper-bowed steam yachts that berthed in Shaw's Cove, and the state pier, where the World War I German submarine *Deutschland* came to dock twice—once right after having sunk a Scott tug and her crew in the Race.

From New London's city dock I could almost see the United States submarine base up the river, and from the deck of Pop's boat or the ferryboat I often watched the whalelike O-boats sliding out to sea for their practice runs, and imagined that I could hear the captain crying, "Taker her down!" just before the last vestige slid noiselessly under the sea, leaving only an ever-widening circular ripple where the submarine had been a moment before.

The Navy and the fishing fleet were in inevitable and never-ending competition, for both needed to operate over waters with smooth bottoms—the Navy, in torpedo practice, so that it could easily recover its torpedoes, and the fishermen so that they would not foul their nets. We were always getting in each other's way.

We got along well together, though, and that summer Pop and I spent a lot of time helping the Navy recover its practice torpedoes. We broke our mast on one of them, but the Navy cheerfully and speedily stepped a brand new yacht mast for us.

During the summer Lieutenant Becker, executive officer of the O-5 had an idea. Since we managed to pick up so many torpedoes in a trawl net, why shouldn't the Navy do a bit of dragging in the same way? The truth was, I think, that the lieutenant like to fish, for after Pop had made two drag nets for him to use in dragging for torpedoes, he and his crew seemed to have a swell time. I don't remember that they dragged up any torpedoes in their nets, but they caught a lot of fish. The best of them they sent to the Navy Commissary; the rest they gave to Pop and me, so we didn't mind their competition.

One day, in a spirit of friendliness, Lieutenant Becker gave Pop a red flag. "Hoist it whenever your net gets caught on anything," he said, "and we'll send a diver out to get it free for you."

Not very long after that we hung out net on a wreck at the bottom, and up went the red flag. Immediately the diver's ship came alongside, the diver went down, and in a few minutes was up again, saying the net was free. Everybody shook hands with everyone else, and compliments were passed around; we went on dragging and finally pulled up with a good load of fish.

A few days later it happened again, and again we put up the red flag and the Navy responded. This time, too, the man was down only a few minutes; he came up, as before, and announced that our net was clear. So we all shook hands again, everybody intimating how nice everybody else was, the Navy went away, and we went on dragging. After a while we pulled up. But this time there wasn't a fish in the net, since it had no bottom at all. The diver had simply taken the easiest way of freeing it and slashed it to pieces with a knife. We never hoisted the red flag again.

During a lull in fishing operations, one warm day in June, while the net was down, I was living in one of my too-frequent fantasies, pretending I was at Ocean Beach walking with a group of young and pretty girls, all of whom were paying me extravagant compliments. I was roused by hearing real girls' voices and pleasant laughter. Looking up, I found my fantasy seemingly almost coming to life in front of me, for coming alongside was Luke Wilcox in his fishing and party boat, carrying a party that included two young and pretty girls. The majority of the party was composed of the family of John Allen of Occum, Connecticut. There were Mr. and Mrs. Allen, five-year-old Harry, sixteen-year-old John, Jr., eighteen-year-old Alma Lily, and nineteen-year-old Thelma.

Thelma was a lovely blonde, and Lily was a brunette with dark eyes whom I immediately labeled with an adjective suitable to my mood—mysterious. The girls' long hair was undone and blowing in the gentle wind—a very attractive style of the time. Luke and my father tied the two boats together, and we visited back and forth while our boat went right on dragging. I immediately forgot all about shore; I didn't even know in what direction it was. Right away I imagined myself a handsome and glamorous sailor and began doing a lot of little unnecessary things about the boat, to show off.

It seemed that all the Allens played musical instruments and were well-known around eastern Connecticut as the Allen Family Band and Orchestra, featuring Master Harry Allen, five-year-old cornet virtuoso. After everyone had been introduced, and in response to their new friends' urging, they picked up their instruments and played a couple of numbers—and played them well, even though the boats tied together were rolling slightly.

After the boats had been untied and each was making its separate way back, my father and I talked about what a nice gang they were, and Pop said, "Any man who marries into the Allen family must be a musician. Mr. Allen told me so."

The following week, after a profitable fishing trip, Pop, who was of a romantic turn of mind himself, and addicted to horns, bought me a silver-plated trumpet, taught me the fingering, and I went to work. Needless to say, after that I spent as much time as possible during week ends and stormy weather with the Allen family. And because of Pop's and Louise's musical interests and Ma's good cooking, the Allen family spent a lot of time at our house.

I huffed and puffed on that silver-plated trumpet for the blonde Thelma and the brunette Lily, and sometimes found it hard to tell whether I was a gentleman who preferred blondes, or just a young fisherman who liked brunettes too. However, after a time the Allens moved to the banks of the Taunton River.

By then I had saved a little money of my own, and I bought myself, as a consolation for my loss, the best darned horn in the show window of New London's leading music store—a gold-plated one this time. I practiced a lot around the Ferguson dock, and after a session of running the scales I put it up to old Nate Lester, who was standing near by with a pained look on his face.

"How do I sound, Cap'n Nate?" I asked hopefully.

He spit tobacco juice in the water below the dock log. Then he answered gently, "Like a third-rate down-and-out Salvation Army cornetist."

I resolved then and there: no more dock playing. In time I took my trumpet on three visits to the Allens' Taunton River farm. But somewhere along the line I had blown my chances. I lost the girl, but the trumpet has stayed in my life ever since. I've had a lot of fun with it, passed many a lonesome hour with its mouthpiece to my lips and my fingers on the valves; and once it probably save the life of my first boat, and maybe my own and those of a couple of other fellows.

Ellery Thompson, Age 20

V. Halfway to Heaven

Although we sent most of our fish direct to Fulton Fish Market in New York, we sold some locally in New London—to the Crocker House Hotel, Cheney and Packer Company, headed by Dad's friend George Packer, some retail at the dock, and many to the famous G.M. Long Company, whose office window directly overlooked the spot where we tied up. Now and then, after Pop had left me, and I was busy as a horse packing and icing fish and cleaning up, I noticed that I was being watched from the window of the Long office.

The G.M. Long Company was the largest buyer and handler of lobsters for miles around; it shipped tons to New York every day, as well as selling a tremendous number locally. Its Mumford Cove oysters were the largest, whitest, firmest, juiciest, best-looking and best-tasting oysters I ever ate. Mr. Maynard, the Long Company's opener, must have opened millions, and left behind him, as a monument to years of hard work, a mountain of shells.

The company at that time was owned and managed by Arthur Greenleaf and Nathaniel Avery. One day, when I was twenty years old, they sent an office boy down to the boat to invite me to come to their office.

"We've been watching you, Ellery," Mr. Greenleaf said, "and wonder whether you wouldn't like to have a brand new boat of your own."

"Sure," I said. "Who wouldn't? But I haven't much money."

They said, "Hang on to what you've got; there's four thousand dollars on deposit in the bank for your use, so go build yourself a boat."

I left their office walking on the softest, fleeciest cumulus cloud that ever drifted across a blue June sky. I had had other opportunities to run boats, but nothing like this. In this case I had everything to gain, and someone else took all the risk of loss. A streetcar or bus would have been far too slow for me that day. I hailed a cab to take me home. The driver, whom I had known all my life, looked at me over the top of his glasses as I opened the door. "What's got into you, Ellery?" he asked. "Spending your money on a cab when you haven't got a girl with you!"

I burst into the house like a ten-year-old kid home from school and shouted the news at them. Morris was too awe-struck even to grin; he gazed at me open-mouthed and almost in reverence, as if I were President Wilson. Pop was delighted and offered to help me build the gear. My mother was worried and doubtful. She said, "Do you think you can handle a larger boat?" All I said was, "No think about it!"

We contracted with Webster Eldridge for a seventeen-hundred-dollar thirty-seven-foot hull to be called the *Grace and Lucy* after Grace Avery and Lucy Greenleaf, my sponsor's daughters. I knew before we built her what kind of engine I wanted—hadn't all that been arranged the day I met James Lathrop?—so we put in a twenty-eight-horsepower Lathrop. How many times that engine, and others of the same breed I have handled, have proved their dependability! Once, with a Lathrop, I ran out of gas far out in the Sound and saw that a storm was coming up. I looked over what I had on board and found that I had a gallon of gas which we kept in a can for priming, a bottle of turpentine, two gallons of kerosene, a quart of lubricating oil, and a bottle of whisky. We poured them all into the gas tank, turned the engine over a few times, and she began to sputter and then run—well, if not smoothly, at least with enough persistence to keep going. She spurted blue flame and yellow smoke and purple smoke and black smoke out of the exhaust, and the oil smudge on the sea behind us looked like a painter's palette, but she took us to Ralph Newcomb's dock, where we got a proper start again.

The total cost of the *Grace and Lucy* was thirty-nine hundred dollars, without insurance, and I owed half of it to the G.M. Long Company, which held the title to it jointly with me. I fished the boat on shares with the company. That first year their share of earnings was eighteen hundred dollars, and before my note for my half of the cost was due I had paid it off. A few years later I bought their half-interest and owned the boat myself.

While she was being built, I kept fishing. The G.M. Long Company owned a large thirty-eight-foot Maine-built sloop with a twenty-four-horsepower Lathrop engine, that they had bought for the purpose of running live lobsters from Point Judith and Block island back to their market at New London to supplement the supply from the local lobstermen. While the *Grace and Lucy* was being finished, the Long Company lent me this sloop. I got Bert Ford (whose nickname was "Peaches and Cream" because of his schoolgirl complexion) to go with me, and we started fishing. Since March is a poor month we didn't catch many fish, but we had a fine time sailing that able-bodied vessel up and down the coast.

Later this old but noble craft, with her large well (a water-tight compartment built into the bottom of a boat for the purpose of keeping sea food alive), struck a rocky ledge off Watch Hill—where a supposedly lighted bell buoy was out of commission—and sank, losing three thousand dollars worth of lobsters. The crew sadly rowed ashore. Alvin Scott and others who lobstered in the vicinity reaped a harvest from ten thousand pounds of extra lobsters crawling around their lobster gear.

Finally the *Grace and Lucy*, with her fresh white paint, powerful motor, comfortably furnished cabin, and new white cotton nets, was ready to leave on her first fishing trip from the City Wharf at New London, where she was berthed. I was the boss now; my backers told me there were no strings attached.

The first night the boat was docked at City Wharf, I made several excited trips between home and boat before finally deciding where to spend the night. Needless to say, the new, soft, springy bunk on the noble-looking craft won.

My father advised me to have an older, more experienced man go with me, and arranged the matter with Tony Enos, a former deep-sea fisherman about fifty years old. So the *Grace and Lucy*, with Tony and me aboard (Morris, poor kid, had to be in school and couldn't go), made her maiden fishing voyage on April 8, 1920, one of the greatest days in my life.

Tony was a good soul, a good fisherman, and one of the earliest risers I have ever known. Every night when I left to go home, he would say, "What time do you want to start in the morning, Cap?" and I would tell him. Usually it was about four-thirty or five, for fishermen like to get an early start in order to take advantage of the good weather which so often blesses the new day just before the dawn, to get a crack at the good fishing spots before the fleet has fished them clean, and, if they should run into bad luck, to have plenty of time left in which to work.

So in the morning I'd come down Hallam Street, my eyes peering ahead in the direction of the dock long before I could see it. The first things I did see every morning were the red and green kerosene lights on the *Grace and Lucy*. Tony seemed to keep them trimmed and burning all the time. Sometimes I'd try to trick him by coming down fifteen minutes or half an hour before I had said I would, but while Tony was with me I never once walked down Hallam Street in the morning without seeing the lights burning before I got there. Tony always beat me. One day I asked him about it, and he said that for years he had been getting up at three in the morning, and he was too old to change his habits now. And he was always restless in the morning, he said, until he got his feet on the deck of a boat.

The first day we operated the *Grace and Lucy* we caught five nice barrels of flounders, the second day five, and the third day seven—along with the usual riff-raff of celluloid collars, monkey wrenches, parrot cages, and a bone or two from some poor soul lost in a wreck—and we had no torn nets. We were off; and, as fish prices were rising at the start of the postwar boom, we made money and bought things we never had been able to afford before. It makes a difference who holds the purse strings, and I wasn't going to have too tight a knot on mine, as I intended to have the frugalities of a New England upbringing take a temporary vacation. Yet, even with new clothes on my body and good times in my memory, I still had money in the bank, and, with an eye on a glorious future, I started to pay off some of my indebtedness to my benefactors.

We took on an extra man and ran some of our catches direct to New York ourselves, more for the fun of it than for any commercial advantage. After fishing two days and part of a night off New London, we would start westward about three in the afternoon, and by two the next morning we would be leaving Execution Rocks Light bound for Throgs Neck and the run up the East River.

I suppose I should have a lot of romantic memories of these entries into New York Harbor before dawn—the sleeping city, the lacy pattern of the Brooklyn Bridge woven against the night sky, the occasional couples we saw sitting on the end of an East River dock. But the thing I remember most vividly is the awful smell which struck us like a blow from a filthy rag as we approached Riker's Island. I had grown up with the odor of the Wilcox Fish Works in my nostrils, but this was something different. It was really putrid, and I have never forgotten it. And I remember Brooklyn Bridge well, too—not because of its appearance, but because of the horses. For some unknown reason the wind always seemed to strike Brooklyn Bridge just right to blow down whatever was lying on the roadway, and horses were still the chief mode of land transportation. So Tony and I always tried to get under cover there.

But there were some pretty things too. There was the amusement park at Classens Point, which always impressed me as a study in contrasts. When we went by in the morning it was quite empty and seemed completely dead; when we returned it was thronging with a colorful crowd of human beings out for fun. And there was the Brooklyn Navy Yard, with its changing population of great white ships, lying still and peaceful.

And there was Hell Gate, not so pretty for anyone who was managing a boat. If the tide was with you, you raced through it at a speed which scared the wits out of you; if it was against you, you had to battle for hours, getting nowhere. On our first trip the tide was against us, and after that I always saw to it that we got there at a time when the tide would help us. But on the second trip, with the tide dragging us through like mad, we almost ran down a dredging scow which was anchored four ways. We were all but trapped between two of the anchor lines, and for a few minutes I felt that, by choosing to run with the tide, I had escaped the devil only most surely to be thrown into the deep blue sea; but we made it by a whisker, and after that I was more cautious.

We reached Fulton Fish Market about daylight and planned to get a couple of hours sleep before the huge wholesale market opened. Tony invariably dropped off in two minutes. But I was always so keyed up and excited that I would just lie awake, or get up and wander about the deck.

Then the market would open and we would get rid of our catch. If it was a high market, with good demand and few fish around, we were sitting pretty. At other times it wasn't so good.

But in any case it was a fine thing to be fishing, and especially to be operating from New London. The Custom House for the surrounding district was handy to the New London water front—on Bank Street, near the center of the city. Bailey's Sail Loft was still nearer the docks, as was the ship chandlery—Darrow and Comstock's, right next door—all places to excite the imagination.

Bailey's Sail Loft was one of the pleasantest places I have ever struck on the face of the earth. The building was old and weather-beaten on the outside, but the floors inside were gleaming white and as highly polished as any dance floor, from the action of the many, many canvas sails which had been dragged across them. There were some big, pleasantly whirring sewing machines; but much of the sewing was done by hand by men who squatted on the floor, the huge sails spread out before them.

John Bailey, the proprietor, was descended from a long line of sail and awning makers, and had the cheery and generous philosophy of Omar the tent-maker. He told us to make ourselves at home in a big room on the second floor, where we took our nets to mend them. He later sold out his business to some old-timers and left to set up an awning business at Fort Lauderdale. But the 1926 Florida hurricane wiped him out, and he came back to New London to set up a new business there—chiefly in awnings. Now those who bought out his old sail loft are all dead, and the building itself has been torn down.

Morris, meanwhile, was becoming a fisherman in his own right. From the time he was ten years old he had haunted the docks. Neither Pop nor I ever did anything to discourage it. We both felt instinctively that it was as inevitable that his life was to be spent on the water as it was that I should spend mine there. I did my best to teach him to swim, but without any luck. Some people just never seem to learn.

When he was sixteen he quit school, as I had before him, and began fishing regularly with Pop, while I was working on my *Grace and Lucy*. But a year later I took him away from the old man, and we fished together. I started using the same tough tactics in training him aboard ship that Pop had used on me—and with the same objective. I loved the kid like—well, like a brother, only when I say it I mean what it's supposed to mean; and, believing in learning the hard way, I wanted him to learn right.

And he reacted much as I had with Pop. One day, playfully, and in the best humor in the world, he flattened me on deck, making me realize that, given the same circumstances and the same relative factors, history often does repeat itself. After that I felt confident that he could take care of himself. And he could, too, and without fear.

I remember the afternoon in early April 1923, when a southeaster struck us between Coney Island and the Fire Island lightship as we were coming in with seventy bushels of scallops in our hold, green water washing our deck as wave after wave hit us. While we were wondering whether the *Grace and Lucy* could make it, our engine suddenly stopped. The main gasoline tank was empty, and the fuel line from the reserve tank—situated where a man would have to risk his life to get to in a storm like that—was plugged up. Morris lashed himself to the after bit and siphoned the gas out and into the main tank, water washing over him as he did it. Eventually we did get in, but not entirely on gas. That ran out while we were still a hundred feet from our Sheepshead berth. The wind blew us in the rest of the way. We had about seventy-five dollars worth of scallops, and the trip had probably cost us eighty dollars. But I had learned that Morris could take it on salt water.

During a part of that year we decided that flounders were easier to catch after dark than in daylight, so we began to sleep during the day and fish at night. One evening, an hour after sunset, we shoved off from "Rat" Wilbur's dock and headed out toward the mouth. About the time the channel lights began winking at us we heard the sound of girlish voices coming from somewhere forward. We looked at each other astonished, each of us thinking he was dreaming, and then, without saying anything, headed for the sound and uncovered two girl stowaways lying under a loose jib on our raised forward deck. They were a little seasick and looked somewhat scared.

Morris, in complete disgust, wanted to head right back to the dock and put them ashore, but I said that we had some fishing to do. The girls confessed that they were fifteen and sixteen years old. Remembering that the last bus left the water front at eleven forty-five, I told them they would be on it, then lit the kerosene lamp in the cabin and told them that would be their quarters until we hit the dock. In a few minutes they were asleep—or pretending to be—and I saw to it that they were back in time to catch the last bus.

Then there were those cakes. I'll never forget them. I've always liked chocolate cake, but Morris loved it. Indeed, he couldn't see any reason for eating anything else so long as there was cake around and something with which to wash it down. Often our provisioning for a two- or three-day trip consisted of nothing more than buying two huge chocolate layer cakes at two-fifty each, and a gallon of milk, and taking them aboard. Sometimes we would run out before the trip was over and have to eat a few fish, but we didn't eat anything but cake and milk until they were all gone.

After a bit Lloyd Gray, a direct descendent of Uncas, and a hereditary chief of the Mohicans, joined us, and Lloyd, Morris, and I fished together. Lloyd had a beautiful wife named Arlene, and lived with her and their small daughter Betty, near the Groton water front, where I spent many happy hours with them.

Lloyd taught me to paddle a canoe Indian fashion, and Arlene taught me how to dance on the floor rather than on her feet. Arlene kept worrying because I didn't have a girl of my own, and kept trying to find one for me. But none which she managed to bring around was half as good-looking as she was herself, and I wanted the best or nothing. Sometimes she and Betty, their child, would go on overnight fishing trips with us, and Lloyd and Arlene would sing soft-toned Indian songs, including some Mohican funeral chants which brought tears to my eyes.

And even when Arlene wasn't there it was fun fishing with Lloyd and Morris. Early one July day, after a run of several hours, we began dragging our net in Block Island Sound, with other boats near by. We made two one-hour tows, which netted us about four barrels of flounders. This wasn't too good, so we continued to work east.

At ten-thirty A.M. we were dragging five miles nor'west of Block Island, which is right along the route of the Boston-to-New York passenger steamers. These vessels cruised at about twenty knots, and heaven help the men who got in their way during foul weather. At ten forty-five a dense fog blew in from offshore and shut out several other draggers just west of us. I knew that the large Boston steamer was due to pass almost any minute just about where we were. I got out my foghorn and gave it a toot. In that pea-soup fog it sounded to me no louder than the squawk of a surprised duck, and I was scared. I asked my brother to go below and bring up my trumpet—the horn which I had bought in a futile attempt to win Thelma's heart and hand. It had failed me then, but now I was going to make the darn thing justify its existence.

Meanwhile, Lloyd darted below to see how his chicken stew was coming along. A minute later he was back on deck with Morris and me, trying to see through the fog, and listening. Morris looked at me, and I could see that he was worried. I grinned at him to show him how little concerned I was. It was probably the worst lie I ever grinned in my life.

We were dragging to the east toward Point Judith. Our compass course was due east. Suddenly we heard the whistle blast of the Boston steamer dead ahead. I realized we wouldn't have time to haul back our trawl net and get out of the way. But maybe, I thought, the Boston boat would pass inshore of us. Her next whistle blast would tell the story. If it came from easy by north it would prove she would clear us inshore if east by south, offshore. The other draggers to the west'ard began to blow their pitifully weak foghorns. The noise wouldn't have wakened a sleeping cat near a dog kennel.

Then the oncoming steamer, which was probably four hundred feet long, let go a blast on her whistle that sent a chill up my spine, because it came straight from the east. The steamer was bearing down on us, and fast.

My trumpet was warmed up, and I let go with "The Star-Spangled Banner" for all I was worth. It wasn't much, but it was enough. The Boston boat blew four short blasts and reversed her engine as she swung to starboard. Her dim gray outline shot past, so close that I thought we were scratching the paint off her side. Then her bow wave, coming and snarling, hit us broadside and rolled us until we picked up green water. Down below, the chicken stew, pot and all, slid off the stove and spilled all over the floor. We heard it go, and nobody cared.

"That was kinda close," Lloyd said.

I didn't answer him. I was looking at Morris. The kid grinned at me, and I grinned back. This time I really meant it.

Later the story got around that during the bad fog that day there had been an excursion steamer wandering around in Block Island Sound, its band playing full blast, endangering all the draggers in the vicinity!

Captain Frank E. Thompson (1873-1936) father of Ellery Thompson. A pioneer Connecticut draggerman and a real salt of the Sound. *Photograph by George Tingley, Mystic, Connecticut.*

VI. Truth and Consequences

The Friday following my first full-fledged fishing trip into New York's Fulton Fish Market with a "hull down" (ten-thousand-pound) trip of black-back flounders, the *Grace and Lucy* lay berthed at New London's City Wharf opposite the railroad depot, with her skipper alone on her in dignified splendor. Father's dragger, the *Eleanor Louise*, lay berthed across the basin from us. My father and his crew of the moment, old Cap'n Nate Lester, were not around; they had driven in the Ford truck to Norwich, fourteen miles upriver, to deliver two thousand pounds of fresh flounders they had caught off the New London coast to a Norwich fish boat which always advertised "We Catch Our Own Fish off Block Island." Lloyd Gray and Morris had gone off on their respective affairs.

It was a warm June day—a fisherman's lazy day—a day to mend nets and talk and see the sights along the water front. But I wasn't mending nets. I had already looked over our gear and watched several groups of passengers embarking aboard the Hotel Griswold's motor ferryboat, and now, in the afternoon, I lay sprawled on the topside of our small pilothouse to watch the world, perhaps to think a little, but chiefly just to sprawl happily. Up the dock toward the depot were the express trains, stopped briefly in their restless shuttling back and forth between Boston and New York. Highballing freights puffed with grim determination up the grade to the Thames River bridge, taking loads of merchandise from New York to Boston, so that they could get loads of merchandise in Boston to ballast them on the trip back to New York. And strolling about as usual, on the docks and across the tracks, were people from nearly every walk of life.

Many of the strollers navigated their way about aimlessly; others were a bit nosy about the other fellow's business; and a few were out for business of their own—seaport business of one sort or another. Not far from my boat, but not looking my way, was an anemic-looking girl, wearing a large picture hat which shaded her small painted face. She seemed to be marking time. Occasionally, she would raise one foot up to the top of the foot-high dock-log, and make a bluff at fixing a slipping garter for the benefit of a tow-boat crew lolling about on the deck of a near-by tug. A moment later the tug near her pulled out, and the girl dragged stakes—silken ones. A stranger, no doubt—a transient—a tramp—poison.

The scene on and across the river was more to my liking. Captain George Crandall was bringing the *Governor Winthrop*, the ferry on which Pop acted as spare captain, in at its near-by slip. The *Corsair*, J.P. Morgan's large steam yacht, was dropping anchor in mid-river where the channel was deep. Not far from the *Corsair* two seine-boat crews from a Wilcox fishing steamer were purse-seining a school of menhaden; and passing in review from time to time were river tugs and barges, submarines (mostly O-boats), Sound steamers, motor boats, and other craft. Captain Silas Marsters was proceeding in his water boat to the port side of the *Corsair*. The captain would find poor business there. Mr. Morgan probably had enough ice and water and other necessities on board for a trip around the world.

The small Launch *Elihu Yale* came in from up-river Gales Ferry—crew training quarters—to dock at the public landing on the north side of the City Pier. Several Yale men jumped ashore and went uptown; ten minutes later they were heading back upstream. Close on their heels came the launch *John Harvard* from Red Top with a Harvard gang seeking a jaunt uptown in New London.

On the shores of Groton, directly across the Thames from my perch on the pilothouse, I could see some of the favorite spots of my boyhood—where I had learned to swim, to row, to scull, to sail a boat, and to string rotten lobster bait for my father's lobster pots.

Again I looked up the dock and saw quite a gathering waiting to cross to the "right" side of the tracks, as a long freight rumbled past. I recognized Captain Pettigrew of the *Lowell*, which recalled many happy memories of the time when I served on his ship, Captain Rose, the famous Block Islander who peddled Island codfish and Island eggs all along the coast in his schooner *Aunt Edie*, and "Nat" Avery, the man who, with his partner, had made it possible for me to own the *Grace and Lucy*, banker, fishmonger, clubman, and the friend and golfing companion of about every worthy professional in the country who ever played Shennecosset.

Lying there, thinking over the sizable packet of memories I had accumulated, feeling cocky in the lore of seamanship and fishing which I had acquired, smug and self-satisfied with having chosen the one life I really wanted to live, with owning my own boat and working it successfully, I felt like an old-timer at twenty-two—a fellow who had learned to know most of what there was to know about life, and could look at the world with a somewhat blasé tolerance.

Already I had had two partners in fishing, in addition to my father and Morris, and now had a third. Bert Ford, who had fished with me on the Maine-built boat owned by the G.M. Long Company, was back in carpentering. Tony Enos, after ten months on the *Grace and Lucy*, had saved nearly two thousand dollars of the twenty-five hundred he had made with me, and had left to build a small boat of his own, on which he could take it easier. Now my mate was Lloyd Gray, "Chief Fleetfoot," who took a fatherly interest in me and sometimes, when he was annoyed at some bit of my foolishness, would say, from the height of his twenty-eight-year-old wisdom, "When you're as old as I am, you'll have better sense." Well, perhaps he was right about that. I didn't know, as I lay on the pilothouse that day, thinking how good life was, and how much knowledge and experience I had accumulated at twenty-two.

Suddenly, right after I had watched the caboose of a freight train flash past, I saw a somewhat faded-looking woman heading toward the *Grace and Lucy*. At first I didn't recognize her as anyone I had ever seen before. Then as she looked up and smiled at me I saw that it was Belle. Her once fleshy body had shrunk to proportions which suggested malnutrition. Her cheeks had hollows in them, and she was pale. She wore the plainest of clothes—a far cry from the fancy duds she had sported in her heyday, only a few years before.

As she eased up to the boat she said, "Hello, young fellow, how's business?" I told her it was the same as ever, dragging, and she smiled faintly. Corny puns weren't really in her line.

I climbed down off the boat, and we sat on the dock log and chatted as we had often done in the past, though I hadn't seen her for some time. A few passers-by cast amused or critical glances at me, but I didn't mind that. Indoors we had always been strangers, but outdoors we were friends. Even before this I had learned that it was easy to avoid the undesirable characteristics of certain people by never going indoors with them, and that out of doors a lot of things didn't matter.

Our conversation touched upon about everything current in the newspapers, along Bank Street, in the harbor, on the relative chances of Yale and Harvard in the coming crew races, and the sourness of the Salvation Army band.

She asked me how I stood on the question of women, and I switched the conversation to fish—in my mind, one of the best four-letter words in the dictionary. She asked about my last fishing trip, and I told her about dragging for two days and a night; the run to Fulton Fish Market, and the difficulty of taking a boat through Hell Gate into New York City. I told her about the swift-running tides of the East River, of the excitement of being at the Fulton Fish Market in the early morning, of exploring New York City, and of the run home through Long Island Sound in fog with several Sound steamers overtaking us so fast they often scared the daylights out of us.

She interrupted. "You seem to know a lot about boats and fishing, but from what I can gather you don't know much about living, do you?" She gave me a somewhat gay, yet motherly smile. I didn't quite know what she meant, so I didn't answer, and she became more explicit, and asked me a very intimate question.

I had been asked the same question before, by fellows along the water front, and had always lied brazenly about it, but now I made an embarrassed confession to her—something any young fellow would be kind of reticent about if it was still true at twenty-two. And suddenly I felt like a deflated balloon. An hour before I had thought I was an old-timer who knew all the answers. Now I seemed like a nine-year-old kid.

She didn't say anything about it then, but after she had given me a pitying look in which there was a lot of real sympathy and understanding we began to talk about other things far removed from New London; and we laughed plenty— and when two people can laugh together, troubles disappear and nothing seems too bad.

I told her a little of my scanty romantic history, and how every time that I had entered the lottery I had drawn a blank.

"It's funny," she said, "how some girl will keep a good guy dangling until one or both of them end up licked.

"Fifteen years ago I made the mistake that many girls make. My mother was a lush—still is, for that matter. And I was determined to make the kind of marriage that would keep me from being the way she was. So I kept putting off a good guy with a decent job and not much money who wanted to marry me. I was pretty crazy about him, too, but not nearly as crazy about him as I thought I'd be about the real Prince Charming when he came galloping along on his white horse and picked me up in his strong arms." She paused, snorting disdainfully at her own foolishness. "And so I waited hopefully; and eventually the Dream Boy, or so I thought, came along out of a cheap circus outfit. He picked me up, and down the trail we went. Finally his horse got tired and quit going, but my man and I kept on going down. Booze helped us along. And, finally, when we got down about as far as we could go, I buried him. Then I came back here where I was born and sort of followed the path of least resistance. But I'm not complaining. Now I have a rooming house with five star boarders who pay their rent promptly and like to play poker at home, so I do all right. At present my only problem, aside from trying to gain ten pounds, is a cute niece—"

She paused and looked at me with an excited light in her eyes, as though she had just got the last word she needed to fill out a word puzzle. "Say, I'll tell you what I'm going to do!" She began to sound like a barker at a circus. "I'm going to have you meet my niece. All in all, she's a good kid, about your age, and I'll bet the two of you hit if off together like ham and eggs. But I warn you, she's unpredictable. Her father was an acrobat—at least everybody thought he was the guy—and her mother, my sister, was a dancer. The girl would make a good stunt woman for the movies. She likes to climb, and if you take her out for a boat ride she'll probably shinny up your mast, tie her handkerchief up there, and slide down like a monkey. Well, I'll bet you she'll bring a sparkle to your clear gray eyes that's never been there before, and to my biased thirty-nine-year-old way of careless thinking, it won't do you a bit of harm."

"What's her name and what does she look like?" I asked with mounting interest.

"You never know her name from one day to the next," Belle answered. "Just now she's calling herself Flo—Flo Jane Doe—and she looks a little like a combination of Mary Pickford and Theda Bara."

Nearly a week later, after one of the most strenuous days of fishing I had experienced, we came in dead beat. We had gone out off New London harbor without any ice or barrels aboard and caught one hundred bushels of flounders in six drags (ten hours' fishing). After arriving back at the dock we had ordered three tons of cake ice, and the whole mess was delivered to us at the dock at five P.M. Then for three hours Morris, Lloyd Gray, and I slaved, packing and shipping the catch. When we finished the others went home and I was alone in the cabin, trying to clean up before venturing through the city streets. I was a mess, and I was tired, mentally and physically. I couldn't have fought my way out of a paper bag.

And then I heard a startling sound. "Yo ho!" The hail came from the dock. I went out on deck and looked up. The sight I saw silhouetted against a setting sun made my heart thump and my eyes blink. I climbed up for further investigation. There was Belle, grinning at me, and beside her was a healthy well-built girl of about twenty-one whose eyes said, "Come on—let's get acquainted." She was Flo. I think I expected her to make a run for it up the dock after she had seen me, but she didn't. She laughed and said, "Hello, lonesome boy."

I told her I wasn't lonesome, I only looked that way because I was tired.

"Well. Aunty and I have come to freshen you up. Aunty said you might take us out in the Sound near Bartlett's Reef Lightship. I love boats—I love anything with speed to it. How fast does your boat go?" I told her eight and a half knots, or about ten miles an hour.

"My God! Don't you get dizzy?" she asked. "Well, come on! Invite us on board and let's go out in the Sound and put some life into the old thing. Aunty's going to act as quarter-master part of the time and steer. And she knows enough to keep her mind and her eyes on what she's doing.

I felt like a kid who was hungry and too scared to eat, and groaned inwardly, but Belle only smiled, like the picture I had seen of "Mona Lisa." Suddenly I realized that there was a lot about being a good New England draggerman that I didn't know. I started to help them on board. Then Flo tore her pearl-gray stockings on a rusty nail in the dock log. She stopped her descent to inspect the damage, and so did I. After that I was lost.

I let go our deck lines, started the Lathrop, and, as the moon was beginning to show over Eastern Point, we headed down the river.

I remember the first time I had become scared of the opposite sex; the scene was the back lot at the rear of our home, where I was a six-year-old) started to play games with a mixed group of eight-year-olds. We played several games; then just before supper time, it was decided by the majority to show bottoms. At first I was all for running home as fast as I could and telling Ma, but on second thought I decided to stick around and see the fire works. And so, without participating myself, I stalled, but finally the sight of so much deformity around drove me home. I didn't recover for along time, or come to think of it, perhaps I never had recovered at all. Maybe it was I who had the wrong slant on things, because I now remembered that while all the other youngsters took the thing in their strides, I was the nasty little boy who yelled "Copper," and gave the show away, so that several hairbrushes were unlimbered that night to go to work on the bottoms that had been bared earlier in the day. And mine, which hadn't been bared, got it too.

I know by now that I had been wrong that day—at least for snitching—but I didn't know yet what was right. As I was trying to figure it out, thinking that after all this might be my last night on earth, and that there were many gaps in my knowledge of the facts of life, and much to be desired in my manner of living, I watched Flo climb, with the agility of a dancer, to the top side of our pilothouse, while her red hair waved at me beneath a tiny ungodly looking hat. And I knew right then that yelling "Copper" or "Uncle" on this moonlit night wasn't going to do me a bit of good.

The morning following Flo's visit on board we started while it was still dark on a fishing trip in the general direction of Block Island. When it became light Lloyd Gray looked aloft to see what the wind was doing to our wind-sock. I waited expectantly for his coming explosion. He said nothing until Morris had gone down into the cabin. Then it came. "Who the devil tied a red rag around our masthead?" Then he saw something else, and added, "And who wrote on the pilothouse, "This ship has been officially christened? And who ate up the rest of our roast chicken? And what the dickens in going on aboard this ship?" He looked at me accusingly and, I thought, a little enviously, as I rubbed out the chalk writing on the pilothouse, before Morris should come up from the cabin and see it.

An hour later, after passing Latimer Light, Napatree Point, and Watch Hill, we entered Block Island Sound. The weather was perfect; it was a great day for fishing. But I was finding it difficult to keep my mind on my job. I was trying awfully hard to remember something, and I couldn't make it. I had a foggy recollection—though I couldn't be sure—that sometime between the embarkation and disembarkation of Belle and her niece I had asked the girl who called herself Flo Jane Doe to marry me; but if I had asked her I hadn't the slightest idea what her answer had been. Was it yes or no, or neither, or a combination of both? For the life of me I couldn't tell. Did I want it to be yes, or no? I couldn't really have told you that, either, with certainty. Details of our conversation, and my feelings about it, were all pretty vague.

The end of the week (fisherman's Friday) found us at our regular dollar-a-day berth at City Pier. After our chores were done I tried to enjoy our ringside seat overlooking the public landing and railroad crosswalk, but my thoughts were centered on a prearranged rendezvous with Flo. Was I ashamed of it? No! Was I proud of it? Yes and no!

I went home and bathed and shaved, dressed up fit to kill, and went downtown. I went in and had my shoes shined—the ones that laced way up over the ankles. I bought four twenty-five-cent cigars for my breast pocket and Sen-Sen for my vest pocket; and then I dallied in the store's back room trying to shoot all the balls into the pool table's leather pockets before a pool shark beat me. Finally I lit out for the rendezvous near the berth of the Norwich Line steamers.

I arrived there and waited, and waited, and two hours went by. No Flo. The tonic on my hair lost its snap, and so did I. Disgusted, I hotfooted it alone to the circus we had planned to see together.

The first show I looked in on was the wrestling exhibition. The savage wrestler was trying to pin to the mat out own Abe the Newsboy (prizefighter, world traveler, and newsboy to the Navy's Atlantic Fleet), but Abe knew two many wrestling tricks, which he used to good advantage. The chagrined grappler nearly blew his top when time ran out with Abe belly down, laughing.

"Try it again tomorrow night,' yelled the bonebreaker, "and I'll murder you."

"I'll be here," hollered Abe. And the crowd yelled.

I looked in on several other side shows: the snake dancer; the mermaid; the fat woman; the thin woman; a half-woman, half-man creature; a "flapjack-mouthed woman," a tattooed woman who boasted that every last square inch of her body was tattooed; and, of course, the belly dancers, who in those days were called the hootchy-kootchy girls. All in all, for once in my life, these girls didn't interest me. The reason was obvious. Flo had something for me they didn't have: a warm smile. But what had happened to Flo? I never did find out.

Lloyd and Morris and I went out in Block Island Sound the next day and ran straight into one of the worst tempests I have ever encounterered, and in a way I welcomed it. There were wind, rain, and hail, and it nearly blew the *Grace and Lucy* and Lloyd and me out of the water. I was scared plenty, and prayed and promised, and good old Lloyd Gray suffered with me, and Morris, who knew nothing about it, and wasn't scared, wondered what ailed me, and by the time we got back to the dock I figured that I had paid my debt to society.

I tackled fishing once more with renewed interest. When we weren't dragging off the coast, we were running lobsters up from Point Judith for the G.M.

Long Company, taking Connecticut College girls out on sailing parties, or ferrying folks who had missed the regular late boat to Block Island.

Late that summer Lloyd showed me an ad in an out-of-town paper. It read
something like this:

*Coming Attraction at the Ball-Park—Caesar's Smoke Ring Circus—Featuring Flo Jane
Doe and Her Suicide Trio—Come and See Three Wild Females (a Blonde, A Brunette,
and What a Redhead!) Ride Motorcycles at Death-Defying Speed on the Inside of an
Enormous Bathtub.*

"Are we going?" asked Lloyd with a grin.

"No!" said I. "I don't like motorcycles or people who try to break their necks
on them; and right now I don't like bathtubs or redheads." But of course we
went. Lloyd wanted to see the motorcycles. And the show was a good one—a
darn good one. How else could it be with Flo in the saddle? I was proud of her.
That girl could ride anything.

That's really all about Flo, though not quite all about her Aunt Belle, who
had started it all for me by fishing a kid out of the water.

Several weeks later I met Belle in front of the First National Bank. We passed
the time of day, and then Belle told me she had just closed out her bank account
and sold her rooming house because she was going to marry "Pollack Joe," her
super-star boarder. She said they intended to move to Hoboken, were the business of stevedoring was much better.

"Joe's a good guy," Belle said, "and I warned him not to expect too much if
he married me. I told him, too, that there wasn't much chance for kids, and you
know what that dumb Joe said to me? 'Don't be too sure, Belle. A woman like
you is like a tramp ship: never can tell what'll come out of her. But anyway, you
and me together, and the hell with 'em all.'"

I noticed that Belle had regained about ten pounds of her lost weight and
was her old flamboyant self. Her hat looked as if it was going to fly away, and
her shoes as if they would fall off, but she looked almost happy. She had found
her answer at last, and his name was "Pollack Joe."

There's a sort of hazy sequel to this story in my thoughts. Often in thinking
back I wonder what really prompted Belle to bring Flo along. And then I see the
enigmatic, kindly, wise figure of Pop in the background. He was an ingenious
soul, and he loved his sons and wanted them to get a proper education in living.
And the more I think of it the more I believe that maybe he whispered something in Belle's ear.

Of course I can't be sure. But after all, he was quite a guy.

VII. Draggerman's Rum

During the twenties the waters off the New England coast became as famous for the activities of the rum-runners as for those of the fishermen. Stories about Rum Row, where heavily laden schooners, safely out of reach of United States law, waited for shore boats to come and buy their stuff, were a dime a dozen. Some of them were true, and some fantastically untrue. But the fantasies were no more fantastic than the facts. And back of fantasy and fact was a coolly thought-out, systematic plan born in the mind of a Southern gentleman as enterprising as he was versatile.

He was really somebody to meet, this gentleman, whom I shall call Captain Bill McCoy. He was a composite of Errol Flynn, Howard Hughes, and Captain Bligh. He was good-looking, courteous, generous, soft spoken, had a charming and ever-ready sense of humor; and he loved money, good boats, and good living. And he had a sense of honor about the relationship between a label and what was inside a bottle. Everyone who knew him said he was a square shooter. He bought fast-sailing Gloucester fishing schooners, took them to off-shore southern islands, and loaded them with the finest liquor obtainable. Then he would sail part way back up the coast, be taken ashore to meet buyers, and later rendezvous at strategic offshore spots—a favorite spot was off Montauk Point—with customers and presents for his rum crews.

Later the gangster type of criminal got into rum-running, and from then on things were murder. It was a tough racket. At the start of this lawless era, daring adventurers ferried the cases of liquid gold from the twelve-mile limit, using small but fast motor boats. Around our district Rum Row was generally twelve miles off Montauk or Block Island or down nearer Noman's Land. Once loaded, the "rummies" would start in toward Narragansett Bay, Long Island Sound, and other neighboring waters, dodging—or trying to dodge—the watchful eyes of the Coast Guard. If they could reach appointed spots on shore, waiting trucks would then try to get through to the large cities. Usually they succeeded—but not always.

As the Coast Guard increased the speed of their fleet of chasers, the booze outfits stepped up their own speed, always keeping a step ahead. Most Coast Guard chasers were seventy-five footers powered by two hundred fifty-horse-power Sterling Petrel engines. The rummies had no trouble getting World War I surplus Liberty airplane motors that developed five hundred horsepower. Naturally they had much faster boats. Some of their yachtlike boats had two Liberty motors.

Sometimes a boat was caught by the Coast Guard, occasionally after shooting it out, although most of the shooting was done by the law-enforcement boys. There was one Coast Guard seventy-five-footer whose commanding officer had a reputation for going right on shooting after a boat had surrendered or was broken down and helpless. He was known up and down the coast, and to put it mildly, was extremely unpopular, even among those who were on his own side.

In Coast Guard circles, a vessel suspected of running rum was placed on the "blacklist," and the Coast Guard did everything to make the life of those aboard such a ship miserable. They stopped them and searched every inch where liquor could be hidden. They passed lines under the vessel's hull, trying to locate portable submerged tanks. They examined the contents of gas tanks, food lockers, etc. They drove long sharp pointed steel rods into fish and ice pens, trying to locate wet goods. When in doubt, or when they could charge such a ship with some trivial infraction of navigation laws, they would tow a suspect to port for further inspection. It was a rotten business all around.

My boats were never on the blacklist, but that didn't prevent us from being shot at or from suffering other indignities. Once we were running before half a gale somewhere west of the Vineyard, bound for friendly Edgartown. I was in the pilot house trying to pick up Gay Head to starboard or Cuttyhunk to Port. Suddenly I noticed sharp splashes in the water ahead of us. Thinking they might be bluefish, although it was out of season, I came out on deck and was surprised to see a Coast Guard seventy-five-footer astern of us, men on her deck unlimbering a one-pounder.

"What the hell are you trying to do, sink us?" I hollered at them angrily as they came nearer.

The patrol boat closed in fast, and as an officer came out of the wheel house I repeated my hail. This time he heard and hollered back, "No, but in another minute we would have blown your pilothouse overboard, and you with it."

The patrol boat was faster than we were, and he could easily have overtaken us and given us a decent order to stop. But just for the hell of it he hung back, so as to have a good excuse for taking a pot shot at us. Perhaps he thought we were a decoy, running one way while another boat with a load ran the other way. That trick had been played plenty of times.

We soon convinced the swashbuckling skipper that we had no contraband on board, and he left us. I wondered whether he had been the skipper of the notorious patrol boat that fired through the fog off Long Island and nearly killed several innocent guests aboard a yacht—the same, apparently, as the one that shot up a rummie, not running and without liquor, so badly damaging an eye of one of the crew that he almost lost it. A friend of mine, Dr. Frank E. Wilson of New London, helped save the man's eye. A few days later Dr. Wilson found a case of Scotch on his front doorstep.

Some rum-runners, trying to make it in, dumped their liquor cargo when the going got tough. A few unfortunate ones sank or ran aground, and the crews swam ashore and ran for it.

Soon after Rum Row was established, trawlers began dragging up some of the dumped bags of liquor, which complicated things still further. Lloyd and Morris and I once "took up" near Block Island and found the net so heavy that I thought it must contain the best catch of flounders for the week. When we got it in on deck we found over a hundred quarts of brandy in it. We had ten bushels of blackback flounders too.

Lloyd and Morris arranged the bottles in single file along the rail, where they made a pretty sight, regardless of what you thought about bootlegging. But just then I saw one of Uncle Sam's patrol boats come tearing toward us., I wasn't going to lose my boat for any brandy, so I started kicking the bottles overboard. Close by on our port side was another Stonington dragger; her crew was watching us and tears ran down their cheeks as I let bottle after bottle go over to Davy Jones. After it was all over I started breathing regularly once more. No danger now of losing my boat, or worse. Then I looked to see where the Coast Guard boat was, and saw it speeding in the other direction. It had turned away while we were throwing the bottles overboard, certainly without suspecting what we were about.

Every fisherman who caught the dumped contraband bottles of spirits wanted to take some of them ashore and home, but many worried for fear of being caught and classified as smugglers. I worried too, so I called up a man pretty near the top in government circles, and asked him about the matter. He told me that although we were powerless to prevent it from coming up in our nets, it would be against the law to land it ashore. "But," he said, "if I were in your shoes, I'd take a chance. Only don't quote me."

At that time everyone connected with water-front activities knew that, besides the professionals, a few fishermen as well as yachtsmen violated the law and compromised the honesty of their craft by bringing in a trip or two of liquor. Eventually many were caught and lost their boats. A few went to jail. I knew perhaps a hundred men who, when not breaking the laws of the United States by trafficking in booze, lived the lives of law-abiding citizens. If there is any marine district along the Atlantic Coast where amphibious-minded mortals over forty say, "No liquor was ever run ashore here," it houses the best liars in the country. I'll bet each coastal district can remember some hectic nights. I remember one such at Stonington, which had become my home port.

In 1922 I had moved my base of operations from New London to "Rat" Wilbur's dock at Noank, because it was nearer the newly developed dragging grounds around Block Island, and also because there was a new school of fishermen working out of Noank, from whom much could be learned—the Mesantes, the Bacchiocchis, and others. But after a while an extra-heavy crop of eel grass began to narrow the channel, and there were other hazards—such as the new water-front factory which employed a lot of girls, and Rat Wilbur's too great generosity in lending money—a temptation which, when not resisted, often spelled poverty, and soon we moved to Nat Avery's dock at Stonington. So we were in a good spot to see the events of the night of which I am writing, and the next-morning aftermath.

We had docked just before dusk. We had a fair catch—ten barrels of flounders, four barrels of haddock, two barrels of whiting, two barrels of trash fish for Alvin Scott, the Watch Hill lobsterman, a half-dozen good-sized (three pounds each) lobsters, two quarts of salty rye whisky, and a chipped thunder-mug obviously out of some ship of long ago.

We packed our fish, took on more ice, gas, oil, and grub, and called it a day. As I was getting into my car, I noticed an unusual amount of extracurricular activity on and around the dock. "Oh, oh," I said to myself, "the birds will fly high tonight, and I'm glad I'm getting out of it. I'm three monkeys. I see no evil, hear no evil, speak no evil." As I drove off I noticed several transient trucks trying to hide their engine hoods under the roof of an old shed, but with their rear ends sticking out of the back as conspicuously as the tails of ostriches with heads in the sand.

As time went on I learned from some local fellows who took temporary jobs that night some of the details of one of the boldest attempts that had ever been made to land illegal liquor practically on the main street of a New England village. The *Bird*, a big eighty-five-foot rum-runner, drove in from sea that night, zigzagged across Block Island Sound, running without lights, and entered Fishers Island Sound by way of Lord's Channel a narrow inlet through Watch Hill reef just east of Wicopessett Island. Ten minutes later the rummie was anchored behind the breakwater at Stonington.

At ten P.M. the right auto lights flashed the proper signal from shore, and things got under way. In no time a small motor and scow were alongside loading up. There were many men on hand to help out. The first loads went shoreward, made contact at the appointed place, and were loaded on trucks which roared away and merged with heavy traffic on U.S. Route I. The motorboat with underwater exhaust prepared to tow the scow back to the *Bird* in the outer harbor;

she was lying in a position where she could make a run for it in any one of three different directions if need be.

The gang climbed aboard the scow, and out they went to the *Bird*. This time the motorboat was loaded first, to deliver a small trip at another rendezvous, and left. Then began the task of reloading the scow in darkness. Someone bungled things; they overloaded one side of the scow and she capsized. Fifty cases of Scotch on the bottom of Stonington Harbor!

But it was only a drop in the bucket. The *Bird* still had over three hundred cases. When the motorboat returned, it was apparent something was wrong, even in the darkness. She looked lopsided and ragged. The gang on her reported, "We hit the bridge as we went under and nearly took the stem out of her. We got the load ashore all right, but someone in the village is wise."

The captain of the *Bird* told the boss from New York, "I know a place near the old fish works where we can unload, and, if we have to, a half-dozen cars can get it up to an old icehouse to stay till tomorrow night."

"Okay," said the boss. "Let's get going, but for the love of Mike don't open these Liberties up, or we'll wake the dead."

What a gang of men on the rummie, so I've been told. Thirty-nine men, and about every one of them good law-abiding citizens except when it came to doing a little smuggling of joy water.

Ten minutes later they entered a small cove and ran aground on a sand bar. The next hour was a nightmare. Twenty men went for a swim to lighten the rum craft; then twenty cases of whisky were dropped overside to rest "temporarily" on a sunken sand ridge. The Bird was finally freed from the bar, the men picked up, and the rest of the rum rushed ashore. Within an hour the right cars had been brought to the scene and the cases put on ice. Then came the dawn, and with it came the darnedest sight I ever saw as we steamed down Stonington Harbor to go fishing.

Though it was not until later that we learned about the happenings of the night just past, we suspected something had gone wrong by the crazy maneuvering of about twenty-five boats—pleasure boats, fishing boats, and rowboats—milling around near the breakwater, some with long poles, others with hooked lines, and one or two with dragnets overboard. A few boats had been successful. Two small craft zigzagged past us toward land, their occupants drunker than hoot owls, a few cases of booze plainly visible. Before long, we later heard, law-enforcement boys got to the scene and "restored order."

And over in the cove, when the tide reached dead low water, there were about ten cases of good Scotch whisky jutting up out of the water like a miniature Statue of Liberty. By seven A.M. they had been liberated ashore into a fish shack owned by two old-time fishermen, whose religious belief—which is in reality the belief of their wives—forbade them more than one drink a week. They got the booze over twenty years ago, and I heard the other day that they are getting down toward the last bottle of Peter Dawson that was salvaged from what is now called Dawson Shoal.

And where were the law boys that night? Well, it seems there was a farmer's barn burning up in the country, which called for a lot of law enforcement; there was a near riot after a bad auto accident on the main highway; and there was a meeting somewhere for police officers about crime prevention.

At the time of this episode, and several others like it, I was firmly resolved to have no part in rum-running—with or without my boats. If once, at another time, I had a more open mind—well, once was enough. But even though I was not in the business myself, I was not spared contact with the boys who were.

One day while the *Grace and Lucy* was tied up at New London's City Pier, four well-dressed men got off the New York Express and began walking over toward my boat. At the moment I was talking with a friend of mine, a pretty and talented Connecticut College graduate, who was not only a fine concert singer and actress, but also quite an athletic outdoor girl.

One of the men asked me if I was interested in making fifty bucks. I said yes. "Then take us to Block Island," he said. I agreed, and then thoughtlessly asked the girl to come along; I told her we would be back at New London within six hours.

On the way over I found out that the men were connected with rum-running when they asked me whether I would run in some liquor for their syndicate for twelve dollars a case. I told them I'd stick to catching fish.

The men seemed interested in the operation of the boat and also in the girl. Occasionally they would talk among themselves, and I saw that one, the decentest looking in the lot, was in violent argument with the others. After a three-hour trip we landed them on Block Island. I was paid off, but the man whose looks I had liked the best asked me to wait ten minutes; he was going back with us. We waited. Finally he showed up. Just before he left us at New London, he called me aside and said, "Buddy, you shouldn't take a girl out with a bunch of roughnecks like us. You know what the other fellows wanted to do?"

I said, "No, what?"

"Your girl friend is some gal," he continued, "and the other fellows were all for pushing you overboard and taking the girl off to the rum ship on Rum Row. It would have put us in solid out there because I know that particular outfit. The vessel's skipper is a great ladies' man—all three hundred pounds of him."

"You mean, hold her for ransom?" I said.

"Ransom, hell." The man laughed. "I mean hold her for the Old Man. He'd ransom her!"

I didn't doubt for a moment that he was telling the truth, for what was the ruination of one young girl to a gang of roving highjackers? And what would the breaking of another law or two mean to a man who lived by breaking the law?

There were many occasions during Prohibition when events were on the borderline between legal right and wrong. For example, take the case of the *Thelma Phoebe*. That boat, loaded to the gunwales with Peter Dawson whisky, grounded on the rocks at the back side of Fishers Island during a pea-soup Block Island Sound fog. It happened just before dawn on a spring morning over twenty-five years ago.

The rummie's crew threw hundreds of cases of good Scotch overboard in a futile attempt to float their vessel off the rocks. Failing in this, they tried to escape ashore. One man, who couldn't swim, jumped into a deep hole alongside the craft. The Coast Guard found him there an hour later, his head just under water—dead. They also found plenty of whisky still in the boat; the rest had either sunk in the bight or was drifting back and forth along the rocky shore. Already the islanders and soldiers from Fort Wright were poling it in and helping themselves. For a while there was confusion. Some got drunk on the spot, others hustled away with case after case.

My father in his *Eleanor Louise* brought Jerry Dillon and other customs officials over from New London. At the time I was at New London aboard the *Grace and Lucy*. The waterfront grapevine whispered to me, and soon, along with another boat, the *Hell Cat*, I was on my way to see what was what, and what we could pick up.

We hove to a hundred yards off the wreck and talked it over with the gang on the other boat. We decided that as long as we had New York State fishing licenses it was perfectly legal for us to set and drag out trawl net, and if any cases of liquor got in the net by accident, it would be just too bad—I hoped.

Custom House officials on shore frantically motioned us away as we nosed in closer and closer toward the stranded craft. Not to be denied, we set our net and dragged it in as close as we dared. The sea bottom was too rocky. Our net caught on a big boulder and we had to pull it back in, but in the cod end where the fish are supposed to be was one flat-fish and one case of Peter Dawson. Hurrah! We were not skunked. The other boat got none. What we'd have done if a dozen cases had been in the net, I don't know. Maybe we'd have gone to jail. So far we had broken no law, but if we took it ashore that would be different. For a while I was fed up with bottle fishing.

A few days later I broke my toe. One of Groton's leading doctors fixed me up. As he started to leave I noticed a quart of Peter Dawson sticking out from his overcoat pocket. How it got there I wouldn't try to explain, but the doctor seemed pleased. Turning, he said, "Now be careful and don't get hurt, but if you do, be sure and call me, rain or shine, day or night."

Later, I was to learn that the *Thelma Phoebe* (she was a British motor yacht) was supposed to have had on board twenty-four hundred cases of whisky when she left Nassau for Halifax. But after the cargo was removed the government had only about eight hundred fifty cases.

The full story did not end with the capture of the smuggler. The island eager-beavers who had "rescued" the largest number of cases of liquor heard that their homes were to be searched. They got scared, so they took the bottles out of their wrapping and burned everything but the bottles themselves. The month was April; everyone had a garden all ready for planting, so they planted, and planted fast. Into one row went corn, into another beans, into the next Scotch. They kept on: a row of potatoes, then a row of Scotch, a row of potatoes, a row of Scotch. Then a row of Scotch, a row of Scotch, and finally the good earth which is no respecter of persons or bottles, covered everything. Little signs were posted at the different rows. For example: beans, Scotch beans, potatoes, Scotch potatoes, etc. One man used a different code: carrots, potatoes, Peter string beans, Dawson cabbage, and so it went.

The expected raid never came off, but the stuff was left in the ground for security. The gardens were nursed carefully all summer. At times there was some pre-harvest picking and sampling. When unexpected guests came it was quite usual to hear a housewife say to her husband, "John, go out and dig up a peck of potatoes, a head of cabbage, and two quarts of Scotch." Good gardeners that they were, their one regret was that there were no perennial species.

It was during these days that I got acquainted with Newport, and Ralph Newcomb, one of the best friends any man ever had. The first time I ever entered port there it was because a squally snowstorm drove me in. I was tired and discouraged and didn't know anything about the place except that it was a millionaire's playground and had three fish docks. As I came into the harbor I saw a reddish-orange glow at one of the docks, and headed for that because it made me feel better. When I got closer I saw that it was an illuminated Gulf Gasoline sign at Newcomb's dock. I found Ralph Newcomb, then a young man, as cheery as the sign. Soon the place became as much home away from home as I could wish. Ralph's father ran a lobster business and Ralph ran the dock and gasoline station, doing a land-office business furnishing fishing vessels and rummies with gas.

"What business is it of mine what they use the gas for?" he asked. "Selling gas is legal."

He liked to seem to be tough. He used to say, "Heard anyone knocking me lately?" And when I assured him that I hadn't he would shake his head sadly and say, "Then I'm slipping."

In reality he was one of the kindest and most generous and honest individuals I have ever known. After I had been in a few times he rigged up a light wire from his warehouse to the ship so that I had only to plug it in and have light aboard the ship while I was in dock without running the generator. The next thing he did was to give me a key to the warehouse, so that if I got in late, after he had closed up, I could walk in and help myself. What a place that warehouse was—nets and ropes and gear, and lobsters and oysters on ice—I loved it!

There were plenty of fish off Newport twenty-five years ago, and those we caught were shipped on Fall River Line Steamers to New York. For a while the world around Newport was bright. But in later years the fish thinned out, many of the boys got married, and the wandering fishermen from the "west" left for homier waters.

I was about the last Connecticut fisherman to stick by Newport as a place to fish from; I nearly called it home. During the spring I would fish off Connecticut and western Rhode Island and work east with the migrating haddock and flounder schools, but for many years my heart remained with Newport. Then during the tough years of the depression, when people weren't buying lobsters and fish, Ralph Newcomb closed up shop, the Fall River Line closed up shop, and so did I at Newport.

It was in the waters near there, five miles from Brenton's Reef Lightship, that, one night after dark, with a pale moon lighting the water slightly, we sighted a creature you might have thought was a mermaid if you had been gifted with that sort of imagination. She was dressed as nature intended people to dress when they are swimming, and one of the things I liked about her was that she didn't seem to mind. All that showed on her face as we came alongside was relief. She was plainly tuckered out and near the end of her rope, but she managed a sort of grin as she looked up at us and gasped, "Thank God you've got a ship under you and are here! I think I've been swimming an hour trying to find that damned buoy!"

Since we were more embarrassed than she was, we tossed her a blanket before we lifted her aboard, gave her a shirt and a pair of pants, made coffee, and then listened to her story, which she told without trying to pretend anything.

Her brother had gotten a tip from "The Hot-Tip Association of Newport" that a rum-runner, frightened by the approach of a Coast Guard vessel, had dumped a load of whisky in fifteen feet of water off the Sakonnet River. He had told her about it, got another man to join them, and they had started out to try to recover it in a twenty-two-foot sailboat. But before they got to the spot where they believed the whisky to be, darkness had overtaken them, and though all of them made exploratory dives they couldn't find what they had come for. Finally, while blundering around, their boat struck a lobster-pot buoy, which stove a hole in it and made it founder. In a moment they were all in the Sound clinging to the boat.

Somewhere in the distance they heard the faint ringing of a bell. It was undoubtedly the bell buoy about four miles south of Brenton's Reef Lightship, and the girl, the best swimmer in the group, decided to try to swim to it, mount it, and ring it as hard as she could in hope of attracting attention from a passing ship. She started out, she said, wearing her bathing suit out of regard for the eyes of her male companions, but as she swam and swam, seeming to get no nearer the sound of the bell—and finally losing it altogether—she knew that she needed every break that she could get, even to shedding the few ounces the bathing suit weighted, and so threw it off.

We got as good an idea as we could of the location of the boat, turned about, and finally found it, with the two men still clinging to it. Soon we had them also dressed in some of our spare clothing, hotted up with coffee, and were on our way to shore with three rescued highjackers, who seemed to us like ordinarily decent and pleasant young people.

We docked at Newcomb's and tied up their boat, which immediately sank. The shipwrecked rum hunters thanked me and said we would hear from them. I never saw them again. A week later, after I had kissed good-by to three pairs of thin pants and three shirts, a Newport laundry truck dumped aboard our boat a heavily wrapped parcel, and pinned to it was an envelope. We opened them up. Our clothes had come home cleaned and pressed, and to keep them company was the envelope with a fifty-dollar bill inside.

Rum-runner
William "Bill" McCoy.
*Photograph Courtesy of the
Mariners' Museum,
Newport News, Virginia.*

VIII. Not the Whole Truth

A while ago I dropped in at George Wilcox's marine equipment store at Quiambaug—not for any very important business, unless it was to tell George that I really would pay my bill before long—and happened to run into Bert ("Peaches and Cream") Ford, shipmate on the first fishing boat I ever sailed without my father. I told Bert that I was writing a book and intended to tell the truth in it.

"Not the whole truth, Ellery!" he said, horrified.

Well, maybe not quite, but in a way this book is a sort of dragging operation, and I'd like to bring up in the cod end of the net as many as possible of the troublesome fish that have muddied the waters of my thoughts. And that's why I tell the following story. It was a once-in-a-lifetime sort of thing, the kind of thing you aren't proud of—and yet you wouldn't like to forget it, either.

The story begins in a seaport sporting club to which I had come by request. The place was crowded with businessmen and hazy with cigar smoke. There were deep leather chairs, and heavy glass ash trays, and the walls were hung with oil paintings which ranged in subject from a beautiful nude to President Harding. Being a young fisherman, I felt out of place. But not for long; the atmosphere was too sociable. After an hour spent in meeting the boys, I was taken to one side and introduced to Captain Bill McCoy, whom I described in the last chapter. We talked of boats and other things, and the evening passed swiftly.

Driving home later, I thought things over in a mixture of doubt and excitement. I had been asked, as a favor, having refused flatly to be hired, to smuggle in a load of whisky for private consumption from Rum Row offshore, and by men who were among the most respected in the community.

And then, the next night, before I realized that I had decided and answered them, we were in Block Island Sound and heading seaward in my dragger. There were three of us—my mate (whom I shall not name), and Captain Bill McCoy, and I. The captain stood by me at the wheel and spoke lovingly of his Gloucester fishing schooner, *Arethusa*, which was loaded with six thousand cases of the finest whisky and waiting for him twelve miles off Montauk Point.

"And I'll make a net profit of twenty dollars a case—a hundred and twenty thousand dollars, and they can't touch me," he said. "After I make a quarter of a million dollars on this coast I want to go to the West Coast and collect another quarter-million off California. Then I'll retire and get some real fun out of life with my family and with fine boats."

Captain McCoy painted a rosy picture. Then nature presented a dirty one— fog. But before Long Island was completely shut out, I got a bearing on Fort Pond Bay. We crept toward it, finally made in there, and stayed holed up by fog for three days. My mate and I ate ashore at a fishermen's boarding house., Meanwhile we saw nothing of Captain McCoy. Though we didn't know it, word had spread to my home in New London that we were lost.

The fog cleared out during the third night. With the dawn Captain McCoy was back aboard. We drove our ship offshore past Montauk. McCoy showed us two presents for his schooner captain—a Colt .38 and a box of fifty-cent cigars. "Both are useful," he said, smiling, "in smoking out the worries a man may have out where there are various kinds of sharks."

We were now far off Montauk and looming up ahead was a heavily laden black-hulled Gloucester-type fishing schooner. Near her were a dozen small boats laying-to, waiting. We had priority, for we had the boss. We went alongside and in a minute were tied up with bumpers overside. To say that she was loaded hardly described it; cases of whisky overflowed her hatches from bow to stern. Burlap-covered "hams" (six quarts) were piled on the cabin aft. The dropped mainsail was serving as an awning for the schooner's captain. McCoy passed a list to the mate with instructions to load us. He then went aft to chat with his captain, a three-hundred-pounder who might have been Rex Stout's prototype for Nero Wolfe.

The tough, unsmiling crew began loading us. It was quite a job; both vessels were rolling in a long ground swell. When we were nearly ready to shove off, Captain McCoy came over and wished us "happy landings." The nautical fat man aft never moved from his chair. As we pulled away, others moved in. Obviously the schooner would do a brisk business, now that the fog had lifted.

We ran to the east-northeast for an hour; then we shut off the motor and drifted. We were in no hurry, not at two-thirty in the afternoon. We ate the last of our fresh grub. Then we discovered that McCoy had left behind his Colt .38, a supply of cartridges, and the box of cigars. I loaded the gun, opened the box of cigar, and lit up a fifty-center. The mate refused. "Get me in a bad habit," he said. "I'll chew on eatin' tobacca."

It was tough waiting for darkness. Our water supply was nearly gone, and the weather was hot. My mate started examining the cargo for something mild in the way of refreshments. He found a case of champagne, opened it up, and withdrew a quart bottle with loving care. With a smile he then tied an end of fish line around the bottle's neck and lowered the quart over the side. "How deep is it here?" he asked.

"Thirty fathom, and don't let it any farther down than twenty or the pressure may break it." He held the line for about ten minutes, then began to seem restless, and I said, "Feel a bite?"

"Yes," he replied, "in my throat," and he began hauling away as though he were pressed for time. We were both disappointed when we felt the bottle. It hadn't chilled much.

A moment later we drank the champagne down like water—the whole works. We put the empty bottle back in its straw container and slipped it back in the case we had taken it from. Then we smashed the bottle and nailed up the case. It simplified matters for us.

The day turned into a July scorcher as the afternoon dragged along. Montauk was nor'-nor'west of us, Block Island plainly visible to the northeast. The slender curving fin of a swordfish poked into view about a quarter of a mile away, and in the opposite direction a school of mackerel were flipping. Looking at them made us hungry. We feasted on canned goods. We had no water, so we tapped the case of champagne again. My mate suggested putting a hinge on the cover. Then he mentioned the possibility of our engine refusing to start, and of being marooned at sea with no water to drink.

"It would mean beginning on twelve thousand dollars worth of whisky," he said, sighing, "and death would come by fever, sooner or later. How much better it would be than freezing to death!" I changed the subject. I got out my trumpet—my spare foghorn—and gave it a couple of blasts that nearly tore the bell off. All fish disappeared, also the gulls that had been hanging around us. I lit up another fifty-cent cigar.

The sun set and we started in, our running lights lit. We had clear sailing and met no patrol boats. Midnight found us at the appointed rendezvous off Eastern Point's Shennecosset Bathing Beach. No shore boat met us, as had been planned. I could see no cars parked where they should have been.

We anchored behind Black Rock, five hundred feet off the beach. Off came my clothes except for my running pants. I strapped an old sou'wester with a flashlight inside it on my head. I then taped several nickels to my wrist and lowered myself overboard. At the last moment the mate tied a string around my waist, and as I swam away I towed a kid-size life preserver behind me. It was "just in case," and though it was a pretty small life preserver, I felt small enough to fit it, if necessary.

In a matter of minutes I crawled up out of the surf, nearly into the arms and legs of what appeared to be Adam and Eve. At that instant the roving beam of a steamer's searchlight hit us. Then it was gone. The two figures scrambled away in nothing flat and disappeared. After catching my breath I hastened toward the beach phone booth and ran right into the night watchman.

"What the devil, Ellery!" he said. "Where'd you come from?"

"Too long a story, Bob," I panted, "I've got to telephone!"

"Telephone's out of order," he said, and there was a wicked note of satisfaction in his voice.

I swam back to the boat, put on my clothes, and started the Lathrop while my mate hauled in the anchor. We went a mile farther and tied up near the Hotel Griswold as bold as brass. I got to a telephone and called up the guy who had managed the affair. I was told there had been a mix-up because everyone thought we were lost; but if we would go back to the prearranged spot, the boys would come right down.

I boarded my boat right in front of a hundred people who were strolling along the waterfront after a midnight banquet. Several gasped as they began reading by the light from the wharf the labels on our cargo. Then we were gone.

An hour later we were being unloaded at a well-known but secluded seaside club. Bankers, merchants, industrialists, lawyers were working like stevedores. One lawyer, who handled two cases each trip, remarked with a grunt, "These are the best cases I've ever had." One of the bankers was quite expert in running toward his car with a case under each arm.

As the night wore on the clubmen slowed down, and with dawn only an hour away there were twenty cases still aboard the boat. I was sweating and mad and tired. Suddenly there was an uproar. Someone had told somebody else that the cops were on the way. In no time there wasn't a man in sight, except my mate and I and the hired man the others had left behind to help us to get underway.

"Well," I blurted, "what now? This stuff goes overboard in half an hour—somewhere. I don't want any straw blowing around my boat after daylight. Any fool will know we haven't been haying."

"Yea," said the worried hired man, "that's the hell of it. Well, we can divide it and plant it. Twenty cases at a hundred dollars a case. Not bad. Not good either. Personally, I hate the stuff; furthermore, I have never swiped anything in my life—that is since growing up."

For a moment there was silence. I was steering the boat up the river, wondering where to go. Then the hired man had a brainstorm. He knew of a place to hide the liquor, and when he named the place, was I surprised! What better place than an inactive naval vessel? It seemed as if he had worked for the right people.

We went there and unloaded, except for a few strays that were in hiding—behind a bunk mattress, in the oven, in the bilge, and so on. And daylight came. Our decks were clear; our worries were over. On reaching home I received a welcome befitting a man home from the sea, from the wars, or from the grave. The rumor that my boat and I had been lost had preceded me. I firmly resolved, "never again"—not for love or money. No, not even for a friend.

IX. *Louise*, the Slack-bilged

I had a lot of affection for the *Grace and Lucy*, my first boat, but she was flat forward, and she pounded so hard that sometimes she'd make the covers of the Shipmate stove hit the ceiling. From watching her and other fishing boats in action I learned that it was the bow and stern which needed modification, and decided that, if ever I built another boat, her forward sections were going to look less like a U and more like a V. But I discovered, too, that if she were too sharp forward, she'd be liable to dive and be wet. It's hard to win any way you plan it. If a boat is full and flat forward, she'll pound; if she's lean, she'll dive; if she's wall-sided, she'll roll; and if she's slack-bilged (that is, narrower at the water line than at the deck line) she won't hoist much of a load without too great a list. When you start out to make a good dragger, you learn that a boat is as complex a problem as a woman, and that your life and happiness may depend as much upon hooking up with a good one in one situation as in the other.

In 1924 I decided to try to do something about it. I had met Louis Steele, president of the Rancocas Construction Company, the year before, and now I went to visit him at his home in Delanco, New Jersey, and went through his shipbuilding works. Then I did some figuring and decided that by scraping up this and that here and there I could have a new dragger.

I made the specification for a forty-four-foot boat with a thirteen-foot beam to be powered by a sixty-five-horsepower Lathrop engine. I tried to incorporate in her the things I had learned from the *Grace and Lucy*, and Jake Smith of the Rancocas Construction Company designed her. I spent as much time watching him as I could, trying to learn how he got the facts of a boat's construction down on paper, storing up in my mind what I saw for possible future use. Later I learned that, despite all my efforts to get a good compromise, we had designed a slack-bilged boat, which was grand going to windward but which had weaknesses that more than once put my heart in my mouth.

I got my new boat in July 1924, and named her the *Louise*, after my older sister. I turned the *Grace and Lucy* over to Morris, who fished her for me for a time, working at first with a seventeen-year-old Italian-American boy named Fred Giri. Pop, meanwhile, disgusted with the too-frequent downs among the ups and downs of fishing, had sold the *Eleanor Louise* in 1923 to the Luke brothers on Long Island, and now spent most of his time on shore, mending nets, doing work around the house, and occasionally doing a bit of piloting and helping out Morris or me when we needed an extra hand.

After a time Fred Giri, lured by the glamour of a new boat, came with me on the *Louise*, and Lloyd Gray ("Chief Fleetfoot") went with Morris. They made a good team, and soon Morris, who had saved over eighteen hundred dollars while fishing with me, bought the *Grace and Lucy* from me for twenty-six hundred dollars and began fishing on his own and giving me the kind of competition I liked. It wasn't long before the kid brother was known as a real high-line Draggerman, and brought in catches which drew admiring grunts from all the old-timers.

Meanwhile I was fishing hard with Fred and others, trying to keep up with Morris. Fred was really somebody to fish with, in many ways. He as one of the hardest workers I have ever met, and often, on a fine evening, after we had fished all day and were preparing to clean up and got to the movies or home, he would look at the star-studded sky—and say, "Oh, hell, let's go out in the Sound and fish until midnight. It'll be more fun than the movies." And we did.

The most fun I had with him was in New York, when we took a trip of fish direct to Fulton Fish Market. I would pick out an expensive restaurant just so I could watch him do the same thing, over and over again. He would pick up the menu and read it straight through—or at least seem to be reading it—with a thoughtful look on his face. Sometimes the dishes were listed in French, but Fred never batted an eye. The waiter, dressed up to look like the best man at a wedding, would stand patiently and quietly, his pencil poised over his order blank, waiting for a man who obviously was a gourmet since he considered each item so carefully. Then Fred would lay the menu down, look at the waiter with innocent boyish eyes, smile, and say, "Bring me four hamburgers and some French-fries." He always did it, and it used to drive those fancy waiters nearly crazy.

Once when the Follies and we were in town at the same time, I thought it would be fun to watch Fred watching the girls. I couldn't get any tickets at the box office and finally found two at one of those holes-in-the-wall around Times Square for thirteen dollars. I didn't mind when I found that Will Rogers, Gilda Gray, Gallagher and Shean, Fanny Brice, Ann Pennington, and many others were all on the same program. Fred liked it as much as I had thought he would, and when we got out he asked me how much it had cost. I told him fifty cents apiece. "Gosh, that's cheap," he said. "It was worth a buck!"

After three years of fishing with me during the twenties, Fred saw a chance to make more money ashore and left me. He now owns the Half Shell, a fine New London restaurant.

Meanwhile I had taken on John Marshall, an ex-Gloucester fisherman, as tough as they come, with a streak of cruelty in his nature. But he was a good sailor and about the best cook I have ever met. "You get it, and I'll cook it," he used to say. "I'll even cook you a mermaid if you'll catch her and get me a pot big enough."

It sounded fine and it tasted fine—at first. But when, week after week, our grub bill was bout fifty dollars for feeding three men—it had been about twenty-five before John came—I convinced him, with tears in my eyes and gas pains in my stomach, that we didn't need seven-course breakfasts. Then the bill dropped back to around thirty-five.

I also took on a lad from Nova Scotia named Henry Landry as third man. The contrast between John and Henry was something remarkable. Henry was young and timid, and visibly scared whenever we ran into any kind of danger. He was a Catholic, and in times like that he would cross himself and you could see his lips moving in prayer. John, the tough guy, had once had an unpleasant experience off the Canadian coast in which a cowardly Nova Scotian had let him down badly. He had never forgotten it, and now he seemed intent on getting even by scaring the pants off Henry every chance he got.

We were fishing hard that winter of 1925-26, off on the mussel bed south of Newport; driving off past Brenton's Reef Lightship in fog, sloppy sou'westers, and freezing nor'westers, rolling our guardrails under half the time, often using words which mother never taught us—and sometimes saying prayers we hadn't learned at her knee, either—and at night aching in every joint. John developed a habit that winter of thinking up all the hair-raising stories he could remember to tell at moments when things looked as though we were close to perdition ourselves. He always watched Henry avidly to see the look of fright come into his eyes and the pallor spread over his cheeks.

One calm foggy morning in early January we were running rather far off-shore to see if we couldn't get in another trip of dab flounders that week. I was thinking about getting another boat and thought I needed the money. What I really needed was more sense.

I hadn't looked at the barometer all morning. When I did look, it was a low 29-50, which isn't good. I began to get ready to head for port, to Henry's obvious relief; but John, seeing what I was about, looked at me somewhat challengingly, I thought, and began telling the story of Howard Blackburn, meanwhile watching Henry in order to get a kick out of the boy's fear.

Blackburn had been fishing in a dory with another man on a winter day when a sudden squall of snow hid the mother schooner from sight, and wind drove the dory astray. Despairing of finding the ship, Blackburn started to row to shore. After miles of rowing his hands became so numb that he knew he would not be able to hold the oars much longer. So he deliberately made his hands freeze in a cupped position, fast to the oars, and kept on rowing. He finally reached land, his dory-mate frozen to death in the stern. Blackburn came out of it alive, but minus most of his fingers.

After John had finished his tale about Blackburn and had spoken casually about other fishermen being hove-down on George's with their vessels' masts awash in a nasty ground swell and crew members trapped somewhere below decks, I couldn't look him in the eye and say we were going in. I felt like Caspar Milquetoast for even thinking about it. By comparison with Blackburn's situation, this was a picnic. In spite of the silent appeal in Henry's eyes, I had to keep going.

Two hours south of Brenton's Reef, or two hours and ten minutes south-by-west of Newport, we swung around and set out net, dragging to the east'ard, blind—nothing but water and fog. John worked vigorously, grinning, and cracking bawdy jokes; Henry was grim, silent, and pale, his feet dragging as though he had to force himself to move. And every now and then I saw him cross himself, and watched his lips moving in a whispered prayer. An hour later we took up with a fair catch, headed back west in the direction of Block Island, and made several other drags westward.

At two P.M. I decided to go in. I didn't like it; the sea was too calm, and the glass too low. We started for Stonington, our home port. We had no departure point after dragging around blind most of the day. We had to guess at it—a poor method of navigation.

The skipper of a well-equipped trawler or dragger of today would have no trouble finding his position. With his radio direction-finder he could get the bearing of Southeast Light, Block Island somewhere to the west'ard, and he could also pick up Point Judith's signal and run directly for the Point, using his sounding machine to feel his way in. Even a portable radio will give a fellow a bearing if he know how to use it. But we had nothing; we couldn't even hear a sound of any kind, except the slapping of the sea against our own planning and the silly cries of the gulls, so we drove her west-nor'west for two hours, then took a sounding with the hand lead. It showed twelve fathoms. We were getting in somewhere, and it was beginning to get dark. In a desperate attempt at making a landfall within the next ten minutes, I followed the last-resort course of Sound fishermen for generations and headed due north, knowing that if you go north far enough along the New England coast you'll eventually strike North America somewhere.

Darkness closed around us, and fog. You couldn't see fifty feet. I shut off the engine and took a sounding which showed us we were in eight fathoms—that was close enough. We were inside the dreaded steamboat lanes, and that was something. Off Point Judith the lanes crisscross every which way, making the area extremely dangerous for passing vessels.

We anchored, then John fixed up a little supper—five courses—but neither Henry nor I was hungry. John ate almost enough for three of us. The faint sound of surf came out to us, which was reassuring, but where were we? On the east side of Point Judith of on the west side? I didn't know.

We decided to stand watches. John was to have the first one, I the second, and Henry the third. If during the night the fog broke, we would make a run for it. At ten-thirty P.M. I went on watch, and the first thing I noticed was an increasing ground swell. The sound of surf was much plainer—too plain. We were dragging anchor, drifting slowly toward the beach. Then all hell broke loose. Wind, rain, and wave hit us all together, right from the east'ard. I called the gang, started the engine, and ran ahead on our anchor warp as the boys hauled it in. Our bow was dipping under green water as we forged ahead. My knees were knocking. So were Henry's, but he was pulling hard right alongside John.

The fog blew away suddenly; the beach and combing breakers were not two boat lengths away. The anchor came aboard, and we drove straight offshore, cold spray sweeping the length of the boat.

"Well, we can jog till daybreak," said John, calm as could be. "I remember a time like this off Sable Island—"

He never finished, for suddenly the blazing lights of a Sound steamer flashed across our bow. It was the Fall River boat *Priscilla*, the "Queen of the Sound," the vessel that often carried our barreled fish from Newport to New York City. Now we had a direction, and with a tremendous sense of relief I set a course directly in her wake.

Our new course was nearly due west. It meant we were to the west'ard of Point Judith and "running up the beach" toward Watch Hill. Then we spotted the white and red flashing light of the Hill. It was about the most welcome sight I had ever seen. We were heading for the front door to Stonington.

In spite of the fact that we were still running in a gale and a sea that could have swamped a less worthy ship—or even the *Louise* if anything went wrong— Henry had now stopped praying and crossing himself, and my knees had ceased knocking together. (It's an ailment which always assails me in times of stress, and is partly caused by too close a relationship between port and starboard knee.) John was making coffee and saying, "God help the folks ashore on a night like this."

As we raced past Watch Hill gas buoy with our tail to the wind, we could no longer see the *Priscilla*; she had disappeared up the back side of Fishers Island. That wind was really pushing us. In seven minutes we were rounding Napatree gas buoy (it usually took us eleven from the Watch Hill buoy), where the water foams and churns in a storm and makes you feel all hell has broken loose under you and the devil is reaching up from the deep to drag you down. I glanced furtively in the direction where I knew the rocks of Wicopesset Island lay, just east of Fishers Island. I could not see them, of course, in the darkness, but in my imagination they looked sharper and longer than ever before. (I swear that in a bad storm rocks like that seem to stretch out crooked grasping fingers toward a ship, and that a boat seems conscious of them, frightened if she is drifting toward them, courageous and gallant and strong when she is fighting away from them.) Maybe I was shivering a little as I put the wheel hard over to starboard to head her up nor'west toward the light at Stonington's outer breakwater. The *Louise* heeled until her scuppers took green water, and I swore to relieve the tension.

"Damn a slack-bilged boat!" I said. "Wait till I get my new one—if I ever live to—"

Just then a savage wave struck us and my sentence stopped in the middle, for suddenly the wheel went loose in my hand, leaving the *Louise* and us helpless before a violent gale. The tiller chain had parted.

If you've ever had a steering-post knuckle in a car break while you're doing fifty down a curving hill, or had your brakes suddenly cease to function in a similar situation, you'll know how I felt. Freed of restraint and driven by the gale, the *Louise* was racing toward the Wicopesset rocks, which would smash her like matchwood.

Instinctively I threw out the clutch and turned the deck lights on. Out of the corner of my eye I saw John leap for the anchor—a good sailor's first thought when a ship is out of control. Then, with the *Louise* broadside to the gale, rolling so that I could hardly stand, I began groping along the bulwarks trying to find the parted tiller chain, searching in vain for it with half-frozen fingers. I remembered the spare tiller cap buried in the lazarette, and dashed to get it, only to find that it was gone. Ahead of us I could already hear the breakers smashing against the Wicopesset Island rocks with thundering force, and in that moment I think I came nearer to panic than at any other time in my life.

Then I heard John shouting at the stern and, looking, saw a sight which brought my heart into my throat. Little Henry, the scared boy, the youngster whose face could blanch and whose eyes could freeze with terror at one of John's gruesome stories, was down on the deck, but all I could see of him was his hips and legs and feet, and one hand, by which he was hanging on. All the rest of him was hanging out over the stern, directly above the hellishly churning tide rip near Wicopesset. By the squirming spasmodic movements of his buttocks and legs and feet I could see that with his free hand he was desperately busy at something. John was there before I was, flopped down bellywise on the deck himself, holding on to the boy's feet to keep him from going overboard, and now both of Henry's hands were at work, and more than half his body out over the stern. Even before I had figured out what he was doing, I wanted to take off my hat to the courage in the heart of this timid one.

It was a combination of his timidity and courage which saved us that night. His fear had made him secretly take the spare tiller cap[*] out of the lazarette and put it where it was handy in case of a need he foresaw as soon as that gale hit us. But in the horrible split second in which we all knew that the *Louise* was out of control, his courage had taken charge. He had silently, and probably with a prayer on his lips, jumped singlehanded to a task which would have been almost impossible for a man to do alone—for nobody could get that thing into place with one hand, and he certainly needed the other to hang on with. And he had almost thrown himself to his death in doing it.

Seeing that Henry was more or less safe in John's strong hands, I got the pole which we kept alongside the pilothouse to use as a spare tiller, rushed aft with it, and we stuck it in place. John and Henry now lay on the exposed stern deck, freezing salt water pouring over them, and worked the tiller with their feet, while I stood watch forward and shouted instructions back to them through the roaring gale, and we finally docked safely at Avery's packing station, right alongside my brother Morris's dragger, the *Florence*.

I was glad to see that Morris had had the sense to stay in port that day. It was more than I would have given him credit for. He was only twenty-one but he was a good fisherman. Only the spring before he had trimmed the pants off me in catching haddock off Newport, and I had pretended that I was quite put out, but actually I was tickled pink, just as Pop had been when I had beaten his catch the first year I had fished alone, in 1920.

What a feed we had that night! John really dished it out for an hour. Now and then, as we ate, I saw him looking out of the corner of his eye at Henry, a puzzled expression on his face. After that night I never heard him ribbing Henry or trying to scare the kid.

The next morning Nat Avery came on board and told us that his house had been nearly blown off its foundations in the terrible gale of the night before. Then I knew that we had really come through something.

Close calls are nothing new in fishing. Every time I hear of a fisherman fed up with life off the coast I'm reminded of a silly story a bunch of us fellows once heard over at the State Lobster Hatchery at Noank, Connecticut. We had gone to the Hatchery to find out how many baby lobsters had been hatched from a nine-pound-egg lobster. The number was one hundred fifty thousand, but we were told not to expect all that number to be crawling around on sea bottom two years later. The mortality rate is high.

Around Noank—the old smack-fishing center—the exploits of men like Captain Ben Latham are the material of household tales. One adventure of Cap'n

---

[*] An iron cap made to fit over the rudder head. On the side facing forward there is a hole into which a pole may be inserted to act as a tiller in an emergency.

Ben's concerned weathering out a storm on George's Bank aboard the *Star*, a fifty-foot schooner that made fishing history.

The *Star*, hove-to, rode out the gale without wetting her decks, but several large Boston schooners lost dories and were partly dismasted. One schooner near the *Star* was hove-down, her masts lying horizontal on the water. The crew of the ill-fated vessel were picked up, and one of them came back to Noank on the *Star*. That night after getting a shore bath, dried out on the outside and wet down on the inside, he told his future plans.

"Boys, I'm through with the sea. I've had enough. From here on in I want no part of dismasted vessels, hove-down hulks, swamped dories, thoughts of being run down, blown up, sliced in half by floe ice, punctured by a swordfish, swallowed by a devilfish, or whitewashed by gulls. All I crave now is to die in bed ashore, with one arm around a bedpost and the other arm, if any, doing any danged thing it has a mind to.

"I've saved several hundred dollars, what's left from my shares in thirty-nine years of in- and off-shore fishing—most of it in the most miserable goldarned weather that the North Atlantic can dish up. Tomorrow I'm going to buy me my last pair of oars; then I'm going to buy me a horse and buggy. The oars I'll lash on the port and starboard sides of the nag; my other belongings I'll heave in the back of the buggy. Then I climb aboard and start driving inland. I plan to keep going day after day, until some old-timer who looks as if he's been around longer than me asks me what those funny-shaped sticks are tied to my horse. Then I'll say, 'Those sticks, old-timer, are oars, and I'll explain about them later. Now you tell me where to drop my anchor.' If he asks, 'What's an anchor?' I'll surely know I'm where I want to be."

But did he go? Not then. The next day he was seen sneaking aboard the *Star* with Cap'n Ben. He lasted with Cap'n Ben two more trips; then he went a season with another Connecticut driver, Captain Henry Langworthy, but after taking a particularly vicious beating coming in from the tile fish grounds near the Gulf Stream, he kept his word—he journeyed inland and bought a chicken farm and married a comely widow.

A year later, according to the story, he died in bed, one arm around his wife and the other around the metal bedpost, blackened from the terrible farmhouse fire that had nearly consumed them.

After the fire the country village fire chief and his helper found something round and made of wood and charred under the bed that puzzled them. They took it to the village schoolmaster to be identified. He didn't know what the object was either. But he looked through a big book until he found a picture of it. A smile crept over his face, and he said, "Boys, that is that they call a life preserver. But the darn thing didn't work."

X. Women Are Lonely

During the spring of 1925 we decided to head for Nantucket and Martha's Vineyard. For years we had been hearing fabulous tales about "eastern skippers"—Danny Mullins, Shirley Nickerson, Stanley Butler, Bob Jackson, Ike Norton, Claude Wagner, the Hillmans, and others—dragging up so many fish that often one kind of fish would be pushed overboard to make way for another—possibly lemon sole flounder—that might bring a better price.

And that was the way we found it; fish were everywhere. So the island waters became familiar grounds for us. Many times after we had loaded up on the shoals near Nantucket and the Vineyard (twenty thousand pounds in ten hours' fishing) we would run into an island harbor for a bit of a rest before heading back west. And in port we found hospitality of which I have fond memories.

The women of the island always seem to be lonesome, and thus to welcome anyone who make port there. The three whom I remember best are Edna, Pattie, and Mattie of Edgartown. Martha's Vineyard—three good, simple, and warm-hearted souls against whose reputation I never heard but one fisherman speak, and he paid for his foolish remarks by a widespread hostility from fishermen all along the coast.

Edgartown is on the eastern tip of the Vineyard and protected from the sea by long, fingerlike Chappaquiddick Island, which gives it a good safe harbor and makes it an ideal place to run in during a storm or for an overnight berth.

Edna ran an ice-cream parlor in this snug harbor, and it was here that the captains and crews of fishing vessels berthed for the night would gather for a sociable evening. It might have been somewhat disappointing to those who are convinced that fishermen and seamen generally are heavy drinkers to see the boys gathered there, drinking round after round of chocolate or strawberry or vanilla soda, "setting 'em up" one round after another. And Edna was always so glad to see us that she would put three scoops of ice cream in every glass. I don't believe I ever spent a night in Edgartown in those days without laying awake most of the night with stomach pains.

Pattie Pease's chief business consisted of being a source of information and good cheer for every fisherman who made port at Edgartown. She was a soft-spoken woman of about thirty whose hobby was fishing boats, their skippers and cooks, and the facts about where each boat around the Vineyard was operating at any given time, what their catches were, and where the fishing was best. She collected her information at the Edgartown water front, where she wandered about, helping take lines of incoming vessels and telling the boys where to shop. Often, when Wally, a runner for a grocery store, wasn't around, she'd see to it a vessel got grub.

If any boat was on her favored list she'd go aboard, have a spot of tea below in the galley, and give out with important information about near-by fishing conditions. However, this inside stuff was imparted only to the skipper. Our boat got to be on her favored list early, and one of my warmest memories is getting her tips while eating supper close by a coal-burning Shipmate range. She never mentioned whether she was married or not, and I never inquired.

During the winter months a dragger's cabin or forecastle can be pretty cozy if it's dry and well heated, and the presence on board of a visiting woman does much for the morale of fishermen away from home.

The clothing Pattie wore on her water-front junkets was out of a world which ceased to exist a generation ago. There were layers and layers of garments, each layer helping to ward off biting north winds that blew down Edgartown Harbor. And once, as Pattie stretched a bit to get on the dock at dead low water, a pair of heavy-duty bloomers were visible that looked as though they might have been made out of a horse blanket.

One old-timer said of Pattie, "What a sailorman Pattie would be if she had only been born a man! Most women remind me of a shoal-water centerboard catboat—quick on the tiller—but Pattie's built like a deep-water vessel."

Among her ancestors, the Peases, were several famous ship captains who wrote glorious pages in whaling history, so Pattie came by her love of the water and boats quite honestly.

The first time I met her she came down the wharf right after we tied up on our third trip into Edgartown in 1926.

"You the skipper?" she called to me from regions of a rotting dock log about on the level with our green side light.

"Yep," I answered.

"Can I come aboard?" she asked.

"I don't see why not. I've never refused letting a good-looking woman come aboard yet." It was cold, so I invited her below.

"What'd you do today?" she inquired.

"Not much," I said. "We fished off the Hooter west of Gay Heady, but the dabs ran small. We hope to try off in the Back Side tomorrow."

"Well," she said. "You're just in time. Ike Norton in the *Catherine* got two thousand pounds of large dabs yesterday, and he also got a thousand pounds of flounders and a thousand pounds of haddock. The January run of haddock are just showing up. Captain Bob Jackson in the *Hazel Jackson* got them even better. But if you get there, keep along the twelve-fathom curve. If you get too far out you'll get those queer fellows, yellow eels." (Today marine scientists call them ocean pout. Sale of them is discouraged.)

The smallest ferry line in the United States runs between Edgartown and Chappaquiddick Island, and often Pattie acted as ferryboat captain. The equipment consisted of a small sharpie (rowboat) for use by passengers, and a scow for heavy traffic like a cow or sheep. If I remember right, fare for a cow was half a dollar; for a sheep it was a quarter—the same for a man or woman, but strangely enough, for a small dog the fare was only a cent.

One day while we were at Edgartown, and talking with Pattie about the April run of flounders off Hedge Fence a half-mile off Oak Bluffs, a lone dog appeared on the opposite bank and barked to attract attention.

"There's Prince," said Pattie. "Wants to come across on a shopping trip for a farmer's daughter. The man at the drugstore ties the package under his neck. The idea is like them St. Bernards in the Alps. Bringing hope and comfort. I'll go over and get him."

She rowed over, got the dog, and brought him back. The dog departed uptown; he didn't have far to go. Pattie wandered back.

"Who pays for the passage?" I asked. "Or is it a labor or love?"

"Call it what you like," replied Pattie, "but the darned dog gets his job done."

At another water front not far distant from Edgartown on the Vineyard, there was another woman who ventured near the docks at odd hours to sell medicines, salves, disinfectants, and such. I never knew Mattie as well as I did Pattie, though I had met her. But I have heard a lot of stories about her. The one I like best concerns also a famous New England fishing skipper whom I shall call Captain Ed.

Captain Ed was a big man and a kindly man who respected the teachings of a much-thumbed Bible which was always visible in his cabin, but if he could get something on you he would kid and worry the life right out of you. His boat was named *Pequot*.

Many a time I've lain at a dock and heard Captain Ed's roaring voice go booming up the water front as he gave some extra-decisive orders on how best to tie up the *Pequot*. In voice and action he was a combination of a Caribbean Sea buccaneer, a Yankeefied Senator Claghorn, and a starving evangelist. During the winter he often fished out of the Vineyard, and he got to know Mattie quite well; because Captain Ed liked to help a person get along, Mattie sold him plenty of goods.

One dark stormy night in winter he brought his vessel into a certain harbor on the Vineyard. He said afterward that there were no other boats in the harbor except two schooners, and as they approached the old wharf they did not know that Mattie was standing in the shadows waiting to come aboard. When they were close enough, the crew member at the stern tossed a bighted line at what he thought was a pile. His aim was good, but what he had lassoed was not a pile; it was the unfortunate Mattie. Before she could call out she was yanked overboard.

The captain, realizing what had happened when he heard the loud splash, bellowed, "You darned cowboy! Think you're lassoing horses? Get a line ashore and fast."

In a few seconds the boat had been snubbed to a stop, and its deck lights lit up the scene. Captain Ed soon had the wildly floundering Mattie alongside. Reaching over, he and two crewmen pulled her out of the water. She was sputtering like the devil, apparently not injured, but wetter than the underside of a tidal wave.

Captain Ed ordered the crew to get her below, help her get wrapped up in bed, and then get back on deck as quick as the Lord would let them. Against her remonstrances they got her below, had all but the innermost garment stripped from her, and a place prepared for her in the cleanest bunk. By this time Mattie had cleared the last bit of salt water from her throat, and, giving the gang of fishermen a withering look, came out with, "What's the big idea, trying to drown me, a poor working girl? What are you fellows staring at?"

Captain Ed handed her a freshly made cup of coffee, then, glancing at the Bible on the table as if to strengthen his will, he made his hands into fists the size of hams, turned, and shouted to the crew, who were standing sideways trying to arrange Mattie's wet clothes for drying. "This woman is a shipwrecked mariner, and that means she is entitled to the best we have to offer. And that includes respect. If any man tries to bother her I'll floor him. Now all of you get on deck; and don't worry, I'll be right behind you."

Mattie watched in surprise as the men cleared out. "Hell," she said, "what do you want to leave me down here all alone for? You got me all wrong. It isn't that I'm bashful. I like company. It's just that I'm so lumpy I hate to have anyone see me with my clothes off!"

Five years later Captain Ed and his crew in the *Pequot* piled up on the back side of Noman's Land during a winter snowstorm. Their vessel, rolling in the surf, started to break up, so the shipwrecked fishermen took to the dory and got safely ashore, leaving behind them the wreckage of one more good and honest vessel.

There is another island woman—not of Martha's Vineyard, but of a small island I shall not name—whom I have never met, though I have always thought I would like to. She is a lighthouse keeper's daughter, and a woman of extraordinary good sense if one is to judge by the story that is told about her.

The other principal character in the story is a sixteen-year-old boy named Ted, who was cast ashore from the wreck of the *Larchmont*, on which both his parents lost their lives. He had no other relatives of whom he knew, and no one ever claimed him, so the whole island adopted him, without going through any legal fol-de-rol.

There was nothing resembling a high school on the island, and the ship-wrecked boy had finished eighth grade before the wreck. The island people got together in sort of a New England town meeting and decided that they must fig-ure out some way to give the boy a chance to win a high-school diploma. After fitting deliberation they asked the seventeen-year-old Lilian, daughter of the keeper of the light, who had recently moved to the island, to be his teacher. She said she would be willing to try it—on her own conditions. Among them was a course of study which she herself outlined, suitable, she said, for a boy growing up in nautical surroundings. Also she demanded subscriptions to the *Saturday Evening Post*, *The National Geographic*, the *Providence Journal*, the *Vineyard Gazette*, *Daboll's Almanac*, and a number of books such as Bigelow and Welsh's *Fishes of the Gulf of Maine*, and Eldridge's *Coast Pilot and Tide Book*. The fathers agreed, and school was begun in the lighthouse.

One the first day the teacher asked Ted if he would like to have a school flag. Ted said he would. For some time he had had his eye on two pennants—one Harvard and one Yale—which the teacher had got one gala day when she left the island to go to the Yale-Harvard boat race. He asked her to stitch them to-gether. It made a swell flag, red and blue, with the large letters Y and H which, Ted and Lilian decided, now stood for Yankee High.

The school flag was flown each day school was in session. It was a large flag and was easily seen from the Sound. Because of the geographical location of Yale and Harvard, the local mariners called wind from the northwest Yale weather, and winds from the northeast Harvard weather. And now when the wind was shifting and variable, they said it was "Yankee High" weather.

When not in school Ted helped island fishermen with their traps and lobster gear. He even did a little fishing on his own, out around the near-by ledges. Lil-ian seemed to know a lot about fishing, too and never let school interfere when Ted could be of help to others as well as to himself. When fish schooled in the Sound, there was no school ashore. The scup would strike in early May, fluke in early August, and mackerel and striped bass in late fall; and when the season was at its height, Lilian and Ted would go fishing.

In school, fish and ways and means of catching them and preparing them were studied and discussed. Sometimes men from Woods Hole Oceanographic Institution came to the island on fishery research, and Lilian always saw that Ted went with them.

Finally Ted's last year of school came. He was now a big fellow and shaving twice a week. Lilian was powdering her nose twice a day and looked younger than ever. And the way Ted was babying Lilian and telling her what to do—but in a nice way—it looked as though he were the teacher and she the pupil.

Graduation day came, and the generous island folk got up a lot of nice prizes for the best of the class in this and in that, including a small dory with dragging gear. Of course Ted won them all—enough fishing and boating equipment to set up a fisherman in fine style. He had everything he could want, except one thing, and by the look in his eyes and Lilian's, he would have that any moment now.

Graduation exercises went off smoothly. Ted did his stuff and did it well; he ended by boxing the compass. Lilian smiled happily and motioned to an old man in the somewhat slender audience. He came forward and taking off his long visored swordfish cap, addressed the six-foot, hundred-and-ninety-pound boy who had just finished high school.

"Ted," he said, "Lillian tells me it's customary for either the oldest or one of the more important citizens of a community to address the high school graduating class. I'm not important, but I'm eighty-two years old, and I've seen a lot of water pass through Quick's Hole. For that reason I'm giving you some advice. It won't be complicated, and it won't take me long.

"Lil tells me you're handy with tools. That's good. I know you're handy around a boat and ain't lazy. When you go fishing, get out early; the best weather is in the morning. The afternoons will take care of themselves.

"Some day you may go to Boston or New York, to the big wholesale fish markets. Certain market-men will show you a good time—perhaps too good. Look out for fast women. They're like a cranky boat, tip over too easy, and that fact has meant doom for many a man. The Bible says it's better not to live alone, so don't you wait too long to get married. By the looks of things it ain't going to be too hard to accomplish that, and do it right, too. Try to live according to the golden rule. It doesn't make too much difference whether you live ten more years or seventy years more. When your time runs out, if you have a clear conscience, you can turn around to the rest of the world and tell them all where they can go. That's all Ted. Good luck."

Yankee High never opened its doors again. A week after Labor Day Lilian and Ted were married. That winter a lumber schooner, rolling heavily in the Sound, had lost part of her deck load, and her hard luck was Ted's gain. From lumber he salvaged he built a cottage on the island near where he kept the small dragger to which the islanders had staked him, and he and Lilian moved in.

One stormy afternoon when he couldn't go fishing he was unpacking and straightening up in their new house, and he came across his final examination papers. He stopped and smiled as he read again what he had written after his answer to the last question: "I love you, Lilian. Ted."

"You were a swell teacher, honey," he said. "But the best answer on this whole examination paper is something I thought up all by myself."

She looked over his shoulder and saw the note to which his finger was pointing. Then she laughed gently to herself, kissed him, and went to the kitchen to put the supper on the stove, saying nothing.

Cap'n Thompson on board *Eleanor*.

XI. Birth of the Lady *Eleanor*

The *Louise* was a grand boat, though a cranky one. She helped me catch an awful lot of fish, carried me on many a good time, and saw me safely through many a near disaster. But actually, thought I had tried in my original plans to make drawings and specifications for a boat that would be easy on the rolling, she rolled much worse than the *Grace and Lucy* had.

So in 1927, after a good dabbing winter off Newport, I decided to try again, this time with a larger boat which I hoped would be even more seaworthy and be better designed for the job it had to do. First of all I wanted a roomy forecastle where my gang and I could rest up, mugg up, or entertain without getting snarled up with one another, night or day, fair weather or foul. Next, I wanted plenty of working space aft; space along the rail to haul in the net without getting knocked overboard; and space between hatches where a bulging cod end could be emptied without myself and crew being buried alive by squirming fish or bottom trash; space to sort and wash the catch; and space below deck to ice and pack twenty-five thousand pounds of fish. It was a large order. It meant putting the pilothouse and dory forward on a raised deck; it meant putting the engine and the winch and a lot else up forward, but not too far forward. What I had in mind was really pretty much the kind of boat which is known today as a Connecticut-type dragger.

I tried to explain all this to some of our more advanced boatbuilders, but they either didn't know what I was talking about or were just plain stubborn about their own ideas. They couldn't see it my way, and I couldn't see it their way at all, so I began to think of the things I had seen Jake Smith do in 1924 when he had laid out the *Louise* on paper; and I remembered how Pop had built that first Connecticut beam trawl of his after trying to get a three-dimensional impression of one from a photograph in a magazine; and finally, feeling kind of desperate like a man before a court of law without a good lawyer, I bought a few drawing instruments, including an old reliable hardware-store yardstick.

Next on the program was a visit to some of the fishing boats in the Stonington and Noank fleets whose behavior in rough water I liked. Then, after a session of flogging my brain cells to increased activity, and after sneaking a few looks at some blueprints of sea-going yachts in *Yachting* and in *Rudder*, I sat down at the dining-room table and went to work on the backs of several well-beaten charts. I didn't want to ruin good paper.

Before I had drawn a line I had decided to call her the *Eleanor* after my little sister, and that seemed to help by making it an intimate and a well-wishing sort of thing. We were all good friends in my family.

Then I rushed home and carefully counted the money in my savings account, and calculated how much I could borrow. Nat Avery at Stonington said, "You can count on me for a thousand and if I haven't got it when you need it, I'll borrow it." At Newport, Ralph Newcomb's father said, "I got a thousand that isn't doing a damn soul any good. If you need it today it's yours." My uncle, Francis Allanac, a conservative businessman, said, "Make your new boat a stock proposition and I'll take ten shares at ten dollars a share. Fishing looks good to me." Mr. Darrow, at this ship chandlery, offered me anything I needed in ship equipment and said it wouldn't be billed to me for six months. How could a fellow lose with such men around?

My mind made up, I went back to the Rancocas yard at Delanco, where we drew up formal specifications for a fifty-foot dragger and signed a contract. Then they started building her and I went back fishing, easy in mind.

A month later I learned the story of the *Eleanor*'s shaft log. The shaft log is one of the most important pieces of lumber that goes into a small wooden dragger. It is generally about eight inches by twelve inches by ten feet. It runs from the engine, through the stern of the boat to the propeller. The propeller shaft runs through it, and there is a stern bearing on the outside of it and a stuffing box on the inside. A lot depends on the shaft log, and honest boatbuilders try to use extra good oak for it. When it came time to find the oak for the *Eleanor*'s shaft log, several of the Rancocas gang went to their own woods and sawmill. They spied a piece laid out to one side and earmarked for a carriage maker in Philadelphia, a beautiful piece of white oak.

"It's too damn good for any carriage. Let's grab it while the mill boss is down in the woods," said one of the gang. And they did. That straight-grained piece of white oak twelve feet long was one specification I hadn't figured on.

Most of the details of the specifications would be meaningless to anyone but a seaman or boatbuilder, but the following two sentences, which are in the contract I drew and signed with the Rancocas Construction Company, show pretty well what I had in mind:

"The boat is to be of a strong and workmanlike character, with no fancy finish....The spirit of these specifications is to produce a fifty-foot overall fishing boat, according to the foregoing specifications and accompanying blueprints, of a strong and serviceable character throughout, and shall be completed by the builder as a commercial boat of this type should be."

I figured that they were, after all, honest men at the Rancocas yard, and that if some of the details of my more or less amateurish designs and specifications were not completely clear to them, they'd know what those sentences meant, and do it.

It took four months to build her, and I was biting my fingernails practically all that time. In fact, after three months, I couldn't stand being away from her any more so I got the Shipmate stove installed, moved over there, and lived aboard her for the last month, even though the cabin wasn't finished yet.

While the painters were working in the cabin, I told them I could help during the evenings if they would leave their stuff on board at night. So they left a lot of good spar varnish aboard, and brushes, and every other night I'd work on her, letting it stand to get good and hard on alternate nights. The specifications called for two coats of varnish, but the *Eleanor* got eight, and it lasted for ten years without touching a brush to it.

Finally the day came, in May 1927, when she was ready for her trial run. Pop, Morris, Howard Shaw, Louis Steele of the Rancocas Company, and I ran her through the inland waterway between the Delaware River and New York Harbor, and while there was no formal dedication or anything like that, the factory girls between Delanco and New York who waved and smiled at us and asked if they couldn't come along, gave us a pretty good send-off. Then we went on up to New London, got the Lathrop Engine people to send a man over from Mystic to check her engine and pronounce it okay, and we were ready to take her on her maiden trip to grounds off Nantucket. It was the third week in May 1927, the week during which Lindbergh made his solo flight to Paris with a sandwich and some letters of introduction he never had to use in his pocket, and I'll bet he got no more satisfaction out of that week in his life than I did out of the same week in mine.

My first crew on the *Eleanor* were Pop—then fifty-four years old—and Sammy. I had planned to have Henry Landry with me, but he made only one trip with Pop and me. Then another boat stole him from me with higher wages, and so Sammy came aboard.

Sammy, like Henry, was a young Nova Scotian, a good fisherman who worked with me for a number of years. Many of our local boats had Canadian crews in those days, especially the trap fishermen who worked off Newport and usually paid their imported help not over seventy-five dollars a month and board. Sammy was one of these, and so it was easy for me to hire him for a hundred and twenty dollars a month, which I did. He was a big eater, and cost me a lot in food, but even so he was such a hard and intelligent worker that I soon raised him to one hundred fifty dollars a month.

Then I began to feel cheap about that, for the other men, the New England men, whom I took on always worked the boat with me on a percentage basis* and were making a lot more than Sammy was. But when I offered to give Sammy, as an extra man, fifteen per cent of the boat's net, he refused.

"I don't care if you make a thousand dollars a week," he said. "A hundred and fifty a month and the grub you serve is good pay and I'm satisfied. Besides, you always give me a bonus when you hit the fish and the market at the same time."

That's the kind of fellow he was, and I always shall remember him for it. I shall always remember, too, the night when a net fouled our wheel and he rowed our dory two miles through a choppy sea to Block Island and brought back Captain Nick Nelson of Noank. The captain towed us in and refused to let me pay him for it. Later I sent him an awfully nice little gadget for his mantelpiece at home—a combination clock and barometer, all set into a ship's steering wheel.

I soon learned that I needn't have worried about the design of the *Eleanor*. She turned out perfect. She would go to windward in a choppy sea with only the murmur of a pound, just enough so she wouldn't dive; she would run off to leeward on the slope of a snarling following sea like a scared rabbit, straight as an arrow, her large outboard rudder acting somewhat like the tail feather on an arrow. And when she got caught broadside to a nasty swell, her degree of roll (or listing) was much less than that of any fishing boat I had ever been on. She would hoist fifty bushels of fish out of water as though it was child's play, not listing more than twenty-five degrees. I've fished her for twenty-two years and expect to make my last fishing trip in her, whenever that may be. Her catches have

---

* The usual arrangement is to deduct the out-of-pocket expenses for each trip from the price received for the catch, take forty per cent out for the "boat's share," and divide the rest equally among the men and the working captain. Thus, if two men and myself made a trip which we sold for three hundred fifty dollars, it might work out something like this:

Check from the market		$350.00
Operating expenses		
Ice	$20.00	
Barrels	16.50	
Gasoline (84 gal. @ .25)	21.00	
Oil (1 gal. @ $1.00) 1.00		
Food	10.00	68.50
		———
Net		$281.50
Boat's share (2/5)		$112.60
Share for each man, incl. myself		56.30

totaled over ten million pounds of fish, mostly flounders and haddock, caught in waters between Nantucket shoals and Long Island Sound. She's getting on in years, like myself, and she looks it; but I regard her as one of the family, and I wouldn't sell her for anything.

The *Eleanor* cost ten thousand dollars ready for sea. One-half of this remained to be paid off in notes. It was, and without too many sacrifices on my part.

The *Eleanor* did change my fishing habits—that is, along with a bit of mild rheumatism. In my smaller boats I had gone pretty much where I felt like going when I stepped on deck in the morning. But when I got the *Eleanor* and found out what a perfect lady she was, and what an imperfect fellow I was, my old ways of fishing seemed a bit irresponsible. For a while I tried to settle down nearer home. I concentrated my fishing on the grounds "down the beach" between Point Judith and Watch Hill. I caught spring haddock and summer fluke and fall whiting and winter flounders.

The nearest and most active fish-packing station was Nat Avery's steamboat fish dock at Stonington, where Nat and his gang of fish handlers and truckmen had built up a thriving business with eastern Connecticut draggermen. When Nat Avery leased the dock property in 1925 (the same day I became a regular out of Stonington) he promised many of us fishermen—Lawry, Lawrence, Kidd, McLaughlin, Edwards, Tuthill, Jones, Thompson, and others—a fish-packing, trucking, and banking service such as we had never seen before. This promise he fulfilled, and his service worked out fine; in work or play, many fishermen including myself, operated out of Nat's dock for years. We had close calls ashore and afloat; most of mine generally happened down around the Vineyard when we fished out of there during the wintertime.

There was a night, for instance, up near Edgartown when I was fishing with Sammy and another young fellow named Markey, a good worker, but strong on wine, women, and song—a sort of lost weekender at sea.

To get from the harbor of Edgartown to fishing grounds south of the island one must go up around Cape Pogue on the northeastern trip and then run down along Chappaquiddick Island and out through Muskeget Channel. This is the channel that separates Nantucket from Martha's Vineyard—or, to be more specific, the channel separates Nantucket's Tuckernuck Island from the Vineyard's Chappaquiddick Island. In a storm it is a good place to keep away from. The shoals before one gets to deep water offshore manufacture waves that are like small steep-sided hills.

We started to head for Edgartown just after sunset that night, a howling gale driving us along. The barometer was falling; seas were mountain-high. We hoped to make in at Mutton Shoal gas buoy. Then everything would be all right, the course to Cape Pogue straight, and the rest of the run into Edgartown in comparatively smooth water.

We were keeping the *Eleanor* on a northeast course, and I figured in another ten minutes we would make the buoy. Suddenly another vessel loomed out of the haze. It was the *Aquidneck*, belonging to Captain Ed Sanchez. They seemed to be steering about north, so, not trusting my own judgment, and thinking that Captain Ed and his gang had either seen the buoy or had made a landfall, I decided to change our course to north-northeast, a sort of compromise between Captain Ed's judgment and my own. When I looked again the *Aquidneck* had vanished, but suddenly right ahead of us loomed a ridge of wildly tossing water. This meant a rip, and many a time a rip means a shoal. Which way to turn to find deeper water? I turned eastward toward our old course, and that deed probably saved the *Eleanor* and our lives.

We ran east for five minutes. Still no end to the rip, so I said to the crew, "Well, boys, say your prayers; we're crossing over!" I kicked off my boots and Sammy did the same. Markey rushed below, dug down in the coal bin, and came up with a half-pint of whisky. Rushing back on deck, he hollered, "No use wasting this." He hit the bottle just before we hit the bar. A giant wave picked us up, then let us down in sand. Another giant wave lifted us, and we were over in deep water. Through the driving mist Skiff Island loomed to port only two hundred feet away.

An hour later we were tied up in Edgartown, and, strangely enough, so was Captain Ed Sanchez in the *Aquidneck*. He said they had dragged across a mile of shoal between Skiff Island and the mainland, with one chance in a hundred of coming safely through, but Providence had smiled on both of us.

That night he gave me some advice. This is the gist of it: "If you have a fair idea where you are, respect your own judgment and stick with it. The other guy may be wrong, as I was tonight. Hell, I was lost, but coming in I had made up my mind I was going to steer the *Aquidneck* due north."

At eight P.M., with the boats securely tied, while a gale wind swept across the marshes outside the village, we were all gathered in Edna's ice-cream parlor, buying round after round of Edna's ice cream sodas, knowing perfectly well that we'd have belly-aches later.

XII. To Be or Not to Be Married

During the year 1929 the Thompson family fortune seemed to reach a new high. Louise was finishing her teacher's course at the New England Conservatory of Music. Eleanor was finishing high school. Ma was finishing two winter quilts, and Pop was finishing three new trawl nets and a case of near-beer. Morris had a dragger and I had two. Fishing was good, and very pleasant checks came daily from Fulton Fish Market.

Good luck had seemed to come in with the new year. In one day, early in January, dragging in fifteen fathoms on the back side of the Vineyard, I had caught sixty barrels of dab flounders, which I sold for over a thousand dollars. In late February we struck the dabs again off the Hooter, west of the Vineyard. In April and May we found huge schools of haddock which extended from the Hell Hole to the mussel bed ten miles east of Block Island. During June we worked the flounders on the beach—from Watch Hill to Point Judith. In July we struck the haddock again, eight miles south-southeast of Montauk near a large clump of rocky bottom. August found us dabbing off Block Island. One day we ironed two swordfish while dragging, and got ten thousand pounds of dabs the same day.

During the summer we worked out of Nat Avery's Stonington fish dock, enjoying the Thompson family in New London and the Riley family near the Stonington water front. In the Riley's two-family house there were fifteen little Rileys, both sexes, with girls—the best-looking chorus I have ever seen—outnumbering the boys.

Stonington, tightly tucked away on a small peninsula that points out across Block Island Sound to the open sea off Montauk Point, is like no other village on the face of the earth—and is better than most. The village streets are narrow and lined with large white houses that were built during prosperous whaling and sealing days. Several houses have widow's walks on their roof tops from which the families and friends of sea captains watched for signs of homecoming ships. And along Water Street (the main drag) beautiful large elm trees, growing half in the road and half up through the sidewalk, are useful regulators for the speed of out-of-town automobiles—so that the home folks can cross the street without undue nervous strain.

Stonington's maritime history dates back to earliest Colonial days and includes trading, shipbuilding, blockade running, whaling, sealing, exploring, fishing, fighting, and Sound steamboating.

During the years that the Stonington Line operated Sound-steamer service between New York and Stonington, a spur track of the New York, New Haven, and Hartford Railroad ran through the center of the village to the steamboat pier. The Line was famous, and a trip to New York on one of the steamers was an event in anyone's life. The service also attracted many schooners and smacks to the port because of the ease with which fish could be shipped into New York City. And for a while Fulton Market and eastern Connecticut were as closely related as first cousins.

I can remember when shipping by steamer had its drawbacks; for one thing, the steamers left on schedule, and there's no timetable to regulate some fishing events. Quite often, especially during the era of sail, a fishing vessel would strike head winds and tide coming in from the grounds, and just miss getting its fish packed in ice and shipped to market. If the weather was hot, the fish usually rotted before they could be packed and shipped. And there have been times—not too long ago, Captain Billy Masante of Noank will tell you—when, after a fishing skipper had been informed of a glutted wholesale market, he would sell his jumbo fluke or lemon sole or bluefish for lobster bait at a dollar a barrel.

Old Tom Wilcox, who fished for lobsters before the Spanish-American War, once said, "I caught lobsters off Fishers Island in water over two hundred feet deep, and I pulled the pots up by hand. Then, after the day's fishing was done, I sailed and rowed in to market, where I was paid seven or eight cents a pound; and I made money. In 1899—I remember the year because I wasn't worrying about the Spanish fleet sneaking in past Montauk—I got paid ten cents a pound for lobsters about ten inches long. That's the size they use in high-class restaurants now, and after they cook it and cover it with some strange sauce, you have to cover the waiter's palm with a five-dollar bill.

There is a legend floating about the Stonington waterfront, and I learned of it through "Skipper" Adams, a stalwart six-footer who helps build Connecticut-type draggers at the shop of Henry Palmer's Stonington Boat Works. The legend concerns the ghost of a frustrated whaling captain who for many years tried to learn the whereabouts of pet whaling grounds of Stonington skippers. On moonlit nights during summer this ghost could be heard stomping about on the narrow streets of Stonington, trying to find a chart which would give him the location he sought. Captain Ben Chesbro, the oldest living whaler or sealer hereabouts, has told me, "I saw the whaler's ghost twice, and both times he stopped in front of Bindloss's office and squinted at the moonlit sidewalk. After a few minutes spent in studying the ground, he would give a deep sigh and disappear. Once I looked at the spot in front of the store and, sure enough, plainly seen by the light of the moon were ghostly markings that looked like an area down around the Antarctic where whales once were plentiful. But with the coming of daylight the signs vanished."

The legend—at least the part about the marks on the ground—is related to facts. Not long ago the last group of Stonington whale men would gather on warm afternoons in front of Bindloss's coal office to argue the merits of favorite whaling grounds. They would draw rough charts in the sidewalk dirt, and often passers-by would have to step out around the drawings into, perhaps, a muddy road. And if a fair lady thus denied the sidewalk should vent a little womanly steam, one of the old-timers was sure to get up and amble away, muttering, "Tha' she blows! She's aspoutin' high, wide, and beautiful!"

It is from the families of such old-time whalers and sealers as these that many of Connecticut's Draggerman come—but not all. During the nineteenth century the numbers of New England fishermen were increased by the coming of Europeans, whose seagoing heritage is as old as maritime history. Many of these, especially the Portuguese-Americans, were quick to adopt the new method of dragging when it began to be used along the coast, and today some of the most prominent fishing families are of this hardy stock. Among the best known of them are the sons and grandsons of Captain Manuel Roderick and Captain Manual Maderia; their number, persistence, and success promise that there will always be Maderias and Rodericks fishing off the Connecticut coast.

As to the relations of the Portuguese-Americans with the old Yankee families—well, the truth is that most New Englanders pay less attention to the names of the boats on which their ancestors arrived, and the dates of arrival, than to the quality of the neighbors themselves, regardless of the tradition of New England aloofness. Some of the most respected and best-liked draggermen in the business are from the families of these later comers.

September, October, and November of the year 1929 found us working out of Ralph Newcomb's dock at Newport and talking advantage of rising fish prices and the flounder schools on the mussel bed ten miles off Newport. Both my boats cleaned up; I cleared four thousand dollars in two months. The future looked bright—so bright that I began to worry. Things couldn't be as good as that!

And then I got a letter from a leading fish dealer in Fulton Fish Market:

Dear Ellery,

Your fish have been coming through in very poor shape. Someone aboard your boat isn't tending to his job. Maybe it's you. Why don't you get married and tend to business?

Sincerely, _____

It seemed a rather good idea. Indeed, the question of marriage had occupied a sort of rainy-day place in my mind for some time, but I had never seemed to have time for it before. Also there always had been a question in my mind as to whether it was fair to a girl for a fisherman to marry her. I had seen too many women waiting helplessly for news of their men holed up somewhere by a storm and out of communication. But now, with everything looking so rosy, I thought I might give the matter more serious consideration. I put it up to one of the old-timers who had never knowingly given anyone a bum steer in his life.

"Why not?" he said. "The trouble with you fishermen is that you're afraid you won't be home long enough to work at it. What about your ancestors who went off on trading, whaling, and sealing trips for months at a time? Gosh almighty, look at the kids they raised! Another thing! I never yet heard of a fisherman's wife starving to death!"

I had to leave my car at the garage for repairs that day, and I walked all the way home, trying to think. As I climbed the hill to our house, my head down, like a man deep in thought, I bumped into someone, and at the same time saw, fluttering between my eyes and the sidewalk, the folds of a sort of what-you-may-call-it dress—one of those things made of yards and yards of bright-colored gingham or something, which sort of billow out around a girl. I had to raise my eyes only a little to meet those of the girl wearing the dress, for the top of her head just about reached the tip of my nose—and I had seen it grow to that height from a place about level with my top vest button.

Usually her eyes were laughing, but now they reproached me. "Sometimes you give me a pain in the neck, Ellery," she said. "You'd've walked right by me if I hadn't stood square in your way. What were you studying so hard about?"

"Getting married," I said honestly. It seemed easier than lying.

Her chin seemed to push forward. "Who is she?" she asked. "I know. It's that—"

"Nobody special," I interrupted quickly. I didn't want any names named aloud on my home street. "I wasn't thinking about marrying any particular girl. I was just thinking of getting married or not getting married—as sort of a general policy, like whether you're Republican or Democrat."

You could almost tell what Nan was thinking by her eyes. Now they flashed. "Ellery," she said quickly in a voice like a tight trawl line, "I'm leaving tomorrow."

I nodded. I knew about that. Nan was an orphan and for some time had been living with an aunt in New London, but now that aunt was sick and was shipping her charge off for permanent safe-keeping to another aunt who lived in Canada.

She came a little closer and put her hand on my arm. "Take me out tonight, Ellery—please!" she pleaded. "Take me out as a young lady—not just as a neighborhood brat dragging along with a big brother."

I knew what she meant without having to go into any of the details. I told her to meet me on the corner at eight, and she turned without a word and began to race for her home. I went on to mine, with no less excitement, but at a pace more suited to my advanced years, and, phoning the garage, made sure that the car would be ready by six-thirty.

Nan—a friend of my sister Eleanor—had crossed the horizon three years before, when she was twelve and I was twenty-seven. The first time I ever saw her was late one afternoon when I came into the house straight from the boat, after packing a day's catch of fish. I was a mess and the way I looked might have scared any kid, but it didn't scare Nan. She was on her way upstairs to Eleanor's room, twisting and turning, almost sliding up the banister, looking down at me curiously out of those flashing black-lashed eyes, first over one shoulder, then over the other. Her long black hair, which had not yet yielded to the new style of bobbing, reached below her shoulders, and was gathered with a single ribbon back of her neck, giving her the appearance of a lovely woman older than her years; her tiny feet were encased in sneakers, her slim straight legs bar, her little newly formed breasts pushing against her thin, too-small blouse. Then, with a sort of whisking rush she had hurried into Eleanor's room, slamming the door behind her.

Even then—never having seen her before, knowing that she was a kid and I was more than twice as old—I wanted to run after her. "Be your age," I said to myself. But another guy inside me said, "Oh, go to hell!"

Nan was an early riser and flitted about our neighborhood hilltop like a bird up with the sun. Pop was an early riser too, and often I would step out of bed in the morning and go to the window in my nightshirt, as one does to get a look at the new day, and there would be Pop in the back yard, mending one of my nets, while Nan hung around talking to him. Pop liked young people, and Nan liked people much older than herself. Sometimes she would look up and see me, wave her hand, and smile.

One morning when I had slept a little later than usual, I suddenly felt a yank and a cold draft on my legs. I opened my eyes and there was Nan laughing at me. She had walked in and pulled the covers off.

"Gosh, you've got hairy legs," she said, staring.

"You'll pay for that," I answered and, jumping out of bed, I grabbed her and kissed her—after all, a little girl, and a friend of my sister's, almost a little sister herself. But I was amazed by the kiss she gave me. It wasn't like a little girl's kiss. After that I told myself to mind my step and tried not to hear the voice of the other guy inside me.

Nan seemed always around somewhere, driving to the store with Eleanor and me when I bought supplies for the boat, standing on the street talking with the mailman, the garbage man, the iceman, even the undertaker while he was waiting for the obsequies to be finished in a neighborhood house—always someone older. Perhaps that was partly because most of the kids her age in the neighborhood were girls. There wasn't a boy anywhere around between twelve and nineteen or twenty.

Another thing about it was that she wasn't pretty in the ordinary sense of the word, and she knew it. (Perhaps that was one reason she liked me. Misery loves company.) She had a pug nose, freckles, and small sparkling eyes; and her ears, like mine, were too big; but those very things, coupled with her inexhaustible store of energy, her quick bright mind, and the initiative and originality born of her vivid imagination, gave her a rare and powerful attractiveness which she was too unsophisticated to recognize.

You never knew when or where she was going to turn up, or how she might get there. One Sunday morning when Harold Lawry—then engaged to Louise—had spent the night with us and we were all at breakfast, we suddenly heard the wedding march being played—amateurishly but with thunder in it—on our old piano in the parlor. I rushed in and there was Nan, playing furiously, as if her life depended on it.

On another day we heard what sounded like a huge coal slide in our cellar. As a matter of fact, that's what it was. When I went down I found Nan half buried under our winter's supply of coal. She had come in through the cellar window, following a stray cat.

A patriotic young couple in the neighborhood habitually flew an American flag from a flag pole in the yard, carefully taking it in at sunset every night. But one evening, when something else pretty important was acutely on their minds, they forgot, and left it out. The next morning at about daybreak, when the doctor arrived to deliver their first baby he found the flag flying upside down. Nan had thought that the house, like a ship in trouble, rated a distress signal.

On another day, when I was at home alone, I heard the shower go on upstairs. I went up, found the bathroom door half open, and the shower going full pace, but apparently no one in the room. As I shut it off, Nan, fully dressed, stepped out from behind the door.

"Don't you wish I had been under it?" she asked. Then she ran out into the hall, slid down the banister and was out of the front door in a few seconds, while I sat down on the top step, my head in my hands, wondering how to cope—not with her, but with myself.

Often I took Eleanor and Nan and friends of theirs out on my boat, from which they would go swimming. I kept my eye on Nan, telling myself that she was the youngest and must be taken care of. And she was quite aware of my attention.

One Friday afternoon I took the girls out in the boat, anchored near the mouth of the Westerly River in Little Narragansett Bay, and, after the girls had changed into their bathing suits in the cabin, rowed them ashore in the dory to swim from the pebbly beach. I was rowing about to no purpose in the dory, killing time, when suddenly I heard Nan cry, "Come get me! I'm in trouble! Oh, save me quick!" There seemed to be real distress in her voice, and I reached her as fast as I could. When I pulled her out I found she had a small cut on one foot which she had got by kicking a piece of driftwood.

She grinned at me. "Oh, Ellery, you're my hero!" she cried. "You saved my life!"

"Like hell I did," I told her, making myself cross to hide from her, and from myself, my confused feelings. "You weren't ten feet from the clam flats and weren't even breathing hard. You could have made Stonington Harbor under your own steam." She could have, too. She was a marvelous swimmer.

"Well, anyway, it was worth a try," she said. "I want to go home."

We all went aboard the *Eleanor*, and started home. On the way in we came abreast of a rowboat with three of the Riley girls in it, out rowing and tired, so we picked them up too, took them aboard, and towed their boat in. As we came alongside Nan looked at them wistfully.

"Gee, they're pretty," she said enviously.

"The prettiest girls in Stonington," I said cruelly, and felt like a stern father who had done the Thing He Had to Do as she pouted and looked away.

One day when we were going out on the boat with Eleanor and some friends, she produced some old-looking painting materials. She was evasive when I questioned her about them. Later I learned that they were some my mother had used as a girl. Nan had found them in our attic and had brought them along without bothering to ask anyone. While the rest swam, she and I sat on a sandy beach at Watch Hill, trying to paint a seascape together, while the gulls wheeled over us screaming their disdainful comments., I painted the sea and Nan painted the sky; as to verisimilitude, it didn't much matter whether you looked at it right side up or upside down.

After a while I said, "You ought to put something on the horizon."

Abruptly Nan put the painting to one side and began to clean the brushes, while her lips went out in an expression of stubbornness which was typical of her. "I haven't decided what belongs there yet," she said. "Maybe I shall some day. But I'm going to keep the painting always."

All of these memories ran through my mind that evening in 1929 as I gave myself the works in the way of a shave, a bath, and the best clothes I had. It was ridiculous, I tried to tell myself. Nan was still just a kid—fifteen, too young to know her own mind—and I was thirty. And yet I was as excited as a twenty-year-old taking out the one and only on the night when he is pretty sure she's going to say yes.

When I met her on the corner I gasped and had to tell myself sternly that

she was only fifteen years old. She had on a new dress I had never seen before—
a young lady's party dress which would have knocked anybody's eyes out, the way
Nan wore it. Her hair had been bobbed since the time she had met me on the
street, and, waved as carefully as Lana Turner's, it concealed all but the tips of
her ears, which had an especial poignancy thus. There was no danger now of
their seeming to be too large. She had on lipstick, but not too much, and her
head was high and proud.

She saw my astonishment and for a moment neither of us said anything,
just looked at each other, and in her eyes there seemed to be a deep, somewhat
sad defiance.

"Like it?" she asked finally. But she didn't smile.

"Too well," I growled. "Let's go."

I had already decided that our evening would not be spent in New London
or Stonington, and now, as I looked at her I knew where we would go. As rapidly
as possible I headed for the Rhode Island border and the most fashionable and,
for a young girl, exciting spot I knew. We had dinner and we danced, and then
we ate again, like a New York couple making a big night of it. All through the
evening I was conscious of the envious eyes of other men watching us, as Nan,
with the grace and poise of a sophisticated young woman in her early twenties,
naturally and with no apparent effort claimed her right to be called the most
charming and loveliest creature there. There was something in the evening
which I had never experienced before, something which the fifteen years' difference in our ages did not seem to affect at all—a rare companionship between
two human beings, a warmth and comfort and naturalness. With Nan in my
arms on the dance floor I was at ease in a way I had never know before, as if here
I was at home, where I belonged, in some subtle way doing what I had been
born to do.

It was not until we got into the car, after midnight, that I began to pull myself
up short again, and made myself become statistical about ages. Firmly I rolled the
window down to let the clean salt air blow in from the sea and clear my mind.

For a long time neither of us said anything. Nan sat in her corner, hunched
down and somber; I tended strictly to my driving. Then, in a voice so low that
I could hardly hear it, she said, "Remember that morning when I came into
your house to see Eleanor, and went into your room instead and yanked the covers off your bed?"

"Yes, I remember, Nan," I said. "And I haven't forgotten either how I jumped
out of bed and caught a startled little girl and imposed a sort of big-brother
penalty. Do you remember that?"

"What do you mean, startled?" she asked. "That was the way I had planned
it would be."

She had whittled me down to size, and I answered somewhat crossly. "Okay.

Maybe I wasn't as big brotherly as I pretended, either, but that has nothing to do with the case."

Nan hunched further down into her corner, not moving an inch my way. "But you're being big brotherly tonight," she whispered, and there was a note of discouragement and almost desperation in her voice. "You act as if I needed protection and maybe a spanking. How old do you suppose Juliet was when Romeo started stepping out with her?"

"In the play I saw in New York Juliet looked about sixty and so did Romeo," I said. I knew that I was being nasty, but it seemed about the only protection I had. For the first time in my life I found myself wishing that I lived in the Kentucky mountains and was mentally deficient and irresponsible. In five years, maybe things could be different, but Nan was going away—to another country— and I was going on fishing at home. And absence, while it may or may not make the heart grow fonder, also brings about changes in circumstances and associates. Nan had to have her chance to grow up and make a clear decision in a matter which could be the most important thing in her life.

We drove back by way of Stonington, and I looked into the shadows of the dock, where the solid, fine graceful outlines of my *Eleanor* gave me a certain comfort. Going down Water Street, our headlights picked up Mark Riley and six of his sisters and nieces walking home from a community dance which I had passed up. I waved at them and they waved back.

"Why don't you marry one of the Riley girls?" Nan said suddenly. "Several of them are older than I am, and—" here she skillfully imitated my voice as she quoted me—"they're the prettiest girls in Stonington."

I answered her sternly. "To cover the matter in a few words, two of those Riley girls we just saw are married, two hate fishermen on general principles, and two are younger than you are. And I don't go around proposing marriage—or any imitation of it—to kids. If it will give you any satisfaction, I'll tell you that there's one I'd like like hell to propose it to tonight, and would if she was five years older—and maybe will in five years if I have the chance, but I wouldn't do it now for a million dollars."

After that neither of us said anything until we got to New London, where I drove to her house and stopped, saying nothing and not touching her as she opened the door of the car.

"Gosh, you're big-hearted," she said, with a little catch in her voice. "I thought you were going to make me walk up the hill. I've got strong legs. Or haven't you noticed?"

"I've noticed your legs plenty," I answered. "and I'll remember how they look long after you're gone. Now go on home and move to Canada and finish growing up. After a few years, if you still feel like it, write me a letter and maybe we'll go out again—either there or here."

"It's a date," she said, and I could hear a little sob in her voice as she turned and ran to the house.

I drove on the short distance to my own house, and went in wondering—as I have so very very many times in my life—whether I had been right or wrong. And I knew then that the question of getting married was not one that could be settled on general principles, like whether to be a Republican or a democrat.

Ellery Thompson's *Eleanor* at the Stonington waterfront. According to Thompson, she cost $10,000 in 1927 and caught 10,000,000 pounds of fish during her career.

XIII. Death of a Draggerman

Morris fished the *Grace and Lucy* for two years and made money. Then he sold her, bought a "post-built" forty-three-foot dragger which he named the *Florence* after my mother, and took on a friend named Howard ("Shorty") Shaw as mate. They roamed the coast, went wherever it seemed a good idea to go at the time, had fun, and caught fish with the best of them. He discovered virgin dragging grounds, and it was he who first "got a trip" out of the great haddock school that migrated in May 1928 to within five miles of Brenton's Reef Lightship off Newport.

Then he had a bad year, as all fishermen do, and sold the *Florence* to Shorty Shaw. Meanwhile I had built the *Eleanor* and had been fishing her as well as my old *Louise*. After I had a sorry experience with a new skipper on the *Louise*, I turned her over to Morris to run. But Morris soon grew restless fishing the *Louise* in company with my *Eleanor*. I think he longed to be sort of a lone wolf in his fishing adventures off the coast. And that can spell trouble—especially for anyone aboard a small boat.

It was at about this time that Harold ("Brownie") Lawry, who had plans to marry our sister Louise (which soon materialized) offered the kid an attractive proposition. He, Harold Lawry, would build two new draggers if Morris would skipper one of them. While the two new boats were being built, Morris was to take over the *Harold L.*, a thirty-five-foot underpowered, cramped-for-space boat which Lawry had been using. (Harold Lawry himself fished the *Mayflower*, a forty-five footer somewhat like the *Eleanor*.) Morris accepted, and turned back to me the *Louise*, which, for a time, I continued to operate under various roving skippers. Morris and his new mate, Sid Stenhouse, began to fish the *Harold L.*, and I began to worry. I knew the *Harold L.*, a fine craft inshore, but a poor one offshore in winter weather. (It is for boats like this that our Weather Bureau— much more efficient now than it was then—issues its "small craft" warnings.)

And so I was not surprised one late January afternoon when, just as a nor'west snow squall struck us in the *Eleanor*, we spotted a small dragger fighting to survive in the turbulent waters fifteen miles south of Montauk Point, making no headway whatever, and recognized it as the *Harold L.* As fast as we could we went to help her, and was the kid glad to see us as we came alongside! We snaked a line to Morris, and he made it fast. Then we began to tow him in, but even the engine of the *Eleanor* was having a pretty tough time in that gale, through rocky-mountain peaks of waves, with the additional weight of the *Harold L.* While I was wondering whether we'd make it, the *Eleanor* rose high on a wave and I saw another dragger heading toward us. The next wave up I recognized it as Harold Lawry's boat.

He came as close to us as he dared and threw us a line, which we made fast to our forward towing bit. We started off again, a three-boat train of draggers, with three engines roaring at top power, and we made it in in jig time, while the temperature kept falling perceptibly with every mile and all of us were thinking, in effect, what Sid Stenhouse, Morris's mate, later said: "I know one thing after that trip: I'd rather die of sunstroke than frostbite."

That night the thermometer registered five below zero, and I lay awake a long time thinking what a narrow line there had been for the kid that day between life and death.

From then on, I knew, I would worry about whether Morris was taking foolish chances. Again I was seeing a demonstration of the fact that kids sometimes show more sense in their teens than they do a bit later, for now that Morris had a responsibility to Harold Lawry to make the *Harold L.* operate at a good profit, he was pushing himself and the boat hard, and often went out in weather which he would have had sense enough to avoid a few years before.

Eventually his new Lawry dragger, a forty-five-foot boat named the *Harold*, was ready, and Morris went aboard as skipper. Harold Lawry fished his new fifty-five-foot boat, the *Weezy May*, named after my sister Louise.

That summer Morris and Frieda Boeson of Noank were married, took a flat in New London across from our house, and started housekeeping. A year later, Morris Jr., was born. Then Morris began to push himself harder than ever. It seemed as though weather made no difference to him. Fair weather and foul, he took chances that older, more experienced fishermen would never think of taking (and that he would not have taken himself a few years before), working as though the devil were driving him, to give Harold Lawry a fair return and to buy those thousand and one things a man loves to buy for his wife and son.

December 10, 1930, was the kind of winter day one may expect off southern New England—bitter cold, and with a nor-west wind which increased to gale force in the early afternoon. I made a run for it early, heading for the handy and friendly harbor of Edgartown. As we eased into harbor I looked around for the *Harold*, hoping that Morris, who had gone out that morning with Earl Caswell and Jimmie Maxon as crew, had had sense enough to go in, and that he had come to Edgartown, but there was no Connecticut boat in sight. We nosed up to the dock, and there the familiar, well-padded figure of Pattie stepped out of the shadows and took our line, while the gale kept trying to push our bow out to sea again. Soon we were tied up and Pattie came below for a cup of tea and a chat. We drank tea, passed the fishing news back and forth, after a bit cooked and ate an early supper, and sat for an hour absorbing the heat from the Shipmate stove very pleasantly.

We were interrupted by the voice of a woman calling my name from the dock log. I hurried on deck and was told that Ralph Newcomb had phoned me from Newport and that I was to call him right back.

It's a strange thing how subtle intimations of disaster can come to you without words. The woman who had told me of the phone call gave me no indication that she knew what the call was about—indeed, I don't believe that she did know. Yet, as I tried to hurry to the corner drugstore, bent over against the snow-laden wind, I found my heart pounding against my chest, my breath coming in gasps, and my feet dragging as if they were trying to refuse to carry me; and I knew it was fear, and not the force of the gale, that was holding me back.

I got Ralph on the phone at once, and without any foolish mincing of words, yet in as kind and gentle a way as possible, he told me that the *Harold* had come into Newport without her skipper. Somewhere between Point Judith and Newport, Morris had been swept overboard and lost.

The mind and heart find strange ways to seek comfort. I remember that, even as my body sagged against the wall of the telephone booth while I fought to retain consciousness, I thought what a tough job it must have been for Ralph to tell me about it, and felt sorry for *him*. That gave me a measure of strength and let me find my voice and my legs again. I told him that I would be there as quickly as I could, regardless of the gale which was still howling; hung up, and left the booth. Outside it was evening; within myself I was walking through the darkest night I had ever known.

Pattie had left the boat before I returned, so I didn't have to go through the ordeal of telling her about it. As soon as we could ready the *Eleanor* we were outward bound for Newport. As we nosed out of Edgartown Harbor the wind suddenly dropped to nothing, and half an hour later the sea was as calm as a millpond. I thought crazily of the old adage about locking the barn after the horse had been stolen.

I had with me that night Markey and Manuel Cruz, a Portuguese fisherman about thirty-five years old, hard-working, honest, silent most of the time, yet cheerful and friendly, one of the most kind-hearted human beings I have known. Manuel said nothing as I told the boys the news, but his eyes filled with pity and pain, and there was in them the message that I might call on him for anything. Markey suggested watches so that I could get some sleep, but I knew that I would not be able to close my eyes. I felt that I would go crazy unless I had something to occupy my mind and hands, so I took the wheel myself and kept it all night as we plowed steadily on toward a thing which I would have given anything not to have had to face. At intervals Manuel brought me hot coffee from the galley, set it down before me, and silently went away.

The *Eleanor* rounded Brenton's Reef Lightship and headed in toward Newport just as the eastern sky became a beautiful rosy pink, promising a fine day. I turned the wheel over to Markey and stood in the bow, peering toward the harbor, where already I could see the shape of the skipperless dragger *Harold*, and, tied up alongside her, Harold Lawry's *Weezy May*. I had a terrible impulse to run, though there was no place to run too—"no hidin'place" anywhere in the world in which I could escape the first major blow which had struck the Thompson family in thirty-five years. Ralph had told me that Mom and Pop hadn't been notified yet, and I suddenly thought of the job I had to do when I went home without Morris.

There were half a dozen Connecticut draggers in the Newport Harbor, most of them having run in at the first signs of the approaching gale, and as we tied up and I stepped onto the dock I was surrounded by a group of solemn-faced draggermen and their crews. There wasn't a lot of futile hand shaking. I don't believe that one of those men said to me, "I'm sorry," or "It's terrible," but every silent, weather-hardened face told me that this was their loss, too, and that if there was anything any one of them or all of them could do to make it a little easier for me, it would be done the moment it was suggested.

Jimmie Maxon told me straight, and in a few words as possible, what had happened. When the wind hit them, Earl Caswell had suggested that they had better go in, but Morris had just grinned and said, "Hell, we're going to catch fish; I promised myself that I'll get the kid a good snowsuit for Christmas! But we'll finish out the day in West Passage."

A little later, while they were dragging, Morris went aft to inspect a tie-down chain (a device for securing the towrope connected with the net). It broke while he was looking at it; one end struck him on the head just as the bow of the *Harold* tilted upward to ride a bad sea; and Morris went overboard.

There are times when a man can go overboard in a calm sea on a hot day in August, when he hasn't much on anyway, and all he gets is a pleasant wetting and cooling off. Yet when a fisherman goes over by mistake or accident, it seems as though it is always a bitter winter weather when the sea water is so cold that it strikes paralysis into the body, and a man is bundled up in as many clothes as he can get on. Of course the truth is that those are the times you hear about. No one mentions the pleasant dunkings.

Morris never had a chance, yet Earl Caswell tried to give him one. Half stripping, Earl went overboard into the icy water after his skipper. It was a good try but doomed to failure. A few minutes later Jimmie cut clear of their dragging net and pulled Earl aboard more nearly dead than alive. Morris had vanished. As the *Harold* started toward port Jimmie tried to pick up bearings by which he could find the spot again, but a snow squall obscured all signs of land, so he couldn't even tell exactly where it had happened.

The group of draggermen skippers and their crews, Ralph Newcomb and I, discussed in short sentences what we had better do. To a casual ear our conversation would have sounded as matter-of-fact as if we had been planning a fishing trip. Soon a fleet of half a dozen draggers was leaving the Newport dock to drag for Morris's body. Jimmie Maxon in the *Harold*, with a couple of emergency crew members (Earl Caswell was in the Newport Hospital in a serious condition from shock and exposure), took the lead to show us, as nearly as he could guess, where the spot was. Harold Lawry in the *Weezy May* and I in the *Eleanor* were close behind him. I thought of another time when the *Weezy May*, the *Eleanor*, and Morris's boat had traveled in close formation. Only that time it had been the *Harold L.*, Morris had been on board, and the outcome had been a happy one. I wished that I could turn the clock back.

For hours we dragged where we thought it had happened, at a spot where every man there knew the bottom was so rocky that it was practically throwing a net away to drop it, but every dragger's net went down without hesitation, and every net in that fleet was riddled on the bottom. (It seems grotesque here to mention that the least expensive net in the lot probably cost a hundred and fifty dollars or more, and to say that that's real money to the average Draggerman, yet it is only telling you in another way what I saw in the faces of those men when they met me at the Newport dock." We riddled every one of the five nets on the *Eleanor* before we quit.

One by one, as their nets were rendered useless, the draggers dropped out and headed back for port, leaving only the *Weezy May* and the *Eleanor*. We stuck it out until late afternoon and even launched our dories and combed the rocky western shoreline of nearby Coanicut Island, but all that remained of the physical Morris—that husky body, those laughing eyes, that unruly mop of hair, the almost arrogant set of the shoulders, and his way of pursing his mouth and sticking a thumb through a buttonhole of his jacket—seemed to have vanished completely.

Finally we gave up and headed back for Newport; we reached there after darkness had fallen. I went at once to the hospital and talked to Earl Caswell. He told me briefly and simply about his futile struggle in the paralyzing water to fight his way back to the boat with Morris's unconscious body, and how finally everything had seemed to go blank, and, when he came to, Jimmie was pulling him aboard and Morris was gone. One consolation I got out of that was learning that the kid was unconscious. He didn't know that he was drowning.

There wasn't anything I could say, except to thank Earl from the bottom of my heart. But there is something that I can say now, without depreciating Earl's magnificent try, which almost cost him his own life. Any man or woman who goes overboard in an attempt to rescue another, without taking along with him the end of a line (if it's handy, and it should be on any boat worth a damn), is asking for trouble of the kind that's deadly.

After I had left the hospital I phoned Pop, and Mom and Frieda (who, with Morris and Morris Jr., had moved across the street just a few months before, to live with us), while Harold phoned Louise (who was now Mrs. Lawry). I shan't try to repeat our conversations. The telling would inevitably be filled with clichés, anyway. Such telephone conversations have been going on in sea-coast towns all over the world ever since there have been telephones, and before that the same conversations for centuries—ever since there have been boats. Only they used to have to be face-to-face. I don't know which way is tougher.

I went to the *Eleanor* to get Markey and Manuel for the sad drive home, and to gather up the five nets which we had ripped to pieces that day, so that Pop could repair them. But I found Manuel squatted on the deck already working on one of them, another lying beside him. "You leave these two here," he said. "I stay and fix."

My voice wasn't very steady, and I'm not sure that I even tried to thank him. "Manuel," I said, "we may have a long job of dragging ahead of us. Maybe it will take all winter. There won't be much in it for anyone who helps me. I wouldn't be sore if you wanted to get a better job."

He didn't even look up, nor did his hand pause in its rhythmic back-and-forth motion as he went on mending the net. "We keep looking till we find the boy," he said.

Three hours later I drove up Crystal Avenue in New London exactly as a church bell tolled nine, and went in to where a group of silent, stricken faces were waiting to listen to the little which I had to tell. We talked for an hour and then Ma headed for the kitchen, to come back soon with coffee and a snack. I haven't the slightest idea now what the food was. I do know that none of us ate much of it, but her simple practical act gave us all new courage.

I remember one phrase which Ma often used when speaking of a child she had met at a friend's or neighbor's. She used it now as she spoke of Morris. "He was such a nice little fellow," she said softly.

For a long time Pop had been silent, seemingly studying about something. Finally he said, "If only I had a couple of boxes of codfish hooks I believe I could rig up something that would bring the boy up—or at least his net, so we would know where we were."

It was late at night now, but without question I went to the phone and called Ellery Edwards of the firm of Darrow and Comstock, ship chandlers. I told him briefly what had happened, explaining my late call, and what Pop needed. Like the men on the draggers, he made no useless remarks about how sorry he was, but told me to pick him up at his house as soon as possible, and he would see that we had all the cod hooks we wanted. An hour late Pop and I were leaving Darrow and Comstock's, which Ellery Edwards had opened around midnight, with a thousand three-inch codfish hooks and a lot of rope and line. When I asked Edwards how much I owed him for the gear, he waved me away and wouldn't let me pay him anything. To tell the truth, I wasn't surprised. That kind of thing wasn't without precedent in fishing circles along the New England coast.

When we got back home, Ma and Frieda and I went to bed, hoping that we could get a little sleep against what we had to face the next day, but Pop went to the garage with the stuff we had got from Darrow and Comstock's and turned on the light. I actually did go to sleep (it had been more than forty hours—the last thirty of them hellish—since I had closed my eyes) but I woke four or five times between then and daylight, and each time I saw that the light was still burning in the garage.

At daybreak we were up. Just as we were ready to sit down to a scanty breakfast, Pop finished his job and stowed his gear, coiled, in his typically workmanlike manner, in three trawl tubs in the back yard. In each section were two hundred feet of three-quarter-inch line—six hundred feet in all—and along the entire working length three-inch codfish hooks were tied at intervals of eight inches. In his bitterest hour he had fallen back on what he knew best—fishing technique. His plan was simple and promised to be effective. What he had fashioned looked like an extra-heavy-duty codfish trawl. With this formidable tool we would sweep the bottom of that area of Narragansett Bay systematically in six-hundred-foot sweeps, and anything loose within our path on the bottom should be hooked.

We loaded the gear in my car, picked up Harold Lawry and Mark, and started for Newport at a rate which had little to do with Connecticut or Rhode Island speed laws. When we got to the dock the first thing I saw was Manuel, squatted exactly where I had left him the night before, his skillful right hand rhythmically weaving back and forth, repairing the second net. The first lay in perfect condition beside him. Like Pop, he had worked all night.

At sea, in the *Weezy May* and the *Eleanor*, we headed for the locality which I had covered with the dragger fleet the day before, then let down the trawl, one end fast to the *Weezy May* and the other to my boat, and started to drag slowly. On the first try we pulled up Morris's net and knew that we had located the right spot. Then we took in the trawl and let down our nets as a somewhat gentler method of taking what we hoped would be our next catch.

After a time Harold took up. In the cod end of his net was the body of Morris Thompson, twenty-five years old and a darned good fisherman.

Perhaps it's well to get all of this kind of thing which belongs in the story over with in one chapter.

In 1935 my sister Louise, Harold Lawry's wife, and the mother of my nephew Byron and my niece Louise, died as the result of an operation. In order to help out at the Lawry home, Ma and Eleanor went to live with Harold and the children, while Pa and I lived together aboard the *Eleanor*. I well remember that winter of 1935-36 as one of the coldest and toughest I ever lived through. Twice the temperature went to seventeen below zero—and that's not a good temperature aboard a small dragger.

Pop, a true salt-water man to his last day, had been helping me aboard a lot since Morris's death, for my own health had taken something of a nosedive. He was never the same after Louise's death. That winter he slipped on deck and threw his shoulder out of joint. It never recovered completely, but Pop wouldn't quit.

Finally spring came and with it the joyful news that Ma was going to reopen the house. On the day set for the great event we entered the New London harbor and tied up. (It turned out to be the last time my boat was ever to be in New London.) We were getting ready to go ashore, when Pop slipped again, this time on the oily engine room floor. Bruno Giri, Fred's younger brother, was on the dock and came to help me. We hauled Pop up, but he couldn't stand. He couldn't talk. He just looked at me and his eyes seemed to say, "this is the end, boy. But it's all right."

"Okay, Pop," I said, and I didn't care that he and Bruno must see that I was crying. "I'll get you some real help."

I got a doctor and an ambulance and then to try not to think and be afraid, I shaved him as he lay in the bunk where we had put him. They took him to the hospital, but before they could begin to undress him, he was dead.

Morris, Louis, and Pop. The Thompson family was pretty well thinned out now.

XIV. Appointment at Dean's Mill

During the 1930's the depression caught up with us. Sales fell off day by day; the more fish we caught, the lower the price fell. The climax came during a fort-night when we had dragged up forty thousand pounds of flounders off Nantucket, shipped them to Fulton Fish Market, and received a check which lacked one hundred and fifty dollars of paying for our gas, oil, barrels, and food, not to mention ropes, nets, and engine repairs.

I had seen plenty of ups and downs in fishing—times when we fishermen had lived like millionaires, and times when, after selling a twenty-thousand-pound trip of fish and paying expenses we had had about enough left to buy a pound of hamburger and a package of cigarettes. But this business of having to pay for the fun of fishing was something else.

Captain George Berg, a high-line fisherman at our dock, had an idea. He said, "It's a damn good time to get some fun out of life. You're going to be dead a long time. I'm going to tie my boat up, go home, get in bed, and stay there for a week."

I thought there was sense in what he said, but wanted something more active than just lying in bed. I thought of the seascape Nan and I had painted—I hadn't heard a word from her since she had gone to Canada—and wondered if I couldn't do better if I tried again. I had always liked nice oil paintings, and for along time had wanted to make a serious attempt to paint some myself. Perhaps, as I had followed my father's example in playing a horn, I was now following my mother's, for, as a girl, she had done quite a little oil painting—pretty pastoral landscapes and still lifes, and things like that.

Now she gave me some good advice. "You get yourself a good box of paint and some good brushes. I know you, and I know you won't be satisfied with anything but the best."

So I went to Brater's Art Store in New London and put it up to the girl who waited on me, telling her to give me the works.

"Something for a beginner?" she asked.

"No," I said firmly. "Make believe I'm Rembrandt."

So she sold me the best paints in the store, and for six months I was making mud pies with expensive imported oil colors which many a starving young genius with ten times my ability would have given his eye teeth for. Mom suggested that I start out with something simple—like some fruit in a dish on the table, or a brace of partridges hanging by their heels—but I wanted action, so I painted a ship at sea in a storm. At least that's what I intended it to be. I don't think anyone would have recognized even the storm.

After I had done everything to it that I could, looked at it judiciously a long time, and decided that there must be something I didn't know about painting, I went to New York and bought a set of English art books which cost forty-two dollars and didn't help me a bit.

Then I went at it the hard way, painting night and day, always pictures of the sea and of ships. I went back to the spot where Nan and I had collaborated in a painting of sea and sky, and did about the same thing as we had done that day, trying to recapture the moment when we had sat there together, trying to remember just how she had painted the sky, and to make the sea as much like the way it was that day as I could. I was tempted to put a ship, hull-down, on the horizon, but then I hesitated. "No, that's Nan's," I told myself, and left it empty. When I got through I wasn't sure whether it was better or worse than the one we had painted, but I put it away and saved it.

But most of my paintings were boats—boats at sea, and usually in a storm, the sort of thing that tests the mettle of a good ship and shows her up for what she is. I love boats and the water, and I wanted to try to do justice to the lines and shape of a fishing vessel. I had been annoyed for too long by the way painters who know nothing about them had crucified them. Boats are real people and should be treated so—realistically. Try this modern, impressionistic painting on a horse and see if you get anything that has the life and spirit of Man-O-War. That's the way it is with boats, too. Impressionism and primitive stuff don't go, unless you want to paint in a bedroom, and I'm no boudoir painter.

So I went on—the *Eleanor*, over and over, and the boats of my friends. And after a while they didn't look like mud pies any more. And then one day I sold a picture and stood looking at the fifty-dollar check I had got for it, not quite believing my eyes, and saying to myself, "Am I really a painter?"

My customer was a famous skipper, known and loved the length of the New England coast, whom I had met in 1920 or 1921 when I made my first trip to Point Judith in the *Grace and Lucy*. Later I was to see the inner harbor there crowded by fifty draggers at a time, but then there was only one, skippered by the gentle and religious Captain Albert Jones, who was often affectionately called "the Parson," and "Jonesy." In his tiny house he had a steering wheel, a reverse lever, which he said he never used ("Never get into reverse," he used to say. "Keep plugging ahead"), a foghorn, a compass, and a Bible. He could, and often did, quote from practically every chapter and verse in the Bible in a way that made his quotation pertinent to almost any situation. He kept the book handy on the starboard side of the compass. He gave Walter Schroeder, who fished with him at that time, the port side for his "literature"—which consisted of what used to be called "art models." They'd be called "pin-up-girls" now, but the change in name hasn't really changed anything about them.

Genuinely, honestly devoted to his religion, he wasn't what anyone would call a superstitious man. But he had one unfailing habit which bordered on superstition. Whenever luck was bad, when fishing or prices fell off, or when he was worried or disturbed about something, he acted like a women who buys a new hat when she's depressed. It wasn't a new hat for Jonesy—though it might have been, at that, sometimes. You never could tell what he would buy. Maybe it would be a hat or a pair of corsets or a fancy apron for his wife, maybe a plaster cast of an ancient naked Greek—decent because it was "classical"—for the mantelpiece, or a fancy footstool, or a pretty little clock, or a picture of a girl about to pop a cherry into her mouth.

And that was where I came in. Because Jonesy was worried about the depression and the almost impossible state of the fishing business, just as everyone else was, I had no difficulty at all convincing him that a genuine oil painting was worth more than the fifty bucks I asked him for one. To him it was the gadget which would cheer him up that week and perhaps change his luck. (Some time later my conscience began to act up, so I gave him another large oil painting, refusing to take anything for it. Then that bothered his conscience, so he gave me an order for a third—to paint his boat, the *Nellie*, which I did, charging him forty-five dollars for the picture complete with frame and hanging wire.)

Jonesy's liking for my pictures was real encouraging, and I kept plugging right ahead. In two years I had quite a lot of pictures of fishing boats and ocean-going ships lying around the house. Then Mr. Willard Keigwin, a singer from Mystic, saw them, liked them, and took me and my pictures to the studio of Mr. Charles Davis, the well-known landscape artist and at that time president of the Mystic Art Association. My first thrill came when I saw Mr. Davis looking at them seriously and with undisguised interest. He told me that he liked them and said, "Keep right on painting what you like. Paint to please yourself."

Well, that visit with Mr. Davis did wonders for me. I began painting like mad, large canvases of Gloucester fishing schooners driving for harbor, square riggers under full sail, Stonington draggers coming in through the most terrible storms. To landlubbers it might look as though I painted the water too rough; but if you want to check on it take a trip on a small dragger fishing off Block Island or Nantucket during winter months.

Soon I found that I was stockpiling pictures—for what, I had no idea. I had to do something about it. I sold some for real money, others for peanuts, and a few were so bad that I had to pay friends to take them away. Still the pile grew, and I had to make room in the house. So I began giving them away to relatives— big ones to aunts and uncles, smaller ones to cousins, and unfinished sketches I had tired of to second and third cousins. By the time I began to realize how large our family tree was, my pile was pretty low again and I stopped being so generous.

Finally, after I had painted several hundred ships, mostly draggers, it got to be sort of monotonous, and I thought I'd better do something about it. I went to Arthur Cammasar in Brater's Art Store and asked his advice.

"Young fellow," he said—though I wasn't any more—"You've been working too much with blues and greens, and that's depressing. Try something with red and other warm colors in it. Red symbolizes blood, and blood means life. What you need to do, my boy, is to try a nude."

We both laughed as though it were a good joke, but he had given me a swell idea. I went out looking for blood. And that word reminded me of the night when ninety-eight Englishmen from Hartford had slaughtered a thousand Pequot Indians on Pequot Hill where I was born. There was plenty of blood around that night, and I decided I could use some of it for my inspiration. I went to the library and got some books and read about it, and then went and saw my old friend Lloyd Gray and got him to tell me all he knew about costumes and shapes and such—not that there was going to be anything much in the way of costume in the picture I had in mind.

During my reading I had been fascinated by the account of the Pequot massacre which I found in James Thatcher's *History of Plymouth*. My imagination was stirred by the description of the maidens and squaws who were spared, and some of whom were sent back to Massachusetts and Hartford.

There was one who particularly took my fancy; she was mentioned in a letter to the Governor of Massachusetts:

"By this pinnace you shall receive forty-eight or fifty women and children, unless there stay any here to be helpful, etc. There is one I formerly mentioned, that is the fairest and largest I saw amongst them, to whom I have given a coat to clothe her. It is my desire to have her for a servant if it may stand with your good liking, else not."

"The fairest and largest I saw amongst them" was the one whom I had picked out to paint—that is, after I had removed the coat the captain had given her, and made sure that there were no beaver skins under it. I put her sitting sort of side-saddle on a large rock next to a lake, mourning for her lost home, her feet dangling just beneath the surface of the cool water, trying to conceal the fact that they would have needed number twelve shoes to cover them.

Even though it did look to me as though there were something a little wrong with the feet, the picture had its points. I thought it wasn't bad for a first try, and took it to Arthur Cammasar, expecting to be praised. He looked at it long and earnestly.

"What's that puckered-up look about her mouth, as if she'd just bitten into a green apple?" he asked.

"She's mourning for her lost home," I told him.

He handed the picture back to me. "Captain," he said (he's just as likely to call you Deacon or Professor or Mr. Whistler, but at least he didn't say "young man" this time), "you'd better stick to painting boats."

That made me mad. It wasn't what I had come there to hear at all. "Not by a long shot," I said. "It was you yourself told me to try a nude."

"But I didn't really mean it. It was just sort of a figure of speech."

"That's not the kind of figure I'm interested in," I said. "I did really mean it, and I still do. This one was from imagination, but next time it's got to be from a live model. If you were a real friend you'd tell me where I could rent one."

He held up his hand and set his mouth firmly. "Not me, brother. I've got hard-to-get paints, brushes, and imported canvases for some of you fellows; I've acted as financial advisor and Laura Jean Libby, but I don't deal in dynamite."

I finally gave up and went out, deciding I'd have to find my own model. I spoke to a couple of other fellows who painted much as I did, suggesting that we combine on the model business, and they agreed. A few days later one of them came to me saying that contact had been established with a perfect thirty-six, willing to model for three tyros such as we were. The arrangements had all been made. She was to meet us at sunup on a specified day in an old barn, where there was plenty of privacy and lots of floor space form which one could view anything from every angle.

It was an ideal choice for a location. Dean's Mill, halfway between Stonington and Mystic, is where the water supply for the town of Stonington is located. It is completely hemmed in by trees that set it off from the rest of the world and make it as a little world itself. Narrow macadam roads built over old Indian trails lead out from the mill in several directions. Down these roads are private estates, good farms, bad farms, and the ruins of several large icehouses. The well-shaded roads are cool in summer, frigid in winter; and in fall, when leaves on the trees are changing colors from day to day, the area is refreshingly beautiful. Famous artists have painted it, and that realization gave the whole thing a professional touch for us. At night the roads around the mill are darker than the hinges of hell—a proper setting for some awful crime. All things considered, it seemed the perfect spot for us.

D-day finally arrived and with my battered paintbox and easel I set out for the spot marked by X in my mind. I found myself fidgeting a little, so turned on the car radio. A pleasant voice came over, extolling the goodness and beauty of some sort of women's undergarment; but that was only scratching the surface, so far as I was concerned that day, so I turned the thing off and drove on in silence.

The road ahead was now spotty with lights and shadows from a red sun hull-down on the eastern horizon. ("Red sky at morning, sailors take warning.") I began to worry. Sure, I had suggested the whole thing, because I really did want to learn how to paint the human figure. And yet, this business of having someone sit around in her skin while you peered and tried to capture her rambling exterior on paper, was foreign to my way of life. It would be all right for those educated along these lines, such as members of an art class, or someone who spent most of the summer lying on the sands at Provincetown or Ocean Beach. But for one brought up in the calm Connecticut woods, not far from the Ann Boradel Dennison Historical Society homestead, and the Pequot Sepos Wild Life Sanctuary (where the privacy of even birds was respected), it seemed to be reaching out a little too far for art. I could sort of see the ghost of a Dennison ancestor hovering over the radio cap of my car frowning at me. Nevertheless I kept on. Art was art, air-conditioned models hard to find, and anyway this was something I had let myself into with my eyes open.

I was the last one to arrive. As I drove in I found three cars parked by the tumbledown barn. In one of them sat a middle-aged woman—obviously the model's mother, or chaperon, or governess, or something. She beckoned to me as I got out of the car, and I walked over and introduced myself, while she looked me over with hard and accusing eyes.

"You don't look like an artist," she said. "Are you?"

"Well, madam," I answered, and my voice was a little like that of a small boy trying to intimate that it was his brother Johnny and not himself who had taken the cookies, "that's a hard question to answer without first defining terms. Some people have called me one, and some have called me other names. That's about as far as I'd go."

That probably made her think I was a harmless lunatic, and she said no more, so I walked over to the open side of the barn, feeling her eyes boring into my back all the way, and set up my easel beside those of the other two fellows. The model, a nice-looking kid, tall, thin, blonde, and with good eyes and a sweet face, was seated on a box, but she got to her feet as I came in, and we were introduced. Her name was Mollie, and it was obviously not the first time, but also not the hundredth, that she had done this sort of thing. She was somewhere in between the strict amateur and the professional. She took off her dress, and then went to work on the sort of things the woman had been talking about over the radio a half hour before.

"Won't you be cold?" I asked.

"With three men around I shouldn't be," she snapped. "And don't think I mean that the way it sounds. It was just a crack to make conversation. Auntie's got a double-barreled shotgun under her coat out in the car and will know how to use it if you three amateur Rembrandts begin to get ideas." Then she smiled charmingly, leaving it anybody's guess as to what she really did mean.

She went on removing the thingamajigs, while the other two guys began grinning in a way I didn't like, and I found my teeth chattering. I suddenly remembered that day when I suggested that we all show bottoms, and I had backed out. I felt the same way this morning as I had on that. When I looked up again I saw Mollie dressed only in rather nice hair, which hung below her shoulders, and a good coat of tan. It was lovely and it was awful!

Now any old salt—or any young one, for that matter—who has been around the water for any length of time, has met up with rugged and delicate situations, like finding bombs and torpedoes in your fishing gear, like being nearly run down by big vessels, like running into blizzards and icing up in winter—this has caused many a small dragger, and some large ones, to capsize—like finding two girl stowaways wrapped up in the jib. These are merely samples of things you can get used to. I had met them all and coped with them. But this thing was beyond me.

I had to do something quick, and knew it. So I made a split-second decision. Saying that I had left a brush I wanted in the car, I got up, leaving my easel and paintbrush where they were, and in a matter of seconds my car was tearing out to the road, with Auntie's eyes probably darned near puncturing the tires.

Five miles due south, and seven minutes later, I was aboard the *Eleanor* at Stonington, and we were soon outward bound for the Hell Hole, where the tides race and roar, where the deep, rock-studded bottom has wrecked many a net, and where you may drag up anything from an unexploded bomb to a five-hundred pound shark, but where I felt at home and at peace.

About this time I had a letter from Nan. She had finished school and was working, and seemed a little more serious and settled down. Her letter said that she planned to be in New England soon, and ended: "I still have the unfinished picture we painted together at Watch Hill, Ellery, and perhaps, if you want to, we can finish it together. I know now for sure what I'd like to paint on the horizon."

Something came painfully to life within me as I read it. The five years I thought about that night when we had been out together had passed now. Nan was growing up. I knew then that, had it not been for the series of tragic events which had quickly followed her departure, I would long since have written her. Now I answered her letter at once, telling her it was a date, telling her all that had happened since last I had seen her, telling her, too, that I was a much better painter than I had been when we had painted together on the sands at Watch Hill, and that perhaps I could help her finish out that horizon.

But she never answered my letter, nor did she come to New England that year, or the next, or the next. Then came a rumor that she was ill, and another that she had died. But I never believed it. Nan, with that pug nose, those flashing black eyes, and that wealth of vitality which surged through her, could never die.

As it turned out she was not dead. But I was not to see or hear of her again for nearly fifteen years.

Professor
Daniel Merriman

XV. High Wind in New England

Hurricane warnings of a tropical storm which was raging off the New Jersey coast and expected to strike across New England by mid-afternoon—that was the weather news which came to us over the radio on the morning of September 21, 1938. But nobody up our way really believed it. At the last minute it would turn out to sea, or so everyone said. Whoever heard of a real hurricane hitting New England?

For three days there had been an easterly storm with winds of gale force which had kept the entire Connecticut fishing fleet tied up in dock, so I was at my home in New London when I heard the warnings. They didn't worry me too much. For once I was among the optimists. The *Eleanor* was berthed at the old steamboat dock at Stonington, in the best shelter in the harbor. My crew, Phil Higgins and John Rix, dependable men both of them, were on board and would take care of her in any save the most unusual circumstances.

And somehow it was difficult to think of either of these men in the midst of anything but circumstances which were at least mildly amusing. John Rix, six-feet-one tall, and thin as a scarecrow, had come to me nearly ten years before, at the beginning of the depression, fresh out of the hospital after a bout with infection of some sort, his black curly hair topping one of the weakest-looking bodies I have ever seen. Yet a few months later I saw him knock the tar out of a water-front bum, who, fooled by his weak looks, egged him on to a fight. His hobbies were cooking and sporty clothes. While he was aboard we ate well and the *Eleanor* was often the background for what might have been a fashion plate of men's flashy attire. John's only complaint against me was that I didn't fish far enough from shore. Disillusioned with the ways of the world, he was happy only when he was out of sight of land.

It was John who brought aboard Phil Higgins, his bosom companion. They were a team and shared joys, sorrows, resources, and confidences ashore and afloat. In many ways they complemented each other. Where John was quiet, Phil was talkative; while John loved to dress "sharp," Phil prided himself on looking like a bum who had seen better days, wearing tattered and torn clothes which had obviously been excellent once; while John was meticulously neat in his appearance, with Phil it was a matter of principle to shave only every other day. He had a long scar under one ear, relic of an attempt to hop a moving freight car which bumped him aside; but except for that, he said, he was a very handsome fellow.

Phil was good company, intelligent, and a good reader. One of his favorite authors was William Shakespeare, and he used to carry a tattered volume of the plays and sonnets on board ship to enliven dull evenings. He had strange habits about food. He would eat scarcely anything until his weight began to fall off, and then eat too much until he had trouble with his stomach. He used to put vinegar into everything he ate, even oyster stew, saying that he had to curdle the milk before he could digest it.

He had a lot of sense about drinking, unless some heavy drinker sat beside him and, by his very capacity, seemed to challenge Phil's. Three times, after a bout in which Phil tried to drink some stranger under the table, he fell off the *Eleanor* and we had to haul him out deadweight. On one of his falling overboard nights, he took out of his pocket a heavy gold watch which had been in his family two or three generations, and dropped it into the sea, thinking its weight was pulling him down. When we got him out he tumbled into his bunk, wet clothes and all, and slept it off. He never seemed to take any harm from such a procedure. He said it was because he was wet with salt water. Fresh water, he thought, would have given him pneumonia.

He was one of the most cooperative men who ever fished with me, in the way of saving me money when the going was tough—sometimes too cooperative. He used to love to chop wood in odd places and pick up driftwood to save the *Eleanor* coal money. Once, after we had left Point Judith, I noticed an unusually fine supply of wood beside the Shipmate stove.

"Where'd all the wood come from Phil?" I asked.

"Oh just a lot of driftwood I picked up, Cap," he said, grinning.

Just then I noticed at one end of a large piece of post the letters E.T. cut deeply and somewhat roughly into the wood, and recognized them as my own initials which I had carved with a pocket knife years before on one of the piles at the Point Judith dock. Examining this heap of wood more closely, I saw that Phil must have chopped up a sizable portion of the dock while I was visiting ashore.

It was Phil, too, who furnished the funniest sight I ever saw while at sea. It was in dead winter, with the thermometer at ten above zero, and we were at that spot where anything may happen—the Hell Hole. Phil, with his usual neglect as to clothes, had on practically soleless boots, not much better than spats. His pants were full of holes, the sleeves of his jacket were practically disjointed at the elbows, and when, after the first drag, he went below to put on something a little warmer, he came up wearing two old overcoats—one of them from a Spanish-American War uniform—and another old coat wrapped around his head like a turban.

He looked warm enough then, until he stooped over to begin to sort the fish that we pulled up on the second drag. Then his pants betrayed him, showing a large expanse of bare bottom, which grew as the treacherous rip progressed. We had about twenty species of fish scattered over the deck, including an extra large angler fish (also called mouth-almighty, pie eater, and mollykite). These fellows have tremendous mouths, and teeth as strong as nails and sharp as needles, and are as savage as small sharks. As I looked, Phil, calmly squatted at his work with his bare bottom directly over the mollykite, which now opened its mouth hungrily.

I shouted, and Phil stood up just before the savage jaws closed. " What's the matter?" he asked mildly.

I was mad. I didn't want any mayhem aboard my boat. "Either you buy yourself some new, extra strong pants, or get yourself married to a good seamstress," I told him.

"Okay, Cap," he said genially. "I'll buy the pants and keep their pockets away from the searching fingers of any woman. I have trouble enough making both ends meet now. If you don't believe me, take a look." And, turning his back, he stooped over again.

But for all these seeming irresponsibilities he was one of the most responsible mates I have ever had, and I had no fear for the *Eleanor* with him and John aboard—that is, unless something happened with which men could not cope.

But along about eleven on that morning of the hurricane prediction I began to think that maybe today was something different. Mother, who isn't a sailor but has more sense than I've ever had, mentioned the low moan in the wind, which had not been there earlier, and I could see that she was really worried.

Sobered, I decided to get to Stonington as soon as I could. If the *Eleanor* was due for real trouble, I wanted to be as near her as possible. Already trees were blowing down, and there was a general air of impending destruction. I took the next bus to Stonington. All the way I peered out the window, getting only occasional glimpses of the terrain between driving gusts of rain which canceled all visibility. Such ponds as I could see were covered with whitecaps and looked like miniature raging seas. Small trees bent almost to the ground before the gale, and several times I saw a big one crash, its roots pushing through the earth behind it like fractured bones thrusting through flesh. At times the bus crawled, and more than once the driver had to detour, or work his way hazardously around an obstruction in the road. Finally we turned and twisted into Stonington and down narrow Water Street, which is difficult enough for a car to negotiate under ordinary conditions., Now, with automobiles blown over, signs from stores lying helter-skelter in the street, and bits of buildings (at one point we just grazed half a front porch which was lying almost in the middle of the street), I thought the bus would never make it. But it finally did, and I got out near the Coffee Pot lunchroom, bucked the wind that almost took me off my feet, and darted in just after I had had to duck to avoid being hit by a large section of house roof which came sailing over my head to make a crash landing against a car, knocking it onto its side.

All about, other people were running into stores and houses, often only to come out again to seek a shelter which seemed safer to them. They were stooping and dodging to avoid an indescribable assortment of material objects which sailed through the air on the wind and rain; the scene was like a witches' storm in a nightmare. I estimated the gale as about seventy miles an hour—not yet of hurricane proportions, but close to it.

Just before running into the Coffee Pot door I had a fleeting glimpse of the dock and saw that all five draggers which had been tied up there the night before were still there—John Pont's *Pal* at the seaward end, then the *Eleanor*, and, in order shoreward, Walter Schroeder's *Ruth*, George Berg's *Lindy*, and the faithful *Louise*, which had been my second boat and which was now owned by George Grogan, who loved her as a well-married man loves his wife. But all were tossing and tugging and straining as though in agony. Then the rain closed in again, a thick impenetrable sheet of water, and visibility dropped to absolute zero. I tried to turn my back to the window, since I could see nothing anyway, and standing there peering into the crashing rain simply seemed to increase my agony; but I couldn't do it.

A moment after I had taken up my post at the window one of the crew members of the *Louise* came staggering in, his face haggard. "The *Louise* is gone," he said shortly. "She's broken all her lines and is pounding against the other dock. You can't do nothing down there. The water's rising, and I had the devil's time getting up the dock myself."

Now I had a new worry: John and Phil, who were, so far as I knew, still on the *Eleanor*. In a moment, however, they came in, drenched to the skin, the flashy clothes which John had put on that morning completely ruined, and Phil's habitual shabbiness a bedraggled mess. There was nothing humorous about the appearance of either of them now. They couldn't have looked wetter or more tired if they had fought their way through the raging seas with all their clothes on. Indeed, at that moment there was little to choose, as to fury, between the surging waters of the sea and the pounding waters and wind in the air.

I greeted Phil silently, my questions in my eyes.

"She hasn't got a chance, Ellery," he said. "None of those boats are going to stay there much longer. The lines are chafing through. John and I made it just in time. The whole dock's under deep water now. We practically swam in."

As he spoke the noise outside increased perceptibly with a terrible whistling howl and the crashing of tin, glass, and parts of buildings. For a moment it became almost as dark as night outside, and suddenly all the electric lights went out. This was it, without question. The weather men had known what they were talking about when they had used the word "hurricane."

I asked Frank, the restaurant manager, if I might go into his apartment, which adjoined the restaurant and had a better view of the harbor. There, braced in an open doorway on the lee side of the building, where the door had blown off, I waited, trying somehow with the strength of my desire for a glimpse of the *Eleanor* to make the rain, mist, and salt spray lift so that I could see what was happening. And slowly the curtain of darkness did lift enough so that I could see the *Ruth*, the *Lindy*, and the *Eleanor*, surging wildly, but still there. Between the time that Phil and John had left the dock and now, the *Pal* had broken her tether and followed the *Louise* to almost certain destruction. The *Ruth's* lines parted as I watched, and she shot into the darkness so quickly that I could not tell the direction of her flight. Only a moment later I saw the *Lindy* rise on a tremendous wave and shoot away, apparently headed for Bindloss's coal shed.

Now the *Eleanor* was left to fight it out alone. She seemed rebellious and eager to follow the others, but still she hung on. Good boat! And good boys who had tied her so well!

Now and then I could see the ghostly outlines of a dragger from another dock go racing past in the mists, over what should have been land, headed for some unknown resting place in the village. On one—I couldn't tell who she was—I caught a brief glimpse of a man clinging desperately to the rail, and then as the boat swept so close to a house that it scraped its sides, I saw arms reaching from a window and the man grasping forward toward them—and then the rain closed down and I could see no more. (Later I learned that he had been pulled to safety through the window.)

Now a new sound joined the medley made by the voices of the storm. It came from somewhere to the northwest along the railroad tracks—a low moaning whistle repeated over and over, clearly a distress signal of some sort.

It's queer what fantastic thoughts can cross your mind at a time when the world is topsy-turvy. As I looked back at the *Eleanor* I had the strange impression that she heard the whistle too, and was trying to answer the call and give what help she could. She seemed straining with a new and purposeful intensity. Then, with a final tremendous heave, she was away like a racehorse in the direction of the moaning whistle, following in general the uncharted overland course of the *Lindy*, headed apparently for the railroad station at the end of Water Street, as if, born to the sea, she would have this one landward fling.

I had a crazy picture of her trying to thread her way along that narrow street through the automobile traffic which had made me swear on many an ordinary day, and then of course realized that there wasn't any traffic there now. It was all awash, a jumble of wrecked cars, boats, bits of buildings, and floating debris, with the surging, wind-driven waters swirling about it as though it were a part of the sea itself.

As a matter of fact the *Eleanor* had sense enough to stay away from that chaotic and congested man-made channel, and to make her overland voyage on a course which was a little nearer her natural habitat, but I was not to learn what had happened to her until the next day.

Over the Coffee Pot there was a rooming house, and there I spent a sleepless night in a darkened and uncommunicative world, for all electric and telephone lines in the vicinity had been broken by the storm. Where the *Eleanor* was I didn't know, and I was equally without knowledge of what had happened to my home and family in New London.

In the morning, as soon as it was daylight, with the storm abated, John and Phil and I started out on our search, like a trio of relatives hunting through the ruins and morgues of a destroyed city for the body of a loved one. Shattered houses, wrecked boats, bits of docking, outbuildings, and debris of every description lined the coast and were strewn up far up the shore inland. In the harbor, masts from boats which had sunk at the dock could be seen sticking up a few feet out of the water. Two large oyster boats which had sought shelter at Stonington a couple of days before lay on a meadow high up on land, both broken in two, never to float again. Two of the larger boats—the *Mary*, owned by Alfred Robello, and the *Marise*, owned by Harold McLaughlin—had sunk at their berths; John Smith's sturdy *Russell S.* was ashore on the rocks. An eighty-five-foot United States Survey vessel was high and dry. Of fifty-two boats which had been in the water the morning before, only two were now waterborne, the rest had either sunk in the harbor or been blown inland. Most of the latter were scattered in pieces over the terrain, some so shattered as to make identification impossible, save for a disconnected piece here and there.

Half a mile from the dock Phil and John and I found what we were looking for. We learned also where the mournful whistles of distress had come from. The *Eleanor* lay on her side on the tennis court of the Country Club, her trawl net thrown like a mother hen's protective wing over a car of the derailed Pullman train from whose engine the distress whistles had come. It looked as though she had done her best to drag it to high ground, but hadn't quite made it. There was quite a nice little catch of coal on her deck, her knocked off rudder lay near by, and over the rudder post hung jauntily the seat of a three-holer. Also near by lay a gallon of paint with the label off, an unopened quart of Scotch, and the *Pal* and the *Lindy*—the *Pal* completely wrecked and worthless; the *Lindy*, like the *Eleanor*, not so badly damaged that she could not be repaired.

Along the sides of the *Eleanor* were vari-colored streaks of automobile paint, showing that she had had brushes with landborne vessels. With crazy nonchalance a Plymouth Rock rooster perched on the pilothouse, looking at us out of rheumy disdainful eyes. Beside him lay a child's china doll. As I looked at the streaks of automobile paint I wondered how the cars had fared in the ship's encounters with them. Plainly the *Eleanor* had done all right.

The Scotch was quickly put to the use for which Nature had intended it and the bottle was thrown back where we had found it. A moment later a Red Cross worker came along, picked up the empty bottle, sniffed it, and said, "Those fishermen have been drinking again."

"Silly ass! When did they ever stop?" John asked pleasantly, and we turned our attention to the gallon of paint.

It was very heavy. We decided that it must be copper paint, exactly what we needed for the *Eleanor*'s bottom, and there she lay, bottom exposed, in an ideal position for painting. But when we opened the can we found that it was white housepaint. Just then we saw a meat man who was out looking for his garage. In one hand he carried a perfectly good ham, unspoiled by its immersion in sea-brine.

"If you find your garage," I said, "you'll need—"

"Sure," he interrupted, "I'll trade you."

So we gave him the paint and he gave us the ham, and we were a little cheered by the thought of ham and eggs on board if we could ever get the *Eleanor* afloat again. Also, since Phil had already done what was plainly indicated by the presence of the rooster, we knew we could count on at least one chicken dinner. Already things were beginning to look up a little.

A thorough examination showed that the *Eleanor* was still tight, and that with minor repairs she would be seaworthy. Piecing together this bit of evidence and that (that bit of back porch railing was from the Old Riley house, the coal on her deck was quite obviously from Johnny Binloss's coal yard, and so on) and partial reports from eyewitnesses, we traced her valiant course. She had left the harbor and gone ashore directly from the dock, pushing troublesome automobiles out the way; traveled parallel with Water Street through the Riley's back yard, nicking their back porch; detoured through John Bindloss's coal yard, helping herself to some good anthracite in passing; ducked back into the harbor again—as if somewhat frightened by her own temerity—where the coastline curves sharply inward; and then had got her bearings and headed overland again directly to her objective. She had thrown her trawl net for the Pullman car in a last effort, and, after a good half-mile run, exhausted by her madness, had dropped in her tracks.

Leaving the *Eleanor* to her well-deserved rest in the elite section of town, I went back toward the center of Stonington, trying to figure out a way to get home without walking. So far I knew nothing of what had happened to the house and family. Bus travel was completely suspended, and many of the streets of Stonington were blocked. But at the railroad crossing I found a policeman routing traffic through the complicated masses of fallen debris to the one semi-cleared way out of town. I told him where I wanted to go and he thumbed a ride for me in an out-of-state car headed for New London. We crawled around trees and other obstacles, detoured through ditches and fields, waited as part of a string of cars more than a mile long at the bridge over the Thames. It took us four hours to travel the fourteen miles between Stonington and New London, but we finally made it. I got out of the car not far from home, and in five minutes was in sight of the house.

It seemed still, thank God, to be sitting in the spot where I had left it. (I think I had half expected that it had tried to go to sea as the *Eleanor* had gone ashore; everything seemed to be happening in reverse that day.) But it looked a bit like a stage set for Tobacco Road. Part of the roof was gone, the front porch sagged drunkenly, our blue spruce trees were flattened to the ground—and wonder of wonders! There was the *Eleanor* peering jauntily from a window, bucking waves as high as herself and riding them valiantly!

I blinked my eyes and looked again, and saw a similar sight at every one of the large downstairs windows—a clipper ship seemed to be rushing under full sail through the living-room window, a Connecticut dragger was at the window of the dining room, and a large steamboat was where the glass should have been in the door. And then I realized that they were my paintings. They looked mighty nice there, framed by the window casings, and though they had taken a terrific beating from the storm they were still intact, except for a hole here and there.

I rushed in to a joyous and damp-eyed family who had worried all night for fear that I had been lost in the storm. After our greetings had been suitably attended to and eyes had been dried, mother told me how, when the storm had broken all the windows, she had gone to the next-door neighbor's house for shelter, and how Mr. Libby had worked his way to our house and had tacked up the canvases to keep the rain out. At long last my painting had proved its practical value, just as my music had, the night my trumpet saved the boat by warning a Sound steamer to keep clear.

Later I sold several of the paintings—including the ones with holes in them, for which I got a higher price because they showed the effects of having come through the hurricane. I was tempted to punch holes in some of the others, but could never quite bring myself to it.

The next morning I went to downtown New London. It was a repetition of Stonington—and worse. Fire had ruined a large portion of the business district. A 200-foot lighthouse tender steamer was lying across the New Haven tracks near the Custom House. Half a dozen trawlers were telescoped together and sunk at a ruined pier. The sixty-foot dragger *Mandalay*, owned by Captain James Lawrence, was high and dry on the dock in Winthrop's cove. The sixty-two foot *Nellie*, pride of that good man Captain Albert Jones, was lying broken on the tracks in front of the railroad station. Trees and poles were down, broken glass, lumber, splintered wood were lying everywhere in a chaotic mass.

But already workers were at the job of clearing up, salvaging, getting ready to rebuild. An army of emergency workers was working to get the electric current flowing again. There were telephone workers, railroad workers, wreckers; the place was a beehive of grim and purposeful activity.

So it was all along the New England coast. At Stonington I had the pleasure of seeing the fellow who had once been the little boy who ate dinner with his father, my father, and me, on the *Rowland Wilcox*, at the invitation of Captain Rowland Wilcox, take a position of determined leadership and get the grim task of reconstruction started. The day after the hurricane John Bindloss stood on a twelve-by-twelve timber, the only visible remains of the Bindloss Fish Dock, and, surrounded by the ruins of young Henry Palmer's new shipyard, several demolished draggers, and the wrecks of several waterfront houses, he said to his audience of bewildered fishermen: "The hurricane has crippled us, but it hasn't licked us. We shall replace every boat lost after we repair those which can be repaired. In time we've have a bigger and better fleet than we have ever had before, and we'll build better docks and shore buildings, too...Now let's all pull together and get busy. We've got a lot of do and little to do it with, but thank God for that little."

The *Eleanor* was one of the first of the salvageable boats to return to the water. George Berg, Jerry La Blanc, John George, Lem Scheller, Phil Higgins, John Rix, Harold McLaughlin, Hap Hudlay, Ralph Gibbs, and others, all lent a hand and worked as though she were her own. Two tunnels were dug under her keel, and in them were placed fourteen-by-fourteen beams—relics of shattered docks—with which the shore was lined. Then she was jacked up and blocked out clear of her soft bed on the tennis court; oak planks (also driftwood) were laid down to form a track; and, using the masts of wrecked ships for rollers, and blocks and falls, doubled and redoubled, we pulled her inch by inch toward the low-water line. Finally a seventy-five-foot Coast Guard boat came as close to shore as she could, gave us a line, which we attached to the *Eleanor*, and pulled her out. Three weeks after the hurricane, she was afloat again.

Meanwhile everyone else was busy too. The Stonington Boat Works was quickly rebuilt on the site of the plant which had been ruined by the hurricane, and soon a fifty-five-foot dragger, the *Carl J.*, slid into the water. Boat after boat followed, setting a pace which has not been equaled by any other New England yard of that size in the past decade. By the time our boys started overseas, after the attack on Pearl Harbor, the fishing fleet was ready to do its share in helping to feed a hungry Army. Needless to say, the *Eleanor* was right in there with the gang, finding fish for fighters.

I spent practically every cent of the first money we made after relaunching on a turkey dinner for all hands, including those who had helped put her overboard. It was a fishermen's feast, served at our house by Ma, who beamed happily and pushed the food at us as fast as we could eat. There was a twenty-pound turkey, a chicken pie with two chickens in it, scalloped oysters, all the Thanksgiving trimmings (because were we thankful!), a case of beer, whisky, wine, soda pop, and coffee. Some of the men who had been expected couldn't make it, but we ate all of the food anyway, and later two of the fellows had to be taken to a doctor, because of overeating. But they said it was worth it. Practically everyone who sat at the table that night had face and hands covered with sores acquired in dragging the *Eleanor* through lush beds of poison ivy which grew between the tennis court and the shore.

Meanwhile, another of my activities was claiming a lot of my attention. Ever since I had designed the *Eleanor* and she had proved herself at sea in all weathers, fishermen friends had come to me at intervals asking that I design boats for them, and I had complied. And now, with half a hundred draggers crying to be born, I worked overtime at my drawing board, in addition to the regular routine of fishing, and occasional relaxation with my paintbrushes and trumpet. And though there have been many disappointments in my life, and there is much which I have hoped to accomplish and never shall, I feel a sense of satisfaction every time I see one of the many boats I have designed behaving like a valiant lady at sea, or standing serenely at her dock, exhibiting her graceful lines and staunch bulk for all who care to look.

So the 1938 hurricane passed into that part of New England history which everyone would rather forget than remember. And yet there is one thing for which I and many others are grateful to the destruction wrought on that fateful day. It taught the fishermen of the New England coast to work together. Before 1938 there had been far too much of a dog-eat-dog attitude among them. And then, faced with cataclysm, seeing individual strength helpless against a force greater than that of all men together, they found that give-and-take means a pretty good way of life.

XVI. Shipmates and Mummychoggs

During the twenty-two years of my *Eleanor*'s life at sea a wide assortment of various-sized feet attached to a number of different kinds of people have trod on her decks, as guests and shipmates—including a nudist who always stripped as soon as he got to sea (last seen limping out of Stonington dressed only in a loin-cloth, his feet sore from the spines of fish which had pierced him because he refused to wear even sneakers on deck or elsewhere); Professor Dan Merriman of Yale University, a frequent and welcome shipmate for the last six years, the toughest seagoing professor who ever lay belly down in the top windward bunk of a small trawler; and, as guest and aspiring shipmate, a charming seventeen-year-old girl, Edna Butlin of Waterford, who for some time has been begging me to take her on as a part of my crew.

And she'd be a good sailor and fishergirl, too. She is long and lean and strong and good-looking. She can steer and pick fish with the best of them, and can take it on salt water in a storm. And besides she plays an accordion beautifully. And what's a dragger without a valve trombone or a trumpet or an accordion or something like that on board to use in case of emergencies?

But how would Frank Muise and Harry Wood—my present crew—and I ever manage to adapt our speech to a lovely seventeen-year-old girl aboard ship day after day? And where would the three of us sleep on those nights when we were stormbound? There are too many pleasant requests in the world that have to be answered with no. Nevertheless I'm sure the time is not far off when there will be draggers manned entirely by women, fishing alongside of those manned by men. And a good thing, too.

A shipmate it has given me more than usual satisfaction to have is Morris Thompson, Jr., my nephew. Young Morris joined me on the *Eleanor* just at the close of World War II, when Charlie Brayman, now of blessed memory, was my mate.

Charlie came from a hard-working family up around Westerly, Rhode Island. At an age at which many boys are still in school he began roaming the country, working in steel mills, on cattle boats, and in circus outfits. During the twenties he came back home and began working with Alvin Scott, the Watch Hill lobsterman, and finally landed on the *Eleanor* where he stayed till the day of his death. Every restaurant-bar along the coast knew Charlie—and everyone who knew him liked him, even though he was the loudest snorer in the Stonington fleet. Often shoes and other weapons of defense (but never any animus) would be thrown at the *Eleanor* in the middle of the night from two or three boat-lengths away, to wake Charlie and make him turn over and stop snoring, so that the rest of the men in the fleet could get some sleep.

Charlie was a good man to have aboard under any circumstances, and especially to have along with a sixteen-year-old kid like young Morris. He jollied him and was a good older buddy, and told stories the kid could listen to without blushing. And if his favorite reading was a nudist magazine, what of it? After all, he dropped it like a hot potato, and began to spend his reading time with the *Atlantic Fisherman*, as soon as the censors stepped in and blanked out places here and there on the models. There were limits beyond which Charlie wouldn't go, and when a picture was just plain labeled "nasty" by a thing like that, he got disgusted.

Finally, on a Saturday night in 1948 his good cheer, his laughter, his friendliness, and his homely wisdom stopped short. He was with the boys until after midnight that day, drinking about his usual Saturday night ration of beer, which was plenty by ordinary standards but never too much for Charlie, and no one saw him go back aboard the *Eleanor*. In the morning they found his body floating beside the boat he loved. He hadn't drowned. Apparently he had had a heart attack and fallen in. Immediately a number of the boats in the harbor put their flags at half-mast, and I was not completely dry-eyed when Phil Riley told me about it. I had talked and joshed with Charlie only the day before. We had spoken of this book, on which I was at work then, and he had said, "You can write anything you want to about me, because I know you won't lie, and you'll buy me a beer or two." Fellow, I'd buy you a dozen cases of beer right now, if they'd do you any good!"

Morris had inherited all the Thompson venturesomeness, and his father's mechanical ability and love for cars. At the time he was my shipmate he was spending the evenings with his cronies in jalopies. Once or twice during the war when gasoline was hard to get he "borrowed" a little out of the *Eleanor*'s tanks without saying anything about it. I didn't mind the loss of a bit of gas— the ration board and I saw eye to eye on the matter of supply for a fishing boat— but I've always been a fool about fires, and I didn't like the hazard that went with surreptitious siphoning from the tanks. So I rigged up a Yale lock which put an end to it.

Charlie stood in the engine room as I did it, watching with a cynical smile on his face. Finally he said, "What are you getting so hot and bothered about? The kid only did it twice. If I'd'a been in his shoes at his age I'd'a took it every other night and twice on Sundays. I'm going up and get a beer." He ended practically every thoughtful statement that way.

During the year that Charlie died, Morris left me to join the United States Navy. Poor kid! They made a dry-land sailor of him. Since he has donned bell-bottom trousers he hasn't once been on salt water, and he loves it! But he'll be out of the Navy in a couple of years, and will probably take over the *Eleanor*.

I remember one summer day in particular when his happy face was evidence enough that the sea was his natural habitat. We left Stonington harbor at two in the morning, starting unusually early in order to make up for time we had lost during a spell of bad weather. I put the *Eleanor* on a south-southeast course, which would take us to an area between Block Island and Montauk Point. Morris looked pretty sleepy, so I told him to turn in and sleep it off while we were getting out to the grounds. Charlie made a good breakfast and we ate it, talking quietly so as not to wake the sleeping boy.

As the sun rose, red and handsome, we were about eight miles south-southwest of Block Island, a good spot for almost every fish in the Atlantic—especially dab flounders on the bottom and swordfish on the surface. We had passed several schools of mackerel on the way out, and just as Morris came up from his nap we passed another. While we watched them a whip-tail shark came rushing in for his breakfast. Thrashing his long whiplike tail in all directions, he killed enough mackerel to feed a creature twice his size; then, as the rest of the school fled in terror, he turned and began eating his kill. He finally swam away with a full belly, leaving many dead fish floating on the water untouched. It was a cruel sight, but a dramatic one, and the kid's eyes shone as he watched it.

Finally we arrived at the point at which we thought we would find dabs, and set out net. Just then a large whale broke water near by, expelled a small cloud of whitish vapor, sucked in air, and went down again. I changed our direction and headed away from him. I don't like whales; they're too big. Once one of them—an enormous one, well known to fishermen, who estimated his length at eighty feet and called him "Old Tom" without affection—came right up to the side of the *Eleanor*, seemed to raise his head and look me straight in the eye balefully. A week after he was cut in two by a destroyer off Provincetown. For years after that I had a recurrent nightmare in which Old Tom was staring at me, barnacles and kelp covering his evilly scarred head, and in my dream not only his eyes but also his mouth was always open greedily. Fortunately I always woke just before he swallowed me.

There are endless whale stories along the New England coast—some true in every detail, some somewhat embroidered. One of the most recent, which happens to be true, is of two young men in a small boat off Nantucket. A whale came up rapidly just under their boat, capsizing it. One of the boys landed square on the big fellow's back, astraddle, and rode him until he sounded, then swam back to the overturned boat. Both boys were soon picked up quite unharmed.

Our whale on this day fortunately made no contact with the *Eleanor*, and that was our good luck, for he was quite a chunky boy—at least seventy feet long, perhaps out of the same mother (and if she had any sense of loyalty and appreciation, by the same father) as Old Tom himself. But later we had a few breathless moments.

After three drags we had ten barrels of fish iced down below decks, and the weather began to clear. As we were well along on our fourth drag we saw our whale again, doing his deep-breathing exercises and wallowing lazily in the ground swell. And almost at the same moment we saw another monster of the deep—one of those new super-deluxe fishing boats—which passed close enough for us to see that she was trolling for tuna or swordfish, or any other fish twice the length of a man and capable of putting up a good fight.

She was a beautiful thing, no question about that, all blue enamel, polished mahogany, and gleaming chromium. She was about forty feet long, extremely wide aft, and with a good deal of flare forward, designed for putting on quite a show by throwing off spray when going at a good clip in a seaway. There was a lot of fancy superstructure and a glassed-in bridge from which a grinning red-faced helmsman was peering out at us. Twin outrigger poles towered over his head, not in use at the moment. From what I could see, the boat carried about every kind of equipment necessary for weekending, show-boating, impressing the ladies, rum-running, rapidly removing the victim from the scene of the kidnapping, catching every kind of fish in the ocean, or scaring them into making a run for safety. There was a short flat bowsprit and a pulpit at its outer end where a man now stood, harpoon in hand, waiting for action. The boat also carried a small deck harpoon gun that probably shot a wired dart and line, connected to a generator below decks that was used to electrocute the fish when a strike was made.

There were six men visible about the deck, dressed in a mixture of clothing designed for yachting and fishing which resembled a little of this, a little of that, and not much of anything—fine outstanding models for a fashion page in *Esquire*. One man, a heavy-set fellow, sat in the after cockpit holding with both hands a fish pole, the butt end of which was the size of his arm. Attached to the pole was a reel just a little smaller than those used on two-ton auto wreckers, and probably containing a small electric motor. Astern from the tip of the pole trailed a fine line or wire. At the outer end, a quarter of a mile back, there was undoubtedly fastened a cunning lure with a hook in the middle and a feather on top, with which to tempt the most reluctant fish. There was a man by the deck gun, one sitting in a plush-lined seat halfway up the streamlined mast, and, to top all this, a fellow standing well forward with a bow and arrow larger than the one Robin Hood used in Sherwood Forest. That boat was loaded for bear!

We were just starting to take up our net when this Taj Mahal for the deep, this dream boat, this Wall Street fisherman's paradise, this flagship for a Hollywood Navy, circled around and came toward us. Suddenly it put on a bust of speed, and as it swept past us at better than thirty miles an hour the red-faced beef-eater in the pilothouse leaned out and shouted, "Swordfish!" I looked in the direction of their course, and, sure enough, breaking the water at some little distance was the telltale fin.

But just then Morris, who had naturally enough left his job with the fish to come to the rail for a better look at the floating haven for the rich, shouted, "Look! The Whale!" Charlie and I looked, and then we too left the fish sprawled helter-skelter on the deck and came to the rail to watch. Sure enough there was Old Tom's little brother, his back just barely showing above the surface, blowing his whitish vapor which, to an untrained eye, might look like a bit of sea spray, directly between the Pride of Battery Park and the swordfish toward which she was racing. I shouted, but it was of course too late. I thought of my trumpet, but decided that even if I could make them hear it, it would only confuse them. We could only stand and watch and wait, our breaths coming short, while the boat headed at full speed for her destruction.

Oh Lordy, Lord! What a mess we were going to see any minute now! I closed my eyes, visualizing whale blubber, splintered mahogany woodwork, yellow sports jackets, yachting caps, silk pajamas, and all sorts of other things scattered all over Block Island sound. I wondered how the steward, who I didn't doubt was below decks would keep his poise. The prospect made me shiver, and I opened my eyes again barely in time to see the whale sound just a few seconds before the boat passed over him. At that I'll bet the old fellow had a scratch on his back from her keel!

Completely unconscious of what they had so narrowly missed, the crew now went into action against the finning swordfish, and it was something to see and hear. The striker-man threw his harpoon-and it made a tiny little hole in the water—some distance from the fish. Then he got tangled in the warp and almost fell overboard. If only he could have established contact we would have had the fun of seeing a real Nantucket sleigh ride. The bow-and-arrow man then tried to Robin-Hood it, and shot his arrow into the air. It fell to the water, we knew not where, but obviously not where the fish was. Through thick and thin, the man with the pole and auto-wrecker-derrick reel kept fishing. And finally we heard a dull boom. At long last their cannoneer had gone into action.

And then we saw the swordfish lazily swimming away; he finally disappeared beneath the surface.

I've caught fish most of my life and made my living at it; and I have developed a highly impersonal attitude toward the finny creatures which, in over thirty years, have piled up literally by the millions on the decks of my boats. I find myself unstirred by their death agonies, and without any tendency whatever to see matters from their point of view. But I confess that, in this instance, I was on the side of the swordfish and felt like letting out a war-whoop of victory when I saw him give them the laugh. Even Charlie heaved a pleased sigh and said," I'm going to have a beer," and young Morris and I grinned at each other and went back to sorting fish.

Well, I sure enjoyed that day's fishing, but the more so because the kid nephew had enjoyed it so much, and I could again live through the delight I had found in the wide-eyed wonder of the kid brother, who had spawned him.

What a pity young Morris couldn't have fished with his father! Such father-son combinations are not at all unusual on Connecticut draggers. One of the most famous of them is that of Captain Manuel Roderick and his seven sons. There are many stories about them, but the most dramatic occurred on a day in February 1945.

The afternoon was cold, with prospects of a storm, as the Rodericks headed to sea from Bindloss's dock in their fifty-five-foot *Alice and Jennie*, for night dragging. The father, a small Portuguese about sixty years old, sat in the pilothouse aft, steering. Two of his boys were the crew. All night they dragged along the Thirty Fathom Curve off Block Island, and by morning had five thousand pounds of fish iced below deck.

After daylight the barometer fell and the weather began to get worse; there was a fresh wind from the northeast. At ten o'clock Captain Roderick decided to go in. But after dragging all night it is difficult to get bearings and select a course. He chose northwest by north, thinking that would bring him to Southwest Gas Buoy by Block Island, from which they could easily set a course for Stonington.

Soon after they had started in, it began to snow. There isn't anything quite so bad as a blizzard for small boat making toward land without electrical aids to navigation. It was soon apparent to the Rodericks that it was going to be tough sledding. Visibility dropped to only a hundred feet. After running two hours they slowed their engine and listened. They heard nothing. George offered to spell his father at the wheel, but the elder Roderick said, 'No, you keep watch. I steer." The boat was rolling now from the increasing size of the sea. The captain hung grimly to the wheel.

Another half-hour passed. They stopped their engine and listened. Nothing—only the howl of wind through the rigging. Snow covered the windows of the pilothouse. George scraped it away. Making a quick, blind decision, Captain Roderick headed the dragger west-northwest in order to be sure that he would safely clear Block Island. Better to be too far to the westward than not far enough.

Again they slowed the *Alice and Jennie* to a crawl, but all they heard was the exhaust of their Lathrop, the wind through the rigging, and the swish of water as it brushed along the boat's side.

George took a sounding. Depth: eight fathoms. He reported to his father, "We're getting close to southwest Ledge. We must be clear of the Island." They went ahead slow.

Then, for a moment, the storm lifted, and high in the sky not two hundred feet away the steep sandy bluff of Block Island's south shore was plainly visible—the barrier against which scores of ships had pounded to death.

It was impossible to turn, because of the rocks on either side. The engine was reversed, but it was too late. The long ground swell was more powerful than even the husky Lathrop, and the doomed vessel kept inching ahead and finally struck and hung on a sharp rocky ledge, helpless as the waves broke over her. The boys made desperate efforts to get her off, but they soon realized she was done for. Their own safety came next and must be looked to quickly, for the storm was closing in again, and large seas were breaking over them continuously. Their small dory, lashed atop the pilothouse, was useless. It was full of snow, ice, and junk. Besides it wasn't large enough to take all ashore, and the way it looked there could be only one trip. So far the Coast Guard hadn't spotted their plight, and the boys were too occupied with the immediate task of getting their father and themselves ashore to bother with distress signals.

George and his brother scrambled and carried their father out on deck, after cutting the straps that had held him to the high pilothouse chair. Why the straps? Well, Captain Roderick had no legs. They had been removed from his body at the hips, in two recent operations.

Then one of the boys went overboard into the icy sea, in a temperature that was five above zero, while the other gently lowered the old man over the side, and then followed. George swam with his father's arms around his neck and eventually, after fighting the high seas and frigid winds, all three made land— three men, if God ever made any!

A half-hour later they staggered into the village of Old Harbor, the two boys carrying their father, the clothing of all frozen in solid ice to their bodies. Here they were well taken care of, and two days later were none the worse for their experience, save for the loss of the *Alice and Jennie*, which was a total wreck, though the engine and some of the equipment were salvaged.

That was the last trip for Captain Manuel, and I think it broke his heart that the boys wouldn't let him go out again after that. He died in 1948, a patriarch in the Old World manner to the end.

I seem to have wandered far away from the subject of my own shipmates, but thinking of the two Morrises made me think of the Roderick boys and how I have always envied Captain Manuel the pride he must have felt in his two sons after that night.

As to my own shipmates, I can't do justice to all of those who have fished with me during my thirty-five years of floundering around. There was Jimmie the Goose, for instance, who was with Charlie and me that day in 1943 when I first arranged to make the *Eleanor* something of an occasional sea-going laboratory for Yale University scientist; but here isn't a lot to tell about Jimmie except his name and the fact that he was a good fisherman and shipmate. Jimmie had got his name from a three-boat fleet on which he had once worked. The boats were named the *Goose*, the *Duck*, and the *Gander* and there was a Jimmie on each of them, so they became known as Jimmie the Goose, Jimmie the Duck, and Jimmie the Gander.

Jimmie the Goose, as I have said, was with us on the day when I found fate dragging me into the hitherto unsuspected intricacies of oceanography. It as a sunny Friday, which saw most of the Stonington dragger fleet in port. Boats were taking on supplies, and the net menders off the draggers were talking, drinking, and repairing nets which had come off second best after being dragged into "some damned Block Island Sound wreck." Some of the men talked in Portuguese, and a few pretty young women visited with them from time to time. "Grub-runners" from a local grocery house were lugging aboard canned goods, sugar, coffee, beer, and what not. The wartime harbor patrol boat nosed into the wharf for water, and to give its crew some time ashore. Blanche Basette, John Bindloss's secretary, waved from her office window at one of the men. All good sights!

Two small boys, the sons of two Portuguese-American fishermen, darted down the dock. No one paid any attention as one of them, about ten years old, cast a line overboard and began a short-lived attempt at catching fish. The other youngster was about seven years old, and he began fiddling around the piling and fell overboard. With the splash there was much hollering and running and swearing. The kid was pulled out, wet and tearful.

"Get the hell up the dock and don't come back," someone yelled at the boy. The other boy reeled in his fish line calmly and said, "I was hoping he would fall in. Now maybe he won't follow me around for a while. But he can swim better'n me. He'd'a been all right if you hadn't scared him with so much hollering." The boys scrammed up the dock. I knew they would be back in a few years, as fishermen on a dragger.

Just then a stranger walked into this Connecticut wartime fishing-port scene. He approached my boat and introduced himself as Mr. Yngve H. Olsen from the Bingham Oceanographic Laboratory at Yale University. He explained that I had been recommended to the Lab by Captain Bacchiocchi of Noank, as the man who could be of help to them in fishing-ground research near Block Island.

"We would like to arrange to go out with you and do some work from your boat," Mr. Olsen said. "Since we are both interested in demersal fish, we thought—"

The word made me quite unreasonably mad. I didn't know until later that it was merely a short way of naming fish that feed on the bottom, and I was pretty sure that none of the other fellows standing around on the dock knew either. I could see them later, kidding me about hobnobbing with a "bug," which is draggermanese for "fish professor," and I became rude.

"Demersals, eh? Fancy that!" Then I'm afraid I rather growled. "Such as what?"

The man from Yale smiled and handed me a typewritten list. Then he sat down on an upended fish basket. A jagged piece of wire pierced his pants, and when he moved restlessly it pierced him. But he only rubbed himself ruefully at the point of puncture and grinned.

I looked down the list of what were supposed to be the names of fish and read such words as *Poronotus triacanthus, Melanogrammus aeglifinus, Glyptocephalus cynoglossus,* and *Brevoortia tyrannus.* There were bold checkmarks in front of *Raja erinacea* and *Pseudopleuronectes americanus.*

"I've checked those in which we are especially interested just now," Mr. Olsen said, "the—"

"Wait a minute," I said. "I left school to get away from that Caesar Augustus Italiano business, et I don't intend to get mixed up in it again, so help me."

"—the little skate and the winter flounder," Mr. Olsen went on quietly, as though I had not interrupted him. "We'd surely appreciate it if we could make a trial trip with you some day soon."

I stuffed his list of nonsense names into my pocket and did some quick thinking. These fellows lived in New Haven, two hours' drive from Stonington, and probably were used to getting up about eight-thirty in order to get to work at nine-thirty. It should be simple enough to leave them behind. But as a further precaution I let my mind run rapidly over the weather indications for the next day and concluded that it would be perfect for the purpose—good enough to go out in, but with probably a raw nor-east wind and a choppy sea—the kind best calculated to make a landlubber seasick. Even if they did get there for one trip, I was pretty sure that would be enough.

"The *Eleanor* usually starts at six in the morning, or earlier," I said sternly. And then I decided I'd be noble, so no one could say I had been unfair. "But I'm willing to give you an extra half-hour. If you'll be here at six-thirty tomorrow morning—"

"If you don't mind, Captain," Mr. Olsen said, smiling, "we'd rather stick to your usual hour. We find the early morning hours best."

I decided that it was a bluff and I'd call it. "Okay," I answered. "Six o'clock here tomorrow morning. And we shan't wait."

"You won't have to," he assured me, grinning, and gave me a handshake which made my bones ache all the way up to the elbow.

After he had left to go back to New Haven I told Charlie and Jimmie the Goose that we were about to embark on a scientific expedition to find out how, why, where, and when (I pulled the goofy list out of my pocket and gave it a quick look) *Urophycis chuss, Lophius americanus, Brevoortia tyrannus,* and a lot of other *icthyofauna* did a lot of things.

"Who cares?" Charlie said. "But that Brevoort dish reminds me. I was there once. I'm going to get a beer."

The next morning, as the time approached, I stood on the deck of the *Eleanor* with my watch in hand, like a commanding officer in a front-line trench waiting for zero hour. I was feeling disappointed, for I knew that my weather prediction the day before had been bad. This was going to be one of the finest days at sea I had ever known. Precisely at six I put my watch into my pocket and turned to Charlie. "Okay. Let's go," I said.

The dear old fellow looked at me in disgust. "Oh, for crying out loud, Cap," he said. "Give the guys a break, will you? Maybe they had a flat or something."

I didn't even bother to answer him, but went into the engine room, with Charlie close beside me, and tried to start the engine. After all, I'd given them fair warning. But the thing wouldn't start. After a few tentative bursts of sound all activity stopped and I couldn't get a poop out of her. I must have wasted four or five minutes that way, and, just as I noticed that Charlie was standing near the valve which controls the fuel supply, and realized that he had shut it off, I head a car roar up to the dock and stop. We both looked and saw two men—who turned out to be Daniel Merriman, head of the Bingham Oceanographic Laboratory, and Herb Warfel, his assistant—unloading chests and bags of equipment.

As soon as he saw me Mr. Merriman came up and introduced himself with an engaging smile. "Sorry we're late," he said. "We were pinched and wasted half an hour."

"How fast?" I asked.

"Oh, about sixty-five," he answered casually. "It's such a good morning, and I didn't think any cops would be out so early. I think the cop who pinched us was probably going fishing himself and was afraid we'd go to his favorite spot and catch all the fish before he got there. We had to go all the way to the station before we could convince him we were headed for Stonington."

Several hours later we were dragging at the Hell Hole. We made a short drag and took up a nice lot of flounders, three small lobsters, a few toadfish, and a bushel or so of skates.

"There you are, professors," I said. "Help yourselves."

"Thanks, we shall," Dan Merriman said, and he and Herb bent over the pile.

Meanwhile Charlie and Jimmie the Goose had already begun to sort them, and Jimmie was just about to throw a skate overboard when Dan Merriman put a hand on his arm. "If you don't mind," he said. "I'd like to give that fellow something to remember us by."

Then he and Herb Warfel went to work, carefully picked out every skate in the catch (by a fisherman's standards a skate is one of the most worthless critters that ever cluttered up bottom sand), pinned little celluloid identification tags to each one, and then threw it overboard.

After watching a moment I turned to Charlie and said in a low voice which I was sure they could not hear, "Can you feature wasting time putting jewelry on anything so low down, ornery, prickly, and useless as a skate?"

"Well," Charlie whispered back, "One man's slippery elm is another's poison ivy. Some people even like to drink water. Nice people, too."

I hadn't intended to be rude, but Dan Merriman's hearing was too acute. He turned to me with his friendly smile. "Looks silly, doesn't it? But there's really a reason for it."

Then he gave me a slant on what fish professors were up to. From forty-five to fifty per cent of the commercial catch along the New England coast consisted of trash fish, he said, fish that were considered inedible and so, for the most part, were thrown back into the sea. One of the most common of these was the little skate, and the professors had learned, he said, that there was an interesting relationship between this fish and the winter flounder—that when flounders were plentiful skates were scarce, and vice versa.

It was apparent that the guy knew what he was talking about. I had noticed it a hundred times—the more flounders the fewer skates; the more skates the fewer flounders.

"We've also found, by examining the stomach contents of both," he went on, "That one of the principal foods of both is a tiny amphipod." He paused and smiled apologetically. "I'm sorry, but the thing has never been given an English name. It's so small that you can barely see it except through a microscope. It's *Leptocheirus pinguis*." His look apologized again.

"We know that the flounder and the skate are in competition for this little fellow, but we don't yet quite know why that inverse ratio in their numbers works—whether the skate drives the flounder out, or their migration habits differ, or what. So we tag the skates, with the request that the tags be returned to us when they are caught, with information as to the dates and places of capture. Bit by bit, we hope to learn more of their habits.

"Meanwhile we're trying to develop commercial uses for the skate so that you fellows can sell them instead of throwing them back to eat the flounders' food and thus diminish the supply of flounders.

"There are other things that we're trying to do." He pulled out of his pocket a list exactly like that which Mr. Olsen had given me the day before. "Now you take this fellow here—" His finger was pointing at one of those Latin names—*My-oxocephalus octodecimspinosus*—but what Dan Merriman called him was exactly what Charlie or I would have—the sculpin—and he began to talk about his feed-ing habits and what effect they had on commercial fishing.

I looked with new interest at the list now, and saw what I hadn't noticed the day before—the list of common names alongside the ten-dollar words. *Uro-phycis chuss*, I saw, was nothing but a fancy name for the snot-head; *Lophius amer-icanus* was a mouth-almighty, the same that had almost done Phil Higgins in one day on deck; and the *sic semper tyrannis* fellow, *Brevoortia tyrannus*, was the menhaden, which had given such a fine rich healthful odor to the Quiambaug air of my childhood. These fellows knew the right names for fish. And if they wanted to put these fancy words down on paper, it didn't mean necessarily that they were *Uroiphycis chusses* themselves. After all, I had known people who called supper dinner and a handbag a reticule, who were all right underneath it all.

And everything Dan Merriman had just said about the skate and the floun-der made sense. If that was what fishology was like, commercial fishing could use a lot of it.

Before the trip was over Charlie and Jimmie the Goose and I found that Dan Merriman and Herb Warfel were two of the best shipmates who ever trod the deck of the *Eleanor*. They never got in the way—which is mighty important on board a working ship; they knew how to lend a hand skillfully; and, in addition, they taught us a lot about fish that none of us had known before, which was mighty interesting—like the puzzling questions of the love life of whales and turtles, and how some poor fish got to be christened with names that sound like swear words, and things like that. They taught us a lot of things of mighty practical use to fishermen, too—like migration habits of certain species of fish, and such.

How many trips we have made in the years which followed that first one in 1943 I wouldn't attempt to estimate, but I do know that I soon came to look for-ward to the companionship of two of the finest fellows I have known, and the others which they brought with them. I was soon having as much fun as they had, helping them pin little identification disks on fish and turning them loose again, examining the contents of their fine-meshed plankton nets for the minute specimens of sea life which they caught, helping measure the temperature and currents at sea bottom with their delicate instruments, and swapping yarns over a meal in the cabin. And they in their turn seemed just as interested in Jimmie the Goose's pinup of Lana Turner in a too-small sweater, and the American flag; and in the instruction sign which Charlie had stuck up in the cabin as soon as he knew that we were going to have professors aboard for guests. The sign said, "If you have to go, walk, don't run, to loo'ard. Go as far as you can, then go."

Finally curiosity got the best of me. In 1944 I decided to see what their set-up was like at New Haven and went to the Bingham Laboratory at Yale, where I wandered around in a world of fish—canned, stuffed, pickled, and dried. One of the latter looked so tempting that automatically I started to obey an impulse born of an old New England habit of "picking," but just as I stretched out my parted first finger and thumb, Herb Warfel said, "Don't do it. That thing's over a hundred years old."

Just then Dr. Bill Thompson came along and invited me to look at the scale of a flounder under the microscope. "It's amazing how much can be told of the life history of a fish from microscopic examination of a scale," he said. "Not take this fellow here—"

I held up my hand. "Don't tell me," I begged. "Let me see for myself."

I looked through the microscope and couldn't see anything to get excited about, though the thing did make a rather pretty pattern all magnified like that. I tried to look thoughtful and said, "Ah, yes! I can see that on Christmas Day last year at—yes, I think about two forty-seven P.M.—the fellow who owned that scale barely escaped being swallowed by a *Lophius amerianus* in twenty-one fathoms south-southeast of Block Island."

Dr. Bill raised his eyebrows with interest. "Really?" he said. "I'm afraid I hadn't got that far in my own investigations. But I do know that he had a mighty hard time of it winter before last."

"How's that?" I asked, because I thought maybe I had missed something really interesting by trying to act smart.

"Because I remember that it was cold that winter—damned cold!" he said, and I knew that we were even and said no more.

A critical event drew us away from the microscope. Miss Louva Henn, Dan Merriman's secretary, came running into the room, her eyes shining with excitement. "Hurry!" she said, "The Mummychoggs are ready!" And without waiting for me to ask who the Mummychoggs were, or what they were ready for, she dashed on to the next room, spreading the news.

Wherever she went work was dropped instantly as the word spread from mouth to mouth. "The Mummychoggs are ready! The Mummychoggs are ready!" It was just like Paul Revere's ride.

We all hurried downstairs where, in an illuminated glass tank, two tiny fish (who, as I learned later, had a long history of coy reluctance) were engaged in a sort of aquatic dance. Although I had put on a rather dumb act at the microscope even I had a pretty good idea of what this was about. As we clustered around the tank, two or three visitors from the Peabody Museum down the street hurried in and blended their ecstatic "Oh's" and "Ah's" with ours.

The male slowly circled around the female, who was plainly almost bursting with her eggs, yet still seemed a bit coy. Now and then Chogg would swim out in front of Mummy with a coaxing little flip of his tail (I had seen less fetching come-on gestures on the water front), turn over and swim upside down, wriggling his fins, to show what a beautiful belly he had, and do loop-the-loops around her; but after ten minutes of acrobatics that would put most circus out-fits to shame, Mummy still said, "No dice!"

I was getting discouraged and was about to make a classic remark about females in general. After all, the little guy had it coming to him after the swell show he had put on, and now, as he hovered motionless, looking discouraged as the devil, I thought he was all through.

But suddenly he flipped into action again. He had just been thinking things over, that was all, and now he put on a new stunt he had just dreamed up—the sixty-four-dollar trick, the sort of thing they'd have given him a drum roll for in the circus. He swam backwards and sideways at the same time!

That did it. Mummy instantly headed for a darkened corner of the tank, and Chogg followed, flipping his tail at us with all the disdain of a thumbed nose. Then they swam side by side for a moment, Chogg to starboard, Mummy on the port, and everyone in the basement almost pushed his nose through the glass, watching. Suddenly Mummy seemed to lean a little to starboard and Chogg to port, there was a quick ecstatic movement, a flurry of bottom sand, a few ripples on the surface of the water, and God only knows how many souls of little Mummychoggs were pulled out of eternity in that moment, eventually to become animate flesh.

One of the Peabody Museum professors was standing beside me. I heard him sigh deeply, and looked around into his beaming face. "I've been looking forward to this for years!" he said happily.

"I'll bet the fish have too," I answered, and then decided that I'd better go before I wore out my welcome.

And as I ended that first visit to the Bingham Oceanographic Laboratory—I have made many since—I kept thinking how very fortunate I had been all my life in my shipmates—Dad, Lloyd, Morris, Manuel, Charlie, Fred, Henry, Edna—the roll is too long to call it here. And among the best of the gang are sea-going professors.

XVII. Very Rich Man

When does a man sum up the evidence and achieve for himself an evaluation of the meaning of his life and life in general? I don't know. I am reminded of the student in Chinese who asked his instructor how long it would take to learn the language. The professor looked at him a little sadly and said, "I don't know. I've been studying it only thirty-five years." Well, that's the way it is. I've been here only fifty years, and haven't found the answers.

There was a time during 1949 when an interlude of enforced complete idleness made me try to find some; but I didn't come to any real conclusions, the way a man is supposed to in distressing circumstances. Except that I did get one thing decided for myself—at least for the moment.

Captain Dennis Cidale, acknowledged leader among the Portuguese-American fishermen of Stonington, wanted to build another dragger to add to the local fleet, and asked me to design her for him on the general lines of my fifty-foot *Eleanor*, only larger. Since every good fisherman is in a hurry for a new boat, once he has decided to built it, I worked night and day, straining my eyes to the uttermost. When I had just about finished the plans Captain Cidale, John Pont, George Berg, and I drove seven hundred miles in one day—round trip—to the Delaware Bay Shipbuilding Company's plant at Leesburg, New Jersey. Here we learned a few of the facts of life in 1949 which astounded us. Shipbuilding prices were something to make a man's hair stand on end. We drove home, and for a week I struggled to revise the plans, trying to save Captain Cidale a dollar here and five there, without lessening the integrity of the boat. Then we drove down again. Meanwhile fish prices had been going down, and boatbuilding prices rising. Everything I had gained in the revisions I had made had more than been lost by increases in prices, and Captain Cidale threw up his hands in despair and decided to forget the whole thing for the moment.

As a compensatory gesture he financed a sort of fisherman's holiday for us at Cape May, Wildwood, and Atlantic City; and I drove them home lat at night in a pea-soup fog. I was painfully conscious of how tired my eyes felt when we got to New London. The following week I spent the days fishing and the nights writing, and out off the Yellow Banks I ate some bad canned sardines which poisoned me and made me think—and part of the time hope—I was going to die. I didn't, but while I was in bed writhing with an agony in my guts, my right eye suddenly put on the worst of its many shows of iritis.

Dr. Wilson ordered me to the hospital and began pumping me full of penicillin and what not, and for over two weeks I lay there feeling sorry for myself. Thirty-five years of hard work, and what did I have to show for it? Ill health, no wife or children, little money.

I remembered a sign which used always to hang in Ralph Newcomb's office in Newport, which just about summed it up; "I started fishing early in life; worked hard through fair weather and foul, caught a lot of fish, and a lot of colds; and when I retired fifty years later I had $50,000. But if my uncle, who had made his money selling lollypops, hadn't died and left me $49,950, I would have retired on %50."

I thought of Nan as I lay there, and wondered whether I hadn't been a complete damned fool that night when the cradle had been extended to ma on a silver platter, begging to be robbed. Oh, a man can have a fine time pitying himself!

Then one day I tuned in on the radio to a talk being given by a fellow who had just returned from Europe and how described a little of what life was like there for the average human being; and I suddenly knew how lucky I was, and revised all of my regrets and desires. All I asked now was that I get well enough again to get back onto the *Eleanor*—I'd crawl if necessary—so that I could hear the sweet music of the Lathrop engine, the voices of Frank and Harry shooting the breeze, the pleasant chuckle of Dan Merriman on one more Yale trip, the fog signals offshore, and the fish flopping on the deck, and smell the salt air and the boiling coffee on the Shipmate stove.

Finally one day Dr. Wilson came in and told me that I could go home—but with certain strings attached.

"Give the fish a break," he aid. "From their point of view there are too many draggers now. I don't want you to design any more for along time. No painting, either, for a while; and no writing. Quit riding your hobbies, or they'll be riding you over the hill. Don't you touch a paintbrush for two months—and then paint me a picture of a Stonington dragger in the worst storm you can imagine, with only one ray of sunlight breaking through a lot of nasty-looking clouds. Let that one ray light up an American flag flying from the peak halyards at the tip of the gaff. Give me the picture, and my bill will be square. Now get up and go home. Stay in the house until I tell you you can go out with dark glasses, and keep the shades drawn."

Two weeks later, in mid-August, the doctor gave me permission to leave the house and go to Stonington and the *Eleanor* just in time to take part in the Stonington tri-centennial celebration. As I started to drive over the familiar roads I felt as though I were going to a homecoming in Heaven, and that set off a crazy train of thought about what a good idea a historical get-together in Paradise could be. There were a lot of fishermen there, and there must be a lot of history. I pictured Pop and St. Peter comparing net-mending knots, and swapping fishing yarns about the Hell Hole and the Sea of Gennesaret. I wondered if maybe Peter wouldn't have some pretty good ones—even some which he wouldn't tell when the ladies were around.

I had just come to the conclusion that the two would probably get along pretty well together, and that the two thousand years which separated them in history wouldn't really be any barrier at all, when I turned into my favorite short cut, the Dean's Mill road, and passed the old barn where I had behaved like a panic-stricken fool, when I noticed a man standing at the right of the road, his hand raised most gracefully, thumb pointing in the direction in which I was going.

I slowed to a stop beside him and he bowed three times. As one smiles in response to a smile, frowns when frowned at, and shakes hands automatically when a stranger's hand is extended, I too, sitting at the wheel, bowed three times, my chest hitting the horn button each time. The three toots of the horn shattered the morning air. He gave no sign that there was anything unusual about that.

As he got into the car I saw that he was a Chinese gentleman, and ransacked the corners of my mind for any scraps of Oriental culture which I might have accumulated while at sea east of Block Island. Just as I was deciding that the cupboard was bare, he spoke.

"It is not an impropriety I commit in your eyes?" he asked courteously.

"No impropriety," I assured him. "Everything's on the up and up."

He offered to pay me what it would have cost him to go to Stonington on the bus.

"Look," I said, "I've just driven past hell and am on my way to Heaven. What would a men do there with fifty cents?"

He nodded gravely, as though he met men every day driving to Heaven, and asked, "You are a doctor? A lawyer? A writer? An artist?"

I thought of the barn I had just passed, of the stacks of unfinished manuscript lying around my house in disorder—which Dr. Wilson had told me I must not even look at—of the half-finished canvases which I had been ordered not to finish for a time, and of the sum total of earthly desires which I had enumerated to myself fin the hospital. I said firmly, "I'm a Draggerman, I own and fish a fifty-foot boat."

"You own house?" His voice was soft, and his question didn't sound at all impertinent.

I said, "Yes."

"You own this car?"

I nodded.

"You rich man," he said.

"Hell no," I answered. "I'm not rich, I'm not even sure that I'd like to be. The house, the car, the boat, they all produce a lot of bills, too, you know. If I owned a lot of other stuff I'd have a lot more bills."

"You have wife?" His question was filled with overtones in which hope and sadness seemed mixed.

"No wife," I answered shortly and a little crossly.

He signed happily and settled back against the cushion, nodding his head vigorously. "You very rich man—very rich!" For the first time he smiled, and there was a look of quiet triumph on his face as he folded his hands across his stomach and lapsed into silence.

I drove down narrow Water Street between throngs of friends and strangers, many of them dressed in Colonial costume or Indian regalia, complete with war paint, and let my philosophic friend off in front of the Lobster Pot. Again he bowed three times, again I responded, and again my horn sounded forth with three blasts, but this time it seemed like a part of the celebration (as indeed it was, in a way) and no one paid any attention.

As he turned away I saw him shake his head, and heard him mutter, "Only three hundred years of history, and they celebrate!"

I turned off Water Street to the Bindloss Dock and the *Eleanor*. Golly, did she look good to my sore eyes! The harbor was full of boats and so were the dragger slips. Practically every vessel was decorated with flags—American flags, Portuguese flags, pennants, colored streamers, and everything else that could be dragged out of lazarettes and attic closets. I counted twenty star-spangled banners on one Portuguese-American dragger alone. For a really patriotic American, look into the heart of a good man who has learned at first hand what life can be like on the continent of Europe, and has traded it for what he could find here.

Many of the draggers had been freshly painted. The *Eleanor* had not. She looked tired and a little shabby. But her beautiful lines were still there, just as I had drawn them on paper twenty-three years ago (and they were reflected in a number of the more recent draggers which I had designed and which were not in the harbor), and I knew that the spirit of youth was still in her good oak. I wished that I could say the same for myself.

I walked down the dock and was greeted like a long-lost brother by Big Barky, Bill Masante, Walter Schroeder, Marion Pont, several Maderia boys, Oscar Kiley—the Stonington Cemetery gravedigger—and the rest. Then the kidding began. Where had I been keeping myself? Did I have a blonde in New London?

Who did I think I was—a gentleman of leisure? It was about time I got back to work before my crew starved! To a bunch of draggermen, when they are talking where anyone can hear, a man has to be laid out with a lily in his hand to be considered sick. But I knew what they meant, and a warm feeling began to fill me up around the chest and throat and eyes. This was what I'd been thinking about when I had listed my wants in the hospital.

I got on board the *Fleanor*, where Frank and Harry greeted me with broad grins and a few unprintable terms of affection. They had every flag flying to the freshening breeze, including the bedding (and about time, too!). I had a surprise for them. Ma had made me a big Yale pennant, three feet by five, and with some difficulty we found room for it and soon had it aloft. I had made up my mind that the *Mustelis canis Centropristes striatus* mummychogg boys were going to be well represented.

The events of the morning included a sixty-vessel dragger parade down Stonington Harbor, and now Captain Dennis Cidale was blowing a signal for the larger draggers to get ready to line up. It would still be some time before the *Eleanor* could nose out into place, and I left the boat for a moment to go to the car and get a cake Ma had baked for us, and which, in the excitement of bowing to my Chinese friend and getting my first glimpse of the *Eleanor* in a month, I had forgotten.

As I walked up the rotting dock I heard Red Kessler, a young blond Draggerman with an observant eye, give with a low whistle and fervent exclamations: "Oh boy! Oh boy! Oh boy! What a doll!" he said. Then I heard an appreciative murmur spread among the boys who were standing near by and, looking up, saw how justified it was.

There she was, coming straight toward me, dressed in clothes that must have cost the price of a couple of good trawl nets, a few freckles still on the face that was one large smile now, the snapping eyes, the slightly pug nose, the pouting Mae Murray bee-stung mouth, the subtle poise and movement of her body which had always intimated readiness for any sort of adventure, the legs still just as shapely as I remembered them, just a little stouter, and—Oh, my God!— a faint streak of gray in the fine hair!

She stopped, not a foot away from me, while the other boys stared in envy.

"Hello, Ellery," she said.

I managed to say "Nan!" And couldn't say any more for a moment, as I felt her hand in mine. I was choked up with a strange mixture of embarrassment and joy that had an unexpected flavor, like something you've looked forward to for a long time, and which, when you put it into your mouth, you find has gone a little stale and doesn't taste the way you thought it would.

"We've god to have a long, long talk," she bubbled. "It's been a long time— too long."

Her eyes were on mine and had that indescribable look of invitation and questioning in them., I repeated, "Yes, long," to make sure that we both understood she had meant to use the word long.

"But just now I've got to go and meet my husband. May we both come aboard dyour boat after a while?"

"Sure," I answered. "Anybody's welcome."

I watched her go up the dock and saw the eyes of every man there followoing her. She had everything she had had that night when I had last seen her, and somehow it had all been accentuated by twenty years of living, and she had the added attraction which a voluptuous woman always gains through experience. For a moment I felt a painful tug at my vitals.

But then I looked back to the harbor, where the upper dock draggers, twenty-five of them, were getting in line for the parade; and my eyes went to the *Eleanor*, where Frank and Harry were waiving and shouting at me, telling me to hurry. It was almost time for us to shove off. I turned quickly to catch a last glimpse of Nan as she disappeared in the crowd searching for her husband. Then I looked again at the fine curving lines of the *Eleanor*, and in my mind's eye saw the staunch oak beneath them. I knew that I might feel differently the next day, but just then, may God forgive me, the *Eleanor* looked the better of the two to me—though of course Nan was in better shape physically than the *Eleanor* is now.

I saw my Chinese friend edging unobtrusively through the crowd and elbowed my way to him. Quite aware that I was probably committing an impropriety, I slapped him on the back, bringing to his face a mild look of rather pleased astonishment.

"Brother, I just had to tell you how right you were," I said, and a happy smile spread over his face as I beat him to the waist-bending act by half a bend.

Three times we bowed together, almost bumping foreheads. Then I ran down the dock to the *Eleanor*, feeling ten years younger, and jumped aboard just as Harry threw off the bow line.

Following are the final four chapters of Ellery Thompson's *Come Aboard the Draggers: Sea Sketches*, published in 1959.

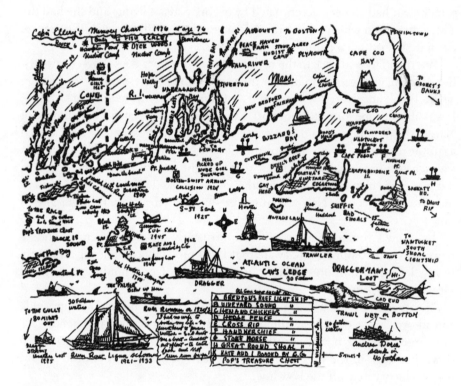

Ellery Thompson's Memory Chart, 1976

COME ABOARD THE DRAGGERS

CHAPTER VI

Rum Row

It all began in the early 1920s when I was fishing my first dragger, the 27 foot *Grace and Lucy*. At the start, when big-city speak-easies and sporting clubs were crying for imported liquors from loaded whisky-schooners, jogging along the 12 mile limit off Long Island, there was little open violence in and around Block Island Sound. But all too soon, southern New England waters became notorious due to the rough actions of liquor smugglers.

Our Rum Row, off the Eastern Seaboard, was the brain child of Captain Bill "The Real" McCoy, a southern gentleman as enterprising as he was versatile; a soft-spoken man noted for loving good able sea boats as well as for mixing business with pleasure, even though the business was shady. Yet Captain McCoy never played rough with guns.

My youthful affairs became involved with Captain McCoy in early summer, 1921, when I ferried him from New London to his rum-laden schooner *Arethusa* off Montauk Point, Long Island. Perhaps this foolhardy trip of mine, in which I came back to port with some broken glass on deck, but not empty handed, might classify me as a rum runner, but I didn't feel like one. At one troublesome point I felt like a damn-fool Yankee.

In 1920 Captain McCoy successfully finished his first Atlantic coast rum running trip up from the Bahamas, using an old schooner for the job. Then he bought the fast-sailing Gloucester fishing schooner *Arethusa*, once the pride of the Gloucester fishing fleet. While sailing his new vessel to southern waters he ran into a terrible storm which proved to him that the seagoing *Arethusa* was a vessel to bring delight to a man's heart, and his body back to harbor in fairly good shape.

In due course of time, Captain McCoy sailed the *Arethusa* north from the Bahamas with a cargo of five thousand cases of assorted whisky and rum. Off Atlantic City he turned his vessel over to his sailing master and went ashore to start drumming up orders for liquor at coastal sporting clubs.

A week later, by appointment, I met him (at a sporting club) in New London. Although when I arrived at the club, Captain McCoy and his seagoing operations were unknown to me, during a confidential chat in a side room I soon found out he was a big business rum runner from the high seas.

"You come highly recommended," said McCoy with a smile, "I need someone like you to put me on board my schooner off Montauk, and by this order in my hand, you can come back to port loaded. How about it?"

How about it, indeed, I said to myself. Twenty-two years old, and faced with a tough question like that.

I glanced at other faces about the table, faces worn by some of New London's most respectable citizens, merchants and bankers, men who had known my father since his steam-boating days, and had known me since I started fishing with Pop.

"It isn't really breaking the law," said a banker, although a lawyer next to him started puffing more rapidly on his cigar, "the whisky is for our own use—what little there'll be."

"That's right, Ellery," broke in a hardware dealer, "and you could save my life. My doctor has been warning me against homemade hootch."

No one laughed and I surely could see no humor in the situation. Through my mind, with no other comparison to go by, was a mental picture of Kentucky and Tennessee moonshiners getting shot up by the "Revenoo boys." One man at this queer round table even tried to tempt me with the private telephone number of his socially inclined secretary, as if a speak-easy girl would influence the course I would take. I had the feeling that I was making a mountain out of the proverbial molehill, but of one thing I was certain, commercially I wanted no financial gain from it. No one told me that rum runners got $10.00 a case for bringing it in.

"What did you say her number is?" I inquired, stalling for time.

"I didn't say."

"I might lose my boat."

"That's absurd," replied one of my best friends, "I haven't steered you wrong yet, have I?"

"You haven't steered my boat," I said flatly.

But the one man to whom I owed my deepest feeling of gratitude, financially and socially, had little to say, as if he knew I was old enough to stand on my own feet and make my own decisions and fight my own battles. Moreover, he well knew some of the things I had thrown over my port-shoulder and some of the things I hadn't.

Again I looked straight at Captain Bill McCoy. Aw, what was the use, sooner or later I would chart a wrong course, so why not see how deep the water was in this offshore one. "Okay, but for medicinal purposes only." Someone laughed. It wasn't me.

Years later in a book written by McCoy, mostly from a jail cell, entitled *The Real McCoy* he mentioned the trip in which a young Connecticut fisherman took him from New London to his loaded schooner off Long Island, at a thirty-fathom spot previously decided upon by his shipmaster and himself.

Our trip offshore with Captain McCoy was one of enlightenment—and of fog. While I was navigating the *Grace and Lucy* as cautiously as possible, McCoy painted a glowing picture about making a rich haul on the high seas without much danger of being caught. He believed that he was within his rights to run rum outside the twelve mile limit; and he spoke glowingly of the future.

"I intend to salt a half million dollars and then quit and sail my boats wherever I wish to go—perhaps into the blue Pacific toward some dreamy island." (Ah, the wishes and dreams of some of us.)

But wishful thinking did not clear away the fog, and for three days we holed up in Fort Pond Bay, near Montauk Point: and it was there, while eating at a fisherman's boarding house, that I talked with a Long Island Draggerman who later was to fish out of Connecticut and be a part of our Stonington gang. His name was Benny Tuthill, and if he knew anything about McCoy's rum ship offshore, he kept his mouth shut about it, the same as I had been doing. Yet, from nervous and smiling glances from several Long Island fishermen, I suspected that McCoy's rum ship was going to do a lot of business in the days to come.

For two days McCoy kept out of sight but as the fog started clearing he was back on board ready for the trip to his vessel. On the way out past Montauk, Captain McCoy showed me some presents he had picked up for his shipmaster—a box of fifty cent cigars and a Colt .38 revolver.

"A good gun can smoke out a lot of trouble," explained McCoy grimly, "but my pet weapon is a fine Havana cigar. There are few laws against firing one."

After sunrise the day turned into a regular "swordfish day," lazy calm with not a cloud in sight. Without question this July day would be hot, perhaps hotter'n hell, I thought a bit glumly. Ah, but why worry, we were heading seaward, not shoreward.

Two hours later we sighted the low-hulled *Arethusa* rising and falling in the heavy ground swell, and with a dozen small boats hovering around her like waiting gulls looking for a handout. The big schooner was laying hove to.

"Ah," said McCoy, "some of the boys got here ahead of us. Those boats look speedy, and speed is what they'll need."

We had priority and went alongside the *Arethusa*, amidships on the port side. A cut-throat crew glared down at us and took our lines. One giant of a man put out a rope-yarn fender, which didn't do much to stop the restless rubbing of the two boats.

It was quickly noticeable that the *Arethusa* had a big load of liquor, for open hatches showed the hold full to over-flowing, hundreds of cases of whisky were piled up on deck; more were heaped on top of the cabin aft. When I spoke about it, one of the more friendly crewmen said that the stuff aft was special—ladies stuff, there so the captain could keep his eye on it.

The *Arethusa's* sailing-master was one of the sloppiest looking fat men I had ever seen, and he lay sprawled under an after sail-awning near the wheel, hardly looking in our direction. The monstrous appearing captain and his piratical looking crew might have made the salty pen of Jack London shiver and shake. However I was doing some shivering on my own hook and in such balmy weather. (To give the devil his due, even offshore on a warm summer day, there seems to be a chill lurking in the air.)

Captain McCoy, after talking with his mate, went aft and talked things over with his skipper. Occasionally the nautical fat man would spit over the rail, but look first to see how the wind was blowing. It was blowing a "Portagee" hurricane—straight up and down the mast.

Suddenly McCoy headed our way. "Start loading him! Here's the list!"

"Sure, we'll load him," growled a thin and bearded crewman. "One more week out here and I could bite the tail off a black mermaid."

"Shut up" bellowed someone, "and start."

Case after case was handed down over the rail and packed away, and I became alarmed.

"Captain McCoy! Captain McCoy!"

McCoy leaned over the rail.

"I only promised to bring in a few cases of stuff for some social drinking. But all this..."

"The list here calls for one hundred cases. Remember, if you're caught, one case can do as much damage as a hundred."

"Yes, Captain, but a fellow can get rid of ten cases much quicker than a hundred before he's caught. I didn't intend to run in a load."

"You'll be all right. And if you get in trouble, let me know. All right boys."

"Sure," I said, "Let 'em come."

"Aye," replied my mate (it wasn't my brother). "Let 'em come and if we get caught I'll scalp the guy who put us up to it."

One man stopped loading long enough to pass a few words our way.

"If you fellows really want to make money, who don't 'cha run out women and run in chinamen. More fun and more money."

"I don't go for that stuff."

"So, good for you, fellow."

As the men labored at lugging cases about, trying not to slip and lose good stuff overboard, I noticed that behind some of their salty hardness there was breeding that might have originated in the average American home. There are times when hard luck, ill-health, greed, do strange things to a man, and when the spirit of adventure complicated matters, most anything can result.

Just as we were ready to cast off with our unlawful load—roped in or not—I personally bought two cases of pinch-bottle Haig and Haig for $45.00 O.T.R.

On New England soil such scotch was worth over $100.00 a case.

"Will you take my personal check?" I hollered at McCoy, as the bearded giant was putting my two cases on board, handling them as if they were cigar boxes.

"Ellery, your check is okay with me. I trusted my life to you in the fog, so I'll trust your name on a check. I'd even take your word. Thanks and good luck. After you get through with this load stick to fishing—someday I hope to do a lot of it. It's a good business."

"If your check shows bilge water," growled the giant at the *Arethusa's* rail, "I'll come after you with my gutting knife and use your liver for shark bait." Mentally I vowed to fatten up my checking account to a high-water mark. I wanted no rum pirates after me. Probably I would have enough troubles without them.

Pulling away from the schooner to the delight of waiting small-craft, we ran off toward Block Island and then drifted about to kill the rest of the daylight hours. Our position about eight miles south-south-east of Montauk is now popular as dragging grounds, but at that time no draggers operated out there, although those thirty fathom bottoms must have been paved with fish.

While we were laying-to, we observed several small boats heading in toward Block Island—possibly with both fish and rum, and it was a good guess that some island hotels would later have just what the summer people wanted.

During the hot nerve-wracking afternoon we drank up the last of our drinking water and finished our slim supply of grub. Any refreshments from that moment on would have to be hard stuff from one or more of the cases.

"This is the moment I've lived for all my life," cried my mate, but we both knew that he was only joking. A steady diet of rum or scotch would either burn a man's guts up or drive him crazy, but my mate and I did polish off a quart of champagne as if it was coca cola.

Meanwhile I had discovered that McCoy had left behind his gun and cigars. With the Colt there was a box of cartridges, so I loaded up and started blazing away at the fin of every shark within range, and while I was shooting I was smoking only the best—fifty-centers, for a moment I felt I was somebody, then I realized who I was, I was a deep-water damn fool.

When the sun dropped behind a batch of newly formed low-lying clouds we started in, and by the time we were abreast of Montauk off Great Eastern Rock, darkness was closing down around us. We headed for Race Rock on the west side of Fishers Island, and then came dark hours that were like a nightmare. If this was rum running, I wanted no part of it after this night was over. And how I wished it was over.

To make a long story short, our lawless nightmare involved running without lights, listening and looking for signs of a Coast Guard patrol boat, dodging all boats and all dark shadows on the water, and finally zig-zagging into a sheltered cover near the mouth of the Thames River, then, anchoring and going for a short swim ashore to locate a telephone. After four days away from home port, all previously made plans were useless. We had to fix a new rendezvous and fast. Daybreak must find the *Grace and Lucy* clean of rum running evidence.

Dumb luck played in our favor and after that important telephone call to the right party, a businessman's girl Friday, we were soon underway again and heading for the west side of the Thames where we docked near a waterfront Casino. Immediately a group of men jumped aboard and started frantically unloading. There were bankers, shipyard executives, merchants, and among others, a well-known lawyer. Perhaps the best criminal cases he ever tackled were those cases of Black and White.

When nearly unloaded a cry of alarm went up. "There's going to be a raid! Someone tipped off the police! Take your boat out of here quick!"

"There's about ten cases left!" I hailed.

"The hell with it. Get going!" And those men vanished faster than had the gulls when I fired McCoy's gun off Block Island. But when we pulled out into the river, with dawn about to break, I noticed one man on board other than my crew.

"I was told to stay on board and show you where to hide this stuff."

"Good, but it had better be close by. Daylight is coming, and in ten minutes this stuff is going overboard, if only into the river."

"We'll make it. Dock just above the Ship and Engine Company. I know of an old destroyer."

An hour later, the *Grace and Lucy* was apparently clean of burlap bagging, wooden case splinters, broken glass, lost labels, and straw never intended for a stable. My own two cases had been taken ashore at the Casino by the friend of mine who helped arrange the entire sorry deal, and I headed for home as gratefully relieved as I could be. Never again, I said. This was it. Yet a few days later my mate and I found about six "hams" of whisky hidden in our bilges. (A burlap ham contains six quart bottles.) When I questioned my mate about this discovery he exploded with righteous indignation: "Sure three slipped out of my hand when we were unloading, and three slipped out of yours."

But, weeks later complications developed rapidly. My mate and I were called into the Custom House and questioned. After my mate had told his tale in a side room, and a fairly truthful one, I was hauled on the carpet and ordered to confess what I knew about running off to the *Arethusa* and what I had seen out there.

Jerry Dillon looked hard at me but as a father might look at his son.

"Ellery, we had your father in here an hour ago, and got nothing out of him. He didn't seem to even know your middle name or the year you were born. You have a darn faithful father. Now, these men here represent Washington They don't go for lying, so whatever you say, just tell the truth."

"Captain," said one of the Washington men. "Did you ever run rum?"

"If I said no, you might think I was lying. If I said yes, I might be a damn fool."

"I think that we'd better seize his boat," said an assistant.

"Ellery, be reasonable. These men know, but they want an answer from you." I knew I had no choice.

"Captain—"

"Yes Sir. I've brought in rum!"

The following hour was rough for my mate and myself. First the law boys got his story, then they pried my version from me. Somehow our yarns jibed and without too much gut spilling on my part, although I confessed to seeing the fishing boat *Lap* astern of the *Arethusa*. I was asked about the men who backed my venture at rum running, how much money I got running in a load, what I knew about other runners.

I knew little or nothing about the other fellow, of whether his boat was loaded with rum or fish. I only knew that my boat had been loaded with whisky for sporting men who paid me hardly anything for running in their booze.

"It wasn't a commercial venture on my part," I said grimly, "I did it as a favor for friends."

"Friends!" snorted a Washington man. "Your friends were steering you toward jail, and we have an idea who they are." The Washington man mentioned a name. "How does that sound. Make sense?"

"Yes Sir," I replied.

There was a lot more but eventually the government men accepted our story as reasonably authentic, and began looking upon us as more fishermen than smugglers. Meanwhile I felt about as small as a herring and as flat as a flounder, and with the realization that we were to get off easy, that is, after promising on my word of honor that I would never again run in rum. A promise I was to keep. I mean from Rum Row.

However, those who ran the *Lap* had their boat seized. But a month later the owners got the *Lap* back, after forfeiting a $2,500 bond. A while later I fell in with the captain of the *Lap* at Fulton Fish Market, and the first thing he wanted to do was to punch me in the jaw. After I accused him of stepping out with a girl friend of mine, he relented, got quite friendly and invited me out to dinner. Later while riding the shoot-the-shoots at Coney Island for the fourth time, I thought of our stormy adventure off Block Island.

Eventually the whisky I had bought at the rail of the *Arethusa* found a natural home at a naval picnic on Mamacoke Island. In fact Lieut. Charlie Becker, an ex-O-Boat submariner, was commanding officer at the big family affair blowout. One thing sure, Navy men, expert at taking a submarine under, didn't flinch at downing a few fathom-busters on their own hook.

As months passed I tried to steer clear of rum running and the stories back of it. It just didn't pay to know too much, for men that knew too much might find themselves on the bottom of the sea with their feet planted in cement. On several occasions I was approached with cash bankrolls about running in a small trip for "worthy people" but my stock answer was, "Nothing doing. Go run it in yourself. So long. See you in jail."

All too soon the running and handling of "liquid gold" from deep water to shore shacks attracted the cut-throat element into whisky smuggling. Then all hell broke loose with plenty of hi-jacking afloat and ashore. Some of us draggermen not only heard bullets speeding through the air, but we heard stories that were literally colored with human blood and immoral conditions hard to believe.

While on a sea-scalloping trip down off New York I overheard vague yarns about a fleet of rum-boats off Atlantic City and western Long Island, whose captains not only tried to sink one another by ramming, but whose crews went ashore in small boats with the idea of hi-jacking or shanghaiing beach-women for purposes only too obvious.

Naturally thousands of cases of whisky ended up on the ocean floor, after being thrown overboard by scared or cornered rum runners who dreaded being caught with the goods. Down off Newport a shipyard deepsea diver was in ten fathoms trying to salvage a load of dumped booze when a Coast Guard chaser hove on the scene. The salvage boat cut clear of the diver and ran for cover, the diver floated in later—dead.

As time passed the Coast Guard made up a "black list" and boats on it were hounded at all hours, offshore and in port. One brand new vessel named the *Whispering Wind* made a dash offshore but was blasted to the bottom by the Coast Guard before completing her maiden trip. Another suspect, while inbound in Block Island Sound, ran into thick fog and then ran ashore on the south side of Fishers Island at a spot only a potato's throw from the Coast Guard Station. Needless to say, the law breakers jumped ashore into the waiting hands of the law boys. This was the last trip of the *Barbara*, and the last one for her skipper.

Suspicious acting or night running yachts and fishing boats were shot at and boarded in rough weather, with innocent craft suffering indignities hard to describe. This happened to me twice. On the least provocation fishing boats were stopped while inbound and searched every which way, even to being keelhauled with weighted lines in a try to detect something unusual at the bottom of the boat. One searching trick was to drive iron rods down through layers of iced fish and cracked ice, as Coast Guardsmen hoped to hear the crackle of broken glass and to smell the fumes of liquor.

For several years most Coast Guard rum chasers were the well-known seventy-five footers, powered by Sterling Petrel engines of 250-horsepower. On the opposite side, many rum runners were powered by either one or two Liberty air-craft engines of 500-horsepower, surplus from World War I, and I would say that more of these gas-hog engines got into rum running than ever got into the air, that is, except the one that blew up one night in the fog near Gardner's Island. That explosion on a loaded rummie sent a father and his two sons overboard, where they drifted and swam about for hours on end. Only one son every reached shore alive.

Gradually the Coast Guard chaser fleets started catching up with bigger and more powerful boats, to bring more and more misery to professional rum runners, and somehow, formerly honest fishermen, the most law abiding citizens on shore, were tempted to become thirty-fathom bottle-fishermen. Most of these misguided fishermen were sorry afterwards, especially those who were caught.

While out on dragging grounds in and around Block Island Sound, draggermen, myself included, got used to seeing ghostly rum runners speeding past in hazy weather, and to hearing the roar of their high-powered motors, as they drove their illegal loads without lights, in hours of darkness toward some remote cover or shore-station where men and trucks would be waiting to tackle their end of it.

Many times, while inbound after dark, did I see strange lights on shore blinking on and off as Post Road bootleggers flashed their coded signals. Although the picture wasn't pleasant, rum running was to stage a 12 year run along southern New England and, without question, some fishermen and fish plants ashore prospered because of it, some fine vessels of today, yachts and fishing boats, owe their existence to the fact that, someone, somewhere, got either ten dollars a case for bringing whisky in from Rum Row, or a few dollars a case for hiding it on shore until the coast was clear for the run to the city. In fact, the stowing of smuggled whisky at fish shack warehouses was a pretty lucrative business.

On the other hand, it is no secret that a few "Law Boat Skippers" nursed unusually large bank balances. Some may have been kicked out of the service as a result.

For several years at the top of the Coast Guard's "black list," was the notorious rum runner *Black Duck*.

"Get the *Black Duck*; she's poison; shoot her down!" was the cry along shore. Then one night the Coast Guard cornered her off Brenton's Reef Lightship, near the mouth of Newport harbor, and the crippled *Duck* was blasted by a hail of machine gun bullets. When the law boys closed in and took over, there was human blood running from the scuppers.

Months later the recommissioned *Black Duck* flew the proud flag of the Coast Guard and drove seaward to chase rum runners. But somehow her notorious reputation remained with her, and there were occasions when even the Coast Guardsmen shunned her as if she had the plague. Somehow I shall always believe that it was the *Black Duck* that shot at my boat one night in hazy weather and with my boat as clean as a whistle, so to speak.

I happened to be on deck to witness the capture at a Rhode Island seaport of a dragger from the fleet I was fishing with. Friends of mine owned the boat, yet they claim they were on shore that night. No one was caught on board; but when the law boys lifted the dragger's hatches, the sight that greeted their eyes was hundreds of gallons of Belgian alcohol.

Although there were some Coast Guard "rum chasers" with a mean reputation, one officer had practically sniffed every bottle in a big dragger's medicine chest, in his desperate attempt to catch someone, violence works both ways. An inbound rum runner down off Newport, bound up a narrow channel, towed astern a dory that contained dynamite, with everything rigged for blowing it up if a Coast Guard vessel followed them in. Luckily these boys got away with it, which probably saved a few lives. Later their boat was caught in broad daylight and without bloodshed.

Around eastern Connecticut where long-distance trucks played a part in transporting landed whisky into New York City, one enterprising truckman got an order to buy $1,000 worth of whisky at Rum Row off Montauk Point—cash in advance. So he chartered a very small fishing boat and left port with the intention of buying and running in the booze. Two days later they arrived in port with long faces but with no liquor. They reported, confidentially, buying 20 cases of whisky (no, they did not remember the name of the rum ship), being chased by the Coast Guard, and throwing the liquor overboard when cornered.

A month later the truckdriver and the fisherman with smiles on their faces left town on a long vacation. Apparently "lost trips" pay off.

The many cases of sunken whisky that were to be caught in the trawl nets of draggermen, throughout the run of Prohibition, is a story in itself, which I may touch on later; for my boat was to drag up plenty of it, to present us with problems galore.

One day I got a note from Capt. McCoy about the Havana cigars and the Colt revolver left on my boat. Of course, I had smoked up his fine cigars, puffing on them like a millionaire, luckily I still had his gun.

Dear Captain:

Will you please leave "the two smoking articles" at Giles Dunn's fish market at Salt Pond Harbor, Block Island. I'd like to pick them up within two weeks. I hope to see you again if only to say thanks and "Keep Fishing."

Cap'n Bill

CHAPTER VII

Salvaged Crop

During the rip-roaring twenties the waters off southern New England became as famous for the activities of rum runners as for those of fishermen. Stories about Rum Row, where heavily-laden liquor schooners, safely out of reach of United States law, waited for shore boats to come buy their stuff, were floating about like cheap toys off a pleasure beach. Some yarns were fantastic fish-stories, but some were colored truthfully, and it was no secret that case whisky (the real McCoy) could be bought at $45.00 a case O.T.R.—over the rail. And once, on a deepsea fishing trip, I bought two cases on my own hook, over the rail of Captain Bill McCoy's notorious *Arethusa*.

Passing time and stirring incidents saw me well fed up with the running of rum—I mean mainly in a commercial sense—and I vowed to never again violate the integrity of my boat with illegal cargo from offshore. Of course lost rum from the ocean floor, stuff that might get in our trawl net, was another matter— as tempting as the devil himself dressed in yellow oil-skins. So we often played host to law-breaking booze without being too aware of it.

On several occasions at island harbors and even at seaports like Newport, Rhode Island, my boat lay alongside craft of questionable nature, and with such beautiful sounding names: *Whispering Wind*, *Glowing Cigarette* (she was to burn up), and *Goose-and Gander*. We generally minded our own business, so I was never too greatly surprised, come morning, to find within the cotton netting of our trawl gear a dawn present of a case of imported Scotch whisky. Some of this would end up in our medicine chest, and then my crew would develop belly cramps in short order and cry for the obvious cure. One complaining fellow had a habit of hollering for a dose of ninety proof tonic at every sign of an ache or pain, but I sort of cured him, I slipped him a mixed dose of scotch and caster oil, and his stomach cramps vanished to loo-ard in faster time than when he got them.

Many people, some the most law-abiding of citizens on dry land, did not consider the handling of Rum Row whisky as really breaking the laws of The United States of America. At least it was so where draggermen were concerned, or where no commercial sale entered the picture. To some of us, mainly fellows in the channel but close to the rocks, the finding of unlawful whisky was comparable to finding pirate treasure. Yet the penalties for getting caught with the goods on board could cost a man his vessel, and possibly his freedom.

During the early years of our Atlantic coast rum running, the liquor smugglers used boats of all sorts—fishing boats, yachts, and about anything seaworthy enough to go out and bring in a paying load. At first the rum runners had the fastest boats, but eventually the Coast Guard vessels started catching up with them. Naturally some rum boats were sunk at sea, others piled up on fogbound shores.

The wrecking of a liquor vessel can create more undercover excitement down along the shores than anything I know. Take the case of the British motor yacht *Thelma Phoebe*, which had come driving up the Atlantic coast from the Bahamas, bound for heaven-knows-where, although Halifax was supposed to have been her destination. During a pea-soup fog in Block Island Sound she got off course and piled up on the south shore of Fishers Island, loaded to the gun'ales with fine imported liquors—mainly Peter Dawson scotch.

The *Thelma Phoebe* was wrecked at dawn on a spring day in the early twenties. After she piled up, the rummies jettisoned hundreds of cases of good whisky in a futile try at refloating their vessel from its rocky cradle; but soon realizing that their vessel was doomed, they tried to escape ashore to prevent being captured by the Coast Guard. All but one made the beach safely. The unfortunate fellow failed when he jumped overside into a deep sand hole alongside his boat, and there the Coast Guard boys found him an hour later, with his head just underwater—deader'n a mackerel, so they said. Meanwhile the yacht captain and his crew made good their escape, probably reaching the north shore by hiring a small lobster boat to ferry them over.

But the big prize was the stranded yacht and its cargo, for the Coast Guardsmen found plenty of good whisky still remaining in the boat, regardless of cases floating and sinking just off the shore. Floating cases and drifting whisky odors, soon attracted the attention of roving Islanders, who passed the word along somewhat in the manner of gulls conversing with one another. Evidently beached liquor was tempting bait and a horde of Islanders soon headed for the *Thelma Phoebe* area, beachcombing as they moved along. Somehow the news of the rum shipwreck leaked into Fort H.G. Wright at the western end of the island, and more than one soldier boy quickly decided to go A.W.O.L.

For a while along the south shore there was more excitement and confusion than one could shake an oar at. Many poled in case after case in grand style, keeping just out of reach of the law boys; some got drunk on the spot; others lugged plenty of stuff away; some hid their recovered liquor along the rocky shores to the west'ard, with the hope of picking up their loot later. Of course some scavengers were chased away, but all in all, the Coast Guard boys had more problems than they could cope with, so a call went out to the north shore for help.

My father, in his *Eleanor Louise*, was the fisherman who brought Custom House officials over from New London, to land them at a north side cover opposite the stranded liquor boat. Strangely enough this cove, and the rum shipwreck itself, were only a stone's throw from Money Pond where Captain Kidd supposedly buried pirate treasure.

At the time I was on board my dragger at New London, wondering where the best fishing might be, but when I heard by the waterfront grapevine about the tempting possibility of good bottle fishing, my crew and I were soon underway to see what all the shouting was about, and to see what we could drag up.

Today, as I look back at it all, my main excuse is that many of us are beachcombers at heart, treasure hunters clear to our soul, and hate to pass up adventuring pure and simple.

However, in those early days of eye-opening excitement, rum was rum and the real McCoy—with a trading value like something out of Fort Knox. Though I realized my connection with Puritanical ancestors, I wasn't going to pass up a good thing, bad though it be. Too often had I tossed over my shoulder something salty and questionably attractive.

In short order my crew and I headed down the Thames, and after an hour's run out around Race Rock Light we were at the scene of the festivities. We hove to a hundred yards offshore to consider our next move. We decided that as long as we had a New York State fishing license it was perfectly legal for us to set and drag our trawl-net, and if any cases of whisky got in the net by accident it would be just too bad—so we set our net. (At that time a New York license cost an out-of-state dragger twenty-five dollars. Today it costs him about five dollars a foot—along the length of his boat. Time limit, one year.)

As we nosed in closer toward the stranded *Thelma Phoebe*, with our net dragging nicely on bottom, Custom House officials on shore frantically motioned us away. I waved back at them in a happy way. One official with a big megaphone ran down the beach until he was directly inshore of us.

"Ahoy aboard that dragger! Get the hell out of there!" came booming across the water.

"We're dragging for flounders," I hailed, as loudly as I could, but apparently the Customs man didn't hear me. He only threw his megaphone into the sand, and for a moment I thought he was going to jump on it. About this time I spotted my father on the stern of the wrecked craft peering down into her after cabin. Later Pop told me that it was so full of choice stuff, it made him dizzy just to look at it.

Suddenly my father looked up and motioned us away. Then our net got "hungup" on bottom, but we hauled it clear and took it on board, undamaged. Probably we had dragged into a large smooth boulder. Our catch was small indeed—one flat fish and one case of Peter Dawson scotch. Hurrah! We were not skunked. If only we had caught ten flat fish and ten cases of scotch, but if we had netted a big haul of booze we might have run into serious trouble and ended up in jail.

When we left the scene, after that one drag, there was relief on all sides. Homeward bound I tried to fathom out some way to not cheat Uncle Sam or ourselves or the next fellow. So far, as we neared New London, we had broken no law. The next trick was to use a little Yankee ingenuity to not break any law too badly. No real deepsea fisherman off our coast really wants to break laws, but state boundary lines and unpopular laws being what they are, a few unlawful acts seem to get entangled in our wake.

The government men in charge of the wrecked *Thelma Phoebe*, at that island beach-head, were Captain Peckham of the Fishers Island Coast Guard Station and Jeremiah Dillon, head man at the New London Custom House. Both men were capable and with marvelous records, and over the years gave many a man the benefit of their expert advice and sincere friendship. I well recall the day that Mr. Dillon told how worried he was about me—and my recklessness at fishing for illegal booze.

"YOU were worried!" I said, "What about me?"

The story did not end with the capture of the *Thelma Phoebe* and her cargo. Years later I heard more of the yarn from reliable sources. While the Coast Guard were restoring law and order at the scene of the wreck, some Islanders were doing a little stowing on their own hook, but when the ones who had rescued the most liquor heard that their homes were to be searched for contraband refreshments, they got scared and went into action as speedily as possible. First, they stripped the whisky bottles of their wrapping and burned all tell-tale evidence of wrong doing. Next they looked at the calendar. The month was April, and it seems that everyone involved had a garden ready for planting. So the jittery Islanders started planting seed like no one had ever planted before.

It so happened that one beachcomber's garden, the largest one of all, overlooked Money Pond and the dim tower of the Coast Guard Station. If only no one would get wise to what was planted in that elaborate garden, not even the ghost of Capt. Kidd...

One family worked with more frantic speed than any of the rest. It was only natural, they had the most to plant, and their small garden stretched out from a grove to the very edge of the sea. One man stood guard on a knoll while his companions planted all kinds of seed—domestic and imported, and the harrowed ground took in seed like a butt-sprung boat takes in seawater. Into one row went corn and rye whisky. Another row soaked up beans and bottled champagne. Then someone planted a row of scotch and string beans—a row of fine wine and watermelon, and so it went, with the good earth swamping all that was tossed into it.

"This isn't really breaking the law," shouted out one old Islander, "anything that the sea tosses up is fair game."

"Aye," replied a younger man. "I've heard that on Block Island an entire ship was once carted away from the beach."

Small signs were posted at strategic spots in the gardens. For example: *Black and White Beans, Rye Corn, Wine Corn, Gin Potatoes.* A near neighbor used a different code: *Imported Sweet Potatoes, Peter String Beans, Dawson Cabbage, Calvert Turnips,* etc. The expected raid never came off, but the stuff was left in the ground for insurance. The gardens were nursed carefully all summer and at times there was some pre-harvest digging and sampling. No outsider got wise, although a few women folk became more than disturbed about the backyard activity of their men folk. One thing sure, no grass grew between house and garden.

Time dragged on. One fall day a certain island family had unexpected company drop in. More food and entertainment fluid was needed, so the lady of the house asked her husband to go out and dig up some vegetables and scotch. "I want one head of cabbage, some lettuce, some new potatoes, and some very old straight whisky," she said in a matter of fact tone of voice.

When some of us heard this part of the story, one fellow said: "Some story."

"Some shipwreck!" I said, "and the wettest that I ever attended—whisky or no whisky."

CHAPTER VIII

Rescue

The reefs and shoals of Block Island Sound have ruined many ships and men; and no woman, to my knowledge, has ever swam to the north shore from a vessel wrecked on Watch Hill Reef. Probably some men overboard there have made it—that is, if the tide was flood.

Watch Hill Reef, off southwestern Rhode Island, lies three miles due south of Stonington. This treacherous reef, at the dividing line between Rhode Island and New York waters, plays a part warding off heaving ground swells from pounding our north shore, but is notorious for the number of vessels that are wrecked along its crags and underwater ledges.

One old ship which hit and drifted clear to sink in deep water is supposedly a pirate ship loaded down with a fabulous golden fortune, but your guess is as good as mine as to her exact location. The scattered remains of other hulks date back to days when Dutch and English ships first coasted off our southern New England shores, when "dead reckoning" navigation was a hit or miss adventure, with plenty of hitting along our neck of the coast. No wonder one channel through the reef is known as Lord's Passage, bordered on the east by a broken-off spindle in an underwater ledge, and on the west by tiny Wicopesset Island.

Today there is a lighted bell-buoy just south of Lord's Passage, which eases the pressure on many local fishermen; but for many years and when I started fishing out of Stonington, the Passage had only a red buoy and a black buoy to go by in clear weather—that is, if one could spot them, with their tips just showing above a racing tide. I recall that one old local mariner claimed that while the good Lord was cutting a deepwater channel through Watch Hill Reef, the devil was busy behind his back piling up rocks and trouble on all sides. I can well believe it, especially on the Wicopesset Island side.

This gull-rookery just above sea-level, is as treacherous as a slumbering rattlesnake. I've always dreaded the thoughts of being shipwrecked on Wicopesset Island, especially with a full gale in progress, for on real blowy occasions even the lives of gulls are in danger, because of storm-tide waves thoroughly house-cleaning the island.

Between Wicopesset Island and eastern Fishers Island is narrow Wicopesset channel, where racing tides imperil boats, large and small. Yet this difficult channel once allowed hard-chased rum runners, dodging in from Rum Row off Block Island, to play hide-and-seek with the Coast Guard. Once a broken-open case of imported but illegal scotch, mixed in with beached food-stuff, got a flock of Wicopesset gulls so drunk, they were practically flying upside down and with barrel-rolls to boot.

Two-mile long Watch Hill Reef, which might have once, when the earth was young, connected eastern Fishers Island to the Watch Hill area of Rhode Island, is a perilous backbone of kelpy surf-washed rock piles, with ledges that flirt with the surface on the flood and expose their worst points on the ebb. Some fishermen have names for its treacherous ledges that wouldn't look good in print. One skipper referred to this off-shore reef as an old whore of the Sound with plenty of damage in her. Without question Watch Hill Reef has tore the bottom out of scores of vessels—large and small.

To me, as a dragger captain, several Watch Hill groundings and wrecks have been outstanding. During my first years in fishing Block Island Sound I got rather used to seeing the full-whitened mast of the steamer *Onondaga* sticking up from the deep waters alongside the reef. She had struck the reef and sunk while loaded with about everything from canned sardines to shoes, even motorcycles; and, after passing up canned sardines, I got rather tired of trying on pre-shrunk shoes that were too small for my feet.

In 1920, the "well-bottom" lobster smack *Hattie Lawry*, a vessel I skippered for a month at the age of 20, hit Watch Hill Reef and knocked a big hole in her bottom, losing 3,000 pounds of Block Island-caught lobsters to the rocks off Stonington. Alvin Scott, Avondale Lobsterman, who had hundreds of pots in the area, reaped a shell-fish harvest, and the following winter visited Florida for the first time.

During the roaring 1920s, rum runners dodging the Coast Guard, were always hitting their bottoms along the perilous reef, but usually got away without meeting disaster there.

Later a lumber schooner lost part of her deck cargo off the reef. With good lumber floating all over the place, many draggers, including my old *Louise*, brought in heavy loads of lumber, but I couldn't seem to be bothered, I wanted to catch fish, not four-by-sixes of western fir. Yet many docks along Connecticut and Rhode Island shores were built from that salvaged lumber, and the 1938 hurricane reclaimed it. The sea gives forth, and it takes away more quickly than it gives. I might add that the tidal waters around Watch Hill Reef claim more lives from capsized outboard motor boats each year than one cares to think about.

During a foggy week end in the mid-1930s, I recall that three small vessels became wrecked on the rocky barriers of Watch Hill Reef, a Nantucket flounder dragger that had been westbound for Fulton Market in New York City, an off-shore "alcohol runner" bound up-Sound, and a small sloop yacht bound for Heaven knows where.

Of course I was among the local draggermen who, after a little fog-shrouded salvage work, was in a position to enjoy a few alcoholic-flavored fish dinners, but as I see the entire picture, the most attractive vessel among the sunken trio was the small sloop yacht, whose plight went unnoticed because of a Wicopesset "haze" and pea-soup fog, for she had hit at the east tip of Lord's Passage, where she sank.

Thick fog had kept the dragger fleet tied up for two days, and several of us skippers started to get restless, eager to get out in the Sound and start dragging our nets. Then on the Sunday morning slack tide I peered down Stonington harbor and caught a faint glimpse of the outer breakwater and Latimer Light. It looked as if the Sound fog might break away. This was the chance I was waiting for, to get in a quick trip and make a fast dollar on a high market.

Most skippers at our dock had called it quits for the day and headed homeward, but not so young Denny Cidale, the new skipper of my old boat, the 44 foot *Louise*. He was hanging around and keeping his eyes cocked down the harbor, hoping to see the fog break away from the outer breakwaters.

"How about it Denny?" I hailed across the docklog. "This fog may clear on the next slack, and maybe we can get in a couple of drags off southeast of the *Larchmont*."

"Sure, Cap'n Ellery. I'm with you. This fog should break away for a few hours, but tonight it will shut down as thick as ever, and we'll be tied up for another spell."

"Where's your crew, Denny?"

"Down below, making a clam chowder."

While I was rounding up my crew—Johnny and Phil—Denny routed out his mate, Jimmy the Goose, and told him what was in the wind—mainly about venturing out to find some holes in the fog.

Jimmie the Goose was a former Nova Scotian fisherman with Grand Bank experience on Canadian schooners and Boston beam trawlers. His real name was James LaBlanc. To leap ahead for a moment. During two years of World War II, when Stonington reached its peak as a fishing port, Jimmie the Goose was to fish with me on the *Eleanor*, and he proved to be one of the best sailormen I'd ever been shipmates with. I also learned how polite he could be, especially in the company of women. Perhaps he wasn't the most bashful man I've ever known, but he wasn't far from it, and all this plays a part in what was to happen during the foggy spell off Stonington.

We soon had the *Eleanor* underway, followed by the *Louise*, but after leaving the harbor we ran into drifting patches of fog. Navigating mostly by dead reckoning, we passed Napatree gas buoy, then Gangway Rock gas buoy, and entered Block Island Sound, watching out for lobster pot buoys at all times to keep from fouling our wheel. We spotted plenty of pot-buoys but nothing else worth mentioning. Most of Watch Hill Reef was obscured from us, at one point, however, when off Napatree, I thought I heard a girlish hail coming from out of the fog, but I charged this off to my imagination.

We made the nearby grounds all right and set our net about four miles southeast of Watch Hill. I called it the offshore Yellow Bank drag, for due north of that fishing spot is the summer colony of Misquamicut, bordered to the east by twin yellow sand dunes, which, in clear weather, we used as ranges.

Denny and I tried to fish our boats as close together as possible for mutual protection (no ship-to-ship radio-phones in those days, in our fleet) and while making two two hour drags we often judged our position by the sound of our exhausts. After all, one's eyes and ears and other senses are pretty good navigational instruments.

Occasionally, however, as fog-shrouded steamboats blew their whistles not far from us, I would pick up my trumpet and blast out a tuneful fog-signal, hoping to scare off any approaching vessel. Of course, it was that old trick of mine—hoping to be mistaken for an unseen excursion steamer.

In late afternoon, after catching about five barrels of mixed fish—some were lobsters from a twenty-five fathom pit—we headed in, hoping to make our Stonington land-fall before darkness and fog shut out everything. Fog in daylight is bad enough, fog at night is not only tricky, it can be "suicide," and I wanted no part of anchoring out that night.

Side by side, each boat a ghostly blur to the other, the *Eleanor* and the *Louise* raced shoreward through drifting fog patches, whose misty fingers seemed to reach out like the devil himself. With old lady luck riding our tail, and with some Yankee cautiousness at the wheel, we made the bell-buoy off Watch Hill and headed westward toward Napatree gas buoy, meanwhile keeping our eyes peeled toward Watch Hill reef to see anything unusual that might appear. For a while, nothing—that is, except swooping gulls and gaily colored lobster-pot buoys in slack-water tide eddies.

But on passing Napatree, with the *Louise* leading the *Eleanor* by several lengths (Denny had been driving her to reach the dock first), the picture of foggy calmness changed rapidly. Suddenly a hole in the fog revealed a small bonfire burning on Wicopesset Island—about half a mile to the southwest. Immediately Denny swung the *Louise* offshore toward the rosy glow, with me wondering about what was up, but heading off to find out, following in his wake. Meanwhile my crew had handed me my marine glasses just in case I might need them.

A few minutes later, we spotted two nearly naked girls dancing excitedly around a tiny bonfire. We also spotted, after they pointed it out by hand waving, the mast of a sunken sloop at the eastern edge of Lord's Passage. The story was plain enough. The stranded girls had burned up most of their clothing in order to attract our attention, and someone was still at the scene of the wrecked sloop. What price womanly modesty at a time like this.

For a while the girls were safe enough, so both draggers approached the sunken sloop cautiously. Suddenly overboard went the *Louise's* dory and with Jimmie the Goose at the oars, it was rowed in close to the sloop, where the bald head of a man was visible as he held to the barely protruding tip of his boat's stern.

Jimmie the Goose reached the man just in time and hauled him in as if he were boating a three-hundred pound tuna. Another five minutes and the rising tide and ground swell would have engulfed him. Meanwhile I might have gone after the girls, but it was the *Louise's* show all the way, we were just acting as insurance. Besides our dory was in poor condition for rescue work, leaky and full of junk, which is a poor excuse.

Darkness was now closing down fast, and it was a race against time. However the fading light of day would benefit the girls in obvious ways and somewhat to my regret. This type of rescue was a pretty rare thing and my crew called me down for not playing a more intimate part in it.

"Take it easy, boys, this ain't the South Sea Islands," I said, as I again followed after the slowly moving *Louise*.

"Well, it sure shapes up that way," replied one fellow dryly.

When the *Louise* got within two-hundred feet of Wicopesset Island, she sort of hove to as Jimmie the Goose threw some fishermen duds in the dory. Then he rowed toward the island, hardly glancing in the direction of the semi-nude girls. As I look back on it now, I'd say it was a picture no artist could paint.

During the following rescue operation, several points bothered me but mostly the darkening picture of fog and night, and I was tempted to get out my trumpet and play some sort of rescue music—something like *Moonlight Bay, Harbor Lights, Nearer My God To Thee, Up from the Grave We Rose*. Instead, I exercised my marine night-glasses, which were just like those once used by masters and pilots of Sound steamboats. A too powerful glass is of little use on a rolling boat, unless a man's hands and nerves are quite steady, and this night my hands were trembly with subdued excitement. I might say that I intended to use my glasses on our return trip into Stonington, so to get them in proper focus I aimed them at the island. I should have known better. I should have been more considerate of female mariners in trouble, especially of the one with silver-colored hair.

The rescuing of the girls went through in fine style, with Jimmie trying not to look at that fascinating bon-fire, now on its last legs, so to speak. But in trying to beach his dory with his eyes to port when they should have been to starboard, he struck a shore boulder and fell over backwards, only to be greeted by two trembling girls who quickly grabbed the clothes he tossed them. About this time my marine binoculars fogged up.

The scared girls were soon ready for the dory trip back to the *Louise*. Meanwhile the misty night was trying to obscure the entire scene, even though both boats now had their deck and running lights on. Then with the girls on board the *Louise*, we started feeling our way toward the bell-buoy off Stonington harbor, which was soon made and passed safely. The trip up the harbor was more of a nightmare, yet we made it safely to the old steamboat dock where we berthed our boats.

When the girls scrambled ashore from the *Louise*, still rigged out in fo-castle castoffs, I only had a foggy view of them, yet as the platinum-haired girl (or young woman, night light is tricky) glanced a bit curiously toward my boat, I had the feeling that I'd seen her before and that someday I might see her again, although that seemed to border on the impossible. All too soon the girls climbed into the roving taxi of Manny Andrews, who had come roaring down the dock, and away they went toward New London and an undisclosed destination.

Even the ship-wrecked mariner still on the *Louise* would say little about the girls—he only smiled and clammed up. Yet he opened up on the subject of salvaging his sloop yacht. Denny called me over to talk about it.

"Give you fellows a quarter of her value if you raise her and bring her in to a shipyard. How about it?" he said.

I shook my head without replying.

"Nothing doing. She's too big a baby for us to tackle. It'd take the mast out of my boat."

"Sure," I added, "there's too much tide around that broken-off spindle, and that spindle is right up through the bottom of your boat. Salvaging her is a job for the big fellows—like Merritt-Chapman & Scott. They'll salvage her for you."

"I know, perhaps too well," said the old yachtsman sadly. "Well, a million thanks, until I can get in touch with you later."

"Say," I blurted out. "Why didn't you get off your sinking boat with the girls—your daughters, I presume."

"No relation—the daughters of two friends of mine. Our little dinghy was built only for two, so I wanted to give the ladies every possible chance... After all, isn't it the old tradition that a captain goes down with his ship."

"I'm not too sure about that," I replied, "and I hope I won't have to face that predicament on my boat, because I would never go through with it if I could help it." And that was that for the evening.

The following day the fog cleared and the local draggers got busy again but at my first opportunity I cornered Cap'n Denny Cidale on the fish dock and inquired further into the identity of those two rescued females.

"Look, Cap'n Ellery," said Denny as he straightened up from the back-breaking task of clamping a chain to the foot-rope of a trawl net.

"I looked enough, Denny. I'm asking. Surely, you should have some idea who they were after being shipmates with them. I'm interested in that platinum-haired girl."

"Girl. She wasn't no girl. She was all of a woman over thirty, and she has snow-white hair."

"Well, she looked like a girl."

"Yeah, I guess she did at that but I don't know anymore about them than you do. You see, coming in from Wicopesset and creeping up the harbor in that pitch-blackness, with a stranded tiller line and a hot-running motor—"

"So you didn't learn much about them."

"No. I had my hands too full of trouble without asking two tongue-tied women who they were or if their ancestors came over in the *Mayflower*."

I thanked Denny in a somewhat sarcastic manner and went about my business. That night I attended a Jean Harlow movie and, after marveling at her beautiful platinum blond hair—her crowning glory, so to speak—I started realizing that a woman's hair could be misleading.

As time went on, with no further sign of the rescued girls, or of any other won-fires I arrived at a conclusion as plain as a gutted codfish. I had better stick with drag fishing, shun thoughts of new girls, old fires and myself as the rescuing hero, and only relive the Wicopesset adventure in my dreams.

CHAPTER IX

Shipmates

Over the years: on the three draggers I have owned and skippered—the 37-foot *Grace and Lucy*, the 44 foot *Louise*, the 50-foot *Eleanor*—I have worked and played at being a roving fishing skipper from Stonington.

During a long run of fishing trips, some with foul weather lay-overs at the islands, I have been shipmates with about all local-species of humans who had either sea-legs to stand on or bottoms enough to sit on; some were from professions low ebb and high tide—male and female. But a person's past history doesn't count for much—not with whistling winds and cold spray whipping across a heaving boat's deck, that is, unless someone's past history can help navigate a boat safely.

In my crews I've had over one hundred men from many channels of life, even to ex-Grand-Bankers and ex-Rum Runners after the tide turned ebb in their old way of life. There was salty John Marshall who had been closely related to "the Marshall fleet of Gloucester fishing schooners," a fellow who was making his first "salt-trip" to the Grand Banks off Newfoundland about the time Boston steam trawlers were first dragging the bottom off New England.

For many years John Marshall sailed out of Gloucester and dory-fished on offshore Banks; he cooked on schooners and he skippered them; but he tired of the long wet and cold trips—trips often with small pay and plenty of grief.

During the early 1920s, John, who had visualized the fading picture of sailing schooners and dory-fishing, had arrived in Stonington to become a small vessel draggerman. He told Nat Avery, who ran the fish-packing and long-distance trucking service on the site of the old steamboat dock, that he had heard about the old whaling and sealing port of Stonington, of how it had a fast-growing fleet of gasoline draggers, of the nearby grounds in Block Island Sound, of the important money being made.

"I don't want to get rich," he said grimly. "I just want to make a fair share without gargling too much salt water on a leaky boat. How about getting me a site on Ellery Thompson's *Louise*. She sort of shapes up rather good; and the skipper looks like fun."

Yes, all during 1926 John and I had fun mixed in with some of the hardest dragging I have ever experienced, fishing off Newport during many a winter blow, holed up at harbors-of-refuge from Point Judith to Edgartown in Martha's Vineyard. This was about the time all southern New England dragging-with-trawl-nets was enjoying its first rapid growth, and in an exciting atmosphere that caught pictures of an expanding Coast Guard chasing hell out of the rum running fleet.

When I decided to build and fish my intended dreamboat in 1927 (my present old lady *Eleanor*) John decided to leave me to my dreams and fish out of Point Judith, where a new dragger fleet was starting to grow. He did, too, and soon drifted into channels even farther east, at and around Woods Hole, where big Sam Cahoon ran a fish-packing and buying station at this very western tip of Cape Cod, where The Woods Hole Oceanographic Institution is located.

Another outstanding crewman who came aboard the *Eleanor* during World War II, was (in addition to fat and frolicsome Charlie Brayman) Jimmie the Goose LeBlanc, A Nova Scotian with Grand Bank experience; also with beam trawler experience out of Boston. Jimmie the Goose was unusually seagoing on board draggers, but he talked little about his past life.

When the Stonington dragger fleet reached its peak during the exciting and fishy 1940's, with fifty draggers landing a thousand barrels of quality fish daily—caught on grounds from ten fathoms to fifty, from Block Island Sound to the Gully near the steep edge of the continental shelf—Jimmie the Goose seemed proud to be a part of it all, and occasionally, at Joe Martin's beer parlor, he would open up to Charlie Brayman about the past when rum running flourished.

It seems to me that Jimmie got tagged "The Goose" after serving as mate on the 85 foot *Goose*, a speedy, low-hulled craft once suspected of being a rum runner, although I can't recall that she was ever caught at it. A sister ship to the *Goose* was named the *Gander*, whose mate was known as "Jimmie the Gander." Last name, unknown.

As time went on after rum running ended along our shores in 1932, I had for crew several ex-bottle-fishermen, one who had known the notorious "Captain Bill the Real McCoy," the adventurous southern mariner who fathered Rum Row off the Eastern Seaboard in 1920, the momentous year I got my first dragger and became a reckless and foolhardy dragger captain.

Although somewhat adrift at this point, the truth is: on July 1, 1921, I was the reckless young fishing skipper who ferried Captain McCoy from New London to his rum ship *Arethusa* hove to twelve miles off eastern Long Island.

It might seem that I'm rather proud of calling attention to the fact that I haven't always sailed about in the best of company, of the fact that my trawl nets have dragged up illegal cases of whisky after it had been dumped over by hard-chased rum runners, and that some of this recovered wet-treasure went into shore-channels of questionable nature.

Nevertheless, no one has ever accused me of sailing about under false colors—not even the Coast Guard who never had me on their "black list" during the Prohibition era—nor the Yale professors and oceanographers who used my boat for research purposes during the 1940s.

The very nature of dragging for a living has a habit of leaving a dragger captain little choice at what course to steer, because crews have some rights in the matter of sharing up the "hauls." More'n once have dragger crews shouted out:

"The hell with the fish in our haul; let's share up the liquor!"

From my point of view as well as from theirs, I've tried to treat all hands fairly, including Uncle Sam, even though Uncle Sam often made things hot for us. None the less, the Coast Guard never had my boats on their "black list" during the era of Prohibition which ended around 1932, although after selling one of my earlier boats (no names, please) she is reported to have run more rum than a "Revenoo-hunted-Kentucky-Mountaineer." By and large, few dragger captains have ever been accused of sailing under false colors. I do not mean skippers from "bottle-fishing-fleets."

Some of this side-channeling has been mentioned in all frankness, to show up our draggerman's life for what it was when some of us were younger.

I recall a September morn just before a change of laws forced rum runners to give up the ghost. Although I had heard rumors about sunken bottle-fish through Hot-Tip channels, my crew and I left Stonington with the intention of dragging for doormat fluke at the channel south of Rosie's Ledge, not far from the Hooter in the path of coastal shipping. We made the fleet and set in, dragging to the east'ard on the strong ebb tide. The weather was fine and the coffee never tasted better, and at the wheel I dozed a bit, as our Lathrop chugged away. Somehow while our net was scraping its wide bottom in 20 fathoms, its mouth wide-open for anything in its path, my boat worked away from good fishing and ever closer to where a lost rum runner's cargo lay on bottom. And while not realizing the loot that lay far beneath our keel, my darn'd old net went to work and scooped up about 20 cases of Peter Dawson scotch whisky.

On hauling in I felt both scared and delightfully embarrassed, and as drunken flounders starting flipping about frantically, I grew more nervous by the minute, especially when I spotted a Coast Guard Cutter steaming our way. My jubilant crew hadn't noticed the Cutter.

What to do? Well, what would you have done? One crew member thought he had the answer. This hard-working but sociable fellow tapped a bottle of scotch and complained about a lack of soda to go with it.

"Look...Jail!" I said. I pointed out he law-enforcing boys coming our way. And a moment later we started heaving bottles overboard to port and to starboard. One crewman was laughing; the other, crying. I was moaning. I didn't want to lose my boat.

We had several good bottles left on deck when the Cutter turned aside, to steam off where she might scare someone else out of their boots. Thankfully the day ended without more lawbreaking, bloodshed, mutiny, and another acute attack of the Thompson flounder-frights. And if I've lied about it, may Davy Jones reach up and grab the keel of my boat and give it a good shaking.

In contrast to the exciting rum running and steamboat-passing and navy maneuvering of Block Island Sound were the more remote and ocean-exposed waters off Martha's Vineyard, where many of us young Connecticut dragging skippers fished. The dragging grounds off Edgartown were fairly free of wrecks and rocks, and fish there were of larger size. Also of larger size were the seas off Mutton Shoal. After a storm they seemed as high as Connecticut hills, and racing shoreward on the foaming crests of them was an experience never to be forgotten. Luckily no Connecticut dragger ever got pooped or swamped down that way. But some bank-fishing Vineyarders marveled, such as Cap'n Bob Jackson on the big swordfishing schooner *Hazel B. Jackson*, and accused us northshore fishermen from Connecticut of trying to commit suicide.

During the mid-twenties, my brother had acquired his own new dragger, the 42-foot *Florence*. My cousin Harold McLaughlin was hard-fishing his 35-foot *Virgie* and sort of planning on his soon-to-be 63-foot *Marise*, slated to be the most widely traveled dragger ever out of Connecticut and Rhode Island.

One stormy day, with the *Marise*, the *Eleanor*, the *Florence*, tied up together at Newport, my brother and I and Harold, in talking things over, decided that when we got married—that is, if ever we were to have any choice in the matter, we would pick out brides who were well-sheered of body and fair of face, and seaworthy enough for the going mate of a dragger. I held out for a girl who might appear capable of bending over and picking up a tub of codfish gear without grunting or busting her seams. This precaution was just in case the dragging of trawl nets went on the rocks.

I may have held out for too darn much, or did I glimpse a domestic picture with some shades of darkness, or a matrimonial sea too rough for comfort or peace of mind. Anyhow, all along the coast between Connecticut hills and island pastures, I fell down on the job of marrying anyone, able-bodied or fragile, fresh or salty, ticklish or otherwise.

It was a different story with Morris and Harold. Both my cousin and brother were to do their manly duty regardless of their calling of going trip-dragging. Perhaps Morris took his duty too much to heart, but no family affairs now except those light enough to rest on my shoulders.

While the exciting and golden twenties were fading I had my observing eyes on several blossoming girls, much younger than myself, although I was not old enough to be their father, not really according to Hoyle.

One was a blond Connecticut Yankee who seemed capable of reading my thoughts and who blushed pleasingly in the reading. Another was a brunette Vineyarder who knew about all the lightships from Newport to Nantucket Shoals, a lass whose father had been a light-keeper. But several acute attacks of the flounder-frights forced me to "starn-all" in a whaling manner when I should have been forward in a courting manner. Perhaps the fair young ladies got a lucky break.

It may seem silly for an ex-dragger captain, who realizes the dignity a skipper should uphold, to speak lightly of such sacred affairs as birth, marriage, death. But some silliness on a hard-fishing dragger is one of the best safety valves I know, and only too true on a tripper away from home-port. Roaming dragger-men are not always the hell-devils they have been cracked up to be. In following migrating schools along the coast, holing up in handy harbors of refuge, most draggermen practice living by the Golden Rule as much as anyone.

What parties the boys used to have in various fo-castles, at harbors from Point Judith to Nantucket, poker playing, musical jam sessions, fishermen banquets, and with such reading matter around as *Vineyard Gazette, Nantucket Inquirer, Providence Journal, Atlantic Fisherman, Fishing Gazette* and *Maine Coast Fisherman* and what have you including *Snappy Stories*, but without much snap compared with today's snap.

Occasionally liquor or a girl friend might come on board. Why not? Why dive into it too deeply. They go into shore homes and on yachts each day. I recall one dry but girlish example. We had been fogbound at a harbor on Cape Cod, and my craft was hostess to two visiting Cape girls. One tore her dress on a protruding nail, and with trembling fingers I got out my old Sailor's Bethel sewing basket and started to sew up the rip in the dress.

"Oh, what will mother think?" she moaned.

The other girl laughed. "She'll think that you fell overboard and a shark got you."

Nervously I sewed away, using a life-or-death stitch taught me by John Bailey, the New London sailmaker. Although I considered myself as a good "twine-man" with wooden seine needles, I was rather fumbly with needles and thread close alongside a ripped and billowing dress, especially as the girl shimmied about nervously.

"Hold still," I muttered, "before I iron you with this sail needle."

"Ouch!" hollered the girl as a near-miss jolted her to a standstill from drifting about.

Finally I finished and in a sleight-of-hand manner I eased a five dollar bill into a tiny pocket on the dress intended to pay for wear and tear. No one seemed to notice my act and I felt good about it. Later I realized some of the implications connected with my gift and hustled those two visiting beachcombing females ashore with more speed than when they came aboard. I wanted no further complications. The mending of torn dresses was completely out of my line, charming though the work might be in comparison to the mending of ripped trawl nets.

To play it safe I crossed that harbor off our port-of-call schedule for summer and fall fishing. It so happened, however, that I ran into the girl at Woods Hole, as she came up the dock from the New Bedford to Nantucket steamer.

Finally after a minute of chit-chat I exploded: "Well, what happened, you know."

"Oh, about the dress, and that awful sewing you did on it?

"Gee, Cap. Nothing happened. I threw the dress away before going home. My girl friend gave me a much better one. My dress only came from the dollar store, so don't looked so worried. Bye. I must catch my bus for Falmouth."

"So long, happy sailing, and fishing," I said.

And mentally I said so long to a five dollar bill. Well, an extra drag in the Sound would square the account. "Extra drags" have a habit of squaring many an account in the away-from-home lives of the draggermen.

Our Thompson way of life was partially exposed in *Draggerman's Haul*, now out of print, but my book didn't tell all by a long shot and letters since ask questions which encouraged me to overhaul my fishy affairs as if I were an old ship with some ship-worms in the keel that must come out to the light of day.

I have had letters from and been the guest of such nice people as the famous radio Fitzgeralds, Ed and Pegeen, Henry Fonda and Daniel Merriman. A.B.C. Whipple, Bianca Bradbury and many others whose interests point to our Atlantic coast wrote to me. One "Islander" in particular, Henry Beetle Hough, editor of the *Vineyard Gazette* on Martha's Vineyard, has encouraged me to write further about our life along our coast, "at whatever cost."

At the dock many others have asked questions about our draggerman's way of life, not exactly as I've lived it, but as a serious day-by-day business.

Some are more specific. "What happened to the Yale gang of oceanographers that you once took out, and were you awed by their educational importance?" No, whenever these doctors of this and that went out on my *Eleanor*, all fancy titles with big letters were left parked on the docklog and all unnecessary rigging back in New Haven. Even when this Yankee skipper visited there by invitation, the professors never threw their importance around where I might run into it. Yet, while holed up at Dan Merriman's Master's House at Davenport College, a gang of students mistook me for a visiting professor of physics from Princeton. "Hell no," I told them, "I'm about as regular as you fellows."

By and large the Yale gang I took out on fishery research trips during the 1940s topped all others, or nearly all, in influencing future courses of my life.

The Yale oceanographers, who ventured seaward with me were all-around good fellows, who furthered their knowledge of our coastal fishery resources without neglecting the craving of their sea inspired bellies. But with red meat points as scarce as teeth in a winter flounder, who can blame them for doing research around the *Eleanor's* grub cupboard. To be truthful, I participated in each and every muggup on board my boat. Some were worth remembering, like the sun-up breakfast that featured boiled short lobsters and short steaks, and with no complaints from the professors about the absence of corn flakes and milk.

One could yarn right through an entire spell of foggy weather about the seagoing gangs from Yale and other Universities.

Well, it's all in the past now, this taking out the college educated fishery experts. And I sort of miss the days when, in company with aquatic biologists and graduate fishery students, I tried hobbying a bit as an amateur oceanographer, in a somewhat futile series of attempts to fathom out underwater mysteries that seemed capable of flooring old Davy Jones himself. For at the Hell Hole I learned that our black-back winter-flounder was a *Pseudopleurenectes americanus*, and that *Myexecphalus octodecimespincsus* was a fancy name for our miserable two-horned sculpin, a trash fish which often ends up as animal food.

True, Latin names may be important to fish scientist in general, but I have never been convinced that the pen is mightier than the oar. Yet after asking a Yale professor if he had ever tried to paddle a dory with a pen, he told me that he had paddled a row boat with a loose book of Latin, and that it had called for all hands on deck to drop anchor and begin splicing the main brace.

And I feel quite sure that Dan Merriman, Jim Morrow, Bill Thompson, Olie Olsen, Herb Warfel, Gorden Riley, and Sally Wheatland, the lady professor, will understand my fogbound point of view. One thing sure, more power to them all.

I've had letters asking about my young nephews, Morris Thompson, Jr., and Byron Lawry. My brother Morris made his wife Frieda a widow early in life. Infant Morris was ten months old. After his fifteenth birthday, keeping alive our family tradition, he went fishing with me on the *Eleanor*. Then came the navy; then the Air Corps; marriage to Lucy, and now there's a Morris Earl Thompson, III, with a calm Atlantic look on his baby face.

My nephew Byron Lawry is now running the 55-foot Dragger *Weezie May*, named for my sister Louise, following the wake of his departed dad, Harold B. Lawry, a pioneer Draggerman. Byron seems to love the sea as well as the next fellow. Good fishing to him!

Along the waterfront the question often arises: What qualities must a boy have to become a Draggerman?

It would seem that to be a Draggerman a fellow must have the eyes of a cat, the strength of a horse, the guts of a camel, the patience of Job, and the willingness to shun shore women in favor of school fish. This is a starter. He should be able to run motors, mend nets, steer by compass, splice wire and rope, cook grub, keep a boat shipshape, lend a hand where needed, and shoot the breeze with the best of them. Drinking the guy off the next boat under the table hasn't much to do with it. In a pinch it should bring no dishonor to one's vessel to be able to carry some liquid ballast.

Each all-season-of-the-year draggerman is a hero in his own hard-earned right. The real draggermen heros have given their lives to the sea. My father and my brother are among them.

High tide or low, I consider it a privilege to be known as a Dragger Captain from Stonington, who has recently developed the peculiar habit of painting pictures of boats instead of fishing them. Along the shore it isn't easy to face away from offshore depth curves, out where the *Eleanor* and I have tossed about in boat-to-boat company with draggermen of Portuguese ancestry who had helped to make Stonington the deep-sea fishing capital of Connecticut.

Years ago I discovered that one man's field can be just as attractive as the next fellow's—afloat or ashore; that loot from the sea and gifts from the valleys are closely related. Yet this isn't the time of tide to examine their relationship, for it's about time to sort of "swallow the anchor," as old timers might say over at Mystic's Old Seaport.

Yet other comparisons still haunt me. Eight years ago I ended my first book by comparing certain characteristics of a beautiful woman friend against the graceful line of my faithful old dragger... and without my boat getting the worst of it. As a young girl the lady in question had stolen a piece of my heart; but my dream boat had soon replaced it.

Sound is vitally important to a Draggerman, or to any mariner, whether it comes from the wind in the rigging, the throb of an engine, the toot of a whistle. Even today I seem to hear the fog-shattering music from my father's old battered trombone, and to hear his long-winded hail that dry-land dangers far outnumbered perils of the sea. And I recall the day he asked me if I preferred slaving on land and leaping from a burning building, or fishing for a living on salt water and jumping from a sinking ship. Naturally I fathomed it out that swimming away from a sinking ship was preferable to crawling away from a burning building. And so for many years I have shunned land areas to haul nets from rivers, bays, sounds, and ocean, trying to keep afloat at all costs.

But now the overall picture of dragging for a living has changed, and though the sky seems clear far overhead, there is fog closing in, over sea and valley, perhaps as nature intended.

Probably each dragger port from Maine to Texas has had one man who fathered the birth of its dragger fleet—others who have nursed its growth. I know little about them. Yet I do have the Custom House records of all documented fishing vessels between New London and Stonington since 1912—a matter for some future tide.

But at this point if I were asked to name some men responsible for Stonington's modest spot on the Atlantic coast fishing map, I might include the following.

Captain Elisha Clark, Stonington's first Draggerman.

Mr. Charles Keller, the 1920 scallop king, a booster.

Mr. Nat Avery, who came to town, bought out Keller dock interests and fathered Stonington's first large dragger fleet.

Mr. John Bindloss, from a sea-inclined family, who became a guiding light during dark days of hurricane and war.

Old Captain George Wilcox, the trawl-net king of Quiambaug, who was a prince of credit during the lean thirties.

Henry R. Palmer, Jr., the Stonington boatbuilder, whose many draggers roam coastal waters.

E.P. York, Jr., our radio-weather man, whose electronic field has modernized the Stonington fleet—in port and out.

Captain Jacobs, the old ship-chandler, who has furnished badly needed wartime supplies and peace-time advice.

Blanche Bessette Stillman, a financial-bookkeeping guiding light from Bindloss's "boating office," who well earned her "navy citation" for coastal defense affairs.

And of course, there was Captain John Smith, the first President of The Southern New England's Fishermen's Association.

Perhaps no list would be complete without good mention of smiling Tony Longo, who, before becoming a fish-dock operator at Stonington, trucked thousands of barrels of fish from Stonington to New York City. Another is John George, who later built the 61-foot dragger *Mildred and Myra*, now run by old seadog Frank Sinnett.

There are of course the home-keeping families of fishermen who keep track of their away-from-home men folk by listening in with shortwave receiver sets to pick up the dragger news and gossip.

And finally there are families such as Roderick, Maderia, Henry, and others, which have given the grasping Atlantic of their young fishermen.

This photo of Cap'n Ellery Thompson and a
crewman appeared in *Life* magazine.

Publisher's Afterword

By Stephen Jones

Headstone of Ellery F. Thompson (1899-1986),
with the inscription "Imagine the excitement on
the other shore."

I. The Hill by the River

Autobiographies are frequently unreliable documents, a fact that biographers enjoy because they like discovering independent information which shows that autobiographers have been sculpting their lives into shapes more agreeable than the truth...

—A. C. Grayling
Descartes: The Life and Times of a Genius

[he] looked sideways up!

—Samuel Taylor Coleridge
"The Rime of the Ancient Mariner"

If you write anything derogatory about a local, everyone will condemn you for betraying a boyo to the Outside. If you talk him up, they'll all be laughing at you behind your back for having the wool pulled over your eyes.

—Edna O'Brien
Mind You Now I've Said Nothing (paraphrase)

The raw April wind blew in off the Mystic River and the hill came as a surprise. The funeral director herded some of us in behind his professionals and we all shouldered the old fisherman in the box to the end of his last voyage. Captain Ellery F. Thompson seemed to have outlived most of his immediate family. Those of us who had managed to follow the body from the funeral home to the grave formed a strange community.

Although the background roar sounded like surf, the fact was that the noise was the trucks running to the city on the nearby interstate. The days when Ellery and his cohorts carried their cargo directly to the Fulton Market by boat were over. It had been those trips to New York, incidentally, that had given the provincial fisherman his idea of fame. It had been a Manhattan writer, seeking out what fed the city, that had made that fame come true.

None of us were official pallbearers. The funeral director worked us in, much as a locomotive or two might be at the last minute pressed into service on a Western freight run. The hoarse cry of the bascule bridge ricocheted around the valley. Some of us lifted our eyes downstream to see the old bridge groaning skyward. We couldn't see from there the nature of the passing vessel, or if indeed there was any boat at all. That early in the season the bridge might have been merely checking its articulation to see if it could function for yet another year. It struck me that decrepit and quaint as the bridge was, the man we were burying had been a robust twenty-three when it was built.

There we were cheek by sweating jowl in closer proximity to each other than we'd ever been. It was not that there was that much left of Ellery himself. Never a heavy man, by his own account he had been *up* to 122 pounds in the nursing home. As is the fashion, the weight was mostly in the furniture. I was looking through the backside of the spectacles of Bernie Gordon, the professor, bookseller from Watch Hill, Rhode Island, who had faithfully kept Ellery's work alive. My shoulder was crushed by the bicep of a burly fellow who ran what he called a "curiosity shop" on New London's notorious sailor-besotted Bank Street. The Curiosity Shop was indeed a Dickensian emporium. In the window a hard-hat diving dress danced with Samurai swords, euphoniums, guitars, sea shells and Japanese knee mortars. Down in the right hand corner of the window, however, was the documentation of the proprietor's claim to fame: a photograph of him grinning midst a harem of hundreds of six inch fish. Across the picture was written: WORLD'S RECORD CATCH OF SMELT. None of these items, of course, were for sale. What kept the business alive were the stacks in the back. Here were mainly World War II foul weather gear which he sold to the local private college girls that the curse of their privilege might be eased by donning the accoutrements of the proletariat. Having the proprietor of such a shop now as a kind of shipmate in this grim task at the cemetery seemed weirdly appropriate. Ellery's life had been a kind of seaport curiosity shop. Certainly, as we neared the crest of the hill, I was grateful for the literal muscle power of the world's smelt record holder.

The roar of the interstate drowned out the minister's words... Something about "colorful, yet courageous..." The minister was an ex-Vietnam Swift boat captain who'd recently come under a different sort of fire by promulgating his criticism of the war. In his more audible eulogy for Ellery at the funeral home he had begun by admitting he had "never personally known the deceased." He had nevertheless, been honored in the past three days to have heard some, "Well ... *stories* and been invited to ah... *share*..." And here, sensing he was at a Yankee funeral about to topple into a Californian cadenza, he halted to shoot a glance at the coffin. The deceased seemed to be winking out from under a brand new yachting cap. "I've been privileged to share... some of the, well, *artifacts*... associated with Ellery's life." From behind the raised coffin lid, like a magician, the minister plucked a painting that had undoubtedly been executed by Ellery. That is, the paint had been applied to the board by him, but the concept was a knock off of one of Charles Robert Patterson's square-riggers running down the monsoon of the China Seas, an image that Ellery had obviously lifted from a 1940s Columbia Rope Company Calendar. "There's more on the back," suggested the Reverend and then, apparently reading for the first time what was actually there, wrinkled his eyebrows and quickly stuffed the painting behind the coffin. This left us with the deceased grinning out from his yachting cap. I was sharing the discomfort of all this until someone behind me laughed and then so did someone in front and soon we all relaxed a bit.

"I believe," said the minister grinning, "we have just experienced a typical 'Ellery Moment.'"

At the top of the hill we gratefully set down the coffin. Nearby stood a weather-pocked blue stone in the shape of a seaman's chest. On the arched lid was embossed a fouled fisherman's anchor and on the beveled side was engraved the name of Ellery's beloved younger brother:

MORRIS E. THOMPSON AUG 6, 1905 DEC. 10, 1930

On a vertical base of gray stone was chiseled:

ON THAT BRIGHT IMMORTAL SHORE
WE SHALL MEET TO PART NO MORE.

The wind continued to blow in off the river. By now maybe a dozen more people had struggled up to the hole. I knew none of them and moreover they did not seem to know each other. And yet, if one did not count the great 19th century bluewater mariners like Captain John E. "Kicking Jack" Williams and Captain Joseph Warren Holmes, who'd rounded Cape Horn 83 times without losing a man—men for whom local streets were named—Ellery had been our most famous man, or at least had been so in the mid 20th century.

Ellery's own stone eventually contained his name and dates (1899-1986) and the words "IMAGINE THE EXCITEMENT ON THE OTHER SHORE." On the lower left of the stone was engraved a fine likeness of his famous boat *Eleanor*, complete with name board, skylight, wheelhouse, ratlines, portholes, mast, boom and all standing and running rigging. Eleanor herself, whose daughter, Nancy Heckland, paid for Ellery's stone, did not join the subterranean assemblage until 16 years later, under her married name of Roath, her stone adorned with two hearts and a simple cross. On the wall in the back parlor of the funeral home where Ellery was sent off, now hangs one of his big oils, gaudily framed like an old master. It shows an *Eleanor*-type dragger heading west, well outboard of Latimer Reef Light in the days when it yet sported its iron canopy above the gallery. Behind the lighthouse, the ocean opens out beyond the Wicopesset Rocks. There are no Coca-Cola calendar mermaids in sight.

Captain Thompson plays his trumpet beneath one of his clipper ship paintings. With him are Barbara, Nancy and Diana, daughters of his sister Eleanor, for whom his boat was named.

II. Mystic in the Early Days of Ellery's Fame

Good navigation consisted of knowing yourself.

—*Draggerman's Haul*, I.

Mystic is yet a small town but back in the 1950s when I first knew Ellery and he was still famous, it was smaller in a different way. Then there was a bigger divide between the summer people and the natives, and just how you took Ellery was largely a matter of whether you were one or the other.

What had originally set off all the fuss had been Joseph Mitchell's two-part profile of Ellery which had appeared in *The New Yorker* January 4ᵗʰ and 11ᵗʰ of 1947. Mitchell's story got legs when collected three years later with Mitchell's other urban waterfront pieces in the Little Brown edition of *The Bottom of the Harbor*. Ellery's story appealed to the whole spectrum. New York's *Daily News*, the daily journal of the Big Apple's strap-hanger culture, visited Ellery in his Mystic lair to snap him in a plaid shirt at home. The photo shoot was dressed with his oil paintings, a female crew member and his trumpet. A 1947 issue of *Liberty* magazine (10 cents) with General George Marshall and Stalin as the Sphinx on the cover, carried a dozen pictures captioned: "Dragger-Artist: Self-taught trawler captain, marine artist, and trumpet player teaches oceanography to college professors." There is a photo of Ellery and Dr. Merriman from Yale shin deep in flounder; another of Ellery supine beneath one of his huge square-rigger portraits tooting a trumpet on a sofa whose upholstery matches the wallpaper. Ellery's fame spread even wider when half a dozen years later *Life* featured him in one of its icon-making "photo essays." This was the same venue in which Americans were first introduced to the handsome young ex-PT boat skipper from Hyannis and his fiancée Jackie Bouvier posing on a small sloop.

Summer people, who set great store by these publications now knew that in Captain Thompson we had a celebrity among us and tended to regard him as a treasure. They were able to buy into this celebrity by purchasing for $10 to $50 his sea paintings. (Professor Gordon records an Ellery painting sale in that period of $400). More often Ellery merely bartered the work for meals, art supplies, goodwill... whatever. Even to this day it is hard to get through downtown Mystic without seeing an Ellery Thompson on the back wall of somebody's office. Ellery did his earliest paintings on stretched canvass, but by the time he burst into fame, he found it more expedient to employ thick brush strokes on Masonite, a new building product that had come to replace beaverboard as cheap dry wall after World War II. Grandma Moses was just coming into national favor at the time and many of us assumed that Ellery was our own local primitive. (One of

Ellery's long-running jokes soon became his reputation as "a *primitive*," the sexual connotations of which, as his body began a dramatic decline, he seemed pleased to claim.)

In the journalism of this time, we read that our man not only fished and painted but played the trumpet. Most accounts specified that this instrument was "a Bb trumpet," as if somehow this was an unusual tuning, which it is, of course, not. Eventually in Ellery's obituary the local newspaper changed the key to Eb! The whole pseudo-precise detailing of the key in which Ellery's trumpet was pitched is perhaps symptomatic of the peculiar blend of the exotic and banal in which even the best of the reporting on Ellery always seemed to indulge.

And then, of course, we were informed that he himself "wrote." In Ellery's obituary April 25, 1986, James McKenna, the Joseph Mitchell of Mystic, said, "When Joe Mitchell wrote those stories it changed [Ellery's] life. He had figured he had a character to live up to. He was living on hope after that. He became less of a fisherman, and more of a media figure... He fell on hard times, and caught less fish. He decided he was going to be a writer, because he was more interested in writing than fishing."

The book which Ellery "wrote" was called *Draggerman's Haul: The Personal History of a Connecticut Fisherman.* and came out in 1950 under the aegis of no less a New York house than the Viking Press, known then especially for being the publishers of John Steinbeck. In this book Ellery asserted that in sketching out Eleanor for the builder he had in effect designed the prototypical commercial dragger that dominated the region in mid-century. It was of this era that town historian Carol Kimball wistfully looked back upon when she wrote in the 1990s upon the occasion of a paperback reprint of Mitchell's book: "It's amazing how our world has changed since these pieces [on Ellery] were published."

Even at the height of Ellery's fame, the locals were, of course, quick to adjust the story. They'd point out that Thompson basically painted only one picture over and over, that of *Eleanor* shoving aside a thick impasto of blue green. Or maybe two *Eleanors* tilted in opposite angles centered about a local buoy. The dragger design Ellery claimed, some locals maintained, had pretty much evolved from Noank fisherman Lenny Allen. Ellery's claim was substantiated only because the image the public saw over and over was the Eleanor as painted by Ellery. As for the "personal history" promised in the book's subtitle, these folks also informed you that they had *known* Ellery's father, Captain Frank E. Thompson (1873-1936) in the old days. They also *knew* Ellery, and this wreck of a man who now shuffled the streets blighted by rheumatism and God knew what other sailor's maladies, was but the sins of that father visited.

Local wits added that like the master and his dog in the old joke, Ellery had become the human counterpart of his boat. This much was indisputable: the famous *Eleanor* was presently on view at Pistol Point just upriver from the New York-Boston railroad line: a hulk, half full of mud and brackish water. Her bilge was, in that cruelly ironic term of art—*in free communication* with the sea... As for the trumpet playing, to local ears the sounds emerging from the battered bell of Ellery's instrument barely qualified as a proper bridge opener. In short, like Margaret Mead with the Samoans, Ellery's big city writer had been largely taken in by his wily subject who had conspired with some resident leg-pullers. Moreover, the gossip was that Ellery's own "writing" had been highly edited in New York, if not ghost written entirely by a New York man.

It wasn't until Ellery was long gone and his fame had more or less appeared to have subsided that I myself came to appreciate his lasting power. One morning I was ushered into in the New London County prosecutor's office where it was my dubious pleasure to be accompanying a youthful relative who had been arrested for what we hoped would be seen as a bit of minor vehicular mischief. The august man himself was seated behind his desk, flanked by the flag of our nation and that of our state. Between them, on the wall above his head, in the spot where one would expect a painting of the state capitol or at least a judge or two, was the largest version I had ever seen of the Ellery *Eleanor*. There she was—pushing through that thick blue-green impasto—coming to our rescue as sure as if she were a U.S. Coast Guard vessel. In no time we had established with the prosecutor a relationship through our mutual admiration of Ellery that resulted in his knocking down the charges. If it weren't for the court clerk's insistence on the business of the day, I think we'd yet be sitting there stoking each other with Ellery's reflected glory.

III. Encountering Ellery

Pop told me that one of the secrets of shore-line fog navigation
was to listen like the devil for the echo of every blast.
—*Draggerman's Haul*, I.

Ellery and I had an odd sort of relationship. (This assumes that Ellery had other relationships that could not be so characterized.) Like him, I was a fisherman and a writer who played bridge opening trumpet. To my mother, a painter who read *The New Yorker*, Ellery seemed to be my only viable role model in town. My father, an excellent trumpet player, and I worked in the boatyard directly across the narrow river from the forlorn *Eleanor* and so daily had warning of the dismal end to which such a career trajectory would inevitably seem to come.

At first I could not believe that this was the boat whose portrait was about the town in so many places, and whose story had been celebrated in the Viking Press book and *The New Yorker*. This sad hulk just had to be a different *Eleanor*. What had happened to her? Why had nobody saved her? After all, here we were in Mystic where a mile upstream at the museum all kinds of less famous craft were not only being restored, but downright coddled.

So here indeed she was at Pistol Point, then the southernmost end of the sprawling Franklin G. Post & Son yard. The Posts had built a wide variety of excellent wooden boats, including the rum-runner *Whispering Wind*. Just what kind of a deal they had made with Ellery was unclear. My colleagues across the river said that Ellery had just walked away from her. The spot where *Eleanor* was more or less beached was the end of the developed part of the property, so I suppose, wasn't costing the Posts any rental space. (Since then, new yard owners broke up what remained of *Eleanor* to expand the yard so that the location of her final coherency is now almost in the middle of the commercialized waterfront.)

I've often thought how painful it must have been for Ellery to have her lying derelict like that right in the middle of the town in which he continued to live, but I never heard him speak of the situation. His answer was to just keep painting her portrait in her days of glory.

After a while *Eleanor* more or less faded into the mud and I thought no more about her, or at least so I would have said. One foggy Sunday morning at high tide, however, before our customers arrived at the boatyard, I found myself sculling the yard skiff across the river. I let her float in over the broken back of the old dragger and glided up to her winch head. This was the device by which Ellery and his crew had gained some mechanical advantage to haul back the otter trawl net and then hoist it high over the deck before letting go the purse strings at the cod end which would dump the bounty of the sea into a marketable posture. Now only a few mallards complained and swam off into the mist. I found myself staring into the wheelhouse whose door was missing. Below was the forecastle in which whatever intimate moments Ellery had managed had taken place. I didn't expect much and yet alone on the Sunday morning with the church bells tumbling through the fog, I was, for an instant—on the verge of the archeological moment.

I peered through the doorway to the dank interior. What had I expected? The jolly gang from *Draggerman's Haul*, I suppose, or at least some "personal history."

There was nothing to see but dark water, nothing to salvage. Before I knew it I had allowed the skiff to drift aft on a curl of back eddy. Hard by the winch, however, there was yet the steering wheel, one of the standard Wilcox & Crittenden galvanized models such as I had on my own little dragger. All of the wooden grips were missing and the iron spokes themselves were twisted, some of them almost it seemed in wicked parody of the rheumatism-wracked spine of the old captain. I rowed back to the yard, grabbed a hacksaw off the bench and returned to cut the helm from the shaft. Sawing through the shaft took surprisingly little time and there I held what seemed, battered as it was, the very soul of the ship in my hands.

"What the hell do you want with that filthy old thing?" asked my yard mates.

They had a point. Here was certainly no mahogany helm to hang over one's bar or mantle piece. Obviously even Ellery himself had chosen to abandon it along with the rest of the vessel. I hosed off the river mud, banged loose some rust or whatever it was. It was no use. Ellery's last artifact could not be made pretty. It seemed the only fit place for the helm was in my cellar, down there in the dark seepage of the broken cistern among other unspeakables. A few years later a neighbor was building a replica of another famous Mystic River boat, Joshua Slocum's Noank oyster sloop *Spray*. Somehow he knew that I had *Eleanor's* helm and asked if he could add it to the collection of odd, old famous bits by which he was outfitting his new vessel. I was almost too ashamed to show him this piece of junk, but he forgave Ellery and me, and swapped it for a steering wheel he'd obtained from a local shipyard that had made rum-runners. We had a friend who had been a lathe operator in World War II and he straightened the spokes and turned out beautiful new wooden grips.

"There," said the boatbuilder. "We have taken the curse of Ellery Thompson off the hardware and yet maintained the spirit of the old *Eleanor*." There was something to what he said. In its new life the helm steered the Slocum replica around the world and now some forty years later, under new management, is still guiding her replica down the waterways of France.

Eventually I met Ellery himself face to face. With Frank, a teenage stern man, I'd been lobstering in my own, smaller version of *Eleanor*. We'd spent a rough morning off the reefs and I hadn't had the leisure to check Frank's measurement of our catch. We'd simply thrown some sopping kelp over the top of the basket, set it in the back of the pickup and driven to market. Grossman's, then as now, is a delightfully funky fish shack out of the 1930s hard by the Mystic-Noank Road. On the front window, there had been a long tradition to cut the English language some slack in soaping up the daily specials on the plate glass—thus *Sord Fish* and *Blu Fish*. Admeasurement, however, was another thing and the proprietor tolerated no sloppiness in the state gauge. As a result he'd rejected about half our lobsters. Frank and I were slinking our way through the back door when out of nowhere appeared Ellery.

Here was a rather a scary looking guy, bent by the years so that like Coleridge's infamous mariner, he had a way of looking at you "sideways up." As with Coleridge's man, his eye was "glittering," hard as the eyes of the alewife that would fall out of the heads of bait fish on winter mornings and bounce about the cockpit like marbles. While in the old pictures you see Ellery with the soft fedora, this day on the back of his head lurked a filthy cap of the sort then favored by men with a flybridge, twin screw sports fisherman, men who presumably on some level were imitating old salts like Ellery. To his legs clung dragger boots half rolled down rendering the effect of an old spraddled doxy in scandalized nylons. A set of suspenders more or less served as halyards to a pair of stained pants three sizes too big.

Through the years since I've thought a lot about exactly how Ellery had known to be there at just that moment. Had he just happened to be passing and spotted us? Had we looked that inept? Or like the sly old fisherman checking his trotline, did he always hang out back there in the morning, knowing damn well that the fishmonger would reject a certain percentage? Later I learned that he himself had not only caught lobsters as a bycatch in his otter trawl, but like many an offshore draggerman actually began his commercial career as an in-shore lobsterman.

In any case, he made no bones about *why* he was there, seeming to conjure up an infinite reservoir of insight into the hearts of those committing littoral crime. It was an aura he enhanced by invoking the name of one Bill McCoy, the notorious rum-runner of thirty years before. (It was the fumes of McCoy's fame Ellery would now have us believe yet flickered blessings sufficient to cover all subsequent occasions of questionable maritime morality.) The logic seemed to be that since Ellery had run rum for "The Real McCoy" he could obtain short lobsters from Frank and me.

Frank, however, was a teenager; the 1920s and Bill McCoy meant nothing to him. He wrinkled up his nose and exposed teeth and I knew he was about to bolt. Ellery could see that the precise connection with McCoy would have to wait for another day. He tried a different tack. He had, he informed us, worked with men of science—from Yale, no less—and that at the moment he wanted our illegal catch for said "science."

"*Yale!*" Frank had grown up as a townie down at that end of Long Island Sound.

It was true that Ellery, had enjoyed that brief career chauffeuring marine biologists aboard *Eleanor*. With the availability of proper research vessels, however, he had now found himself more or less put out to pasture at the Mystic Seaport Museum. There he functioned as what more sedately might be termed a "docent." One thinks of those infinitesimally fragile elderly women who are called upon to stand between the momentary unruly mobs and the scrimshaw and the harpoons of eternity. I believe Ellery's official title was "interpreter." What he interpreted was the fishing industry and his principal prop was a brand new version of Grossman's. The shack had been made to look authentic with some ancillary barrels and the obligatory tatters of trawl net. Inside lurked a tank sipping from the Mystic River. Ellery's mission was to now and again plop in a fresh "scientific" lobsters and then stand back in his yachting cap and justify their creepiness to tourists.

"It's all right, boys," he now whispered. "It's all FOR SCIENCE." His skinny hand reached for the handle on our basket.

I've often wondered what made Frank move so fast with that basket. Perhaps it was all those Grimm's Fairy tales he'd overheard me reading to my sons. In any case, he was taking no chances of being himself scooped up in some old man's scam at the market. All I could do was shrug and trot off after him to the pickup.

From behind me I heard the crusty old pipes: *"Well, I see that some boys just isn't ready yet for 'SCIENCE.'"*

My later encounters with Ellery were more dignified and even somewhat literary. By then I'd actually read Ellery's two books, *Draggerman's Haul* (1950) published by Viking Press and *Come Aboard the Draggers* published (1958) by the Stonington Publishing Company. In the library of the Noank Marine Lab across the street from where I lived, I'd come across a copy of Joseph Mitchell's *The Bottom of the Harbor*, the collection of *The New Yorker* pieces in which Mitchell's two-part profile of Ellery had appeared.

Thinking back to our adventure at the fish shop, I was especially interested in Ellery's written encounter with the rum-runner McCoy. In checking out the Ellery oeuvre, however, I noticed that his two versions of his meeting with the great 1920s icon did not quite jibe. In the Viking Press book one gathers that while Ellery is a bit star struck and wet behind the ears, he at least holds up his side of the illegal pact. In the subsequent 1958 take, however, he seems to have something to get off his chest.

In this version, Ellery begins by rendering pretty much the same account of meeting McCoy in the New London "sporting club" and "ferrying" the great man out to Montauk where they hunker down during a three day fog before motoring on to the schooner on Rum Row. The picturesque over-the-rail scene is also pretty much the same, Ellery merely substituting Jack London for the Nero Wolfe allusion of *Draggerman's Haul*. In both accounts there are some minor discrepancies with what we know about the rum running schooner from McCoy. Ellery insists that McCoy's schooner was "black," whereas McCoy tells us (and photos bear this out) that he had painted *Arethusa* "a dazzling white" so contact boats (painted black) could find her out beyond the limit. (McCoy also ran a number of schooners less famous.) In *Draggerman's Haul*, Ellery carefully avoids identifying the schooner as actually *Arethusa*, saying merely that McCoy had talked "lovingly" of her. (In any case McCoy had by 1921 changed her name to *Tomoka*.) In *Come Aboard*, Ellery no longer is so careful. He insists his experience was with what by then has become widely known as an American icon, the *Arethusa*. Also, largely the same is the charming comic idyll where Ellery and his mate loaf and invite the enlarged sense of their selves on McCoy's cigars, cartridges and champagne while waiting for dark to make their run home. The real discrepancy, however, is in Ellery's own accounts of what happens after they make shore in New London and most notably in the consequences weeks later.

In *Draggerman's Haul*, Ellery merely cuts off the McCoy adventure at the end of chapter eight:

> ... and daylight came. Our decks were clear; worries were over. On reaching
> home I received a welcome befitting a man home from the sea, from the wars,

or from the grave. The rumor that my boat and I had been lost preceded me. I firmly resolved, 'never again'—not for love or money. No, not even for a friend.

Apparently it was nowhere near that simple. In *Come Aboard*, Ellery continues the narrative of the night coming back to New London in greater detail and then adds:

> But, weeks later complications developed rapidly. My mate and I were called into the [New London] Custom House and questioned. After my mate had told his tale in a side room, and a fairly truthful one, I was hauled on the carpet and ordered to confess what I knew about running off to the *Arethusa* and what I had seen out there.

Ellery names the Custom House man who during the inquiry informs him that they already have had his father in for questioning, but had got nothing out of him adding, "You have a darn faithful father." But there are men from "Washington" who ask Ellery point blank if he has "run rum." When Ellery equivocates, one of the Washington men suggests they seize Ellery's boat.

Ellery blurts out, "Yes Sir. I've brought in rum!"

It seems only fair to quote Ellery's next moves verbatim:

> The following hour was rough for my mate and myself. First the law boys got his story, and then they pried my version from me. Somehow our yarns jibed and without much gut spilling on my part, although I confessed to seeing the fishing boat *Lap* astern of the *Arethusa*. I was asked about the men who backed my venture at rum running. How much money I got running in a load, what I knew about rum runners.
>
> I knew little or nothing about the other fellow, of whether his boat was loaded with rum or fish. I only knew that my boat had been loaded with whisky for sporting men who paid me hardly anything for running their booze.

Ellery reports he then told the Washington men, "I did it as a favor for friends."

> 'Friends!!' snorted a Washington man. 'Your friends were steering you toward jail, and we have an idea who they are.' The Washington man mentioned a name. 'How does that sound. Make sense?'
>
> 'Yes Sir,' I replied.
>
> There was a lot more but eventually the government men accepted our story as reasonably authentic, and began looking upon us more as fishermen than smugglers. Meanwhile I felt about as small as a herring and as flat as a flounder, and with the realization that we were to get off easy, that is, after promising on my word of honor that I would never run in rum. A promise I was to keep. I mean from rum row.

The boat Ellery sold out, which in this account he calls, "*Lap*," however, was confiscated, to be returned a month later after forfeiting a $ 2,500 bond. (About a year's wages.) In his unpublished manuscript *Draggerman's Loot or Bachelor Dragger Captain*, Ellery tips his hand on the contact boat's identity. "Two Long Island fisherman friends of mine, in their Noank built 40 footer—I'll call her the *Lap* (don't spell it backwards)— and they began a career of rum running." Malcolm Willoughby in the official U.S. Coast Guard history of the era, *Rum War at Sea*, has a *Pal*, seized by the marine patrol in New London in 1924, but she is a sloop. Nor is this the end of the matter.

> A while later I fell in with the captain of the *Lap* at Fulton Fish Market, and the first thing he wanted to do was to punch me in the jaw. [Later Ellery notes: 'It just didn't pay to know too much, for men that knew too much might find them- selves on the bottom of the sea with their feet planted in cement.'] After I accused him of stepping out with a girlfriend of mine, he relented, got quite friendly and invited me out to dinner.

The two then ride "the shoot-the-shoots at Coney Island" four times. Ellery would have us believe that this was a simple reunion of old friends. One thinks, however, of the nerve-wracking scene with Harry Lime and Holly Martin on the Ferris wheel in *The Third Man*, where the issue of who is to survive is left to the final moments when the ride is over.

Ellery goes on for a few pages sketching other aspects of rum running, especially the "bottle fishing." This was a semi-innocent pastime in which he and other draggermen dabbled in the normal act of tending their nets on grounds where contact boats had happened to have jettisoned cargo in a chase. His "boat was to drag up plenty of it, to present us with problems galore."

He ends the chapter thus:

> One day I got a note from Capt. McCoy about the Havana cigars and the Colt revolver left on my boat. Of course, I had smoked up his fine cigars, puffing on them like a millionaire, luckily I still had his gun.

> Dear Captain:
> Will you please leave "the two smoking articles" at Giles Dunn's fish market at Salt Pond Harbor, Block Island. I'd like to pick them up within two weeks. I hope to see you again if only to say thanks and "Keep Fishing."
> Cap'n Bill

While Ellery writes another chapter about "bottle fishing" and finding his "boat lay[ing] alongside craft of questionable nature..." he says nothing about returning McCoy's gun through the handy Giles Dunn's fish market at Salt Pond, nor does he in- dicate that his ratting out of McCoy, or at least one of his contact boats, ever causes him any real hardship.

To substantiate his acquaintance with McCoy in *Come Aboard*, Ellery states: "Years later in a book written by McCoy, mostly from a jail cell, entitled *The Real McCoy*, he mentioned the trip in which a young Connecticut fisherman took him from New Lon- don to his loaded schooner off Long Island, at a thirty-fathom spot previously decided upon by this shipmaster and himself."

First of all, there is no record that McCoy "wrote" any versions of his life "in prison." Frederic Van de Water *wrote* the only McCoy memoir. In 1930-31, several years after McCoy's release, the veteran writer held a series of interviews with the "foghorn" voiced McCoy. In these 305 pages of *The Real McCoy* the closest McCoy comes to substantiating Ellery's claim is the account of being rushed out of New London to Martha's Vineyard at the beginning of chapter four:

> My bed in the New London hotel [probably the Mohican] was still warm when the Treasury agent's men searched the room, but the launch into which [companion] Weatherly and I had jumped was spilling the miles over her stern en route to Gay Head...

Ellery's boat would be, at best a ten-knot dragger, and would hardly match a "launch spilling the miles over her stern en route to Gay Head" a distance nearly twice as far as Montauk Point, most of it in open ocean.

It could be argued, of course, that McCoy, giving his story to print two years before Repeal, was protecting the "young draggerman." Furthermore, there is plenty of documentation in the form of indictments alleging that William F. McCoy "between July 1, 1921 and July 31, 1921... did arrive from a foreign port, to wit, some port in the British West Indies to libelant unknown, at the Port of New York and/or Bridgeport and/or the subports of New Haven and/or New London in the State of Connecticut..."

Since it was McCoy's standard procedure to employ local craft to get out to his schooners on Rum Row, he well might have used on some occasion the "young draggerman" and not bothered to note this particular instance. After all, from the older man's point of view, what had been to the young man the defining moment of a lifetime, would have seemed merely routine. And yet Ellery insists there is all that business of the box of cigars and the pistol and McCoy's note to him arranging for the return of the items. Nor have we yet come across in Ellery's archive what surely must have been his proudest possession, the actual letter from McCoy.

As for McCoy's pistol, the only record we have of Ellery with a sidearm occurs in regard to a shark. On August 12 of 1921 the *Hartford Courant*, under the headline "SEVEN-FOOT SHARK KILLED WITH REVOLVER BY GROTON FISHERMAN/ MONSTER GIVES ELLERY THOMPSON TOUGH TUSSLE OFF BLOCK ISLAND" reported that Ellery "caused his neighbors to rub their eyes... when he reached home on his smack, *Grace and Lucy*, having on board a fine specimen of a sand shark measuring seven feet from nose to tip of fin... Several attempts were made to capture [the shark] with tackle but this was abandoned and Captain Thompson got a revolver..." Considering the timing and the likelihood of Thompson acquiring ordinance from any other source, one could hope that the pistol might well have been McCoy's revolver. The only question is: why in years later did Ellery pass up this marvelous opportunity to once again rub off a little of the King of Rum Row's glory?

Ellery took many cracks at the McCoy tale. His Stonington Historical Society editor put it this way: "In the chest of manuscripts he left, this encounter crops up again and again, like an old Saturday morning movie serial, with the big moment just about to come." Perhaps his happiest resolution of his betrayal of his alpha figure McCoy is in a bit of verse he left behind in which the morally dubious rum running is morphed into the less evil "bottle-fishing," and the father is called a father:

> Our net was slowly raising
>> We'd get a fathom—then a spell
> The wind was up and raging:
>> The tide raced past like hell
> At last we got the boards
>> And hove on the lazy line—
> But even then—Good Lord
>> I'm glad 'twas brand new twine,
> We finally got the wings aboard.
>> Pop was panting and so was I
> We hoisted out the bulging cod end
>> And what a catch—rock on rye
> I looked at Pop, he looked at me
>> Then we culled rock from our gifts from the sea
> I wrote in my log on the first of May
>> Caught today: scotch on the rocks down on the bay

Southeastern Connecticut in the days of Ellery Thompson was pretty much a cultural backwater, but it is a rare moment in *Draggerman's Haul* when Ellery misses a chance to accrue some stardust. New London had had its moments of affluence in the days of the Harknesses and Morton F. Plant. Eugene O'Neill's reactions to some of this heady stuff provided the juice of the productions that won America's only Nobel Prize for drama. But about all that was left in Ellery's day were the brothels of Bank Street and each June the Yale-Harvard rowing race, America's oldest collegiate sporting event.

There was a Frank Merriwell story about the big boat race, but the Yale-Harvard was not so much about muscular young men in skinny boats as the spectator fleet which at its height numbered in the thousands, ranging from two-hundred foot steam schooner-yachts to improvised rafts. Steam trains with observation cars followed the progress of the race on both sides of the Thames River. The Mohican Hotel was jammed as were all the summer boarding houses. Morton F. Plant built the Griswold, a huge hotel for his guests. For Ellery this festival seems to have been largely a matter of dredging up a Yale pennant or an undergarment he variously identified in his works as a "shimmy" or a more stately "corset" and which he would have us believe was the symbolic bycatch of sophisticated reveling on the part of the moneyed class. (The salvaged undergarment would seem a precursor to the more legitimate Eli glory that Ellery acquired after the War when he was chosen to transport on *Eleanor* some of Yale's scientists.)

The Fulton Fish Market on South Street in Manhattan was more substantive than New London as a gateway into the wider world. For most of the 20th Century, fishermen in Southeastern Connecticut knew more first hand about New York, or at least South Street than they did the state capitol in Hartford. The Fulton Fish Market was the distribution point not only for New York City, but the majority of the Atlantic seaboard. In the days when Hart Crane was attempting to invent a new poetic language out of the "wide leeward-ings" of lurching sailors on South Street, a no-less wide-eyed young Ellery from the provinces was at the helm of his dragger chugging up to the same dock.

Ellery gives us, however, very little of this Big City material directly. In reading be-tween the lines and in talking with him through the years, I got the sense that he thought that some of his value to us locals was that he had seen the bright lights and not as a mere tourist, but as part of the big-time buzzing flow of the Great Port. Most of the local commercial fishermen, of course, carried at least a little bit of this aura about. Only Ellery had been officially blessed by the nation's most sophisticated publi-cation as himself worthy of notice as actually part of the pulse of Gotham.

In 1947 and 48 when Joseph Mitchell was publishing his waterfront pieces about Ellery and other colorful denizens of the littoral in *The New Yorker*, Malcolm Johnson was issuing a series of 26 articles in *The New York Sun* that exposed the uncolorful cor-ruption of the port in the hands of such gangster icons as Albert Anastasia, Frank Costello and Lucky Luciano. Johnson received the Pulitzer Prize for his work and the attention of Budd Schulberg and Elia Kazan who put together *On the Waterfront* with Marlon "I Coulda Been a Contendah" Brando, Karl Malden, Lee J. Cobb, Rod Steiger and Eva Marie Saint.

While the images of the Johnson waterfront were mainly of the cargo-hook carrying longshoreman, no less a riparian racket was being run at the Fulton Fish Market by many of the same names. In the 1920s and 30s Ellery was docking there in his prime. Long-time Manhattan reporter Herbert Mitgang writes in *Once Upon a Time in New York*, "To manufacture, sell or move anything in New York during the 1920s and early 1930s, somebody had to be paid off." Mitgang documents how Samuel Seabury, the man who brought New York's Roaring Twenties mayor, Jimmy Walker, to resign, made one of the centerpieces of his investigation [Walker's] D.A.'s failure to stop the shake-downs in the Fulton Fish Market. (More than a half-century later, efforts were still being made to eliminate payoffs to racketeers there.)

At the controls of the Fulton Fish Market was one Joseph A. "Socks" Lanza (1904-68). "Socks," known for his fists more than his sartorial extremities, was ultimately a member of the Genovese crime family. He began his rise in 1923 when he organized Local 359 of the United Seafood Workers union, originally a Lucky Luciano operation with a Joe Ado-nis and Frank Costello connection. The Fulton Fish Market was an enterprise from which Lanza was able to wring profits of $20 million. Even though he had been convicted in 1938 of labor racketeering, Lanza had direct contact with the Office of Naval Intelligence and networking with fishermen, tracked German submarines during the 1940s. He was nevertheless sentenced to from 7-1/2 to 10 years hard time. Released in 1950, he went back to running the Fulton Fish Market scene until he died October 11, 1968. It would seem impossible that Ellery could have missed him, or at least his torpedoes.

Aside from claiming on his death bed that he had helped catch Nazi submarines, however, Ellery seems to have avoided the remotest reference to Lanza and the darker side of the Fulton Fish Market. Even the yarn in *Come Aboard the Draggers* of his en-counter with a rum runner on South Street he treats entirely within the context of Pro-hibition and at that lightly.

It was during the time of Ellery's fame that he put his head down at night in a second floor apartment on the south side of Mystic's Main Street. The area had not yet become the exclusive site of fashionable shops and many store fronts were soaped over. Later Ellery's living space was occupied by a dentist office that later got itself closed down because of hepatitis. Below, at street level, was a Western Auto Store, the owner of which did himself in by abusing one of his own products. The river that ran directly under the first block was an open sewer, the recipient of up-river homes whose notion of sewerage consisted chiefly of the straight pipe.

Of more cheerful aspect was an Army-Navy Store with a Boy Scouts of America franchise and a shoe shop run by a trout fisherman who actually could and would repair shoes. Only a couple of blocks over the Bascule bridge, was Ellery's favorite breakfast spot, Archie's Soda Shop, a place of nurture that extended him a kind of rolling credit against the paintings of *Eleanor* Ellery hung on the walls.

At least as important to Ellery was his location directly over a paint store. When Ellery had lived in New London he had made use of Arthur Camassar's downtown shop. Camassar gave him technical advice and sold his work. In Mystic Ellery substituted The Maxwelton Company which not only carried art supplies but bottom paint for boats and seam compound. The Maxwelton Paint Store became a place where Ellery's products met their public. Edward Maxwell, the store's proprietor, estimated that at the time of Ellery's death the fisherman-artist had "completed more than a thousand pictures of local scenes." It was in buying bottom paint for my little dragger, however, that I again met Ellery.

On the surface, Princeton graduate Maxwell might seem to come from an unlikely background to become a confidant for a decrepit, old fisherman. Before the Stock Market Crash in 1929, Maxwell's father, J. Rogers Maxwell, had been commodore of the New York Yacht Club. He had owned a 126-foot steel Herreshoff schooner named *Queen* which he moored in Hempstead Bay behind the breakwater that J. P. Morgan had constructed for *Corsair*. When Ed was a child the chauffeur used to take him and his brother "Cooch" for walks out along that breakwater where they sometimes made efforts to fish. Of the Maxwell's *Queen*, her builder's son, L. Francis Herreshoff, wrote:

> Her plating was as fair as the shell of an egg, without the least unfairness where the rivets pulled the plating up to the frames... while her cabinet work was quite plain, it was beautifully finished, mostly in hand rubbed butternut. *Queen* was the best kept-up yacht I was ever on, and I have been on a great many of the very best including [the royal yacht] *Britannia*.

Commodore Maxwell had been one of the prime forces behind the invention of "Corinthian" or amateur, one-design yacht racing in North America through the auspices of the Seawanhaka Yacht Club in Oyster Bay. The family mansion in Glen Cove is now the Russian Embassy. The Maxwell family were, and now in the fourth generation of this tradition, are still top drawer sailors. No less an expert than H. A. Callahan, author of a series of definitive how-to books on sailing in the mid-twentieth century, had acknowledged in *Rigging* his technical debt to Commodore Maxwell.

In the back room of Maxwell's store, set on the floor and propped up precariously next to the paint shaking machine, there was a huge, boardroom style, gold-framed oil painting of the Commodore. "That was back when my family had *dough*," explained Ed. He ran the paint shaker by inserting the plug in the wall and then yanking it out in a fiery apocalypse after it had done its dance. "I got tired of buying new switches for the damn thing."

In the manner of Ted Williams who was said to be able to give you the count, pitch and location of every home run he'd ever hit, Ed could share with you the current, wind coordinates, set of sail and nearby competition for every buoy he'd ever rounded in a race. In several of these occasions H. A. Callahan figured prominently. In this total recall of the precise maritime conditions surrounding his success, Ed then was much like Ellery who, according to *The New Yorker* writer Joseph Mitchell, had risen to prominence on the basis of his phenomenal memory for the key minutiae in fish migration and the precise setting of his otter trawl net.

"You ought to go up and visit Ellery some time," said Ed. "Better knock first."

PRIVATE STUDIO
CAP'N E. F. THOMPSON
NO VISITORS OR CHILDREN

The sign, which I now have in my hand nearly a half century later, was mounted on a piece of brown poster board with peel-off lettering. Scrawled in his favorite red between the words "No" and "Visitors" is what seems to be the word "social." In other words, only adult, business visitors were permitted.

"Ed sent me."

"Come on in. Don't pay no mind to that sign. That's just to—." A ragged collection of bone and twisted joints encased more or less in a glove of distressed flesh waved me through the dust motes.

There were a few old-time artist's easels set up. One had a square-rigger he'd copied off a Charles Robert Patterson Columbia Rope calendar. Another had Ram Island Bell with a Coca-Cola calendar girl tip-toeing about on the acetylene tank. Against the wall leaned several more Coca-Cola girls in a variety of bizarre yet somehow wholesome encounters with aids to navigation.

In *Draggerman's Haul* Ellery had written "I'm no boudoir painter," and indeed these were outdoor girls, kept well out of doors. Even by 1950s standards these women were chaste enough, being faithful replicas of the smooth enameled young women in mid-century found advertising America's most refreshing soft drink. Ellery had merely removed them from their usual venue of gas stations and office calendars. There clinging to the iron structure of an aid to navigation they would in their skimpy sun suits hail passing versions of a crewless *Eleanor*. In a few depictions, such as the one featured upon the big easel, the girl had been abandoned to rock and gong in imperturbable solitude. By way of explanation, Ellery announced, "Ya know, it's violating a fedr'l law to tie up to an aid to navigation."

In a corner well away from the Main Street windows were other images: photographs—*self portraits*, one might accurately say. These were guarded by a sign:

WHAT YOU SEE HERE STAYS HERE

I was never sure whether Ellery recalled the incident at the back door of the fish market and I certainly did not insist upon revisiting that uncomfortable moment. In any case, by now I was more interested in him as a writer. He had even then filled a large, shaggy steamer trunk with typewriting on paper. The principle part of the bulk, he said was accounted for by his "Artists & Models Novel." He hung fire for my reaction with a defiant leer. When I finally blinked, he confided that there was also the rum running novel and leaned forward to cup a bony hand to his lips. "You ever hear of Bill McCoy, the *real* McCoy?"

"What happens if there's a fire?" I said sitting up straight.

"I'll just heave the whole business out the window."

"God help the fireman coming up the ladder."(I'd recently joined the local volunteers.)

"He'll just have to duck."

Nor was this steamer trunk the end of his literary production. Years later Ellery had moved down river to the ground floor of the salt box on the grounds of Ft. Rachel Marina. There in the War of 1812 a woman named Rachel was said to have kept the impromptu militia entertained with coffee and doughnuts the night they repelled British Admiral Thomas M. Hardy's fire barges. On my way home in my pickup at the end of a day on the lobster boat, I'd swing down Ft. Rachel Place and there in the dusk hear Ellery gunning his typewriter behind the drawn oil cloth shade of Rachel's house. It was an awesome sound that would have put the fear of God in any Lewis gunner cringing in the trenches of the Great War. To think that instead of bullets these were words adding to the already bounteous trove of inscribed paper was at times daunting.

Up in Ellery's apartment over the paint store I asked him about the rumors that a movie was to have been made of his life. The *Hartford Courant's* Martin Masters reported that Ellery had told him Henry Fonda had read the book and wanted to be him. Fonda had recently scored as a mariner in the Broadway version of *Mr. Roberts*. I'd heard Ellery preferred Gary Cooper. Was it true he had been holding out for Gary Cooper to play the part? (By then, Cooper had died.) "I got tired of waiting for him," said Ellery.

Why hadn't he published other things?

"My writer died."

"?"

"His name was Pope, a heart attack. "

Ellery seemed proud that he had had "a writer."

I was shocked. After all, no less a maritime writer-seaman than William McFee had written in *The Christian Science Monitor* of May 22, 1950, that unlike "... one of these 'as told to' confections, in which a journalist writes up the material he has extracted from a man of action, Captain Ellery wrote the book himself, just as he has painted scores of oil pictures of ships and seas and plays what he calls the trumpet for his own pleasure if not for the neighbors." McFee goes on to cinch his point by concluding that "[Thompson] is no great writer, and he makes no pretense to be. But he tells his story with unflagging zest, and he gets through his story of New England fishermen and whaling men without mentioning *Moby Dick*. This is a real achievement."

That Ellery had been the real thing, writing his own tale, was also an assumption carried on by the New London *Day* obituary writer who lauds our man's honest, homemade seaman's prose. More finicky scholars pay Thompson the respect to try to sort out the issue of authorship by comparing the Viking Press *Draggerman's Haul* with *Come Aboard the Draggers: Sea Sketches*. The locally published book would seem to have had no "writer." In any case, *Hartford Courant* 's Masters reports that Ellery told him *Draggerman's Haul* was the product of "three-years of hard work."

But there is something even more curious about Ellery's tale of the catastrophic untimely death of his "writer." The mysterious Mr. "Pope" surfaces nowhere in what ultimately turned up in Ellery's own files as kept by Marion Krepcio. What she documents is the true story of Ellery's collaboration with Viking editor Robert O. Ballou, who incidentally did not die until 1977, some dozen years after Ellery's statement about Pope's death and three decades after their work on *Draggerman's Haul*! Krepcio concludes that Ellery wasn't so much "ghost-written" as "heavily edited."

A perusal of the Krepcio file containing Ellery's correspondence with his Viking editor Robert O. Ballou bears out her thesis. In the years long before computer searches and cut and paste, years before even the organizing mind of Marion Krepcio wrought order out of Ellery's paper chaos, the job of assembling Ellery must have been formidable. Ellery himself warns his editor that he is likely to mail him anything: "Don't mind what I send you. I might even send you the mortgage on the old homestead." Another time he says, "I hope I'm not confusing you with some extra junk I'm sending you. Some of it was written a few years ago without much planning. But you may find something in it that may help. There is so many anecdotes about leading fishermen (including Pa and Morris) that perhaps, someday we can do a smaller book about them. Who knows? There is so much ground to go over even I find myself confused. But I remember it all clearly." Sometimes he admits, "I'm just rambling." Perhaps his best sense of working in the material emerges one day when—mixing his maritime metaphors—he refers to his emendations as "caulking material that will balance things more for the people hereabouts."

Ellery was often concerned with "the people hereabouts," anxious to reward them with thanks and praise, nervous he might offend, obsessed as your old maiden aunt with tediously nailing down all the familial connections. He was randy to make any alliance he could with the larger world, in any dimension available. He urged his editor to make sure that Hank Palmer, who ran the local boatyard, was connected—Ellery wasn't even entirely sure himself—with Nathaniel Palmer. In 1821 Palmer was the Stonington lad who at 21 had been given credit "by a Russian admiral" [Bellinghausen] for discovering the continent of Antarctica. Some two generations before such pan-ethnic embracing became fashionable, Ellery wanted his editor to know and maybe work in stuff about what were then called "Indians:"

Did you know that Lloyd Gray (Chief Fleetfoot) had a beautiful wife [Arlene] who often visited our boats with goodies she cooked... I spent many hours with them on the Groton waterfront... There I learned to dance and paddle a canoe. Lloyd taught me to paddle Indian fashion, on one knee, and Arlene taught me to dance on the floor and not on her feet. Arlene had perfect teeth, then and now...

Ellery hands his editor another possible addition to the book, having "just remember[ed] more "about Lloyd and Arlene." This little suggestion becomes a two-page mini-epic that commences with the Indian family, including "four years old Betty... braving a dense fog on the way home from Block Island. (We crawled home that trip feeling our way past Watch Hill and up dangerous Fishers Island into New London." The boat trip conflates with "I knew Arlene had been 'expecting' for quite a while..." and races into a frenetic automobile trip in Ellery's "old Cleveland" up into then difficult roads of the Indian reservation at Lantern Hill. They seem to be on a search for a tribal mid-wife. The back roads produce a car that bounded "up and down" with the feared results upon the expectant mother "and me a bachelor..." Somehow "by careful steering, Indian fortitude and plain guts of Arlene" they find a place with "children in the yard, a good sign." Eventually a helter-skelter relay of people manage to get Arlene to the hospital and Ellery home to his bed. Unfortunately, the infant son died." Arlene "was okay." Ellery concludes: "There must be a moral here, but it isn't for me to say." In a scrawled addition to the typing, Ellery at some point added: "Arlene proved her worth on both these trips, land and water—a true New Englander."

Ellery wants to get the music in, not just his trumpet and his dad's trombone, but his mother's "piana." He stresses that the whole family atmosphere was built on sharing musical performance. "We had lots of fun at home—music etc.—in an era when the piana was the main artical of furniture. (Don't mind my spelling.) No wonder we were so slow in marrying, especially the girls."

There are the landmarks of his childhood whose beginning coincided with that of the 20th Century. As in the case of those, in Ben Hecht's phrase, born "a child of the century," the moments often strike Ellery as cosmically in step with the turning points in a larger history. Perhaps these coincidences are what gave Ellery a special sense of the confluence of his times and destiny, the local and the epic, the background and the foreground, the trivial and the crucial. After all, right out there in the front yard, ripe as an apple tree for boyhood boarding, there was "the brand new flag ship of the Atlantic fleet, the battleship *Connecticut*. And Charlie Davis, the slickest driver around, driving a span of white horses... and important, too, was the trolley line just opened and running past our house, but not too many nickels [available] for exciting rides... There was Luke Wilcox's invitation to witness our first movie, only to be disappointed at Stonington by an electrical failure." Disappointing, too was the pivotal moment when "inspectors condemning our cow and giving up hope for our horse..."

On the whole, Ellery often complimented Ballou on these editorial "smoothings out" a number of times, praising Ballou's work as "smooth as silk." This was no cliché to a roughly epidermalled and often-amorous fisherman in the days just after World War II when rationing had made even more remote the more iconic female accouterments.

It was the "love stuff," of course, that gave author and editor the most problem. As Ellery put it, "I may have to live here the rest of my life." In the years when *From Here* to *Eternity* and *The Naked and the Dead* were breaking new ground in the novel, Ballou had no good solutions for non-fiction. Neither of them ever found the right tone for this "love" material. (Almost 70 years later, I still have problems explaining to my college students Steinbeck's apology for the bawdy in the 1941 *Log of the Sea of Cortez*.) It's hard to know exactly whom the author was trying to please. "The love stuff was for your entertainment," he writes Ballou. "If no part of it has a place, I'll have one less worry." There is certainly a legitimate place for the ribald side of waterfront life, especially as I recall it even in the 1950s in the ports that Ellery's haunts. One day, as an afterthought, Ellery comes up with an exemplum for Ballou:

> There is one man... small with funny face, whom I forgot to mention. He works at odd jobs about the village when he's not working in the machine shop. He's married with three children. He has a hard time making ends meet. This summer he took care of my boat while I was sick and worked in the cemetery digging graves. Yet he is the most cheerful fellow I ever heard tell baudy [sic] jokes. The day of the boat parade he was dressed in sailor hat, sport shirt, overall (jumper) coat, full dress pants, and sneakers, one brown and one white. He would scare the devil. But when he strikes bones digging a grave he's done for the day.

What Ellery offers as his own contribution to bawdry is in response to Ballou's query about a technical term in cartography. He begins with an entry worthy of Barry Lopez's recent project on topographic terminology, *Home Ground*:

> About the book: 'Holes' are the names given to narrow channels between islands in the area near Cape Cod... (Small settlements opposite a Hole often take its name.) But all this is E.F.T. school of thought... That's all I know about them. Menhaden fishermen used to chant (and excuse the poetry)

> > *I lost my hat off Barnegat*
> > *And where do you think I found it ?*
> > *Upon a pole at Holmes's Hole*
> > *With a dozen whores around it.*

Such were the challenges facing Robert Ballou, editorial worker on William Faulkner's *Sound and The Fury*, John Steinbeck's *Pastures of Heaven* and Ellery Thompson's *Draggerman's Haul*.

Oddly enough for those days of tender sensibilities, it was a female who became Ellery's literary executrix. "I grew up around navy men," Marion Krepcio told me. "I'd heard it all." Krepcio certainly knew Ellery as well as anyone, having evolved from a paralegal taking down his will to a *de facto* caretaker in his last years. "When I went in there the first time, I thought, 'Oh, my Gawd! How can anyone live like this? I started to turn around and walk out, but my parents had always raised me to look after the old folks. I decided to brave it out. I asked him if he were aware that he had mice. He had to think about it a while and concluded that there could be this possibility of mice. I said, 'Well, look on your stove. There's Papa and now look, here comes Mamma, and now look—here come all the kids.' We had to scrape the stuff off the stove. Some of it was food slopped over the rims of his pans. Some of it was food after it had gone through the mice. When you consider there were all those old derelict barges down there then, not a hundred feet from his door, it's a wonder they were *only* mice."

Krepcio went from sweeping up and scraping off to trying to straighten out Ellery's papers. He could not have found a better person by training and temperament. Her commitment was staunch. "I went into the hospital two times because of the mold."

A number of people would look in on Ellery in this phase, bring him food and whatnot. Tuck Jones, who had succeeded Ed Maxwell at the paint shop, says he used to carry a bag of stuff down to Ellery every Friday. "The apartment over the paint store had been condemned. There was no heat up there but a kerosene stove. The Ft. Rachel place was at least on the ground floor, though I don't think the heat was much better."

Ellery heated by wood in the fireplace that must have been the same way Rachel had done it when she entertained the ragtag militia that gathered the broken bottles, nails and clam shells that made up the grape shot they used to repel Thomas M. Hardy's fire barges in 1813. Furthermore, the fireplace was no less insidious in its danger than the kerosene stove. One night Ellery's chimney got out of control and there was a fire that burnt a hole in his ceiling that remained until David Leavitt had it fixed for him.

David Leavitt had made money in the bakery business and took on a kind of *noblesse oblige* role as Ellery's patron. He had also assumed responsibility for another famous old maritime wreck, the North Dumpling Lighthouse precariously perched on a classic glacial drumlin that overlooks the island of Flat Hammock a couple of miles off the mouth of the Mystic River. Leavitt rebuilt the abandoned light station, adding some ancillary buildings. He permitted the U.S. Coast Guard to take down the ugly skeletal tower that they had been using for the beacon and reinstall a proper lantern atop the mansard roof of the station house. Leavitt devoted one of the rooms to Ellery, decorating it with his paintings in time for Ellery's 85 birthday party.

"It was the last time Ellery went to sea," recalled Krepcio. "He was terrified to go out there. 'Don't worry,' I said. 'There'll be lots of people to keep you from drowning.' We had a great crew... We made a kind of traveling seat out of a plank and carried him into the boathouse which was right there at sea level. To get him up the steep drumlin to the lighthouse itself would have been too much of a problem."

It was a great crew indeed: fellow dragger captain Jimmy Lawrence, of the *Mandalay;* Noank's Captain Adrian Lane, who'd skippered the Coast Guard barque *Eagle*, the Wood's Hole Ketch *Atlantis* and the Mystic Seaport's *Brilliant;* Professor Dan Merriman of Yale and a wonderful doctor from Mystic who lived on a boat and had become, in effect, Ellery's personal physician, Roger Ryley.

"Doc" Ryley lived with his wife aboard the *Pequot*, a wooden Penobscot Bay trawler-yacht designed by the boating writer Carl D. Lane. The *Pequot* was moored starboard side to at the Cottrell Lumber Company dock on the east side of the Mystic River between the two bridges, a couple of hundred yards upstream from where *Eleanor* met her end. Roger Ryley is himself a legend, a local hero who deserves a statue more than the Civil War soldier down the street from the *Pequot's* berth. He delivered most of the babies in the Mystic area between World War II and his retirement in the 1970s. He was the last physician I knew of who made house calls. In fact with one such visit he saved my father's life employing a technique for high blood pressure out of the middle-ages. Twenty years later and long after Ryley had retired, my father was faced with his imminent death. Presented with the opportunity of being ministered to by the latest in hi-tech apparatus, he called out, "To hell with all that. Call Doc Ryley!"

In the words of Roger Ryley's son, history teacher and namesake, "Dad was one of the go-to guys who kept Ellery going in his last years, of which there were many more than anybody expected, including Ellery himself. Ellery was not a mean drunk, but he had the tendency. He was one of my father's many patients who had more years than teeth and his libido had pretty much run out. Dad kept him moderated by rowing down to Fort Rachel and visiting him on a regular basis. He would sound Ellery's heart and go through the usual low-tech stuff of the day and they would spend a lot of time just talking about boats and the old days. From time to time Ellery divvied up by presenting my father with a painting, sometimes an old one he had kicking around. Sometimes he'd say, 'Let me whip you up one.' We have, along with a classic *Eleanor* portrait, a Wilcox menhaden steamer.'"

Eventually, even with all the go-to help, Ellery could not be maintained at Ft. Rachel. "He started to hallucinate," said Krepcio. "We'd moved his bed by the window and he got terribly upset like I'd never seen him. He wasn't just joking. 'You can't have a man's bed by the window on the ground floor," he hollered. 'Someone might harpoon him through the window.'"

It was Krepcio with Doc Ryley who made the decision to get Ellery out of Rachel's old house on the river and into the nursing home in Colchester when the time came. "Colchester," she says apologetically, "halfway to Hartford. It was as close to the sea as I could get him."

It was Krepcio who saw to it he received the best care there. It was she to whom he referred in his late jottings as his "Guardian Angel."

Marion Krepcio lives on one of the rocky points that jut down into Fishers Island Sound from the northern shore where for years she has collected and written about sea shells in the great amateur tradition of the 19th Century naturalists. As was the case with Ellery, professionals with fancy degrees often consult her. It was this mutual interest in the sea that helped form the bond between the patient and the caregiver. As both caretaker and literary executrix, Krepcio has become the expert on the nooks and crannies of Ellery's life, a role she does not duck. "People ask me if Ellery died of syphilis. He did not."

Krepcio has used her paralegal training to discipline her nerve in facing the fierce challenge of parsing Ellery's unpublished oeuvre. Recently she has braved the famous steamer trunk and many boxes of manuscript, sorting through pounds and pounds of Thompson manuscript, culling promising materials. "Ellery told some stories many times in many different forms, both oral and in writing. Sometimes the variations are more interesting than published stuff. Some of the local fishermen told me that Ellery 'embellished' the truth, you know—stretched it considerable. One story, especially the one about him dragging up a car in his net, they had trouble with. But then in one of the boxes, what do I see? A snapshot of a Volkswagen dripping in his net!

"But it's the ghost writing thing. His editor at Viking was Robert Ballou as we see by the correspondence. I would like to see Ellery published in his own words. I see the *Draggerman's Haul* as a fair account, but I keep saying to myself, '*These are not his words.*' Ellery had a wonderful way of putting things. I used to love to listen to him. The way he said the stuff. There are some of his writings in the boxes that show this quality. You wouldn't want to mess with that. They deserve to see the light of day and I promised Ellery on his death bed, I'd work to see that they would. 'Promise me never to let the romance of the sea be forgotten. Keep studying the sea.' And here's this old guy at 85 still wondering about it all."

It was Krepcio who found one of the most delectable of Ellery's posthumous works. "He was grateful in some ways to Joe Mitchell because he understood what Joe's articles had meant. But there was always part of Ellery that didn't exactly care for the way that he got described in those pieces. So he went to New York and interviewed Joe Mitchell. He turned the tables on him! You've got to read it to see how he did it."

Ellery's version of the Joe Mitchell treatment consists of a rambling parody which begins as does Mitchell's piece with a kind of tour of Mystic, goes on to interview the man who owns the Stonington Fish Dock, the librarian, and stray docksiders. It is not so much a pastiche of Mitchell as a relentless struggle to comprehend a standard journalistic method which seems to have astonished Ellery much as his scientists' guests amazed him with their perverse need to note the catch of the day in Latin. As such the Mitchell parody seems to be another battle in Ellery's good natured war to determine just how his life was to be packaged for the market.

It wasn't Marion Krepcio, however, who sent a load of Ellery's work posthumously to New York. After Ellery's death I was approached by my editor at Viking Press to "go through" Ellery's literary remains. "We can't do anything with it as is and thought of you because of the subject and the area." Ellery's literary remains were presumably made up of the stuff I'd seen twenty years earlier in the trunk up over Ed Maxwell's store plus all the stuff I'd heard being machine-gunned off down at Fort Rachel for a dozen years. No doubt in there somewhere was "the [wink-wink] Artists and Models novel." (The *Courant's* Martin M. Masters quotes Ellery as saying one of his future books will be *Never the Twine Shall Meet* "'A book about New England Men Whose Nets Go Down to the Sea.'" Whether this was just a bit of Joycean jiving on our man's part or not remains to be seen.) At the time I found the task of re-assembling Ellery daunting. Finding no takers, Viking returned the literary remains to "the woman who had sent them." Recently a few pounds of manuscript was on view at Ellery's exhibit at the Stonington Historical Society. Three pages or so of a bucolic memory of youth were mined for the Society's newsletter along with a what seems to have been yet another shot by Ellery at the McCoy affair, but with no additional material.

Up in his quarters over the paint store we did not discuss his literary influences. In *Draggerman's Haul* Ellery talks about the influence of his childhood reading as the "Frank stories," that is a serial character with that name who a la the Hardy Boys engaged in wholesome, outdoor adventures. (Was he referring to Frank Merriwell?) In *Come Aboard the Draggers*, he lists his shipboard reading in distant ports exclusively in the context of alternatives to sin:

> *Vineyard Gazette, Nantucket Inquirer, Providence Journal, Atlantic Fisherman, Fishing Gazette and Maine Coast Fisherman* and what-have-you including *Snappy Stories*, but without much snap compared with today's snap.

Ellery kept Mitchell's photostats of *The New Yorker* accounts which report on the reading matter in *Eleanor's* forecastle, *Sunshine and Health* and *Popular Mechanics*. In *The New Yorker's* layout, Ellery's book list is surrounded—like a jeering chorus of sophisticates—by ads for stage productions of Frank Fay and Joe E. Brown in *Harvey*; Judy Garland, Van Johnson, June Allyson, Robert Walker and "many other stars" in *'Til The Clouds Roll By*. There is Clifton Webb in Noel Coward's *Present Laughter*; Cornelia Otis Skinner in Oscar Wilde's *Lady Windermere's Fan* and Garson Kanin's *Born Yesterday*. The movies have Lawrence Olivier in *Henry V.*

When I asked Ellery about literary style, he looked out the window at the great counter weights of the Bascule bridge that spanned the Mystic River.

"College professors," he said, as if they were out there now, crawling about on the counter weights.

"Ah," I said, recalling all those marine biologists from New Haven of which he speaks so familiarly in *Draggerman's Haul.*

"I was trained by college professors to write," he said. "Yale men. Scientists."

"Yes, marine biologists."

"Yessir. They would instruct me to use *active* words."

"*Active* you say?"

"'Active,' *they* said. For instance, instead of writing 'I *stepped* down from the wheelhouse and *walked* aft,' they'd tell me to write, 'I *jumped* down from the wheelhouse and *ran* aft.'"

"Scientists said that."

"Yale men."

I fortunately found out that it was not necessary to beard Ellery in his quarters. He spent part of each day in Ed Maxwell's store where he'd sit on the counter, hat on the back of his head, long legs dangling. It was understood that there was somehow a connection between the merchandise and Ellery.

Half the store's shelving was devoted to bottom paint and seam compound. "It's the only way I can afford to keep afloat," Ed would say. The object of all this attention was the ancient, wooden Atlantic Class sloop *Avenger*, a survivor from the 1920s, all that was left from the great days of his father's Herreshoff *Queen*. None of Ed's skills had eroded, however. At least every time I paid attention to such things, it seemed that Maxwell was winning another race with the old girl. Aboard her he fought a rear guard action against the oncoming fiberglass revolution. *Avenger*, held together, so it would appear, by every product in the paint store, lived up to her name, not only locally at the poor end of Long Island Sound, but back down at the western end where Ed took her to challenge the "Gold Coast" competition of "the boys who had been able to hold onto some of their dough in the Crash."

The other half of the store Ed had surrendered to art supplies. His wife, Lil, was a graduate of Connecticut College where she majored in art. The fancy camel hair brushes and tubes of cerulean blue and burnt umber were for her students. It had been Ellery's mother who had originally got him interested in art, bringing home the supplies. Later, before Arthur Camassar, Ellery himself found Ed Grader's in New London. Now Maxwell's was equally handy for him to get what he needed, especially as he'd worked out a deal to swap supplies for a more or less finished product. These Ed could put in the window and theoretically have the rights to actually sell. Even if Ellery's work sold slowly, the store's marketing notion was something like: *if this beat up old fisherman can do this, think what you could do with our products.* At least such was the excuse for the relationship.

While there were interruptions by customers with leaky boats or aspirations to capture local scenes, one got the feeling that most of the hours were consumed by conversations between the odd couple. "My mother never approved of Ellery Thompson," one of Ed's daughters recently told me. "She figured he wasted Dad's time telling stories, most of which she considered, well—*unsuitable.*"

At Princeton in the 1930s Ed had been a history major and after graduation had come to Mystic to work for the military-industrial complex in the form of the intense maelstrom that was General Dynamics Electric Boat. The shipyard was the successor to the relatively bucolic New London Ship and Engine Company of which Ellery speaks in *Draggerman's Haul.* Just what a Princeton history major did in this hi-tech government submarine-building operation was never clear to me, but Ed had one of those steel-trap minds for technical detail. I have blundered into his shop many an afternoon to find myself in a grinding debate between Ed and some other student of naval matters. One day I remember standing there forty minutes while the details of the stern turret of a certain British cruiser of the pre-war era were worked out, or more accurately—not quite worked out. After Ed's death I was able to locate some of the database for these discussions in his battered volumes of *Brassey's Naval and Shipping Annuals* and *Jane's Fighting Ships.* On the page of these tomes, however, such details never came alive the way they did in the old paint store.

In Maxwell's there was the residue of other reading material that had been temporarily abandoned on the counter. I recall seeing *The Rise of the Dutch Republic, Vol. II.* "How was Volume I.?" I asked.

"I don't know," said Ed. "That one wasn't on sale."

The next day on the counter I came across a ratty paperback, something like *Christine Keeler: Her Own Story of Her Own Sex Change In Her Own Words..*

"Oh that," laughed Ed. "Ellery left that."

"Ellery?"

"He wanted my opinion."

"You mean as literature or medicine?"

"Well, you know Ellery."

IV. The Science of Ellery

> If that was what fishology was like, commercial fishing could use a lot of it.
> —*Draggerman's Haul*, XVI

Actually, despite Ellery's jokey way of referring to the scientists, his connection with Professor Daniel Merriman at Yale was a long and mutually rewarding one. The work, most of which they performed in the midst of World War II, was of the utmost national, even international importance. Many of the issues raised were to haunt the field down to the present day. Joseph Mitchell does go into considerable detail about Merriman's work. It had, after all, been the most of which was the original focus of *The New Yorker* story. What is lacking in the reporting, however, is the sense of urgency that the scientists must have felt. Reading Mitchell's "Dragger Captain" now, most readers see the Yale excursion as just another Nova field trip. I had myself forgotten that the work actually took place *during* the war in submarine infested waters, not after it in some rising research boom.

Part of the blame must fall to Viking editor Ballou who seems to have steered Ellery onto the shoals of his new author's weaker side. The Viking book replaces the kind of legitimate drama that might have been the science with a bit of pubescent satire on the breeding of mummychoggs down at the Yalie lab. As a result, many of the subsequent contemporary accounts that fed on this version followed suit. They seem to treat the fact that a commercial fisherman could have a viable working relationship with a major scientist the way one might think of a talking dog. As Samuel Johnson said, it is not the specific eloquence of the discourse at which you marvel, but that it exists at all. In *Draggerman's Haul* Ellery pretty much limits Merriman's appearance to what strikes the author as the professor's amazing punctuality on the pier and the willfully perverse insistence on the employment of scientific vocabulary. It's easy to blame Viking for not coaching more of the richness of the scientific collaboration out of Ellery, but when you consider the times, in the late 1940s there was no tradition for a John McPhee type of treatment that would honor the subject. There was also the problem of the war itself as Ellery reveals in his notes:

> Incidentally my *Eleanor*, rigged with some electronic Navy gear was a sort of spy boat for the Navy, a matter I would not explain to any big city writer... After a German Sub had sunk the steamer *Black Point* close off Point Judith, our armed forces afloat and in the air—blasted the enemy *U-853* to the bottom with all on board, now a skeleton brew. But Joe was back in New York pondering

over what to write for his intended Dragger Captain stores which appeared in
The New Yorker...

Some of the momentum of understandable war-time reticence, however, seems to
have carried over into the attitude three years after the cease fire in the 1948 Viking
book.

Marion Krepcio's Ellery archive reveals the true nature of the science done aboard
Eleanor. Merriman himself was a graceful writer who acknowledged Ellery in his work.
Ellery saved to his dying day the paper Merriman gave him in which "The authors wish
to acknowledge the patient and kindly cooperation of Captain Ellery Thompson, whose
help has made possible the preliminary analysis, and on whom the success of the con-
tinuing investigations is dependent." Merriman and his research assistant Herbert E.
Warfel's "Studies of the Marine resources of Southern New England—A Preliminary
Analysis of the Connecticut Trawl Fishery" was done under the august auspices of Bingham Oceanographic Laboratory, Peabody Museum and Osborn Zoological Laboratory,
Yale University. Merriman presented the paper at the Ninth North American Wildlife
Conference held at the American Wildlife Institute Investment Building in Washing-
ton, D.C. in the penultimate year of World War II.

It is especially ironic that Merriman should be trivialized in the aftermath of the pub-
lication of *Draggerman's Haul*. Ellery saved a piece by Charles Clapp Jr. in the Sunday
edition of *The New Haven Register* of June 25, 1950 in which Clapp reports hearing the
story of the inception of *Draggerman's Haul* through the mouths of Merriman in his lab
at New Haven:

> Even before [Mitchell's *The New Yorker* pieces] Ellery had considered writing
> a 'sort of history of dragging' and had made notes about things he would in-
> clude. [Mitchell's] profile spurred him on and for the next couple of years he
> kept grinding out pages of manuscript which he mailed to Merriman for criti-
> cism. As Ellery's writings began to take on the form of a book, Merriman's sec-
> retary typed some of the revised drafts...

As for Merriman's own style, it was certainly no constipated, number and jargon infested prose of the type that came to be cultivated so assiduously by the practitioners of
"rigor" in the post World War II grantsmanship era. Nor was it, contrary to Ellery's account of "Yale scientists," mindlessly "active."Merriman harkened back to the leisurely,
but not wordy style of the pre-war era in marine biology. The son of a Harvard historian,
who as Ellery noted "taught a lot of history to Franklin D. Roosevelt," Merriman was
not only a careful observer of Ellery's catch, but had written a monograph *Challengers
of Neptune: the 'Philosophers'* for the *Challenger* Expedition Centenary in which he delivered at the celebration in Edinburgh in 1972. It was a paper that helped kick off the
growing awareness of the history of bluewater scientific exploration. The juxtaposition
of *Challenger* and *Eleanor* must have given Merriman a kind of wry amusement. Thirty
years after *Eleanor* had served as Merriman's *Challenger*, he sent Ellery a copy of the
'Philosophers' monograph: *"For Ellery—all the best in 1974—Always, Dan Merriman."*

Merriman also passed on to Ellery his account of a 1950s expedition to Cabo Blanco, Peru, aboard Ellery's friend and cousin Harold McLaughlin's Stonington dragger. The expedition was in search of game fish as a food source, but Merriman's twenty page monograph on the grounds is both informative and a delight in the manner of Steinbeck and Ricketts' *Log of the Sea of Cortez*. The Cabo Blanco marlin fishery became the inspiration of Montauk game fishing notables Royal Knight and S. Kip Farrington, leading to the building of special, twin-screw sportfishermen under 35 feet that were shipped on freighters to work the inshore waters off Peru. It was to Cabo Blanco that the film makers who shot Hemingway's *Old Man and the Sea* took Spencer Tracy to catch his marlin.

Merriman's introduction confirms that there is no question that Ellery and *Eleanor* were engaged in serious, important science. As part of establishing his scientific protocol, Merriman analyzes the Stonington fishing fleet as a whole, then zeroes in on *Eleanor*:

> The present study, covering the period from July 1943 to January 1944, is an analysis of the catch of a moderate-sized vessel, the *Eleanor* of Stonington. This boat, 50 feet overall, consistently used a modified otter trawl 80 feet in width with a 4-inch body mesh and a 3.5-4 inch cod end mesh. The depths fished ranged from 10 to 26 fathoms. The dragging time varied from 1 to 2 hours (mean effort, 1 hour 26 minutes)... After a preliminary period of observation, the authors went aboard for at least one trip a month and often at more frequent intervals. On those occasions data were collected and one complete haul, typical of the day's effort, was purchased and taken to the laboratory. Every fish in such a haul was then weighed and measured; samples of each species were also examined in regard to parasites, stomach contents, and stage of sexual maturity, and in addition scales, otoliths (ear-stones, calcareous deposits in the inner ears of fish).

Merriman and Warfel report, "The accumulation of data on the relative proportions of marketed and trash species in the catch; studies on the life histories of the individual components of the catch; the analysis of total fish populations" and include charts, graphs and conclude with the transcript of a discussion between participants. They begin their discussion with a back and forth about the waste of fish thrown over the rail because they happen not to be marketable on a particular day.

> Chairman Allen: I have been out on some of these fishing boats and have seen them check them off as they catch fish that certainly look very good, and if you ask a fisherman whether they are good fish he shrugs his shoulders, or says, 'maybe' but they aren't the fish that they were out for.

One of the participants points out that the Borden Milk Company, then a household icon, was using some of this product for cattle feed. There are comments about setting up laboratories to study ways to utilize the "waste." In the first decade of 2000 my students keep bombing me with papers making the case for the evil that otter trawls do. Some of the more sophisticated ask me how the famous scientists from Yale could not have pointed these evils out to Ellery. When Merriman and Company were aboard *Eleanor* of course, it was decades before underwater cameras spied on the bottom chains of otter trawls. These men aboard *Eleanor* were concerned with two things: Nazi submarines and a stopgap solution to world hunger brought on by the Depression and the War.

The man Ellery called "Herb Warfel" gets to what would seem to be the heart of the conference. "I would like to see more technological laboratories established along the coast... I think we could use a half a dozen now very advantageously, because here is protein food, and the world is crying now for it."

We know that the relationship lasted to the end of Merriman's life. On Memorial Day, 1983, from his home in Bethany, Connecticut, Merriman writes a bread and butter note to the Krepcios for their work on Ellery's birthday re-union. He apologizes for not writing sooner because of a bad back, the "cure (?)" for which was "worse than the disease and one of its side effects (prednisone) is to disrupt the calcium metabolism so that my back feels as though one of *Eleanor*'s trawl doors had run over it on a drag through the Hell Hole." He thanks the Krepcios for the:

> ... wonderful birthday-party you gave Ellery. Not only did it give Ellery pleasure and fun, but the rest of us (especially ME) got a huge kick out of it right down to the last detail including the cake (both to look at and eat.) The two of you are just great, and of course the fact that you care so much for Ellery means a great deal to me. We are lucky people to have known Ellery over the years, and I'd say he's a lucky guy to have you two for neighbors.

The very last thing that Ellery wrote on his bed at Colchester was upon hearing of Merriman's death:

> It was Dan Merriman of Yale who encouraged me to write. He said 'Yes, Ellery, you can.' Dan was internationally known. He studied the oceans. Oceanographer, they called him. I called him Dan. Dan Merriman became ill and now lies dead. I hope to God he didn't die in vain. He told me by phone his time was due. One of the finest men I ever knew. 'Keep living,' he said, 'I know you can.'

In Krepcio's archive Ellery reveals how it was when Mitchell, on his usual prowl through Fulton Fish Market, came across one of Merriman's tags and became aware of Ellery. In Ellery's memo documenting the beginning of the Mitchell connection it would seem that the "tide" that he refers is not, as it might seem, a tale teller's metaphorical trope, but literal. He is aboard *Eleanor*, jotting stuff down in a beat up notebook to kill time as he waits for the tide to turn so he can set his net in a particular direction:

> But before the tide turns ebb I want to bring in Joseph Mitchell of *The New Yorker* who came up from New York, via the oceanographic portals of Old Eli, to gather material about Yale professors going down to the sea on Stonington fishing boats.

The fish activities of the Yale men from the Bingham Oceanographic Laboratory in New Haven attracted the attention of Mitchell. He was an expert at nosing out stories of lower Manhattan, especially around the Fulton Fish Market district along South Street near the Brooklyn Bridge. While browsing around the stalls of Fulton Fish Market hobnobbing with various fishmongers, including Jim Coyle of John Feeney Company, he spotted a tagged flounder [another Ellery take has it that Mitchell 'caught a tagged flounder'] that arrived at the shipper by me from my boat at Stonington. Naturally, Joe Mitchell followed the scent east through the oceanographic portals of Old Eli to the deck of my dragger *Eleanor*. What followed is too long a story for here on this tide.

Joe made several trips out on the *Eleanor*, sometimes in company with Dan Merriman and his research assistant Herb Warfel—other times with my crew and me. Somehow, Dan Merriman got permission from the port Captain at New London for Mitchell to go out on my boat.

It is only when reading the reference to the "port Captain's" permission that we are brought back to the realization that all this science was done during the War. There were submarine nets between Avery Point and Ocean Beach to protect our own Groton-New London submarine base from the U-boats, which were indeed from time to time well inside Long Island Sound. Ellery remarks casually, "Incidentally, my *Eleanor*, rigged with some electronic Navy gear, was sort of a spy boat for the Navy." There is certainly a good deal more to this involving not only Naval Intelligence and U-boats, but the Fulton Fish Market Mafia with vectors to "Socks" Lanza, Lucky Luciano and even up to the beleaguered governor of New York, Thomas Dewey, who eventually, as the *Chicago Daily Tribune* so infamously had it, "won" the 1948 presidential election over Harry Truman.

One of the underreported aspect of the Second World War is this coastal work done by an unholy mix of citizens, and there certainly was important anti-submarine work going on in the fishing fleet. Mystic's Joan LaBlanc McLaughlin tells the story of her father working as "a radioman" on the Stonington dragger *The Old Mystic* at this time. "Draggers didn't have 'radiomen,' as such in those days. That is, someone on those small boats whose whole job was to just tend to the radio, but that was my father's job all right. So you know that something special was going on. It had to do with anti-German submariner stuff and he even received a certificate from the government thanking him for his efforts as a radioman in the War."

But what is more immediately interesting here is Ellery's attitude toward Mitchell and writers from New York:

One thing sure: I did not spill my guts about the part my *Eleanor* and other Stonington draggers were playing with the navy in our coastal defense system. No way... [it was not] a matter I would explain to any big city writer.

Of for what we now perceive as Ellery's ecological sins, neither he nor Merriman say anything. The issue of otter trawls and resource management was not on the table in the era of what in retrospect would seem to be his greatest depredations. The period when his father introduced the otter trawl to Connecticut waters, a technique which Ellery so proudly in the name of family wisdom extended and enhanced, was two generations away from the moment when SCUBA diving cameramen rode the gear that revealed the evils wrought upon the benthic community. My colleague at Avery Point, Helen Rozwadowski, points out that when the initial research by the divers on otter trawls was performed, it was to improve efficiency, not document depredation. As for the waste incurred in bycatch, Merriman did address that during the War, based on research largely aboard *Eleanor*. So endemic, however, is this tangle of market, science and regulation, that over half a century later policy and management experts still wrestle with it.

Herbert Warfel and Dan Merriman on board *Eleanor*, circa 1943.

Ellery Thompson with
flounder. *Photograph by
Bernie Gordon.*

V. Ellery as a Literary Subject

> I shan't try to repeat our conversations.
> The telling would inevitably be filled with cliches anyway.
>
> —*Draggerman's Haul*, XII

There came a time, however, when Joseph Mitchell's focus began to drift from the Yale scientists hook. Ellery felt the shift:

At first [he] aimed most of his attention on the professors and the 28 species of fish that came up in our net. But somewhere along the line he sort of switched pens in mid-air and began pumping answers to a thousand questions from me.

Furthermore, looking from subject back to author, the Krepcio Archive reveals that Mitchell was not at all what Ellery expected either:

When I first spotted him coming over the dock-log onto our deck, I thought, here is no writer of popular yarns, but a professor who looks the part. I had expected our super-cargo to be a much older man than in his mid-thirties appearance. His full figure suggested no under-nourishment... At first I couldn't put my finger on just what [made] him appear so professionally dignified and reserved. Was it because his kind but penetrating eyes frame behind horn-rimmed glasses? Or was it because his face was quite un-tanned or was it his need of a haircut ? No I sensed it was deeper than that—to me, unfathomable.

Yet I had the feeling that as he spotted me at the wheel, realized I (a thin, and perhaps mean looking Yankee) was the skipper [that] he was the most disillusioned "newsman" to ever step foot off Eastern Connecticut soil.

And indeed when Mitchell's *The New Yorker* pieces came out, Ellery remarks somewhat indignantly, "I was pictured as a skinny sad-eyed rheumatic Yankee fishing skipper who lay in his bunk at night planning on how to outwit the flounders in Block Island Sound." (Again the layout of *The New Yorker* ads comprise an ironic chorus with a 2/3 page ad announcing that "Brooks Brothers Sporting Department Is Based Upon The Knowledge of the Sport... because their cut, colors, materials and workmanship are so perfectly designed and specified for the work they do in the field... Cold Weather Parkas, $35 and $40, Wool Shirts $10 and $11.50.")

Slowly, in spite of all this sophisticated baggage, Mitchell, the veteran newspaperman, now working for the fancy magazine, won over the southeastern Connecticut fisherman.

Some of the journalist's success seems to be because Ellery eventually discovered that Mitchell was not really a city boy after all, but the son of farmers from what Mitchell himself later refers to as "black-ankle country in North Carolina." Then there was, of course, the magic of a bond with McCoy:

> It seems that after college in North Carolina, Joe had hit New York City, to write for the *Herald-Tribune*, during the closing years of Prohibition, and somehow, in his wanderings around Fulton Fish Market, had not only become intently interested in Atlantic ocean and Hudson River fishing but in the early days of rum running when Bill McCoy was a name held in respect.

Ellery found his moment with the Big City writer when he could trade on the McCoy legend:

> One day in 1945 at Hell Hole grounds when Montauk Point on eastern Long Island was in view to the S. S. W. I pointed it out to Joe Mitchell (as the Yale gang worked our last haul) 'Out there, Joe, 12 miles beyond Montauk Light was one of Bill McCoy's favorite jogging locations along Rum Row. Contact boats from eastern Long Island did a lot of business along the Row.'
> 'How about you?' quizzed Joe taking out his notebook.
> 'Hell, Joe. I was no rum-runner, not really, although I may have been suspected of being one.' 'You knew Bill McCoy?' 'Yes, I knew him. I was once a shipmates with him. I ferried him out from the north shore to his schooner *Tomoka* [a.k.a. *Arethusa*] at sea. I bought two cases of Haig and Haig scotch for $96.00. I wrote him a check.'
> 'Didn't you run in a load of whiskey?' Joe was trying to pin me down, and I was fearful; about what he might write for *The New Yorker* in his planned Dragger Captain story. I must shoot the breeze to wind'ard.
> 'Mr. Mitchell, if I told you that I never smuggled a boat load of booze from Rum Row, you might call look upon me as a skinny Yankee liar. But if I confessed that I once stood accused by treasury men of landing a trip of whiskey on the good earth of Connecticut, I would be a damn fool Yankee—true or false.'
> Joe Mitchell looked at me with a friendly smile, as if he thought a bachelor Yankee fisherman was an expert at evading the truth.

Maybe the key to the bonding of Mitchell and Ellery was based on something a good deal less glamorous than the lore of marine life and the aura of Bill McCoy.

Somehow I had noticed that Joe Mitchell didn't go out of his way to impress people by engaging in "high class" conversation—with or without wise cracks. He spoke his mind slowly and without fanfare.

Nor was it eventually a sympathy based merely on Mitchell's modesty, as Ellery noted in his random jottings: "We had many things in common. Most of them were ills, imaginary and real capable of tormenting the human body."

While neither man in this dour duo was at the time over fifty, Ellery's sensibility seems to have chimed with Mitchell's own self-proclaimed "graveyard" style, a manner which the reporter confesses to the public in the valedictory preface to his final collection *Up in the Old Hotel.* He had confided his ills to Ellery, however, half a century earlier in a hand-written note on *The New Yorker* stationery and Ellery treasured it to the end:

> *July 29, 1947*
> *Dear Ellery:*
> *I got back today after spending some time with my family in North Carolina. I had some trouble with my stomach again and knocked off work for a few weeks. I'm feeling better and am going back to work tomorrow. I'm behind schedule (I'm always behind schedule, it seems) and I guess it'll be deep in the winter before I see daylight, but I've stopped worrying about it. Anyway, when and if I ever do get straightened out, I'm going up to see you. I'll let you know in advance.*

After a paragraph acknowledging that he'd seen the article on Ellery in *Liberty* and lamenting the poor quality of the photos ("too blurry"), he concludes:

> *Hoping you are feeling fine and that fishing is good. Give my regards to Mrs. Thompson,*
> *Sincerely,*
> *Joe M.*

There was the natural, if not foreseen battle between subject and writer for just who owned Ellery's story. It would indeed seem fatuous to align *Draggerman's Haul* with the classic excursions into autobiography such as Augustan and Rousseau, and yet a form is a form, a least initially. As Brian O'Nolan said in the process of inventing Flann O'Brien, "The first thing a writer needs to do is to create someone to tell his story." Any attempt at what we now call the presentation of the self must start out suffering from a common set of limitations. A. C. Grayling, in contemplating one of the iconic contemplators, René Descartes notes:

> [While] autobiographers have been sculpting their lives into shapes more agreeable than the truth... perhaps [it is] closer to what they felt was (so to speak) the real reality, which only they could see because only they lived it.

It is, of course, for the sculpting rights of this very "life" as he lived it that Ellery is desperately (if comically, with little boy weapons) fighting Joseph Mitchell—and for that matter, from his grave by the Mystic River, and the Krepcio archive, yet contending with all the rest of us who come after.

The first skirmish in the war between the fisherman and the big city writer for the fisherman's life story began with the species by species semantic struggle:

> Although I had caught about every sea critter that had swum or crawled into the path of our nets, Joe knew more about these creatures from the deep than me. But I told Joe: 'I bet I know where to find them on the bottom more than

any seagoing professor from Yale.'

'Don't be too sure, Ellery. Mr. Merriman is a smart ichthyologist.'

'Right, Mr. Mitchell, but why in blazes do they have to call our plain flat fish or winter flounder a *Pseudopleuronectes americanus*... I left school to steer clear of Latin.'

At one point Mitchell seems to have been brought to a lower, non-semantic level, though the brawl remained oral. The resulting narration seems more Paul Bunyon, than *The New Yorker*:

Joe put down his fork and looked straight at me. "Look. One summer on Block Island I won a clam eating contest."

"So!"

"My total was 70," said Joe proudly. "But if I had been as hungry as I once was at an East Side Beef Stake Supper, I would have made a better showing."

The two men began to relax a bit, in each other's company and revealed something of their domestic sides: Mitchell came up from New York. After entering my house where he was welcomed by my mother, he opened the most tightly packed briefcase I ever did see. Like an assorted jack-in-the-box, out tumbled a sporty pair of pajamas, a roll of notepaper, a box of pencils, two books on European fishing, and an autographed copy of *McSorley's Wonderful Saloon*...

Ellery seems amazed that the books are actually signed over to him. "'Gosh Joe, thanks!'" I stuttered, as I read the inscription in my gift books. Ellery concluded that "This Joe Mitchell was quite a guy;" and charges it up to where the Big City reporter really comes from. "...immediately I began to respect the South for spawning some pretty decent Americans. Hurrah for Dixieland, I thought." Ellery began to put fishing books aboard *Eleanor* as reference work along with similar contributions from Merriman. Mitchell's slim literary volume of Lower East Side pieces, complete with its dust jacket, remained by him until the day he died.

Eventually Mitchell and Ellery got around to talking about writing. At first it was Mitchell's methods and accouterments that impressed the fisherman:

In some respects, Joe Mitchell was one of the most interesting people ever to embark on the *Eleanor*. With his pencils and a roll of note paper big enough to shame a new roll of toilet tissue, he could ask more questions in one hour than a small boy asks in a week. Pointed questions too, that prodded deep within. Although [his] reputation as a first class New York reporter and writer barely registered in my mind, I had no knowledge of his Profiles in *The New Yorker*... Yep, he was a reporter all right, and from certain accounts, a mighty good one. One that might bear keeping an eye on.

Later Ellery noticed that despite "[my] romancing with winter fishing around islands off Cape Cod... Joe wasn't one to stray far from the hub of his story, centered in Block Island Sound." In peeking over the writer's shoulder Ellery noticed Mitchell's note book was dense with "a hodge-podge of invertebrates that came up in our draggerman's haul."

"Ellery, you should write your own stories, and don't overlook calling on Mr. Merriman for help." Joe pocketed his large pad of note paper and handed me his pen. "Try this one: it writes underwater."

When Mitchell's eventual product, "Dragger Captain," appeared in *The New Yorker* in January of 1947, Ellery knew all the shop keepers in Mystic and so was able to track the demographics of his burgeoning fame:

> The few copies that arrived at Mystic newsstands were bought up within minutes, chiefly from artists and writers living on Masons Island. [An island connected by causeway to the east bank of the Mystic estuary and which has routinely been referred to as "an enclave."] It was the same elsewhere in southeastern Connecticut. News of Joe Mitchell's story had preceded its publication.

Oddly enough, it was not Mitchell but Merriman who sent Ellery, not exactly a *New Yorker* subscriber, his first copy. Despite the scientific endorsement, Ellery was able to fend off actually reading his profile. His excuse is typically Elleryian in its baroque complexity and would no doubt fuel a Freudian or even more likely, a Jungian for a whole season. "Due to a winter bout of my old eye trouble (Iritis) I asked my mother to read it to me while I lay in bed blindfolded."

Hadn't he given in to the temptation of the Big City in a way far more insidious than anything suggested in the Baptist hymns with which he loved to torment his mother and the fog? The forty-eight year old Ellery must hide behind a blindfold and a disease with a fancy name in a bed in his widowed mother's house. In the manner of Beatrix Potter's heroine, she spoon feeds him in the manner suitable to the naughty Peter Rabbit after his raid on the big city garden of Mr. MacGregor. When she has fed him all the chamomile tea he can take, he slinks back to his boat like the thieves in the *Bible* under the cover of darkness.

Ellery's reluctance to hear how he came out in the Big City didn't end with his mother's voice coming to him in bed from beyond the blindfold. His small-town fears seem to have almost seeped into him through his mother's milk. "As she stumbled nervously in the reading and I knew she had run into embarrassing paragraphs." Once again the old classical trauma comes to the rescue. "Mother was a darn good reader but some Latin fish names threw her for a loss. "Never mind, Ma," I said, "I'll read it later."

In all his writing, no matter how edited, and certainly in his actual dockside discourse, Ellery, like a draggerman flirting the net near a wreck, senses the action is at the edges. Some of this, of course, is simply a kind of bad-boy, approach/avoidance stuff; much is schtick: the self-styled lanky Yankee salt playing to the Big City audience.

> I had the feeling as he [Mitchell] spotted me at the wheel... a thin, and perhaps mean looking Yankee... And here I was trying to show off at every turn, just because I might be written up in a magazine story...

But most of Ellery's darker side seems real. Mitchell writes, "He is deeply skeptical.

He once said that the older he gets the more he believes that humanity is helpless... It's the blind leading the blind out of the frying pan into the fire, world without end." (Which also happens to be a fine example of a favorite Ellerian rhetoric trope in which he elides a crescendo of cliches until he produces a Biblical finale.).

At some point Ellery must have summoned up the courage to read the piece himself and write his review for his journal:

> In his "Dragger Captain" story, Joe Mitchell did fairly well by a colorful description of Stonington-by-the-sound, and of the local old-time salts who had fished, sealed and whaled on distant seas.

Even for a man given to clichés, this is so densely packed that one can feel him warding off the pain of being fully depicted by a stranger talking to strangers. "Old salts," and "distant seas" aside, the sobriquet of his homeport as "Stonington-on-the-sound" is a slogan hardly then even known to the most commodity-minded real estate broker. It must be charged up to something close to Ellery's unique manner, something too wistful for sarcasm. Mitchell notes the style: "When he does get into a talking mood, much of what he says is ironical. He is deeply skeptical."

There were other repercussions when word got out on the waterfront that Ellery had been singled out for Big City attention. "I reached the point," he confides to his journal, "when I felt like sneaking into Stonington after dark to board *Eleanor*." Ellery's complaint about Mitchell was not confined to stylistic points, or even the portraiture of himself as the "sad-eyed" Yankee bedding down with dreams of fish. It was his perceived insults to his Stonington colleagues. "Joe should not have said that some Stonington draggers were powered with old automobile engines." (The closest I can come to this slight in Mitchell is: "Half have gasoline engines, the newer ones have diesels.")

But even though Ellery is talking to his journal, he wants to set the record straight. He wants to be fair: "Make no mistake; it was a top-notch story, with plenty of Mitchellism."

It is not clear exactly what sort of "top-notch" ingredients went into a "*Mitchellism.*" Most admirers of the reporter praised him for his transparency of style, for *not* intruding his mannerisms into the story. What idiomatic color readers might find in a Mitchell piece was usually that of his subjects. In the case of "Dragger Captain" the "isms" presumably would be mainly "plenty of" Elleryisms. Did Ellery, as many subjects do of interviews, simply not recognize his own stuff in the mirror? Or was he saying that Ellery, as told to Mitchell, came out not quite Ellery? It seems to me from knowing Ellery in person, reading his books, various interviews with various reporters and the Krepcio file that Mitchell came closer to the true Ellery than the Ellery of Viking's "editing."

Of course, like most authentic mariners, from William Dampier to Joshua Slocum, Ellery was always playing to a gallery in the respectable front parlor. He even pitched the stuff that was in his journals, which were actually not so much diary or journal entries, as drafts for the future eyes of some Big City target. That a Stonington fisherman might see his ultimate market in Manhattan should not come as a surprise or even necessarily be seen as an automatic "selling out" in the Holden Caulfield sense. As Helen Crandall says in her short history of Stonington, (a point Mitchell picks up on), it was, after all,

Stonington fishing families that founded the Fulton Market!

In any case, Ellery solaces himself by remarking: "Luckily, few of the Portuguese and old Yankee fisherman wasted time reading from slick paper magazines."

The demographic of the magazine owned by the Fleishman gin company, would not be, of course, the fellow commercial fishermen but the members of the Wadawanuck Yacht Club located snugly by its tennis courts at the inboard end of the harbor. This was the target audience for Mitchell's Ellery piece when it was republished in what Ellery calls "pamphlet form" "to meet" what Ellery admitted was "the demand." Wouldn't it be interesting to be able to sip one's martini *on the* club lawn and know all about what was taking place in the middle distance, out there where the summer southwest wafted just that nip of pungency to mix with the bite of the juniper berry? One hundred and fifty copies were sent to Ellery "to pass around to those who wanted the story." The image of him hawking these on the lawn of "the Wad" is intriguing, if unlikely. Exactly what happened to these copies is somewhat of a mystery. In the half century left of Ellery's life this particular format of the Big City representation of himself seemed to have vanished, whether by his distribution or his jettisoning.

What is clear is that Mitchell helped Ellery become an author. Not only by loaning him his pen and all that that implied, but by networking in the Big City publishing world and also writing in his behalf to the film industry.

Although Joseph Mitchell proved to be the most enduring author in Ellery's life, there was a literary personage who sailed with the Thompsons and impressed his mother more. This was Francis Hopkinson Smith (1838-1915.) Smith wrote a whole shelf load of floridly phrased travel sketches such as *A White Umbrella in Mexico* (1892), *Gondola Days* (1897) and fiction, *The Tides of Barnegat* (1906), which went through various editions culminating in a monumental, uniform "set," after the manner of such early 20th Century luminaries as Joseph Conrad and Henry James. Like Conrad, Smith had one foot in literature and the other in the actual maritime world, in his case, not as a sailor but an architect of iconic coastal installations.

The great-grandson of Francis Hopkinson, a signer of the Declaration of Independence, Smith started his constructor career as an assistant superintendent of an iron foundry during the Civil War in New York. After the war he acquired a partner, James Symington, and set up the engineering firm that lasted thirty years. Among Smith's more notable achievements was the design of the Mosquito Inlet Lighthouse in Florida (an important landmark in Stephen Crane's great short story "The Open Boat"), and the base of the Statue of Liberty on Bedloe's Island in New York Harbor. More routinely, but of great significance to Ellery, Smith engineered the breakwater at Block Island's New Harbor.

Smith's crowning achievement, however, was also up in Ellery's country, Race Rock Light. Perched precariously on a submerged rock between Fishers Island and Orient Point, Long Island, this structure has to endure currents running five knots which when moving against a strong wind create fearsome turmoil. So great is the rip that the old charts refer to the passage as "The Horse Race" after the image suggested by the flowing manes of the galloping seas. Smith not only designed the tower with the best of 1880s technology, but supervised the building. Furthermore, he wrote a best-selling novel about the project, *Caleb West: Master Diver* (1897) featuring a thinly disguised view of the chief constructor Thomas Scott of New London of Meritt-Chapman & Scott.

More to the point, Ellery's mother had one of those F. Hopkinson Smith sets and according to a note by Ellery in the Krepcio file, read them all to Ellery for style as well as content. In the last year of Smith's life, Ellery's mother somehow persuaded the famous author who, after retiring from the construction firm , was apparently still cruising for literary material.

While we were fishing near Race Rock Lighthouse that summer day in 1913 when dragging was in its infancy. I was a boy spending my vacation aboard my father's small fishing boat. A famous writer of the day Mr. F. Hopkinson Smith, took a trip out with us. Besides being a romantic novelist catering to the whims of the heart-throb crowd, he also was an eminent engineer, and was associated with Captain Tom Scott in the building of Race Rock Lighthouse. With the small schooner of Captain Tom Bebee anchored nearby [and] bushy-bearded Captain Tom hauling in black fish from time to time, the tall silver-haired Mr. Smith began talking about writing a new seacoast novel with my father and Tom Bebee two of his characters, as the old Bank fisherman and Pop as the steamboatman again going down to the sea to teach Morris and me how to make our living at sea without tempting old Davy Jones to grab us,

Homeward bound he called me aft near the tiller. "My lad, never be ashamed of being a fisherman and let no true fisherman ever be ashamed of you. Jesus loved all fishermen. Jesus loved all toilers of the sea. Fishing the Atlantic can be a glorious way of life. Fishing is a romantic business and I intend writing a novel about it, and have several fishermen in mind. Who knows? Someday, someone may come along and write you into a honest sea story."

Mr. Smith died the following year, his sea novel unwritten. Some one is now writing about me—ME!

VI. The Making of *Draggerman's Haul*

> It doesn't take a very vivid or poetic imagination to consider
> that speech as something composed of metaphors...
>
> —*Draggerman's Haul*; IV

The "me" who wrote Ellery's story, however, had to evolve over a long time from that day out by Race Rock when the famous lighthouse designer/novelist had planted the notion that a fisherman's career might be of literary use. It took a midwife in the form of Mitchell's two-part *The New Yorker* profile to interest a New York publisher in the potential that F. Hopkinson Smith had seen nearly a half century before.

Based on an interest in Mitchell's pieces, Robert O. Ballou of the Viking Press sent Ellery a contract to publish *Draggerman's Hail* on March 15, 1949. Among other writers in the stable was John Steinbeck.

It is not enough to drop Steinbeck's name next to Ellery as yet another brush with greatness to lend candlepower to his spotlight. In the 1930s the rocky relationship between Ballou and the then young, hardscrabble California writer forms an interesting foundation for the editor's later relationship with the unknown fisherman writer. Born in Illinois in 1892, Ballou first surfaces in the literary world as book review editor of the *Chicago Daily News*. At the end of the 1920s he is with book publishers Cape and Smith heading up the design and production of William Faulkner's *Sound and Fury* (1929), *Sanctuary* (1931) and *As I Lay Dying* (1930), (The books that built the foundation upon which ultimately rested Faulkner's Nobel Prize). Like Ellery whose best days were in the 1930s and 1940s, the man who was to put his pencil on Ellery's prose was forged as an editor in the publishing adversities of the Depression.

Ballou had begun with Steinbeck in 1932 when the editor was working for Cape and Smith. Steinbeck's agents, Elizabeth Otis and Mavis McIntosh, picked out Ballou to tend the young, unknown writer because, as Steinbeck's biographer Jackson T. Benson notes, they felt he had "good taste and a reputation for being concerned with literary quality." Almost before their relationship could begin, however, Cape went bankrupt, leaving the fledgling Steinbeck without a publisher. Benson tracks Ballou scrambling to the new firm of Brewer, Warren and Putnam, taking with him Steinbeck, who had "formed a high opinion of Ballou on the basis of reports from Otis and McIntosh." At the time, Steinbeck had written none of the books by which he is now known, but was working on *The Pastures of Heaven*. Ballou sent him the routine publisher's request for biographical information. This was the sort of thing that Steinbeck fought all through his famous career and at this early stage he merely wrote Ballou, "I don't remember what is true and what might have been true."

In being cast back upon his youth for Ballou's assignment, however, Steinbeck, so Benson speculates, came up with the material for his short story collection *The Red Pony*, his first mature work. Once again, however, Ballou and Steinbeck had their horses shot out from under them as Brewer, Warren and Putnam went broke right after *Pastures of Heaven* came out in 1933. By mid-February 1933 Steinbeck himself was broke and wrote Ballou that he and his wife were going to "get in the car and drive until we can't buy gas anymore." Before they ran out of gas, the Steinbeck's found a tar paper shack near the Pacific at a cheap rent. Even at that, however, the first month's rent consumed all their money so that Steinbeck was forced to pry off two shingles from the roof to bind the manuscript of *To A God Unknown*. The manuscript was now so heavy, however, that he had to borrow the postage, to send it to his agents.

This time Ballou forms his own company and once again Steinbeck sticks by him, their correspondence characterized by Benson as "one man who couldn't pay his electric bill writing across the country to another man who was afraid he couldn't pay the printer."

While Ballou tries to pull together enough money to publish *To a God Unknown*, his option runs out, and Steinbeck's agents, sensing another disaster, send the book to Simon & Schuster who offer a firm contract. Steinbeck, however, remains loyal to Ballou and won't sign with S & S. It is at this time that the author's mother goes into a long, melodramatic and ultimately fatal decline. Steinbeck sets himself up at the kitchen table and tries to polish the draft of his "pony story" for Ballou. Between managing the bedpan duty for his mother in the next room and throwing up, he ekes out "a few pages a day." Soon Steinbeck's father is also dying and the author writes Ballou speculating on which will go first. Ironically this domestic misery inspires Steinbeck to his best, early stretch of writing, all of it possible because the faithful Ballou is waiting to justify the effort by publishing it. Alas, Ballou's own firm goes bust. Once again he manages to leap to another house and takes Steinbeck's contract for his next book with him.

A peculiar thing then happens. Steinbeck completes *Tortilla Flat*, a short, comic book about Mexican immigrants done pretty much as a *joi d' esprite* after a jug wine party. Ballou sees it for what it is: a thin attempt at a subject in questionable taste. He turns it down and Steinbeck is suddenly back to square one, a struggling young writer without a contract. Steinbeck's agents send *Tortilla Flat* out to a half dozen publishers with no success. By chance Pascal Covici, who heads up a small firm Covici-Freide, finds Steinbeck's two earliest books *Cup of Gold* and *Pastures of Heaven* on a remainder table while he's on a book selling trip to Chicago. Talked into the books by the store's enthusiastic owner, Covici takes them back to his hotel room, reads them and is impressed enough to get in touch with Steinbeck as soon as he returns to New York. Much to his delight, Steinbeck's agents inform Covici that Ballou has just set Steinbeck free.

Covici immediately signs Steinbeck up. *Tortilla Flat* becomes Steinbeck's first big seller and his first of many films. Covici goes on to publish Steinbeck's first critical success *Of Mice and Men* and now has the author's loyalty so that when Covici-Freide goes broke, Steinbeck takes him to Viking in time for *Grapes of Wrath*. Continuing the emotional attachment to his editor that he had begun with Ballou in the days of his mother's illness, Steinbeck writes long "journals" of the composition of *Grapes* and of *East of Eden* in the form of a conversation with Covici. Both volumes transcend their original impulse and become fascinating glimpses in the workshop of the creative process. It is Covici then who goes down in history as perhaps the second great American editor of the mid-century after Scribner's Maxwell Perkins (Hemingway, Scott Fitzgerald, Thomas Wolfe, Marjorie Rawlings, and James Jones).

Meanwhile Ballou scrambles over to Viking. Thus, when Ellery Thompson arrives at Viking just after the War, some ten years after *Grapes of Wrath*, he has Steinbeck's first editor, but not the editor Steinbeck has at Viking. Benson sums up Ballou's contribution to Steinbeck: "Ballou shall be given credit for sticking with Steinbeck at a critical time, and the irony of his loyalty was that it didn't last quite long enough. If he had stayed with Steinbeck for one more book, he might well have recovered his losses and gone on to share in Steinbeck's success. Nevertheless, he was one of the few who backed Steinbeck during his hard times."

Just how did Ellery himself arrive at Viking? Oddly enough it was through his painting and his science. It will be recalled newsman Charles Clapp Jr. had reported that Professor Merriman's secretary was typing up drafts revised by the scientist and the fisherman at the Bingham Lab in New Haven. In gratitude, Ellery "presented her with one of his paintings. Through a curious series of circumstances one of the heads of Viking Press saw this painting at her house, commented on it, learned about the book, and—"

Was it Viking founder Harold K. Guinzburg who scouted Ellery through the painting? In any case, shortly thereafter Ellery receives a note from Guinzburg thanking him for just such a painting. (Guinzburg has a cozy relationship with his authors. It is he who hosts Steinbeck's third and final wedding at his home and it is his daughter who plays "Here Comes the Bride" on the Guinzburg parlor piano). In later years Viking publishes a host of prize winners including Nobel Laureates Saul Bellow and Samuel Beckett. Jacqueline Bouvier Kennedy Onassis joins the staff as an editor through her friendship with Guinzburg. Clapp remains Ellery's friend, writing him a letter counseling him on how to deal with the enigma of best-seller lists and reviews, a process it seems especially baffling to one who is used to selling his wares in Manhattan under more tangible, if damper arrangements.

In spite of the chumminess between Steinbeck and Covici and Guinzburg it would be a mistake to think that Viking editors let even their most famous authors run wild. Benson remarks: "Steinbeck was just another author and authors can run astray without an editor's considered judgement." Benson speculates that Marshall Best, the chief editor, was always lurking over Covici and the other editors. It was Best, who in Benson's theory, pushed Covici into challenging the soon to be infamous ending of *Grapes of Wrath*. Steinbeck stood up to the editors; the book went on to be the basis for his Nobel Prize after the War and is a perpetual candidate for that perpetually elusive designation as "The Great American Novel." *The Grapes of Wrath* ending, however, is, to this day, yet getting high school English departments into trouble with school boards.

The character of Robert Ballou and the politics of the Viking office are important when we come to sorting out the way *Draggerman's Haul* got put together. The first drafts, after all were pecked out on a typewriter by a man who barely had a middle school education and had at the time not so much published a letter to the editor of the New London *Day*. We are dancing along the edge of the larger problem of the man of action and his ghost writer. The establishing of authorship is particularly an issue with maritime writers, one that goes back to Alexander Selkirk and Daniel Defoe, William Dampier and *his* writer, on down to the bluewater sailor "logs," "journals" and "diaries" of the 19th Century, through Joshua Slocum's 1900 *Sailing Alone Around the World* and a host of others. None of this would matter as much if Ellery had not received praise by reviewers from William McPhee to the New London *Day* for his genuine seaman's prose.

The manuscript of *Draggerman's Haul* was not yet anywhere near finished when Ballou began to work on the project and there was nothing in Ellery's background to persuade an editor that this colorful subject was in control of the expression of his own life. For a start, Ballou felt the need to explain clause 6c in the standard contract. Addressing Ellery as "Captain Thompson," he writes: "When one starts out on this kind of collaboration there is always the possibility that it will not work out as well as we hope. Because of that possibility—though we don't anticipate its happening—we feel that we ought not to commit to publishing the book if the manuscript does not come up to our expectations."

So far this is merely a down-home translation of the standard author's contract. What follows, however, suggests that what Ballou meant by "collaboration" was not merely office-speak for teamwork, but a recognition that his role in the preparation of the manuscript as anticipated by Viking was to be closer to a partnership between a ghost writer and "author." The question in New York was what to do with some sort of performance that was halfway between a seaman's rambles and a publishable product. "Naturally we would have every incentive to publish it, for we would already have a large investment in it in the form of my salary and expenses..." The editor goes on to inform his prospective author just who is going to be the decider: " but if you and I could not turn out together a book which we all thought rated enthusiastic production, it would be better for all of us if Viking were to abandon its investment and turn the project back to you." Having let that sink in, Ballou hastens to add in a new paragraph "None of us believes that this will happen if you are willing to go ahead on the basis we have suggested above."

It is not until five weeks later that Ballou writes "Captain Thompson" again. It is not clear if this delay was caused by the editor or the writer or a combination of both. In any case, it would not seem that Ellery had been distracted by being at sea as Ballou says he's "Sorry the weather has been troublesome for fishing." Ballou expresses his gladness that he is "considering favorably signing one of the contracts, and that you are writing more," which implies that this is not going to be an "as-told-to" but more of a heavy edit job.

By Ballou's reaction, what seems to have held up things on Ellery's end is a combination of a writer yet living at home with his mother and his own lack of confidence in his literary technique for indirection. "I have known from the first that there might be some conflict in your mind between your desire to paint a picture of life as you have really seen it and lived it, and your desire not to offend friends like... and your mother.

There is no doubt in my mind that you will tell the story as you see it, and that is as it should be. I think, too, that you will find that you can do it in ways that are not in any way offensive. Life isn't just a bed of roses, nor is the human race a congregation of angels, and I think that most people accept this fact by now." Ballou goes on to applaud an interest that *McCall's* seems to have expressed directly to Ellery "in the material" and invites him to come to New York to visit "Mr. [Harold K.] Guinzburg" the chief editor, and himself. He concludes "With best wishes to your mother." (Apparently Ballou is not aware that Guinzburg has already met Ellery through the painting.)

By August 12, the editor and his writer are cooking. On stationery that now ignores the Viking letterhead, but has what is presumably his own address, Ballou writes: "Dear Ellery: I've meant to write you before to thank you for the good, and rewarding, [sic] day you gave me a week ago, but I've been pushing ahead on the book—and other things—and there never seems to be enough time." He proceeds to ask a half dozen questions which Ellery answers in a combination of type-written responses and his sprawling handwriting.

Ballou's first letter in this series asks Ellery to straighten out a genealogical tangle involving the Wilcox and Bindloss family (Eventually Ellery tells Ballou "You have the Wilcoxes down pat—perhaps too pat for their own good."). Ellery makes the connections and launches into some judgements on the folks, one of whom had "tremendous" stature in the community "But he was okay, a good Baptist. He didn't run [hire?] Pa money or no money." Ellery includes the morsel that his "grandmother Thompson owned stock [in the Wilcox menhaden fertilizer company]. It was good stuff and hard to get." He begins "a remarkable story about Pa making a thousand hook trawl line 500 feet long—working all night while the family tried to sleep—" He promises "to go into it later." Was this how Ellery backed into the moving chapter on the retrieval of Morris's where such a hook line was used to fish the body?

Ballou wants to know the year Ellery's father was hurt on the *Panuco*. Ellery types in that this was 1911, corrects by hand that it was 1912 and promises to send Ballou "a chapter on it this week. I think it funny ???"

Ballou has a question about distances between points and another one on crew personnel which elicits an interesting typed comment by Ellery that resonates today: "During the late 1920s many of our local boats had Canadian crews. They were good fishermen. Finally they were not allowed to cross the border to U.S.A. to fish. Then we began developing our own 'fishermen.'" In pencil he promises "more on it."

Six weeks later (9/30/49), Ballou shows how he tried to turn an inevitable problem in biography into a literary asset. While there are few other documents that show the strategy, and this one is thin on tactics, it at least shows what Ballou's contribution was. "I was especially glad to get the chronology of your various family moves, the places of your births, etc., straight. It looks on paper like a merry-go-round, or more like a snowball which gathered size whenever it moved."

Ballou then traces some of the moves. Now into the rhythm, he ventures a tone which if you think about the actual sadness of what he's talking about, the displacement of the family caused by the bread winner's inability to keep the roof over its head, is anything but "bright." "Whenever Pop was there was apparently a B. B. Gardner moving van waiting. I've tried to make it sound that way in using it, and it brightens up the story."

So much for facing up to Ballou's dictum that "Life isn't just a bed of roses." Apparently it is a "merry-go-round" instead.

The movie business by now has begun to intrude and Ballou gets an opinion from Viking's lawyers on the contract Warner Brothers wanted Joe Mitchell and him to sign. A week later Ballou's next letter is also largely taken up with the Warner Brothers matter which Ballou (misspelling his boss's name) has now taken to Harold "Guinsburg." Meanwhile the job of editing still must go on. In the margin of Ballou's letter, Ellery notes that the manuscript he's just sent Ballou is "a little over 60,000 words... probably 2/3 of the book."

On October 14, Ballou writes Ellery two sympathetic paragraphs about the movie deal, mentioning that he hasn't "seen Harold [Guinzburg] this morning, but I talked to [agent] Mark Hanna on the phone" setting up what he hopes to be a meeting with Ellery aboard *Eleanor* in Stonington. Ballou adds a long paragraph which gets into the nitty-gritty of the book's composition. It is the best single document that survives of what went on between editor and writer that effected *Draggerman's Haul* in "things that matter." Moreover, given Ballou's experience going back to Faulkner and Steinbeck, his remarks would seem to reflect what seems standard practice between editors and authors in mid-twentieth century America:

> I'll work in about Arlene and as much as I can of the others you want to mention. The thing that has to be guarded against in this is seeming to drag people in by the heels just for the sake of mentioning their names. What I'm doing is saving all these bits which have come along after I have written the parts where they belong, if anywhere, and others which I have missed, and keeping them all together.

Ballou goes on to outline his idea of the ongoing working relationship between himself and his author:

> After we have an otherwise complete ms. I'll go back and work in as many of the bits as I can. If you will make notes of other things you think of, and corrections on the copy of the first 204 pages I sent yesterday, and keep the copy safely, then later we ought to have a session of a day or two maybe together, and I can take off from your copy the things which should be in the final copy.

In splicing together the narrative that Ellery has already typed, Ballou finds himself into some areas that have him worried about his own maritime expertise. Trying to sort out the matter of establishing literal, historical truth, he then backs into an interesting theory of "proper embroidery" which anticipates so much of our current discussions of the rules in "creative" or "literary" non-fiction:

> I'm sure that I must have made some errors of fact—by which I don't mean proper embroidery of facts—I'm sure there are lots of things in the book which tell the truth at the expense of mere facts—but the things that matter.

First Ballou gives an example of the "things that matter." It is the topographical discussion of "holes," without the ribald factor.

> For instance I remember in one place I tried to describe what a "hole" was and I was vague in my own mind and said it was a channel between islands [such as Wood's Hole, or Quick's Hole between the Elizabeth Islands off Cape Cod] or a washed out bottom at the mouth of a stream, which, thinking of it later, seems probably wrong as hell to me. That is the kind of error we mustn't make.

Then as a kind of throwaway parenthetical at the end of the postscript, Ballou reveals a hint into the kind of "proper embroidery" in the service of "the truth at the expense of mere facts."

> (Incidentally—Blowing my Own Horn Department—tell me what you think of the ending I put on the Ted and Lillian, Yankee High, story. [Last five pages of Chapter X, "Women Are Lonely."] I like it. In fact I like the whole story. I was almost tempted to suggest to you that we might hold it out of the book and try to make a good short story out of it to sell to a popular magazine for a thousand bucks. But that's not the way to write a book. This thing ought to have the best we've got. If there's anything left over that doesn't belong in the book, then we can think about what to do with it.)

If by "the ending I put on" Ballou means the last three paragraphs of what ended up as Chapter X, then one can only marvel at the taste of the man who turned down *Tortilla Flat*, edited *The Pastures of Heaven* and *To A God Unknown*, designed Faulkner's *The Sound and Fury* and championed *Sanctuary* to the film industry.

In any case Ellery answers promptly the next day: "I've gone over the manuscript pretty well and it's swell. I think it's darn good reading. You've done a wonderful job... And the rum business is as smooth as oil but twice as potent." And then he gets into one of those maddeningly bifurcated meanings he falls into from time to time: "Putting myself as someone far removed from this scene, the book seems to be one that can be read over and over again with equal enjoyment. I'll go into in more carefully later on." Does this distancing refer to the "scene" in the preceding sentence—the rum running about which in 1941 he felt might yet be too close to some sort of perceived statute of limitations? It was a topic about which, in any case, he was to coyly play both ways to his dying day. Or does he refer to the major topic of his letter—the experience of having "gone over the manuscript?" In this meaning he would be telling his editor that he finds himself in that most desirable of writer's position: the reading wherein he no longer winces at the personal scent of his own prose. This position may not quite be the young James Joyce's ideal creator removed from the scene of his creation, "... beyond or above his handiwork, invisible, refined out of existence, indifferent, paring his fingernails," but it would celebrate a major step in Ellery's development as a writer.

A week later Ballou replies with more stuff about Warner Brothers putting pressure on him to show the book, which is now at 204 pages. "Incidentally, the *Saturday Evening Post* is going to take a look." Ballou is still tracking the prose, however, and adds a p.s.

in pen in which he tries to balance the needs of narrative consistency with the historic facts in regard to Nan and Ellery's interest in each other and in painting. It also shows the degree to which Ballou is thinking of himself as someone who has come to be *saying* in Ellery's story exactly what it was Nan did:

> It occurred to me in your story about Nan that this was long before your serious interest in painting began, as we had it before. Because of that I said that Nan had brought along painting materials. Is that ok? It can, of course, be arranged any way that seems best, so long as it hangs together—but we have to explain how there happened to be painting materials along that day.

Again the film industry intrudes upon the book and Ballou sounds off: "But what stinkers, honestly, to need a thing like our entry into the field with the book in order to begin offering you a little real dough. I simply haven't the capacity to understand those guys." The hovering specter of Hollywood was to follow Ellery into his old age.

It's not that the book in itself hadn't its own lime light. *Draggerman's Haul* was a Book-of-the-Month Club selection for July 1950. Ellery kept his copy of the BOMC *News* until the day he died. It is interesting to see the company into which Ellery was suddenly thrown. One can well-imagine him leafing through the catalogue of his new stable mates. The cover of the BOMC *News* featured a painting of *Fourth of July Parade* by A. C. Howland, a comic mixture of ancient vets and small-town urchins in the manner of Norman Rockwell. Fellow literary selections and their blurbs which have survived for various reasons to our day included: *The Last Cruise* by William (*Ugly American*) Lederer, (a "noble canto in the greatest epic of man against the sea") about a W.W. II submarine; Clyde Brion Davis' *The Age of Indiscretion*, ("a scathing denunciation of the prevalent view of a large group of present-day intelligentsia, that our own period is in decline"); Columbia history professor Jacques Barzun's *Berlioz and the Romantic Tradition*; *Scottsboro Boy* ("It is now nearly twenty years since nine Negro boys were brought into court at Scottsboro, Alabama, and were tried—if the proceedings that followed could be called a trial—on the charge of rape."); *Understanding Your Boy* by Father Flanagan as told to Ford McCoy; in which the "well-know founder and director of the famous Boys' Town... sets before the reader his proved technique of how to replace bad behavior tendencies with good behavior tendencies."

The backlist was daunting, especially with its urgent annotations but was probably as close as Ellery came to possessing a syllabus of high culture. The list included no less than three more books by Winston Churchill; a biography of the Marx Brothers; Catherine Drinker Bowen "flawless and magnificent literary achievement *John Adams and the American Revolution*;" Marchette Chute's *Shakespeare of London*; Henry Steele Commager's "much-praised interpretation of American thought and character" *The American Mind*; John Hersey's *The Wall* ("one of the major novels of our generation"); Norman Mailer's first book *The Naked and the Dead*; Laura Z. Hobson's "widely-praised best-seller has to do with anti-Semitism" (later the movie with Gregory Peck) *Gentleman's Agreement*; Graham Greene's *The Heart of the Matter*, Alan Paton's *Cry, The Beloved Country*, Arthur Miller's *Death of a Salesman*, Gilberth's *Cheaper by the Dozen*; Toynbee's *A*

Study of History, ("... seeks to find a pattern in the rise and full of all the colorful civilizations of the past. It is a book that is a must read by every person who feels the need of formulating a philosophy for himself."); Robert E. Sherwood's *Roosevelt and Hopkins*, ("Based on Hopkins' forty filing cabinets of secret papers"); Eleanor Roosevelt's *This I Remember*; Fleet Admiral Leahy's *I Was There*; F. O. Matthiessen's *The James Family*, Eisenhower's *Crusade in Europe* and E. B. White's *This Is New York*. Interestingly enough there was also Joyce Cary's *The Horse's Mouth*, the marvelously written tale of a waterfront artist-rogue who lived on a derelict barge, "the spryest, maddest, most delightful old man that one can remember in recent English fiction," later memorably played by Alex Guiness. (While Gary Cooper and Henry Fonda were considered for the role of Ellery, no one seems to have thought of Guiness.)

The Book of the Month Club also flogged classics such as Dreiser's *American Tragedy*; Nordhoff and Hall's *Bounty Trilogy*, illustrated by no less than N. C. Wyeth—more thrilling men against the sea stuff; Fielding's "masterpiece" *Tom Jones*; Dostoevsky's *The Brothers Karamazov* ("one of the most penetrating psychological studies ever written, with unforgettable episodes recently selected and edited by W. Somerset Maugham."); Dickens' *David Copperfield* ("Charmingly illustrated"); Tolstoy's *War and Peace* ("considered by many critics the greatest novel ever written") and Emily Bronte's "strange tale of passion and doom among the violent and undisciplined people of a remote English countryside" *Wuthering Heights*.

There were also numerous self-help books: Catholic Vincent Sheean's latest; Protestant Norman Vincent Peale, D.D. *The Guide to Confident Living*; Fulton Oursler's *The Greatest Story Ever Told*; and *The Bible to Designed to Be Read as Living Literature* (King James version). Perhaps of more practical interest to Ellery was *Sex Questions and Answers: A Guide to Happy Marriage*, ("Especially valuable for parents with growing children, and for young people about to be married."); two cookbooks, a home repair guide and a sewing book.

Ellery's own book was reviewed by the reigning suburban taste diva Dorothy Canfield, who also took on the Father Flanagan as told-to about bad boys. She concludes her hundred word summary: "All this comes to us with the salty directness of a man who knows his stuff because he lived it." The review featured a thumbnail photo of "Mr. Thompson" in layers of plaid shirts, his soon-to-be-famous "sad eyes" over a ok-if-you-must grin. The price was $ 3.00.

Many of the selections in the Book of the Month Club with Ellery were being made into movies. It was natural therefore, that while *Draggerman's Haul* did not really have an obvious dramatic narrative line in the way of *Cry, The Beloved Country*, *Cheaper by the Dozen*, *Mutiny on the Bounty* or even *The Horse's Mouth*, there might yet be something in the book that could be mined.

VII. Ellery and the Film Industry

I didn't mind when I found out that Will Rodgers, Gilda Gray, Gallagher and Sheen,
Fanny Brice, Ann Pennington, and many others were all on the same program.
— *Draggerman's Haul*, IX

The percentage of movies that are finally made from scripts that even get as far as being commissioned, completed and paid for is minute. This is because scripts are commissioned for movies that are not only never made, but are never seriously intended to be made. Such a process is not to be confused with profitless poets and novelists toiling in proverbial garrets. The film script not-to-be-actually-made has come to be a profitable sub industry. Apparently following John Keats' line that "unheard melodies are sweetest," there are even some films that seem to grow greater reputations for not having been made, such as James Agee's script for Stephen Crane's great short story "The Blue Hotel."

This curious process is true now as it was true in Ellery's time. It certainly seems to have been the case with *Draggerman*, starring Henry Fonda (or Gary Cooper), directed by John Ford (or ?) The degree to which Ellery's life was either sustained or ruined by the possibility of not only his book, but his "story," that is, his *life* being turned into an American icon is a subject of much debate. Again, as close as we can come to the truth seems to be in the Krepcio Archive.

The film interest in Ellery actually started with the Mitchell articles in *The New Yorker* and Joe Mitchell himself jumped into the action. On April 21, 1948 Mitchell writes Ellery on *The New Yorker* stationery revealing that he has "some news on the movie matter, although it is of a rather indefinite nature." Evidently Harold Ober, Mitchell's literary agent, has gotten Warner Brothers sufficiently interested in *The New Yorker* profile plus "about 10,000 words of notes" that Mitchell had jotted down on the "fish market and fishing articles" he'd done. The film writer is to use "this material as background" and "make an attempt to devise a plot." If the "plot suits them, they will buy the material." The drop dead date is August 1 and the top price for which "we can hope for is $15,000." Ober has advised Ellery not to get his "hopes up." The chances are nothing except some option money will come of the work. Mitchell recommends to Ellery that they put the whole project out of their minds until August.

Ellery evidently passes this offer on to Robert Ballou his editor at Viking who, as we have seen, is in the midst yet of editing *Draggerman's Haul*. Ballou has shown the "agreement you signed with Joe Mitchell on February 19, 1949" to Viking's lawyers. Ballou has had experience running interference for authors with the film industry as long ago as April 1932 when with Cape and Smith he'd corresponded in behalf of William Faulkner over the film rights of *Sanctuary*. "Of Viking's lawyers," Ballou wrote Ellery, "they are a very good firm, very cautious and conservative, and this is, on the whole, a pretty strong statement for them to make. Of course it is only an opinion, but I would bank on any court taking the same view. Not that it will ever come to court—we hope." One can only assume that Viking's lawyers were advising their two writers to get out of the Warner deal.

In the meanwhile Ober advises Mitchell to say nothing about anything to outsiders. Ellery devises an end run:

> Whenever my morale would hit the doldrums, I would head for the home of Danny and Alma Robertson. Danny had often fished with me on the *Eleanor* and Alma (wife, mother of three, writer) offered me encouragement I seemed to crave. Later Alma was to write a letter to Henry Fonda, who after acknowledging it, called me on the telephone and invited me to visit him backstage at *Mr. Roberts*. He even set aside four "producer row" tickets for a performance. Naturally I went and took along the Robertsons and my sister Eleanor. After a swell show, Henry Fonda and I talked about the making of a Draggerman movie. "Someday, I'll do it," he said.

The Madison Avenue agent Mark Hanna wrote Ellery May 3rd, 1950 at the Thompson home on Crystal Avenue. It is clear that Hanna is about to have a meeting on Monday night with "Hank" who is once again making a name for himself, this time in the Broadway *Mr. Roberts* role. After thanking Ellery for "a very nice letter," Hanna expressed his pleasure that Ellery had such a good time at *Mr. Roberts* and in meeting Fonda. They both agree that Fonda is "a helluva nice guy." (Ellery's phrase.) Hanna says he doesn't expect Fonda to commit himself because of the *Mr. Roberts* engagement which he was locked in until 1952. Fonda, of course, actually became committed to the *Mr. Roberts* role well after that date when he took on the film version, then an unknown project. Nevertheless, Hanna thinks "a mild 'goose' won't do any harm," but "certainly not Monday night" but in the near future. The hope is to get the actor to take an option. Hanna concludes by saying he himself has "seen the book" and thinks it's "an outstanding job" though, of course, in true New York fashion, he has yet had a chance to actually read it. (He's evidently going by the jacket and the inside covers.) He promises to write after Hank and he have had their little meeting on Monday night. A month later Fonda writes Ellery by hand on a sheet of pale blue paper simply headed:

Henry Fonda

Ellery preserved the letter. Fonda begins by apologizing for the long delay in responding to Ellery's letter, which, like Hanna, he characterizes as "nice." He's been rehearsing replacements in the cast of *Mister Roberts* and concludes that there just aren't enough hours in the day. He thanks him for the book (evidently *Draggerman's Haul.*) Which he says he "thoroughly enjoyed" and can't thank him enough for "the pleasure in reading it."

The "little meeting" on Monday with Hanna apparently was indeed not long. Fonda characterizes it as "brief." He hopes to see him again when he can. In the meantime he's sent the book off with a letter expressing his "enthusiasm" to no less than John Ford whom Fonda hopes will "share it." This is, amazingly enough for Ellery, the same John Ford who pretty much invented the modern Western and who had directed Fonda in the Academy Award role of Tom Joad in Steinbeck's pre-war *Grapes of Wrath*. Fonda signs off to Ellery "hastily but sincerely."

Fonda, however, is off to Hollywood to make the film version of *Mr. Roberts* with Jack Lemon and James Cagney. The very success Fonda has had in the role of the laconic, lanky executive officer of a World War II vessel caught in the backwaters of the Pacific war mitigates against his freedom to take on being the lanky, laconic fishing skipper now pretty much caught in the backwaters of Eastern Connecticut. Neither Ellery nor Mitchell give up.

In the summer of 1957 Ellery somehow gets involved in an agreement with a Hollywood script writer whom I will call Nelson Falorp. On October 14, Falorp answers a letter from Ellery who has evidently sent him some pictures which Falorp finds "charming." He puts them up over the mantel of his library where "I can glance up and look at them as I work." In his cover letter to the agreement, Falorp says he "did not realize until I saw the contract which I am returning unsigned that Mr. Ober is your agent as well as Mitchell's." Falorp has relatives in Connecticut and hopes that "you and they can get to meet each other and that you and I will meet in the not too distant future." He assures Ellery he is "still deeply interested in the Dragger Captain project, but in the meantime states that he is "more than ever unwilling to sweat it out to the profit point and then find profit and pleasure both blocked by shrewd agenting."

Getting down to the business in what seems to be another shot at the agreement, Falorp reminds Ellery that it was he who initiated the proposal to Falorp on April 6 to which Falorp responded on July 25 and which Ellery accepted by telegram sent from Stonington at 2:58 PM on August 4. (This sequence unfortunately is missing from the Krepcio file.) In Falorp's letter of agreement he promises to "follow the true pattern of your life as narrated by you as closely as possible." He says he will "take personally and through recognized agents and attornies [sic] all steps to sell and exploit it." He offers to split the profits fifty-fifty. "And I will use the best efforts of myself and my agents to secure for you assignments as technical expert in any and all productions arising from my efforts "

Apparently unbeknownst to Falorp, however, Ellery has been writing to Harold Ober who indeed is now his literary agent as well as Mitchell's. On August 21 Ober himself is "out of town" but his assistant is not very happy with the mess Ellery seems to be sailing into. She warns him that the July 25 agreement with Falorp is committing Mitchell and *The New Yorker* and that "they need to know what the arrangements are."

Ellery gets around to answering Ober in October 24. Ober himself is now out with "the Asian flu," but his assistant is still on the job. She reports that Falorp has written "to Mr. Ober on October 21st about the option agreement, to which he took certain objections, and we have another letter from him this morning." The Ober office takes strong objection to Falorp's request for a three-year option. The office policy is one year and "Mr. Mitchell has authorized me today to tell Mr. [Falorp] that he will not consent to... these arrangements. Mr. Mitchell has your own interest very much in mind, and I would like to point out to you that neither you nor Mr. Mitchell has the promise of any money... and we cannot see that any advantage would accrue to you under this arrangement."

A month later Falorp writes Ellery, again from Hollywood. "As you know, Dragger Captain has always been close to my heart and both my agent and I have kept watching for a place to use it." Because "feature motion picture making, of course, has practically stopped here" Falorp suggests a one hour TV feature with the possibility that "a series might grow out of it." He thinks he can get $1,000 for a single show, but warns that "television is an odd and touchy medium and it has a short attention span." He asks for Ellery to write him as soon as he gets the letter to give him "the authority to go ahead." He closes by once again hoping to meet Ellery face to face.

Later there was an unsuccessful scenario involving Gary Cooper. In any case, the image of Ellery Thompson as the second incarnation of a kind of *Mr. Roberts*–Tom Joad–*High Noon* filmed by John Ford certainly sustained Ellery for some time. Eventually, about the time I came to know him, it had become obvious to even him that reasonable as all this Hollywood stuff had once seemed, it was just never going to happen. The New York-Hollywood hocus-pocus came to strike Ellery as at best a mystery, well-suited to his lugubrious schtick, "hardly the way you did business with your product at the Fulton Market, though Lord knew that was often a bit discouraging." The way the film-publishing axis works these days, however, has hardly changed.

Ellery's interest in dramatizing his life did not begin, however, with the film industry. In his miscellaneous memoirs, Ellery relates that the first New York cultural experience that his father exposed him to was the baseball at the Polo Grounds where the histrionic manager John McGraw held forth. Readers of *Draggerman's Haul* will note that Ellery had a lifelong interest in what might loosely be called New York theater. For the young fisherman from Eastern Connecticut, the theater was merely an extension of the sophistication of Manhattan that he had first encountered on South Street when his father took him to the Fulton Fish Market followed by a walk uptown to the *Follies*. In the twenties Ellery retraced the path through lower Manhattan leading his own crew. It was a particularly ripe moment for such an endeavor. As Tom Dardis reports in his biography of the Broadway producer-publisher Horace Liveright:

> The twenties were the most exciting period in the history of the American theater... with seventy-six theaters putting on more than two hundred new plays and reviews each year—a staggering number by today's standards—there was something for every taste. On the lighter side were Florenze Ziegfeld, and his perennial *Follies*, twenty-four from 1907 through 1931, filled with feathers and rhinestones, beautiful girls, and comedians such as W. C. Fields, Eddie Cantor, Fanny Brice, and Will Rogers, and Jerome Kern's *Show Boat*, which outran everything else produced in the decade. The early Noel Coward and Cole Porter musicals were just beginning to appear.

[243]

Like his father, Ellery seems to have delighted in corrupting the boys from Eastern Connecticut and "thought it would be fun to watch Fred watching the girls." In fishing for hard-to-obtain tickets, he displayed the skill and determination he usually reserved for hunting down fish:

> I couldn't get any tickets at the box office and finally found two at one of those holes-in-the-wall around Times Square for thirteen dollars.

Although Ellery's early fascination with the theater may have been primarily anatomical—more "rhinestones and feathers" than stagecraft—after World War II, with the aid of Bernie Gordon's brother, Joseph, he put some of his experience as an audience to work and composed two versions of his life to be "performed with music." At one point Joe Gordon wrote Disney on behalf of Ellery and elicited some interest that ultimately went the way of the other Ellery show biz productions. To demonstrate that Ellery was closer to W. C. Fields than to the New London waterfront of Eugene O'Neill, one of the songs in the Gordon-Thompson script contained a lyric rhyming "Ellery" and "celery."

Ellery painting a picture of a dragger at the Stonington docks.

VIII. The Art of Ellery

"Something for a beginner?" she asked.
"No," I said firmly. "Make believe I'm Rembrandt."
—*Draggerman's Haul*, XIV

Most people felt more comfortable with Ellery's paintings than his narrations, whether encountered in print or in a more precarious "glittering eye" encounter. I kept my own eye out for these paintings and discovered that he had actually done a wider variety than his critics had given him credit for. The subjects were not only *Eleanors* caught broadside, but also *Eleanors* head on. Moreover there were Eastern rigs, the usual way in which schooners were modified into engine boats by down-rigging the masts and building a wheelhouses aft. (*Eleanor*, being designed for engine power from the conception, had her wheelhouse forward in what is sometimes called the Western rig.) Sometimes Ellery varied the backgrounds, taking his models further offshore. At times he got as far off as a spinachy smudge with a salt shaker on top that you could be easily persuaded might be Montauk Point complete with lighthouse. There were also those Gloucester schooners like *Arethusa* or *Bluenose* and those square-riggers that might recall to those who hung around pot-belly heated carpentry shops in the 1940s and 50s as the Columbia Rope calendar. Most bodacious of Ellery's sea paintings was "A view of a harpooner ready to iron a giant sperm whale" produced as an Ansochrome® postcard by Bernie Gordon. For the price of the postcard the purchaser got: two whaling barques, one portside profile, one head-on bearing down; two whale boats with six crew each including a red shirted harpooner; lots of thick, blue green waves; a spouting sperm whale grimacing on top of the waves like a fat man on a mattress and four gulls heading our way, plus space for a message and address on the obverse. A few years ago in the back room of a local insurance agency I found an Ellery of the pre-war Wilcox menhaden steamers of which he writes so lovingly in *Draggerman's Haul*. (Ellery was a Wilcox descendent.) My friend Jack Steele is the fortunate owner of Ellery's painting of Bill McCoy by the steering wheel of what is presumably *Arethusa*. McCoy scholar Robert McKenna suggests that the basis of this depiction is the 1944 *Ripley's Believe It Or Not* drawing, itself a variation of the photograph of Bill McCoy that is the frontispiece of the 1931 *The Real McCoy*.

Early Ellerys, before he got into high production on masonite, had actually found their way onto stretched canvas. Just the other day (2006) I saw in the window of a local frame shop an *Eleanor* being buzzed by a Navy TBM of the sort I recalled flying over my house in the 1940s and which recalls the valuable WW II chapters in *Draggerman's Haul*.

The price on Early Ellerys varied with what he needed at the moment or thought he could pry out of a customer. Judging from what you saw on local walls, the majority of his paintings in the first twenty years went as barter for professional services or restaurant privileges. The hard cash exchanges usually began at fifty bucks in the 1950s. I'm not sure how he arrived at this price. Fellow Mystic artist S. Jerome Hoxie always kept track of his hours on the back of the painting, "just like any other craftsman," as he explained to me one day on the pier back of his shop. Of course, Ellery had not been used to toiling that was tied to time, but pounds, hardly a helpful metric for a picture. When it came to things such as the world of art, Ellery tended to key on *outre* models. As for fifty dollars, I recall a match box at the time that advertised a career in radio that would net the graduate of the proffered course exactly that much per week. As with most painters, death is a good career move. One of the downtown historic Mystic shops now sells a strictly maritime Ellery for from five to eight hundred depending upon condition. "That is," says the shop keeper, "when we can lay hold of one. They pretty much fly out of here."

Despite the fact that Ellery was no longer living over the paint store, the new proprietor of the paint store, Tuck Jones nevertheless succeeded Ed Maxwell in the role of confidante and general factotum during Ellery's Fort Rachel period. It was Tuck's duty, it seems, to bring Ellery a proscribed bag of goodies every Friday night which included a magazine, a tube of alizarin and a number six brush. The number six brush Tuck figured Ellery used for the finer work. "Yes, there *were* some finer points in an Ellery painting," Tuck reminded me. "Ellery employed the watercolor brush because he could get that detail. In applying oil paint on the rough side of the Masonite, he wore down the number six every week. The alizarin is made from the red in the madder root ($C_{14}H_8O_4$). Ellery used alizarin straight: the lips on the women, distant roof tops, bell buoys and I think he mixed it, too. The red shirt on those harpooners in the whaling postcards. Those sunrises and sunsets, too, there you have the mere hint of alizarin. Of course, it's what he did his signature with."

Judging by the paintings that cropped up in this period, the magazine Tuck delivered each Friday seems to have been one of the 1960's version of the old *Snappy Stories*.

"He used some of the pictures of women as his models," said Tuck. "They seem to have replaced the Coca-Cola calendar girls on the bell buoys. In fact there was a favorite one of his he had copied and would cut her out and paste her right on—and not just our old friend, Ram Island Bell, but all kinds of even more improbable venues. And then he'd do his own painting of her right *over* the silhouette. I mean—*yeah!*"

The employment of Hugh Hefner's 1960 vision of the female body was a sad descent from the days when, as Ellery had written Bob Ballou, "past Dean's Mill in the thickly wooded section where in early morning with a chill about, I got frightened by a chilled model who began to do more shimmying than shivering."

Even back then, however, it seems Ellery's sense of the female form was filtered by what we now call Pop Culture, in this case *September Morn* meets Little Egypt. It's hard to say whether he actually perceived that way or was merely catering to what he had created as an audience, or, as is clearly the case in his painting, merely lacked a more nuanced technique.

It was about then, at Ft. Rachel, in an effort to keep body and soul together, that Ellery began taking other short cuts with his artwork. The long-range effect was that he developed the reputation as somewhat of a waterfront trickster. He sensed that the *Eleanors* were pretty much in about every home that they were going to be for a while. Noting the trends in the Annual Mystic Outdoor Art Festival where out-of-towners were cleaning up on bluewater stuff, he started copying Patterson's deep sea, square-riggers, work already knocked off one generation on the Columbia rope calendars.

The irony is that Ellery might have had the opportunity once to study with Patterson or at least come face to face with him. Charles Robert Patterson (1878-1958) combined nearly a decade of deepwater seafaring experience with academic art training. Between 1920 and his death in 1958, he did more than 400 paintings, capturing the sea and its artifacts and workers as only a fellow maritime professional could. Among his clients was Ellery's old hero William McCoy for whom he did a painting of the *Arethusa*'s infamous encounter with U.S.C.G. Cutter *Seneca* off New Jersey in November of 1923. It was Patterson who put McCoy and the rum-runner's eventual writer Frederic Van de Water together. For Ellery his own encounter with Patterson was, for reasons he omits, demurred:

> In the spring of 1921—following my first successful year as a Connecticut draggerman—Captain Langworthy (a Noank schoonerman of considerable note) and I visited a Boston fish pier to view the new fishing schooner *Mayflower*, a fine appearing vessel to be denied "racing privileges" to square off against the Nova Scotian *Bluenose* (the committee had declared her "too yachty." It was at this point that McCoy scandalized the committee by offering *Arethusa*). Langworthy invited me to accompany him on to Gloucester, with the chance of meeting his "close friend" Charles Robert Patterson the artist and viewing the newly launched Essex-built schooner *L.A. Dunton*. I refused and returned to New London to head out on another flounder dragging trip. I can still recall Captain Langworthy's words: "Ellery, you'll be sorry. Who knows? Someday you may take up oil painting, perhaps of a Gloucester schooner. I hope they will never die."

"As Ellery got older," said Tuck, "it got harder for him to keep up with what he saw as the potential market. He began taking black and white photographs of his own work, some of which were the rope calendars. He'd reduce them on a copier which in those days were all—locally anyway—black and white. So he'd color them in. 'Hand tinted, by the artist,' I suppose you could say. But a real, first generation Ellery painting is always large, and these copies were eight by tens. A fellow came into the shop one day bragging that he had just 'stole' a 'rare Ellery, *one of the small ones*', for a mere $ 200 at a local gallery. I'm thinking: oh no, what, *small ones*? I had finally to say I suspected it was only a colored-in photograph. 'Oh, no,' this guy says. 'This is a genuine Ellery.' So we go around on this. He's a great big guy, very loud and sure of himself. Big handle bar moustache. Looked like a Gay Nineties weight lifter. I ask him to let me take the framing job apart from the back if I promise to redo it professionally for nothing. When I show him that it's just a colored-in photograph, and of a painting not even originally *by* Ellery, this guy hits the roof. Ellery was dead by then, but I feared for the life of the gallery owner."

Like the great eccentric American painter of moonlight and sea, Albert Pinkham Ryder (1847–1917), Ellery was a deep night worker. "The thing about Ellery's paintings," said Krepcio, "is that the colors get better under poor light. You look at them in the day and you say, 'Oh, those greens and blues!' I have my Ellerys so I can turn down the lights. Then the colors are more realistic—they glow. After all, at Ft. Rachel he painted them at night under a sixty watt bulb. He'd often start after midnight."

As jokey as Ellery usually was about his art, and often is *in* his art, he began to receive serious attention. He won a couple of prizes in the Mystic Outdoor Art Festival, one for "Most Popular Painting." Rudolph Schaefer, long-time chairman of the board at Mystic Seaport, heir to the brewery fortune and owner of the America's Cup replica, the Schooner *America*, gave Ellery a complete set of plans for the vessel with the intention that he paint the ship's portrait. The official history of the Mystic Art Association *A Time To Remember: Art and Artists of the Mystic Connecticut Area 1700-1950*, bears the notation that "Ellery Thompson of Mystic, a retired dragger captain who has become well known for his portraits of famous ships, is among those joining the ranks (of those who like Henry Ward Ranger (1858-1926)) formed an important contribution to the record in the Mystic area."

We have seen that it was through a painting by Ellery that he came to the attention of Viking Press. In later years his painting was even more important. As he confided to editor Henry Beetle Hough in June of 1981, the fact was that "without my painting I might have starved to death. Painting has supported my writing over late years."

Painting of Bindloss Dock, Stonington, Connecticut by Cap'n Ellery F. Thompson.

Ellery with one of his paintings of the Fall River Line's *Priscilla*.

IX. The Art of Courtly Love

Now and then Chogg would swim out in front of Mummy with a coaxing little flip of his tail. (I had seen less fetching come-on gestures on the waterfront.)

—Draggerman's Haul, XVI

The life amorous of Yankee watermen in the mid-century is perhaps best not too closely looked into. In wrapping up his second book, *Come Aboard the Draggers*, Ellery says "Why dive into it too deeply?" Ellery, himself, however, frequently brings up the subject, at least obliquely, if not a bit coyly, in *Draggerman's Haul* and *Come Aboard the Draggers* and it seems almost compulsively in countless interviews. Even at 85 when flat on his back in an up-country nursing home, he dictated to a woman (presumably the "Guardian Angel" referred to) a letter intended ostensibly for a fellow mariner:

> Tomorrow, my Guardian Angel is bringing one of my clipper paintings to hand in front of my bed. Later, I may be terrible and have her bring up the last nude woman on a seascape that I painted. It may shock some of the younger nurses aides, but they see me nude every day.

The topic of Ellery's love life, real or imagined, is approached obliquely by Kathleen L. Barber reviewing *Draggerman's Haul* in the *Washington Post* May 28, 1950:

> This unusual mariner, whose autobiography we have here, also paints, plays a trumpet (his radar in fog) and rejoices in bachelorhood. His material is first rate... But the captain's smirking and bridling will make even the staunchest of Connecticut Yankees wince.

I'm not sure what Barber means by Ellery's "bridling," and the "rejoicing in bachelorhood" would seem to have to be ironic. Mitchell, who had the advantage of spending time with Ellery in person, refers more accurately to Ellery's "sad-eyed" countenance. Women did like Ellery, that is to say there always seems to have been those willing to mother him. Bachelorhood, in so far as it was really a choice for him after thirty or so, seems to have been a necessary distancing technique from what might have become a stifling relationship. Ellery, like so many American authors from Mark Twain to Steinbeck and Hemingway liked to see himself as a "bad boy" in the Huck Finn mold. In the less skillful hands this naughty lad image could indeed easily slip into a kind of cloying smirk. The alternative in the mid-century to giving in to the smother-mother seems to have been the pathology dramatized so popularly then by Tennessee Williams and Alfred Hitchcock.

Here's how Ellery handles the subject in his second book, *Come Aboard the Draggers*:

> One stormy day, with the *Marise*, the *Eleanor*, the *Florence*, tied up together at Newport, my brother [Morris] and I and Harold, in talking things over, decided that when we got married—that is, if we were ever to have a choice in the matter, we would pick out brides who were well-sheered of body and fair of face, and seaworthy enough for the going mate of a dragger. I held out for a girl who might appear capable of bending over and picking up a tub of codfish gear without grunting or busting her seams. This precaution was just in case the dragging of trawl nets went on the rocks.
>
> I may have held out for too darn much, or did I glimpse a domestic picture with some shades of darkness, or a matrimonial sea too rough for comfort or peace of minds. Anyhow, all along the coast between Connecticut hills and island pastures, I fell down on the job of marrying anyone, able-bodied or fragile, fresh or salty, ticklish or otherwise.

He goes on to note that "it was a different story with Morris and Harold..." but even alluding to the death of his brother aboard a dragger which Ellery maintained had been fishing in bad weather, concludes, "Perhaps Morris took his duty too much to heart."

This is an interesting point because while Ellery's account of his brother's death in *Draggerman's Haul* is rhetorically restrained and close to the facts in the U.S. Coast Guard reports, his subsequent interviews on the subject stipulate the kind of bad weather that justify his statement in that chapter:

> Then Morris began to push himself harder than ever. It seemed as if weather made no difference to him... working as though the devil were driving him... to buy those thousand and one things a man loves to buy for his wife and son. [There is a fuller discussion of the death of Morris in the Appendix.]

Born in 1899, like Hemingway, Ellery's continues to remind us that his life corresponds exactly with the Century.

> While the exciting and golden twenties were fading I had my observing eyes on several blossoming girls, much younger than myself, although I was not old enough to be their father, not really according to Hoyle.
>
> One was a blond Connecticut Yankee who seemed capable of reading my thoughts and who blushed pleasingly in the reading. Another was a brunette Vineyarder who knew all about the lightships from Newport to Nantucket Shoals, a lass whose father had been a lightkeeper.

Ellery gives the impression that it was he who resisted the marriage. "But several acute attacks of the flounder-frights forced me to 'starn-all' in a whaling manner when

I should have been forward in a courting manner. Perhaps the fair young ladies got a lucky break."

In *Draggerman's Haul* Ellery would have us believe that his activities were confined to a single platonic relationship with an under-age girl he calls "Nan," and some inno-cent flirtations with female pals on the New London waterfront, relationships he says, that have been entirely misunderstood by busybodies.

In preparing a paper entitled "The New London Waterfront Was Salty," to deliver to the New London Historical Society at the Custom House, Marion Krepcio managed to cull some relevant Ellery:

> Chapter after chapter could be written about New London harbor in the days of my youth, of the scores of saloons along the waterfront. I visited many while trying to locate crewmen on local or visiting draggers and line trawling schooners. Why mention names to embarrass descendants, although the wettest was the bar in the Nutmeg Hotel on Bank Street, strategically located near ship chandleries and Bailey's Sail Loft and the Seafood Lunch restaurant where Pete's bowl of clam chowder at 10 cents; beef stew at 15 cents; roast beef dinner at 30 cents. Of course these were pre-war prices.
>
> The only women allowed in many of these swinging door saloons were Sal-vation Army gals selling their *War Cry*, usually on Saturday night. Never did I wit-ness any rudeness aimed at the ladies. As for waterfront mugging, it was something unknown, except for rolling a drunk.
>
> ...The old time characters along the New London waterfront appear just as fresh in my mind today, in the 1970s, as in my 19th year prior to 1920—the year I put out to sea in my flounder dragger. And the women were as numerous as the men. At this point I'll just mention the names I knew them by: Annie The Lean, the thin-woman alcoholic; Lightning Bolt Sadie, who always ran for cover at the first flash of lightning—usually toward a fire house or livery stable; Flo Jane Doe, the gal who opened my eyes to one fact of life (sex); Eight Bell Nell, the prettiest and friendliest of them all—Queen of the Sporting Girls... whose sweet face reminded me of Mary Pickford on an off day. [Unfortunately he does not gloss Nell's sobriquet.]

As usual Ellery seems to want it both ways. In complaining about Mitchell's "thin-sad-eyed bachelor Yankee fisherman" portrait, Ellery also manages to bring in a defense of his own love life. "I was pictured as a fisherman... who would rather sleep with a rolled up coastal chart than a woman other than a legal bunkmate." But then he admits that "Mr. Mitchell had inquired little about my love life, because I had discouraged that line of questions from the very beginning."

This is a curious line for Ellery to take. Mitchell worked under perhaps the two most prudish editors in the history of major, American 20th century journalism, Harold Ross and William Shawn. I believe I have read all of Mitchell's published work at least once and can recall nothing more in "that line" than that which emerges in the Ellery pieces.

This salacious New London territory is, of course, the same lurid district that caused so much misunderstanding in the life and letters of Nobel Laureate Eugene O'Neill. Bill McCoy refers to the female denizens of Rum Row, the off-shore district of New London, as "The Daughters of Joy."

Toward the middle of the century Ellery shifted his grounds to Mystic, ten miles east of New London to the town in which he had lived his first five years. My own observations of Mystic and even Noank in the 1940s were also given to misunderstanding. I recall waiting in the backseat of the car for my father on Water Street in Mystic while he worked on his boat. Across the narrow street from the boatyard was a gloomy ark of a house with shaggy green asbestos siding. From each of its upper windows looked down plump, pale women, their bare arms flowing over the window sills, their pink, poxed faces smirking beneath crooked oil cloth window shades. Occasionally they would wink or wave at me, a gesture that was as close as I ever observed them coming to what might charitably be called "joy."

One day I asked my mother why these women could just sit there all day without working. I don't recall her answer, but the next time we visited the boatyard my father parked in another place. George McGugan, who ran a boatyard on that street, told me years later that there had been "stand-up cubicles all down that lane before World War II" and that "all the doors had numbers on them." Down river a couple of miles, there was a narrow, crooked lane on the back side of Noank that was known as "Cat Alley," and not necessarily for the prevalence of the four legged variety. My neighbor in Noank took to her grave the names of the families in the village that ran "houses" during the 20s and 30s. That an unmarried fisherman of heterosexual orientation would come to be associated with these enterprises would seem inevitable.

As for these casual, waterfront encounters it is fair to recall Ellery's comments in *Come Aboard*: "... we heard stories that were literally colored with human blood and immoral conditions hard to believe... [rum running] crews went ashore in small boats with the idea of hi-jacking or shanghaiing beach-women for purposes only too obvious."

Less abstractly he gives us his own experiences with what he calls "beachcombing female:"

> But some silliness on a hard-fishing dragger is one of the best safety valves I know, and only too true on a tripper away from home-port. Roaming draggermen are not always the hell-devils they have been cracked up to be. In following migrating schools along the coast, holing up in handy harbors of refuge, most draggermen practice living by the Golden Rule as much as anyone.
>
> What parties the boys used to have in various fo-castles, at harbors from Point Judith to Nantucket, poker playing, musical jam sessions, fishermen banquets...
>
> Occasionally liquor or a girl friend might come on board. Why not? They go into shore homes and on yachts each day.

He goes on to "recall one dry but girlish example." It is the story of a how "at a fogbound harbor on Cape Cod... my craft was hostess to two girls." One rips her dress on a nail and Ellery goes on with a chaste story about how he sews her up "using a life-or-death stitch taught me by John Bailey, the New London sailmaker." All this maneuvering, since the girl is still in the "ripped and billowing dress, "involves a lot of "fumbly" proximity "especially as the girl shimmied about nervously."

To add to the risqué nature of this "fo-castle" event, Ellery "in a slight-of-hand manner... eased a five dollar bill into a tiny pocket on the dress intended to pay for wear and tear." Later, Ellery has second thoughts when he "realized some of the implications connected with my gift." He "hustled those two visiting beachcomber females ashore with more speed than they came aboard. I wanted no further complications." Ellery's charity, however, goes unnoticed, as he discovers weeks later when actually attempting to avoid the girl, he runs into her miles away at another port. "After a minute of chit-chat," Ellery finally "exploded" and asked about what happened to the dress and the girl merely tells him that she had bought it at the dollar store and changed it and threw it out before she ever got home, presumably with the $5.

Paradoxically, as these waterfront brothels faded, driven out by rising real estate values as much as vice squads, the "sexual revolution" permitted risqué depictions of women. *Draggerman's Haul*, however, is a product of the late 1940s, an awkward no-man's land between the more or less obvious cat house and the era of Hugh Hefner and his imitators. Images of desirable females were limited to the leering illustrations of *Snappy Stories*, the grainy robustness of *Sunshine and Health* and its imitators, flip books, dirty playing cards and the occasional "bachelor" movie shown on the bartender's apron of a local "club." Now days, just walking into the local drug store Ellery would be confronted with more images of exposed four-color, female flesh than he had suffered in a life time.

My favorite of all the Ellery *in flagrante* yarns is one that allegedly took place at one of the Noank docks. When I first heard this story the *mise en scene* was said to be the Town Dock at the foot of what was then called Store Hill, but I suspect it was more likely the venue Ellery himself speaks of in *Draggerman's Haul*. While he is ostensibly telling us about waterfront logistics, the inevitable bycatch of amour slips in sideways:

> In 1922 I moved my base of operations from New London to "Rat" Wilbur's dock at Noank... But after a while an extra-heavy crop of eel grass began to grow in the narrow channel, and there were other hazards—such as the new waterfront factory [presumably the branch of the Rossie Velvet Mill whose women turned out thread. Later the structure became the State Lobster Hatchery, then the University of Connecticut Marine Laboratory. It is now the Town of Groton Shellfish Co-op.] which employed lots of girls...

Now the Noank waterfront is largely a matter of neatly trimmed lawns running to sea walls where yachts repose and the village beach is a wholesome site, at least by daylight, where young mothers are wont to bring their babes for beneficial sea bathing. In the old days the waterfront was what the locals call a "good deal rougher." There was a fisherman named Sweet who was famous for his casual, al fresco castrating of cats, the begging yowls of which had intruded upon his hangovers. The woman from whom I bought my house had remained an old maid after her fiancée from Mulberry Street in Manhattan was shot in front of the town pump. Whichever pier Ellery performed upon this infamous night, the time was before the Depression and the 1938 Hurricane, so the structure was yet of sufficient strength to support a number of *Eleanor* size draggers all rafted up to one another on the down stream side. On this sultry evening *Eleanor* herself was the inboard vessel, the only one actually tied to the pier.

At first an observer would conclude that there was no one aboard any of the boats. The only man in the scene, at least at the beginning, was the fellow coming down Front Street toward the dock. His solitude was not for long, however, which should not have surprised him as he was shouting and waving his arms. His voice was soon caught in its own reverberations among the buildings crowding the end of the street, several of which have now been torn down by the University of Connecticut in the interests of science and so the conditions of this event cannot be precisely reproduced.

Just who this shouting man was and what his relationship to the female allegedly aboard *Eleanor* has been lost to history. Perhaps he was her father, for these Ellery narratives, when not positing professionals, favored youth. Perhaps he was her brother or her husband or her lover. None of this really matters. The only important person in this tale is Ellery.

Exactly how he managed to get up on deck, adjust his wardrobe and cast off the dock lines is a bit unclear. We do know that the tide was ebbing strong and that there was the combined weight of several draggers on the *Eleanor*'s straining warps. We also know that it was the custom on these draggers to have a steel band around the mast to which the boom was attached and that in back of this band was enough space for the thin blades of the fillet knives, blades kept razor sharp. Such a knife would have come easily to the hand of anyone emerging from the wheelhouse. The only solution to freeing the lines under all this pressure would seem to be to hack quickly, or perhaps take just a little more time and saw. In any case that is the way the story is usually told, with emphasis on Ellery's technique applied to the cutting of the dock lines.

The reason why so much attention gets placed on the dock lines is perhaps because no one, not even after all these years, can really account in detail just how Ellery managed to handle the rest of his escape: an elaborate procedure commencing with the starting of *Eleanor*'s engine, proceeding on to the towing on the hip four or five unoccupied draggers—off into darkness—to exactly where?

And what of the woman below? Perhaps she never existed. Like the females in so many classic maritime narratives by Melville, Conrad or Childers, women do not quite seem to have an independent existence outside the needs of the masculine narrative. The "Nan" in the pages of *Draggerman's Haul*, for instance. Surely she is not the woman below at the Noank dock. Yet who is she ?

Thompson scholar Sandy MacKay of Stonington has put forth an interesting theory about Ellery and "Nan" which he has promulgated at the Stonington Historical Society show of Ellery's paintings in 2005 and in my honors seminar at the University of Connecticut at Avery Point that year. The basis for MacKay's meditation is a huge Ellery oil in his possession that uncharacteristically contains no *Eleanor* or even any other boat. There is simply a wide view of Watch Hill Bell looking in from the Passage showing the lighthouse and some boulders and a pair of sea birds. To Sandy, "it is clearly a seascape waiting to be inhabited." He sees the scene is *suggestively* sufficiently populated. As he points out, there are actually *pairs* everywhere: boulders, birds, bells, buildings... "It's the painting Ellery writes about in *Draggerman's Haul*, the one he and Nan begin together, but never finish. They are, nevertheless, in it because this is what they see—what they are looking at *together* and this is as close to consummation as they get. Hell, perhaps it is as close as anyone really gets."

Ellery & Nan together gazing at the Watch Hill Lighthouse is indeed a pretty picture, rather in the genre of Lady Brett's impromptu taxi cab fantasy of her life with Jack Barnes at the close of Hemingway's famous 1920s novel of impotence *The Sun Also Rises*. In any case, Viking editor Ballou's back and forth to Ellery trying to straighten out the chronology of the advent of Nan and Ellery's interest in painting would seem to mitigate against such a scene in real life.

My 21st century mixed-gender students at Avery Point seem to find Ellery's "attitudes toward sex merely pre-pubescent." They are very kind about this and manage to find plenty of other things in *Draggerman's Haul* of interest. One does not expect a Molly Bloom, or even a Judy Bloom. Sometimes it seems as if Ellery's just caught up in something near the Madonna complex so prevalent among Mediterranean fisherman and their descendants in Stonington and Noank. Ellery's first half Twentieth Century Protestant Yankee take on sex, however, is not so simply bifurcated. Nor does he seem quite Victorian. It is almost as if he, or his ghost writer, subscribed to the code in *The Art of Courtly Love* a how-to book at the time of Queen Eleanor's of Aquitaine at Poitiers in 1174. I have no reason to believe that as in the case *of Christeen Jorgenson: Her Own Story* this handbook had found its way onto the paint store's counter, but there are passages strikingly sympathetic in their piscatorial imagery:

> Love gets its name (*amor*) from the word for hook (*amus*), which means "to capture" or "to be captured," for he who is in love is captured in the chains [nets] of desire and wishes to capture someone else with his hook. Just as a skilled fisherman tries to attract fishes by his bait and to capture them on his crooked hook, so the man who is a captive of love tries to attract another person by this allurements.

The little book's author, Andreas Capellanus, gives us much talk of "love" bringing "his sailors into the quiet port after they had been soaked by many tempests" or in other moods, leaving "his sailors in the mighty waves." Most of all, of course, like the literary Ellery, we are comforted by the delicious unattainableness of the love object itself.

As with Sandy MacKay's theory of Ellery in love, maybe what we have here in the pages of *Draggerman's Haul* and its appendices is what the old guy was looking at and if it is not exactly what we would see of him, it is at least a sufficient suggestion of what there was he wanted us to see.

Certainly more wholesome is Ellery's relationship with Edna Butlin who worked aboard *Eleanor* in the early 1950s. While she is mentioned in *Draggerman's Haul*, it is through Professor Gordon's priceless archives we find three other vectors on the relationship. News articles insist that Edna was the first woman to go to sea as a paid hand in the Stonington commercial fleet. More cautiously, Professor Gordon points out, "Nineteen-year-old Edna Butlin was one of the first female crew persons, not related to members of the crew, to be seen working on a Stonington dragger." The reaction to the attractive young woman's appearance was a sign of the times. Martin M. Master's in his September 23, 1951 *Hartford Courant Sunday Magazine* interview reports Ellery informing him that "Stonington fishermen were 'pop-eyed' last winter when they saw eighteen-year old Edna Butlin of Waterford working for him." Edna was also featured in the New York *Daily News* piece in which she is photographed aboard *Eleanor* playing accordion to Ellery's trumpet.

More significant is Butline's own matter of fact take on the experience, unfiltered by Ellery's perspective. She had gone to work in the policy department of a large insurance company whose house organ interviewed her upon seeing her in the *Daily News*. It seems she was brought up from a young age on her father's sloop on Long Island Sound and when eighteen went aboard *Eleanor* with her father to help Ellery out as "spare hands." At some point Ellery was later laid up with rheumatism and working on *Draggerman's Haul*, and had to let his regular crew go. When he was able to go to sea again, he was forced to press Edna into service as a first mate. He told her, "I can't get a dependable one who can get out early in the morning." As an amateur engine mechanic and experienced deckhand she more than fulfilled the requirements of first mate. She also took over Ellery's job as cook and as he told her, kept the galley a lot cleaner. Furthermore, with her accordion she could join the Captain's trumpet in those jam sessions while they towed the net. In a throw-away parenthesis in one of his unpublished ms. Ellery remarks: ("I nearly ended my fishing with an all girl crew.") All of this gender prejudice seems strange in an era of fishers such as Linda Greenlaw and Vivian Volovar and the number of female captains in the windjammer fleet these days. It is strangely poignant that in all of Ellery's depictions of *Eleanor*—with and without the Coca-Cola girls, Edna Butlin working aboard *Eleanor* was an image he does not seem to have attempted to capture.

X. The Legacy of Ellery Thompson

When does a man sum up the evidence and achieve for himself an evaluation
of the meaning of his life in general? I don't know.

–*Draggerman's Haul*, XVII

Joseph Mitchell got Ellery's second life off to a flying start by saying in *The New Yorker*
flat out that "The biggest fishing fleet in the vicinity of New York City... works out of
Stonington, Connecticut" and "The most highly respected captain in the Stonington
fleet is a Connecticut Yankee named Ellery Thompson..." Unfortunately within a dozen
years, Ellery's iconic vessel *Eleanor* was what was on the bottom of the harbor and his
reputation as a fisherman with it. If you had not witnessed Ellery's physical decline in
middle-age from the rheumatism already at work in Mitchell's account, it would be easy
to conclude that here was yet another case of fame in America ruining its subject. The
fact is that while *Draggerman's Haul* was an alternate selection in the Book of the Month
Club, both the Fonda and the Cooper movie deals never materialized and there was really very little cash coming in to corrupt our man. What he gained was just enough
fame to keep his paintings moving at low prices and barter for meals and professional
favors. He was taken under the wing of the Mystic Seaport in 1965 with a steady, but
low-paying job, giving tours of the 1921 Gloucester Schooner *L.A. Dunton* (which he was
fond of likening to McCoy's *Arethusa*, and the launching of which he had himself actually witnessed). His main gig was running the "New England Fishing Shanty" in which
he sometimes managed to round up a few lobsters, some of which he claimed were
"over 22 pounds." He could not, however, save his boat. The way he liked to put it to
Krepcio was, "They said they'd take either me or the *Eleanor*. They couldn't take both."

The witticism dances past the sad truth. There was no way the Seaport would have
been able to afford to salvage *Eleanor* off the mud bank, especially in those days when
their mission did not really escape the confines of preserving the 19th Century "whaling
village" and relevant artifacts. It was only at the turn into the 21st Century that the Seaport was able to restore the Thompson family dragger *Florence* to fill the gap in the
recent fisheries collection.

As Ellery's reputation drifted from fisherman to artist, people seemed to need to see
him as either a fisherman who happened to write and paint or a writer-painter who
happened to fish. On a more grandiose level this is the sort of mariner versus artist
controversy that students of Melville and Conrad have long outgrown. In Ellery's case,

however, locally and in the short run, such amphibiousness struck many people as *prima fascia* evidence that Ellery was a kind of waterfront cadger.

Legitimizing what might otherwise seem as his eccentricity, he wrote regularly for the local weekly, sometimes as a semi-official columnist, sometimes in the Letters to the Editor section. A letter he kept demonstrates that he still had the knack of hanging a bit of nostalgia on the hook of an ongoing controversy and wrapping it all up in his old themes. Unpacking "Reader Takes Issue with Dave's Age," *Mystic Compass*, August, 16, 1977, we find Ellery defending his territorial rights to local sea legends based on his years at sea which have been endorsed by the death of his brother Morris, his collegiality with Dr. Merriman, and his connection with big city journalism, all this salted with the nomenclature of the trade and the obligatory joke about the otherness of women:

To the Editor:

Please strop publicizing that 17 and-a-half pound lobster as being 122 years old. I believe you're all adrift, and should have checked with a reliable expert before sounding off about a poor lobster outliving a normal man by 40 years.

I've handled lobsters up to 25 pounds in weight. The first 20-pounder was caught by my brother Morris Thompson in 1930—his last year among the living—age 25 and his big lobster was not much older.

In 1950, I dragged up an 18-pounder in Block Island Sound, which I sent to the editorial offices of *Life Magazine*. His age was estimated to have been less than 35 years. While I had charge of the New England fishing shanty at Mystic Seaport in 1965, I had several lobsters above 22 pounds in weight crawling about in the circulating water tank.

After being exhibited over the weekend, the jumbo lobsters were boiled and eaten. The Modern Grill boiled up the 26-pounder. Mrs. Roy Perkins (widow of lobsterman Ray Perkins) made up a lobster salad that fed 14 people. This granddaddy lobster was probably less than 50-years old. One expert said less than 40.

Even world record-sized lobsters of 45 pounds were not of a greater age than man. I have this from experts at a leading oceanographic institution.

Recently I called by telephone Dr. Daniel Merriman, now retiring from Yale, although still active on federal projects. And he laughed when I told him about the "medium" size lobsters reported to be more than 120 years old. Don't quote me, he said, but I would say the Stonington lobster "Old Dave" wasn't born until after World War II.

I called another expert, "Ellery, any lobster hatched a few years following the Civil War (1865) has been dead for 50 years or more."

It may take five years for a lobster to grow to one pound, but it doesn't take him five years to grow the second pound, and at age 15 some lobsters may weigh all of 10 pounds. It's the same with the human race. Some youngsters can weight 300 pounds in their teens.

Even Abbot's in Noank was all adrift by posting the sign about a 20-pound lobster being a 100 years old. They just multiplied the weight of the lobster by five. It doesn't work out that way, according to my biased opinion.

One thing is certain. Never would I eat any critter older than myself—not even if I were a cannibal recovering from a hunger strike. But my opinion is only one. How about some others? Now I must knock off. I'm having a three pound lobster for lunch—age eight years. It's a she lobster, so she may have lied to me about her age.

> Ellery F. Thompson
> Water Street [Ft. Rachel Place]
> Mystic

P.S. I'm glad old Dave is going back into the sea to, someday, reach a reasonable old age.

Nor did Ellery ever give up on the idea of the other books. Writing to International Marine publisher Roger C. Taylor in May of 1977 he reveals what the original Viking plan had more or less been:

> Several years ago, a New York publisher viewed much of the material in much rougher form than it is today, and offered his opinion that there was enough stuff for three books. He said some of it hit the mark; some didn't. But to work on it and see what develops.

To Taylor Ellery admitted:

> I have been doing a lot of writing [the subject matter] dating back into the 1890s, when the 38 foot male sperm whale came ashore on Quiambaug Beach (midway between Mystic and Stonington). Although writing about forty chapters on my life and life around me into the sixties when I joined the activist staff at Mystic Seaport, has, as a hobby, kept me out of mischief, I do believe there is enough substance in most of it to be worthy of being printed. But I worry that the quality may not be of professional caliber, at least, for publication by you. One thing sure: I'll be 76 in April and time is short for me. Anyhow, I sure wouldn't want to see years of work—labors of love, really—wasted.

What Ellery seems to have presented to Taylor, by means of an intermediary, was the infamous steamer trunk, which Taylor refers to as 'the suitcase.' Bravely he promises Ellery 'to getting at it as time permits.'

Charming as Ellery's local journalism was, as the rheumatism took over, his in-person appearance could scatter a wedding crowd. Like his Coleridge prototype, however, he always seemed to manage to "stoppeth one of three." To those of us with whom he had that magic there was his irrepressible ebullience, which he seems to have carried to the end. Albert Murray, in writing about the "basic elements of American behavior" quotes Constance Rourke who says it is the role of the American writer "to provide emblems for a pioneer people who require resilience as a prime trait." While it is at times tempting to see Ellery as a kind of waterfront con man, no one I know, from Ed Maxwell or Bernie Gordon, Joseph Mitchell—on down in time to Marion Krepcio—no one has ever confused what Mitchell recognized as Ellery's waterfront skepticism with a cheap cynicism. He constantly sought to hurt no one. Without the help of grants or any of the other aids to citizens designated as national treasures, Ellery managed to support himself by his wiles.

As early as Sunday January 19, 1967, Ellery had set his spiritual house in order with a one page "Religious Impressions." After a mildly begrudging admission as to the use of formal religion as a useful "crutch" and a more willing acceptance as to its role as "a harbor-of-refuge lashed by violent storms," the former Baptist hymn tooter opted for a generalized golden rule, "From the mouth of Confucious [sic]: 'What you do not want done to yourself, do not do unto others.' 'Love all men. Know all men.'" From the Scriptures of Taoism he adds: "'Keep on good terms with all men. He who loves the world as he does his own body can be entrusted with the world.'"

He concludes somewhat cryptically:" Fables believed means history indeed. The true religion of the future will be the fulfilment [sic] of all religions of the past, the true religion of humanity. God Bless us every one." He signs it "Cap'n Ellery."

In June of 1982 he wrote Henry Beetle Hough, the longtime editor of the *Martha's Vineyard Gazette*, who had blurbed *Draggerman's Haul* nearly forty years ago. Calling across the decades to the far reach of his usual run to Edgartown, Ellery's tone to the peripatetic old editor was elegiac: "I hope you are well and up and about, walking your favorite trails. Now I wish I could visit all the ports and inlets where I sought security from the elements, especially Edgartown. Never in my wildest dreams did I think that this reckless old Yankee would outlive all other fishermen of my generation."

While Ellery died as a ward of the state, he always made sure to credit those who helped him, adding paragraphs to his books and when they were no longer available to him for this purpose, at least writing appreciations into his journals. To Marion Krepcio and others he was an inspiring lover of the sea. If nothing else, like the sea, he is an ex-emplum of resilience. From the nursing home he dictates to Krepcio one of his many communications to his old friend Captain Howard Burdick:

> There are so many stories I wish time to tell... But life is cruel. No human should spend their last years on earth in pain and dismay. Ah, but what a life I have lived for 85 years! I have lived longer than my mother and all my male relatives. Had lots of cards and visitors today. It is great to have friends, old and new. Everyone seems to have trouble, but the miseries only make the delighted more heavenly.

And then, he borrows from the old stock-in-trade funeral elegy about the deceased's departing from his friends on the familiar shore and selects the punch line for his epitaph: "IMAGINE THE EXCITEMENT ON THE OTHER SHORE."

Today, walking along the wind-blown banks of the Mystic River in the season's first snow flurry, I come across that line chiseled into the local granite of his tombstone and can only shake my head and smile. As he had said to Marion Krepcio near the end: "Disgusted and disappointed? Yes. Discouraged? No."

As Ellery points out in *Draggerman's Haul*, his reputation has at times suffered from the company he kept. It is interesting to see just what sort of company he is presently keeping. A recent issue of *The Portersville Press*, the official organ of The Mystic River Historical Society (vol. xxiii, issue vi) shows him with the following entourage:

> Among the items we have seen in the last few months were a Civil War sword owned by General S. D. Lee, an Allyn musket used at the Battle of Groton Heights, a diagram of family pews in the Union Baptist Church, an Ellery Thompson painting of a dragger, a Greenman needlepoint foot stool and Thomas Courter's honorable discharge Civil War document.

Just as I thought that Ellery had been thus safely retired to the bric-a-brac of historical preservation, however, I had yet another encounter with the old goat, one that seemed more in keeping with the man I had known. I was in the barbershop across the street from where Doc Ryley had lived on his boat. In fact, the shop was within a few hundred yards of most of Ellery's later day haunts including the bones of *Eleanor*. The barber shop itself had been in existence all during those days. It did not surprise me to see there, sharing space on the back wall with images of the 1950s New York Yankees, one of Ellery's schooners. In the mood for serious research, I asked the proprietor, "What's the story on how you came by that painting of Ellery Thompson's?"

The barber, a fine singer when in church, let out what sounded like a wild turkey warble which modulated into the aria of a barn owl. An elderly customer with his hand on the door knob, joined to make a remarkable duet. The rest of the customers broke out in a chorus of knowing laughter. All this raucous reaction some two decades after the man's demise! The closest translation I can come up with is: *Hey, with Ellery,—you don't even wanna know!*

Stephen Jones
Schooner Wharf

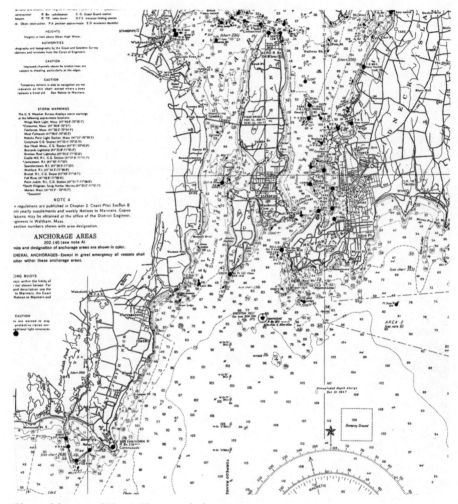

Chart of the area of Morris Thompson's drowning.

APPENDIX I

THE DEATH OF MORRIS THOMPSON

Ellery's greatest love seems to have been reserved for his younger brother Morris, (1905-1930) to whom he dedicates *Draggerman's Haul*. It is, however, as Thompson scholar Andrew Burnett suggests, "a relationship marred by what can only have been feelings of guilt." Early in *Draggerman's Haul*, Ellery announces the birth of his brother accompanied by this charge by their father: take care of him:

> "You're going to spend a lot of time around the water with the kid. And you'll have to look out for him especially there."

Thompson's father asks Ellery to teach Morris to swim as it is "something I can't do."

Despite Ellery's own aquatic proficiency and his best attempts to transfer his skill, he was never able to teach his brother how to swim. While it is true, as Ellery's father indicates, in those days it was probably more common for New England seamen not to know how to swim, Morris's failure to learn how would seem to have been a sword of Damocles. All accounts of Morris' demise indicate that whether Morris could swim or not, was irrelevant. Unnoticed for several minutes, he was either "swept" or knocked overboard in cold water several hundred yards from shore.

As with many of Ellery's stories, however, there are alternate versions and the differences are significant. Although Ellery's account in Chapter XIII of *Draggerman's Haul* is moving in part because of its rhetorical restraint, it contains the seeds for the subsequent conflation. Ellery begins the chapter by carefully explaining how his brother came to be skippering the "thirty-five foot underpowered, cramped for space... poor [for] offshore in winter weather" *Harold L.* and not his Franklin Post-built *Florence* which he had sold.

To illustrate the poor bluewater, seakeeping abilities of the *Harold L.*, Ellery tells a fine story about how he in *Eleanor* with another boat, tow Morris in from a bad position off Block Island. Next we hear of Ellery in *Eleanor* hunkered down in Vineyard Haven, Martha's Vineyard expecting another storm. While in his cabin, he is visited by someone who tells him that Morris has been lost in the West Passage of Narragansett Bay some 40 miles to the east. Ellery fires up his engine, throws off his lines and departs in *Eleanor*. After steering all night, Ellery arrives at Newport where the *Harold L.* has been brought by her crew, Harold Caswell and Jimmie Maxon. Caswell is now in the Newport hospital suffering from exposure after his attempt to save Morris by jumping overboard. There follows a harrowing day in which Ellery and the half a dozen Connecticut draggers that happened to be docked in Newport at the time attempt to recover Morris' body by using their otter trawls in the West Passage. They even send a party ashore on the west coast of Conanicut Island which forms the right hand side of the Passage a mile across from the Bonnett Shores. After an unsuccessful day of searching, during which the fleet rips all of its nets on the rocky bottom, Ellery goes home to New London, presumably having begged a ride by car. That night he puts his father to work fabricating a long-line trawl rigged with cod hooks donated to the cause by the New London ship chandler, Darrow and Comstock. The next day the two Thompsons return to the West Passage, equipped with the hook trawl. Augmenting this gruesome device are two of their otter trawl nets from the day before that *Eleanor* crewman Manuel Cruz has repaired in an all-night effort aboard the boat at Newport. In tandem with brother-in-law Harold Lawry in *Wheezy May* (named for one of Ellery's sisters Louisa) the *Eleanor* crew puts over the new hook trawl and in spite of the strong currents, they manage to recover Morris's net which had been cut loose by Maxson in his attempt to facilitate the maneuvering of the suddenly short-handed *Harold L.* "Then," Thompson writes, "we took in the trawl and let down our [otter trawl] nets as a somewhat gentler method of taking what we hoped would be our next catch. After a time Harold took up. In the cod end of his net was the body of Morris Thompson, twenty-five years old and a darned good fisherman."

The report on 12/13 in the *New London Day* concludes:

> Although a comparatively large number of searchers failed to find the body Thursday, the relatives of the deceased resumed the quest.

Some forty years later I ran across a man who claimed to have been aboard the boat when Morris was lost. The man's name eludes me, so it is worth at least establishing the provenance. I was having my own little dragger *Lawrence* rebuilt up at Whitford Marine on Whitford Road at the northern border of the town of Groton. Late one afternoon I found two men, a generation older than I up the ladder peering into my boat. "This reminds me of a dragger I used two fish on," said one. That vessel turned out to be Morris Thompson's *Florence* (now rebuilt by Walter Ansell and the shipyard crew at Mystic Seaport.) The retired fisherman proceeded to tell me that he had been in fact aboard the afternoon Morris had died. At the time I thought he meant *Florence*, but Burnett's research reveals conclusively the vessel was not *Florence* but the *Harold*. Far from being "off Point Judith in a gale," as so many accounts have it, Morris, my source claimed was steaming placidly up the West Passage of Narragansett Bay well inside Pt. Jude. It as was around Thanksgiving 1930, and there was snow in the air. With the otter trawl set, the crew (3 or 4) went down below to play cards around the warming of the Lathrop engine. The wheelhouse was such that you could stick your head up from time to time to adjust course and still have the lower part of your body in the card game. At some point Morris went out the aft door of the wheelhouse to relieve himself over the stern. The card playing continued until it was his turn again. Somebody stuck his head out the wheelhouse door and there in the snowflakes there was no Morris. The crew immediately hauled back and found him in the net.

The Westerly *Sun*, and the New London *Day*, have Morris "off Point Judith," some ten long miles to the south and in open sea condition which combined with the turbulence for which the Point is notorious would have hardly been conducive to a placid game of cards below.

Joseph Mitchell who, considering he worked for *The New Yorker*, accepts a remarkable number of facts based solely on interviews with Ellery, buys into the offshore version:

> While working in a December *gale off Newport in 1931*, Morris was knocked senseless by a *huge wave* that broke on the deck of *his* dragger; the wave, receding, sucked him in and he drowned. [My emphasis]

As will be seen there are no less than five errors so far in Mitchell's report , presumably based on what Ellery told him. Mitchell goes on to get Morris' story from Ellery:

> "He shouldn't have been out there," says Ellery says, "but the poor boy had just started a family and prices were dropping and he was fighting hard to make a living." Ellery and his father and several friends of the family took the *Eleanor* out while the gale was still in progress and began to drag for Morris's body. On the morning of the third day, when they had almost decided to quit and go in, it came up in the net. (*Bottom of the Harbor* p. 144)

Andrew Brunette, whose grandfather managed the cemetery in which Ellery, Morris and Eleanor are all buried, has researched the accident. Brunette's find consists not only of the Thompson family tombstones with dates, but the obits in two local papers, The New London *Day* and The Westerly *Sun* plus the U.S. Coast Guard reports. The *Sun* has the *Harold* rigged as a "schooner."

> Morris L. Thompson of 265 Crystal Avenue, New London, Conn. Skipper of the fishing schooner "Harold" was washed overboard and lost off Point Judith early yesterday [12/10/1930]. The schooner reached here late yesterday to report the loss of Thompson and to leave Earl Caswell of Newport, who attempted to rescue Thompson, at a hospital to recover from exposure.
>
> Thompson lost his balance when the schooner pitched in rough sea and was seen to fall by Caswell. The later dived after him but the sea was so rough and the water so cold he was soon in danger of drowning. James Maxson of Stonington, Conn. threw a line toward Caswell and maneuvered the schooner so the later could be pulled aboard.
>
> Thompson is survived by his wife and eight-months-old child. He was accompanied on the fishing trip by James Maxson of Stonington Monday morning for a week's fishing.

Burnett has also turned up the report of Picket Boat C.G. *2343* as filed with the Commander 3rd Coast Guard District December 13, 1930: The Brenton Point Coast Guard Station reports the temperature at 2:30 p.m. to be 44 Fahrenheit at Newport, a bit warm for "snow in the air." The tide was ebbing, against the wind which was Southwest at force 4 on the Beaufort scale: "Moderate breeze 13-18 knots raises dust and loose paper; small branches are moved." This is hardly the Force 10 of the Whole Gale "55-

63 knots. Trees uprooted, considerable structural damage occurs." While tucked up in the lee of Bonnett Point on the Boston Neck section of Narragansett Bay in the mile-wide West Passage, the boat could have encountered close to a twenty mile an hour wind against the tide but with probably no more than a half-mile fetch.

Captain Geoffrey Jones, however, reminds me that a southwest wind coming up the West Passage would have been straightened out by the hills so that the Bonnett Shores would have offered no lee. The sea would be rolling in directly aft from the open ocean. Furthermore, such a sea meeting the ebb in a narrow passage would have been not huge, but certainly abrupt.

> At 2:00 p.m. received a telephone message from Newport Police Department stating that Morris E. Thompson, master of the fishing sloop (Harold) of New London, Conn. was lost overboard while dragging for fish in the West passage, Narragansett Bay at about 2:00 p.m. December 10, 1930 about 1-mile N. of Beaver Tail Light West passage, and about 50-yards off Conanicut (Island) shore and asked our assistance to locate the body. M.[achnists] M[ate]. 1c (L) W.E. Nickerson, Mo. M.M. 2c (L) F. J. Harper and Surfman W.A. Brindle left Fort Adams dock cruised to Newport dock and picked up a James Maxson one of the crew of the Harold and went to scene of accident. Sent surfman W.A. Brindle ashore with skiff to patrol the beach and after dragging the vicinity for several hours trying to locate the body returned to Fort Adams dock at 6:30 p.m.

The Day contains the most complete report although it insists on the "off Point Judith" scenario. The line-thrower, previously identified variously as "James Maxon of Stonington" and "James Maxon" seems to have been a James Mexon of Newport. (My friend James Maxson of Mystic confirms that neither he, nor his father James, were candidates for this particular heroism.) What remains a mystery is why the Coast Guard Station at "Prices's"(Prince's Point ? Castle Hill?) ten miles north east from Point Judith should have been summoned *first* for a body that had been in a man's clutches only an hour before off Bonnet Point in the West Passage. *Eventually*, the southwest wind and the ebbing tide might have taken the body that far east.

LOCAL FISHING BOAT MASTER
DROWNED OFF POINT JUDITH
FELL OFF BOAT IN ROUGH SEA

> Morris E. Thompson, 24 years old, master of the fishing boat Harold, lost his life off Point Judith yesterday when he pitched from the deck of his vessel and drowned.
>
> Mr. Thompson lost his balance when the fishing boat rolled in rough seas. Earl Caswell of 7 Gould Street, Newport, is in Newport hospital suffering from the effects of exposure suffered when he dived into the icy seas in a vain effort to rescue Thompson, who could not swim. Casewell [sic], in turn, was saved by James Mexon [sic] of 24 Gould Street, Newport, who threw him a line and pulled him aboard the Harold.

According to members of the crew, Thompson was at the wheel when the *Harold* was passing Pt. Judith shortly after 2 p.m. The rest opf the crew were below. Suddenly they heard a call for help from Thompson.

COULD NOT SWIM

Knowing that Thompson could not swim, Caswell immediately dived after him and managed to grab him. The cold water numbed and exhausted Caswell so that his hold on Thompson relaxed before the boat could be maneuvered to seize the two men. He barely had strength enough to hold the line thrown by Mexon and he was dragged aboard with difficulty.

The boat put into Newcomb's wharf in Newport, arriving about an hour later. City Physician Dr. Francis A. Keenan was summoned. After giving first aid to Caswell he sent him, to Newport hospital, where he was reported resting comfortably last night.

COAST GUARD SEARCH

The police were notified and Sergt. Samuel Dugan and Patrolman Fred W. Foerber of Newport the police and a state trooper from the Portsmouth barracks responded. They notified the coast guard authorities at Prices Neck where a crew under the direction of Capt. Ellesworth Latham and accompanied by Mexon set out in a coast guard launch to seek Thompson's body. At the coast guard station today it was reported that the attempts to recover Thompson's body had been unsuccessful.

Notice of Mr. Thompson's death was received by members of his family last night. They were grief stricken.

Among his survivors are his wife, Frieda and an eight months old baby; his parents Capt. and Mrs. Frank E. Thompson; two sisters, Miss Eleanor F. Thompson and Mrs. Harold Lowrey, and a brother, Ellery F. Thompson, all of this city.

NATIVE OF GROTON

The young man had been a resident of this city for a number of years and had many friends here. He was a native of Groton. Of a seafaring family, he had followed the water most of his life, and first assumed command of a fishing boat when he was only 18 years old.

The boat which Mr. Thompson commanded at the time of his death is owned by his brother-in-law, Capt. Harold Lowrey.

Fishermen from Newport and Stonington were searching for Mr. Thompson's body today.

Of contextual concern are two articles that share the page with Morris' tragedy. "Trawler Deckhand Arrested Today is Irish Alien" and Liquor Seized by C.G. Destroyed at Providence."

It is possible that my alleged eyewitness source at Whitford Marine had merely said that he had fished on *Florence* with Morris and had been with him on the boat off which he fell. There is no way of reconciling the state of sea and the whack on the head with my source's flat-calm scenario. The Brenton Point Coast Guard Station report of finding Morris' body in the West Passage does conform to the general location, but is not compatible with the original card-playing crew finding Morris that day in the net they were towing when he was at the helm. Whether Morris was *swept away* in some grand bluewater fandango or merely eased on a snowflake off slippery deck with his apparatus in hand, certainly makes for a genre difference. (One of the great pseudo statistics of search & rescue industry is the preponderance of drowned men found with their flies open).

There is also a significant discrepancy between the reported locations from which the Coast Guard boat departed. Price's Point to the Fort Adams pier may seem just around the corner on a large scale chart, but that "corner" can make for some slow going against the wind, especially in the rescue vessels of the era.

There is a parallel potential for exaggeration in Ellery's chapter "The Slack-Bilged *Louisa*" where Ellery insists they were almost up on the rocks at Wicopesset. I have gone through the relevant paragraphs for three autumns with my students using the H.O. Chart, aerial views, current charts etc and we can find no way, given Ellery's own data, how an easterly gale would have put *Louisa* up on Wicopesset. These rocks are due south, 90 degrees from his rhumb line as she rounded Napatree Bell Buoy and headed up into his berth in Stonington. Ellis Reef, perhaps, or Ram Island Reef, but not the more juicily named Wicopesset. "Fishermen are licensed to exaggerate," my students remind me, and the episode does what it is supposed to which is illustrate the bravery of the youthful crew member.

APPENDIX II

OTTER TRAWL

The technical side of Ellery's fishing career has often been reduced, following his lead, to something of a crop dance with arcane remedies and rare cures thrown in. He claimed his father was the first to bring the otter trawl method of bottom dragging to Connecticut waters. This may have been true. Innovation in vernacular waterfront technology is difficult to document as intellectual property. Much of it does develop the way folk music did, by a jury rigging of emulations, some acknowledged, more filched surreptitiously. Ellery did live in one of the major periods of transition, from sail to power over the grounds. The back half of his career teetered on the edge of the electronic revolution.

The most interesting aspect of trawling is not so much the pedestrian fact of the open-mouthed bag bumping along the bottom, gulping all before it, but the method by which that maw is kept agape. A simple device, the otter door works in a Zen-like manner by converting the opposing force of the stream into a energy that powers a controlled sheering action that pries apart the jaws of the net. The evolution of the "otter" board or door is a curious one. The use of boards to guide fishing gear underwater begins with poaching in the British Isles, finds itself adopted by high tech naval men in World War I and returns to the commercial fisheries where it undergoes various permutations on through Ellery's time down to the present.

Something of the "otter's" furtive nature begins with the word's Greek origin which does not stand for the cuddly aquatic animal beloved of nature films, but the water snake. In 1860, according to the O.E.D., a correspondent for *Vacation Tour* who went by the initials G.H.K. noted that "Certain Philistines have increased their mischiefs by permitting their gillies [guides] to use the otter." The otter was "a thin piece of board about four feet long and a half a foot or so broad." The board is "weighted at one edge to make it float upright, to which is attached a line, so arranged that when it is pulled, the angle between the otter and the line causes the [otter] to move parallel to the shore."

This elegant method which allows the fisherman to control his gear by proxy is behind the most complex modern application. Once the otter principle has been mastered it is but a short step to attaching fishing hooks, nets or mine sweeping cutters to the board. A manuscript in the Welsh Folk Museum quoted by J. Geraint Jenkins in *Nets and Coracles*, states: "The otter (*styllen*) was usually used on lakes, after dark between the months of May and September. The implement being used was the *styllen*: a plank of wood 14 inches long by 10 inches with a strip of lead on one side, so that it floated upright... Instead of following the shore, the otter would travel towards the centre of the lake and would return to the bank according to the length of the fishing line. I can assure you that it was (and is) a most profitable method of fishing." So profitable indeed that it was made illegal in 1861, but continued in use in various forms. The *O.E.D.* records a report in 1890 stating that the salmon fisheries have already been "well whipped over or ottered for by the local fishermen." This was a well-known poaching method in the old country well into the next century. Irish born, West Mystic Shipyard manager William Smyth , an acquaintance of Ellery's, still recalled it fondly it in the 1960s. Smyth explained that vectoring an otter out in the stream from the bank "was very much like flying a kite. I even experimented with an actual kite in the air, trolling a salmon hook from on high. It worked well enough to prove the point."

By 1910 the otter technique had gone bluewater and legit. The deepwater fisheries have adopted the technique as the *O.E.D.* records the London *Daily News* report stating that "The steam catchers... are of the most approved type, with special steam winches and 'Otter' fishing gear." By 1910 the *O.E.D.* has the June issue of *Blackwoods* noting that the navy is interested in the technique: "We might adapt to naval use those poaching expedients, the 'cross-line' and the 'otter.'" Sure enough, by the time the Germans have sewn the waters from the North Sea to the Orkneys Commander Burney has his mine sweeper *Oropesa* rigged out with what is now called a paravane to which is fastened a wire cutter. When the unmoored mine pops to the surface, snipers on the deck of *Oropesa* finish it off.

In the 1930s, my Noank neighbor Antonio Pezzolezzi employed a similar paravane concept using a farmer's scythe to adjust what he considered an unfair imbalance in the lobster fishery. More recently beach fishermen at Ocaracoke, North Carolina, one-upped their fellow Outerbank neighbors to the north in setting out their seine nets during the run of the sea trout by replacing the two-man Hatteras dory with an un-manned otter .

In any case the concept of controlling a fishing device underwater by use of otter boards had a long history prior to the Thompsons. What they did was apply the para-vane method to the bottom fishing bag net. While there have developed many nuances over the past century, here is John C. Salisbury's *Commercial Fishing Methods: An Intro-duction to Fishing Gear*: a mid-century description of the basic otter trawl which is close to what Ellery was up to:

> The trawl net is basically a large bag made of netting which is drawn along the sea bed to scoop up fish on or near the bottom. Depending on the manner in which the gear is constructed and rigged, its operating characteristics can be altered to permit use on various types of bottom for many species of fish.
>
> [The trawl net] can be seen as a large bag-shaped net, wide at one end, the mouth, which is open, leading to the body of the net which tapers to the closed end. Fish that enter through the mouth are trapped in the 'cod end'. (Which is of a smaller mesh than the body.)
>
> The mouth takes up an oval shape when viewed from the front, and two wings stretch out in front on either side to increase the area swept and to guide fish in the net's path down to the cod end. Around the upper edge of the mouth runs the 'headline' to which are fixed a number of floats [cork in the earlier days, plastic post World War II], and around the bottom of the mouth is the ground rope or foot rope, which is in contact with the bottom and is weighted.

The combined effect of the floats on the headline and the weighted ground line keeps the mouth open vertically.

The ground rope may be weighted with chain, or it may be merely wire, when the net is being operated on clear bottom. When used on rough bottom, iron or rubber rollers are rigged to assist its passage.

As this account is of Ellery's day, it ignores the fact that it is the ground rope that does the damage to the sea floor. To protect the ground rope and the whole leading edge of the net itself from its own rapacious sins, Ellery and others sewed in baggy wrinkle chaffing, that is, scraps of rope ends.

The headline and top of the mouth usually overhang the footrope and the bottom of the mouth to ensure that fish disturbed by the groundrope do not [escape by heading straight upward], but hit the top of the mouth and are shepherded down into the cod end.

Horizontal spread of the mouth is attained by 'otter boards' or doors towed ahead of the net and set at an angle of attack to the towing direction, so providing the outward force necessary to spread the wings to which they are fastened...

The common otter board is a rectangular wood and steel structure... The two wires forming the backstrap to the ground cable are fastened to the upper and lower corners at the outer face of the rear edge. Towing brackets are fitted to the inner face of the board to provide a towing point some two-fifths of the length from the leading edge. From the towing point, the steel warps lead up to the towing vessel.

The cod end is a funnel of netting closed at the rear end [the purse] by a rope looped through the meshes or rings tied with a special cod end knot which is easily released [and for some not so easily recalled to retie].

The speed at which the trawl is towed over the bottom varies, depending upon the species being sought, from about one and a half knots up to four and a half to five knots for fast swimming fish. Both vessel and gear must be designed and arranged to suit the species being caught, and wide variations in the size and rigging of the net doors may be used to provide the correct combination and maintain the desired net geometry. Towing a particular trawl too slowly may cause the otter boards to close together, so provide insufficient spreading power to the net which [then] tends to snag the bottom. On the other hand, towing too fast could result in the net lifting off the bottom and 'floating', quite possibly leading to it turning over, and becoming 'foul gear.'

...When at the fishing grounds, the trawling operation is a continuous sequence of setting out the gear from aboard, towing the net (usually for between two or three hours) and then hauling back the net, emptying the catch from the cod end, and setting out again for the next tow.

What Salisbury does not take into account is that boats like Ellery's did not have speedometers, but only r.p.m. indicators so that "speed" had to be adjusted for current, both rate and direction which usually resulted in the need for a seat of the pants vector analysis. The type of bottom, although not as much a factor as in oystering, is also a consideration. It was in recognizing the nuances of these necessary adjustments wherein actually lay Ellery's glory. All the rest was pretty much clowning.

Capt. Ellery Thompson and crewman
Phil Higgins of the 50-foot *Eleanor*.
Photograph by Bernie Gordon